Chinese
Phrasebook

LAROUSSE

Editors
Julie Kleeman, 谢曦 (Xi Xie)

with

Valerie Grundy, Elisabeth Hallett, Christy Johnson, Donald Watt

Supplement on Chinese language and culture
Julie Kleeman

Publishing manager
Janice McNeillie

Design and typesetting
Sharon McTeir

© Larousse 2006
21, rue du Montparnasse
75283 Paris Cedex 06

ISBN: 2-03-542155-1

Sales: Houghton Mifflin Company, Boston

Achevé d'imprimer en Mai 2006 sur les presses de « La Tipografica Varese S.p.A. » à Varese (Ital.

Introduction

This phrasebook is the ideal companion for your trip. It gets straight to the point, helping you to understand and make yourself understood so that you don't miss a thing. Use it like a dictionary to find the exact word you're looking for right away. And at each word we've provided a selection of key phrases that will help you in any situation, no matter how tricky things may have gotten.

The English–Chinese section contains all those essential expressions that you'll need to get by in China. In addition to the Chinese characters, each translation is given its *pinyin* equivalent. *Pinyin* is the official Chinese system of phonetic writing using Roman letters.

And because you need to be able to pronounce the words you see on the page properly, we've provided a simple and straightforward phonetic transcription that will enable you to make yourself understood with ease.

The Chinese–English section provides all the most important words and expressions that you might read or hear while on vacation. It's arranged by subject for ease of look-up.

And that's not all: we've added practical and cultural tips for getting by, a supplement on Chinese language, life and culture – everything, in fact, to make your trip go as smoothly as possible.

Pronunciation

So that you can say what you want to say in Chinese without running any risk of being misunderstood, we have devised a simple and straightforward phonetic transcription to show how every Chinese word or phrase used in this phrasebook is pronounced. This phonetic transcription, which is shown in brackets after each Chinese word or phrase and its *pinyin* equivalent, uses as many standard English sounds as possible, so that it is virtually self-explanatory. The following list provides further clarification:

[a]	as in man
[ang]	as in hang
[ay]	as in say
[ch]	as in child
[eah]	as in yeah
[ee]	as in bee
[eow]	as in meow
[eun]	as in broken
[ew]	as in dew
[i]	as in sit
[igh]	as in sigh
[j]	as in jet
[o]	as in drop
[oh]	as in oh!
[oo]	as in soon
[ooh]	as in ooh!
[ow]	as in cow
[ue]	as in wet
[uh]	as in huh
[un]	as in butter
[ung]	as in hung
[z]	as in yards

English–Chinese phrasebook

able
- to be able to... 能...... **néng**...... [nung]
- I'm not able to come tonight 我今天晚上来不了了 **wǒ jīntiān wǎnshang lái bù liǎo le** [wo jin-tyen wan-shang ligh boo leow luh]

about 大约 **dàyuē** [da-yue]
- I think I'll stay for about an hour 我想我大约会呆一个小时 **wǒ xiǎng wǒ dàyuē huì dāi yī gè xiǎoshí** [wo shyang wo da-yue hway digh yee ge sheow-shir]

abroad *(live, travel)* 在国外 **zài guówài** [zigh gwore-wigh]
- I've never been abroad before 我过去从未出过国 **wǒ guòqù cóng wèi chūguòguó** [wo gwore-choo tsong way choo-gwore-gwore]

absolutely 完全地 **wánquán de** [wan-chwan duh]
- you're absolutely right 你完全正确 **nǐ wánquán zhèngquè** [nee wan-chwan jung-chueh]

accept 接受 **jiēshòu** [jyeah-shoh]
- do you accept traveler's checks? 你们收旅行支票吗？ **nǐmen shōu lǚxíng zhīpiào ma?** [nee-meun shoh looh-shing jir-peow ma]

access 通路 **tōnglù** [tong-loo]
- is there disabled access? 有无障碍通道吗？ **yǒu wú zhàng'ài tōngdào ma?** [yoh woo jang-igh tong-dow ma]

accident 事故 **shìgù** [shir-goo]
- there's been an accident 出事故了 **chū shìgù le** [choo shir-goo luh]

according to 据...... 叙述 **jù......xùshù** [shoo-shoo]
- it's well worth seeing, according to the guidebook 据旅游指南介绍，那值得一看 **jù lǚyóu zhǐnán jièshào, nà zhíde yī kàn** [joo looh-yoh jir-nan jyeah-show na jir-duh yee kan]

address *(details of place)* 地址 **dìzhǐ** [dee-zhir] ◆ *(speak to)* 向...... 讲话 **xiàng......jiǎnghuà** [shyang...jyang hwa]
- could you write down the address for me? 你能把地址写给我吗？ **nǐ néng bǎ dìzhǐ xiě gěi wǒ ma?** [nee nung ba dee jir shyeah gay wo ma]
- here is my address and phone number, if you're ever in the US 如果你来美国的话，这是我的地址和电话号码 **rúguǒ nǐ lái měiguó dehuà, zhè shì wǒ de dìzhǐ hé diànhuà hàomǎ** [roo-gwore nee ligh may-gwore de hwa juh shir wo de dee-jir huh dyen-hwa how-ma]

adult 成人 chéngrén [chung-reun]
  ▸ two adults and one student, please 请给两张成人票和一张学生票 qǐng gěi liǎng zhāng chéngrénpiào hé yī zhāng xuéshēngpiào [ching gay lyang jang chung-reun peow huh yee jang shue-shung-peow]

advance (money) 预付金 yùfùjīn [yoo-foo-jin] ◆ **in advance** (pay, reserve) 事先 shìxiān [shir-shyen]
  ▸ do you have to book in advance? 是否得事先预定? shìfǒu děi shìxiān yùdìng? [shir-foh day shir-shyen yoo-ding]

after (in time) 在......以后 zài......yǐhòu [zigh...yee-hoh]; (in space) 在......后面 zài......hòumian [zigh...hoh-myen]
  ▸ it's twenty after eight 现在是8点20分 xiànzài shì bā diǎn èrshí fēn [shyen-zigh shir ba dyen er-shir fen]
  ▸ the stadium is just after the traffic lights 过了红绿灯就是体育场 guòle hónglǜdēng jiù shì tǐyùchǎng [gwore-luh hong-looh-dung jew shir tee-yoo-chang]

afternoon 下午 xiàwǔ [shya-woo]
  ▸ is the museum open in the afternoons? 博物馆下午开放吗? bówùguǎn xiàwǔ kāifàng ma? [bo-woo-gwan shya-woo kigh-fang ma]

aftershave 须后水 xūhòushuǐ [shoo-hoh-shway]
  ▸ a bottle of aftershave 一瓶须后水 yī píng xūhòushuǐ [yee ping shoo-hoh-shway]

afterwards 过后 guòhòu [gwore-hoh]
  ▸ join us afterwards 过后来找我们 guòhòu lái zhǎo wǒmen [gwore-hoh ligh jow wo-meun]

again 又 yòu [yoh]
  ▸ the train is late again 火车又晚点了 huǒchē yòu wǎndiǎn le [hwore-chuh yoh wan-dyen luh]

age 年龄 niánlíng [nyen-ling] ◆ **ages** 很久 hěn jiǔ [heun jew]
  ▸ what ages are your children? 你的孩子几岁了? nǐ de háizi jǐ suì le? [nee duh high-zir jee sway luh]
  ▸ we've been waiting for ages! 我们已经等了很久了! wǒmen yǐjīng děng le hěn jiǔ le! [wo-meun yee-jing dung luh heun jew luh]

agency 代理处 dàilǐchù [digh-lee-choo]
  ▸ what is the contact number for the agency? 代理处的联系电话是多少? dàilǐchù de liánxì diànhuà shì duōshao? [digh-lee-choo duh lyen-shee dyen-hwa shir dwore-show]

ago 前 qián [chyen]
  ▸ I've been before, several years ago 我几年前去过那里 wǒ jǐ nián qián qùguo nàli [wo jee nyen chyen choo-gwore na-lee]

agreement/disagreement

- absolutely! 当然是！ dāngrán shì! [dang-ran shir]
- that's fine by me 我没意见 wǒ méi yìjian [wo may yee-jyen]
- you're right 你是对的 nǐ shì duì de [nee shir dway duh]
- go on, then 那就继续吧 nà jiù jìxù ba [na jew jee-shoo ba]
- I'm not at all convinced 我一点儿都不相信 wǒ yīdiǎnr dōu bù xiāngxìn [wo yee-dyenr doh boo shyang-shin]
- I disagree 我不同意 wǒ bù tóngyì [wo boo tong-yee]

agreement 一致 yīzhì [yee-jir]

- we need to come to some agreement about where we're going next 我们得就接下来去哪儿达成一致 wǒmen děi jiù jiēxiàlái qù nǎr dáchéng yīzhì [wo-meun day jew jyeah-shya-ligh choo nar da-chung yee-jir]

ahead 在前 zài qián [zigh chyen]

- is the road ahead clear? 前面的道路是否通畅？ qiánmian de dàolù shìfǒu tōngchàng? [chyen-myen duh daoloo shir-foh tong-chang]

air *(wind)* 空气 kōngqì [kong-chee]

- the air is much fresher in the mountains 山里的空气清新得多 shān li de kōngqì qīngxīn de duō [shan lee duh kong-chee ching-shin duh dwore]

air-conditioning 空调 kōngtiáo [kong-teow]

- do you have air-conditioning? 有空调吗？ yǒu kōngtiáo ma? [yoh kong-teow ma]

airline 航空公司 hángkōng gōngsī [hang-kong gong-sir]

- no, we're traveling with a different airline 不，我们乘坐另一家航空公司的飞机 bù, wǒmen chéngzuò lìng yī jiā hángkōng gōngsī de fēijī [boo wo-meun chung-zwore ling yee jya hang-kong gong-sir duh fay-jee]

airmail 航空邮件 hángkōng yóujiàn [hang-kong yoh-jyen]

- I'd like to send it airmail 我想寄航空信 wǒ xiǎng jì hángkōngxìn [wo shyang jee hang-kong-shin]

airlines

There are several international and domestic airlines operating in China, as well as a number of new private air companies offering low-cost flights. *Okay Airways*, which was founded in 2005, is one such example.

airport 机场 jīchǎng [jee-chang]

▸ how long does it take to get to the airport? 到机场要多久？ dào jīchǎng yào duō jiǔ? [dow jee-chang yow dwore jew]

airport shuttle 机场巴士 jīchǎng bāshì [jee-chang ba-shir]

▸ is there an airport shuttle? 是否有机场巴士？ shìfǒu yǒu jīchǎng bāshì? [shir-foh yoh jee-chang ba-shir]

air pressure 气压 qìyā [chee-ya]

▸ could you check the air pressure in the tires? 你能检查一下轮胎的气足吗？ nǐ néng jiǎnchá yī xià lúntāi de qì zú ma? [nee nung jyen-cha yee shya lun-tigh duh chee zoo ma]

airsick 晕机的 yūn jī de [yun jee duh]

▸ can I have an airsick bag? 能给我一个呕吐袋吗？ néng gěi wǒ yī gè ǒutùdài ma? [nung gay wo yee guh oh-too-digh ma]

aisle *(between plane seats)* 通道 tōngdào [tong-dow]; *(plane seat)* 靠过道的座位 kào guòdào de zuòwei [kow gwore-dow duh zwore-way]

▸ two seats, please: one window and one aisle 请给两个座位：一个靠窗的座位和一个靠过道的座位 qǐng gěi liǎng gè zuòwei: yī gè kào chuāng de zuòwei hé yī gè kào guòdào de zuòwei [ching gay lyang guh zwore-way yee guh kow chwung duh zwore-way huh yee guh kow gwore-dow duh zwore-way]

aisle seat 靠过道的座位 kào guòdào de zuòwei [kow gwore-dow duh zwore-way]

▸ I'd like an aisle seat 我想要一个靠过道的座位 wǒ xiǎng yào yī gè kào guòdào de zuòwei [wo shang yow yee guh kow gwore-dow duh zwore-way]

alarm (clock) 闹钟 nàozhōng [now-jong]

▸ I set the alarm for nine o'clock 我把闹钟定在9点 wǒ bǎ nàozhōng dìng zài jiǔ diǎn [wo ba now-jong ding zigh jew dyen]

at the airport

▸ where is gate number 2? 二号登机口在哪儿？ èr hào dēngjīkǒu zài nǎr? [er how deng-jee-koh zigh nar]

▸ where is the check-in desk? 哪儿是办票柜台？ nǎr shì bànpiào guìtái? [nar shir ban-peow gway-tigh]

▸ I'd like an aisle seat 我想要个靠过道的座位。 wǒ xiǎng yào gè kào guòdào de zuòwei [wo shyang yow guh kow gwore-dow duh zwore-way]

▸ where is the baggage claim? 哪里是行李提取厅？ nǎli shì xíngli tíqǔtīng? [na-lee shir shing-lee tee-choo-ting]

alcohol

The Chinese traditionally drink beer and white wine or spirits, but are starting to drink more red wine and cognac. The Chinese alcoholic drink with the best reputation is 茅台酒 máotáijiǔ [mow-tigh jew]. It is made from sorghum, is more than 50% proof, and is believed to have been made for more than 4,000 years. The Chinese love making toasts during the course of a meal with friends, colleagues or business associates. You say 干杯 gānbēi [gan-bay] (bottoms up) when you drink. To show respect, when you clink glasses your glass should be at the same height as or slightly lower than the glass that is being held out to you.

---

alcohol *(for drinking)* 酒 jiǔ [jew]; *(for medicinal use)* 酒精 jiǔjīng [jew-jing]
  ▸ I don't drink alcohol 我不喝酒 wǒ bù hē jiǔ [wo boo huh jew]

alcohol-free 不含酒精 bù hán jiǔjīng [boo han jew-jing]
  ▸ what kind of alcohol-free drinks do you have? 你有哪些不含酒精的饮料？nǐ yǒu nǎxiē bù hán jiǔjīng de yǐnliào? [nee yoh na-shyeah boo han jew-jing duh yin-leow]

all 所有的 suǒyǒu de [swore-yoh duh] ◆ *(the whole amount)* 全体 quántǐ [chwan-tee]; *(everybody)* 每个 měi gè [may-guh]
  ▸ all the time 始终 shǐzhōng [shir-jong]
  ▸ all English people 所有的英国人 suǒyǒu de yīngguórén [swore-yoh duh ying-gwore-reun]

allergic 过敏的 guòmǐn de [gwore-min duh]
  ▸ I'm allergic to aspirin/nuts/wheat/dairy products 我对阿司匹林/坚果/小麦/奶制品过敏 wǒ duì āsīpǐlín/jiānguǒ/xiǎomài/nǎizhìpǐn guòmǐn [wo dway a-sir-pee-lin/jyen-gwore/sheow-migh/nigh-jir-pin gwore-min]

allow 允许 yǔnxǔ [yun-shoo]
  ▸ how much luggage are you allowed? 可以带多少行李？kěyǐ dài duōshao xínglǐ? [kuh-yee digh dwore-show shing-lee]
  ▸ are you allowed to smoke here? 可以在这里抽烟吗？kěyǐ zài zhèli chōuyān ma? [kuh-yee zigh juh-lee choh-yen ma]

almost 差不多 chàbuduō [cha-boo-dwore]
  ▸ it's almost one o'clock 差不多1点了 chàbuduō yī diǎn le [chao-boo-dwore yee dyen luh]

alone 单独的 dāndú de [dan-doo duh]
  ▸ leave us alone! 别打扰我们！bié dǎrǎo wǒmen! [byeah da-row wo-meun]

along 沿着 yánzhe [yan-jir]
  ▸ along the river 沿着河 yánzhe hé [yan-jir huh]

altogether *(in total)* 总共 zǒnggòng [zong-gong]
  ▸ how much does it cost altogether? 总共多少钱？ zǒnggòng duōshao qián? [zong-gong dwore-show chyen]

always 总是 zǒng shì [zong-shir]
  ▸ I always stay in the same hotel when I come to Shanghai 我去上海时总是住在同一家宾馆 wǒ qù shànghǎi shí zǒng shì zhù zài tóng yī jiā bīnguǎn [wo choo shang-high shir zong-shir joo zigh tong yee jya bing-gwan]

ambulance 救护车 jiùhùchē [jew-hoo-chuh]
  ▸ could you send an ambulance right away to...? 你能马上叫辆救护车去……吗？ nǐ néng mǎshàng jiào liàng jiùhùchē qù......ma? [nee nung ma-shang jeow lyang jew-hoo-chuh choo...ma]

ambulance service 紧急医疗救护服务 jǐnjí yīliáo jiùhù fúwù [jin-jee yee-leow jew-hoo foo-woo]
  ▸ what's the number for the ambulance service? 紧急医疗救护服务的电话号码是多少？ jǐnjí yīliáo jiùhù fúwù de diànhuà hàomǎ shì duōshao? [jin-jee yee-leow jew-hoo duh dyen-hwa how-ma shir dwore-show]

America 美国 měiguó [may-gwore]
  ▸ I'm from America 我来自美国 wǒ láizì měiguó [wo ligh zir may-gwore]
  ▸ I live in America 我住在美国 wǒ zhù zài měiguó [wo joo zigh may-wore]
  ▸ have you ever been to America? 你去过美国吗？ nǐ qùguo měiguó ma? [nee choo-gwore may-gwore ma]

American 美国的 měiguó de [may-gwore duh] ◆ 美国人 měiguórén [may-gwore reun]
  ▸ I'm American 我是美国人 wǒ shì měiguórén [wo shir may-gwore reun]
  ▸ we're Americans 我们是美国人 wǒmen shì měiguórén [wo–meun shir may-gwore reun]

ankle 脚踝 jiǎohuái [jeow-hwigh]
  ▸ I've sprained my ankle 我扭伤脚踝了 wǒ niǔshāng jiǎohuái le [wo new-shang jeow-hwigh luh]

announcement 通知 tōngzhī [tong-jir]
  ▸ was that an announcement about the Shanghai train? 那是有关上海火车的通知吗？ nà shì yòuguān shànghǎi huǒchē de tōngzhī ma? [na shir yoh-gwan shang-high hwore-shuh duh tong-jir ma]

another *(additional)* 又一的 yòu yī de [yoh-yee duh]; *(different)* 另一的 lìng yī de [ling-yee duh]
  ▸ another coffee, please 请再来份咖啡 qǐng zài lái fèn kāfēi [ching zigh ligh fen kigh-fay]
  ▸ (would you like) another drink? (你想)再来一杯吗？ (nǐ xiǎng) zài lái yī bēi ma? [nee shyang zigh ligh yee bay ma]

answer 答案 dá'àn [da-aan] ◆ 回答 huídá [hway-da]
- there's no answer 没有人接听 méiyou rén jiētīng [may-yoh reun jyeah-ting]
- I phoned earlier but nobody answered 我早先打过电话，但是没有人接听 wǒ zǎoxiān dǎguo diànhuà, dànshì méiyou rén jiētīng [wo zow-shyen dagwore dyen-hwa dan-shir may-yoh reun jyeah-ting]

answering machine 电话答录机 diànhuà dálùjī [dyen-hwa da-loo-jee]
- I left a message on your answering machine 我在你的电话答录机里留了口信 wǒ zài nǐ de diànhuà dálùjī liliú le kǒuxìn [wo zigh nee duh dyen-hwa da-loo-jee lee lew luh koh-shin]

anti-dandruff shampoo 去屑洗发露 qù xiè xǐfàlù [choo shyeah shee-fa-loo]
- do you have anti-dandruff shampoo? 你有去屑洗发露吗？ nǐ yǒu qù xiè xǐfàlù ma? [nee yoh choo shyeah shee-fa-loo ma]

anybody, anyone 任何人 rènhé rén [reun-huh reun]
- is there anybody there? 有人吗？ yǒu rén ma? [yoh reun ma]

anything 任何事物 rènhé shìwù [reun-he shir-woo]
- is there anything I can do? 我能帮什么忙吗？ wǒ néng bāng shénme máng ma? [wo nung bang sheun-muh mang ma]

anywhere 在任何地方 zài rènhé dìfang [zigh reun-huh dee-fang]
- I can't find my room key anywhere 我什么地方都找不到我的房间钥匙 wǒ shénme dìfang dōu zhǎo bù dào wǒ de fángjiān yàoshi [sheuh-muh dee-fang doh jow boo dow wo duh fang-jyen yow-shir]
- do you live anywhere near here? 你住在这附近吗？ nǐ zhù zài zhè fùjìn ma? [nee joo zigh jir foo-jin ma]

apartment 公寓 gōngyù [gong-yoo]
- we'd like to rent an apartment for one week 我们想租一个星期的公寓 wǒmen xiǎng zū yī gè xīngqī de gōngyù [wo-meun shyang zoo yee guh shing-chee duh gong-yoo]

apologize 道歉 dàoqiàn [dow-chyen]
- there's no need to apologize 没必要道歉 méi bìyào dàoqiàn [may bee-yow dow-chyen]

---

apologizing

- excuse me! 请原谅！ qǐng yuánliàng! [ching ywan-lyang]
- I'm sorry, I can't come on Saturday 对不起，我星期六来不了了 duìbuqǐ, wǒ xīngqīliù lái bù liǎo le [dway-boo-chee wo shing-chee-lew ligh boo lyow luh]
- that's OK/it doesn't matter/don't mention it 没关系 méi guānxi [may gwan-shee]

appetizer 开胃菜 kāiwèicài [kigh-way tsigh]
- which of the appetizers would you recommend? 你推荐什么开胃菜？ nǐ tuījiàn shénme kāiwèicài? [nee tway-jyen sheun-muh high-way tsigh]

apple 苹果 píngguǒ [ping-gwore]
- could I have a kilo of apples, please? 请给我来一公斤苹果好吗？ qǐng gěi wǒ lái yī gōngjīn píngguǒ hǎo ma? [ching gay wo ligh yee gong-jin ping-gwore how ma]

apple juice 苹果汁 píngguǒzhī [ping-gwore-jir]
- I'd like some apple juice 我想来点苹果汁 wǒ xiǎng lái diǎn píngguǒzhī [wo shyang ligh dyen ping-gwore-jir]

appointment 预约 yùyuē [yoo-yue]
- could I get an appointment for tomorrow morning? 能把我的预约安排在明天上午吗？ néng bǎ wǒ de yùyuē ānpái zài míngtiān shàngwǔ ma? [nung ba wuh yoo-yue an-pigh zigh ming-tyen shang-woo ma]
- I have an appointment with Doctor... 我和......医生有个预约 wǒ hé......yīshēng yǒu gè yùyuē [wo he...yee-shung yoh guh yoo-yue]

April 四月 sì yuè [sir yue]
- April 6th 四月六日 sì yuè liù rì [sir yue lew rir]

area (region) 地区 dìqū [dee-choo]; (small) 地方 dìfang [dee-fang]; (of town) 区 qū [choo]
- I'm visiting the Beijing area for a few days 我要在北京呆几天 wǒ yào zài běijīng dāi jǐ tiān [wo yow zigh bay-jing digh jee tyen]
- what walks can you recommend in the area? 在这个地区你推荐哪些步行的路线？ zài zhège dìqū nǐ tuījiàn nǎxiē bùxíng de lùxiàn? [zigh jir-guh dee-choo nee tway-jyen na-shyeah boo-shing duh loo-shyen]

area code (for telephoning) 区号 qūhào [choo-how]
- what's the area code for Beijing? 北京的区号是多少？ běijīng de qūhào shì duōshao? [bay-jing duh choo-how shir dwore-show]

arm 手臂 shǒubì [shoh-bee]
- I can't move my arm 我的手臂动不了了 wǒ de shǒubì dòng bù liǎo le [wo duh show-bee dong boo leow luh]

around (in all directions) 在周围 zài zhōuwéi [zigh joh-way]; (nearby) 在附近 zài fùjìn [zigh foo-jin]; (here and there) 到处 dàochù [dow-choo] ◆ (encircling) 环绕 huánrào [hwan-row]; (through) 越过 yuèguò [yue-gwore]; (approximately) 大约 dàyuē [da-yue]
- we've been traveling around China 我们环游了中国 wǒmen huányóule zhōngguó [wo-meun hwan-yoh luh jong-gwore]
- I don't know my way around yet 我对周围还不熟悉 wǒ duì zhōuwéi hái bù shúxi [wo dway jo-way high boo shoo-shee]
- I arrived around two o'clock 我大约两点到 wǒ dàyuē liǎng diǎn dào [wo da-yue lyang dyen dow]

- I'd like something for around 15 yuan 我想要15元左右的东西 **wǒ xiǎng yào shíwǔ yuán zuǒyòu de dōngxi** [wo shyang yow shir-woo ywan zwore-yoh duh dong-shee]

arrive 到达 **dàodá** [dow-da]
- my luggage hasn't arrived 我的行李还没有到 **wǒ de xíngli hái méyou dào** [wo duh shing-lee high may-yoh dow]
- we arrived late 我们晚到了 **wǒmen wǎn dào le** [wo-meun wan dow luh]
- we just arrived 我们刚到 **wǒmen gāng dào** [wo-meun gang dow]

art 艺术 **yìshù** [yee-shoo]
- I'm not really interested in art 我对艺术并不怎么感兴趣 **wǒ duì yìshù bìng bù zěnme gǎn xìngqù** [wo dwy yee-shoo bing boo zeun-muh gan shing-choo]

as *(while)* 当......的时候 **dāng......de shíhou** [dang...duh shir-hoh]; *(like)* 像 **xiàng** [shyang]; *(since)* 因为 **yīnwei** [ying-way]
- the lights went out just as we were about to eat 当我们正要吃的时候，灯灭了 **dāng wǒmen zhèng yào chī de shíhou, dēng miè le** [dang wo-meun jung yow chir duh shir-hoh dung myeah luh]
- as I said before 就像我以前说的一样 **jiù xiàng wǒ yǐqián shuō de yīyàng** [jew wo yee-chyen shwore duh yee-yang]
- leave it as it is 别动它 **bié dòng tā** [byeah dong ta]
- as... as 与......等同 **yǔ......děngtóng** [yoo...dung-tong]
- as much/many as 和......一样多 **hé......yīyàng duō** [huh...yee-yang dwore]

ashtray 烟灰缸 **yānhuīgāng** [yan-hway-gang]
- could you bring us an ashtray? 你能给我们拿个烟灰缸吗？ **nǐ néng gěi wǒmen ná gè yānhuīgāng ma?** [nee nung gay wo-meun na guh yan-hway-gang ma]

ask *(question)* 问 **wèn** [weun]; *(time)* 询问 **xúnwèn** [shoon-weun]

asking questions

- is this seat free? 这个座位有人吗？ **zhège zuòwei yǒu rén ma?** [juh-guh zwore-way yoh reun ma]
- where is the railway station? 火车站在哪儿？ **huǒchēzhàn zài nǎr?** [hwore-chuh-jan zigh nar]
- could you help me get my suitcase down, please? 请问您能帮我把手提箱拿下来吗？ **qǐng wèn nín néng bāng wǒ bǎ shǒutíxiāng náxialai ma?** [ching weun neen nung bang wo ba show-tee-shyang na-shya-ligh ma]
- could you give me a hand? 你能帮我一下吗？ **nǐ néng bāng wǒ yī xià ma?** [neen nung bang wo yee shya ma]
- could you lend me 10 yuan? 你能借给我十元吗？ **nǐ néng jiè gěi wǒ shí yuán ma?** [nee nung jyeah gay wo shir ywan ma]

▸ can I ask you a question? 我能问你个问题吗？ wǒ néng wèn nǐ gè wèntí ma? [wo nung weun nee guh weun-tee ma]

aspirin 阿司匹林 āsīpǐlín [a-sir-pee-lin]

▸ I'd like some aspirin 我想要些阿司匹林 wǒ xiǎng yào xiē āsīpǐlín [wo shyang yow shyeah a-sir-pee-lin]

asthma 哮喘病 xiàochuǎnbìng [shyow-chwan-bing]

▸ I have asthma 我有哮喘病 wǒ yǒu xiàochuǎnbìng [wo yoh shyow-chwan-bing]

at 在 zài [zigh]

▸ our bags are still at the airport 我们的行李还在机场 wǒmen de xíngli hái zài jīchǎng [wo-meun duh shing-lee high zigh jee-chang]

▸ we arrive at midnight 我们是午夜到的 wǒmen shì wǔyè dào de [wo-meun shir woo-yuh dow duh]

ATM 自动取款机 zìdòng qǔkuǎnjī [zir-dong choo-kwan-jee]

▸ I'm looking for an ATM 我在找自动取款机 wǒ zài zhǎo zìdòng qǔkuǎnjī [wo zigh jow zir-dong choo-kwan-jee]

▸ the ATM has eaten my card 自动取款机吃了我的卡 zìdòng qǔkuǎnjī chīle wǒ de kǎ [zir-dong choo-kwan-jee chir-luh wo duh ka]

attack (of illness) 发作 fāzuò ♦ (person) 袭击 xíjī [shee-jee]

▸ he had a heart attack 他心脏病发作了 tā xīnzàngbìng fāzuò le [ta shin-zang-bing fa-zwore luh]

▸ I've been attacked 我被人袭击了 wǒ bèi rén xíjī le [wo bay reun shee-jee luh]

attention 注意 zhùyì [joo-yee]

▸ may I have your attention for a moment? 请大家注意一下！ qǐng dàjiā zhùyì yī xià! [ching da-jya joo-yee yee shya]

attractive 有吸引力的 yǒu xīyǐnlì de [yoh shee-yin-lee duh]

▸ I find you very attractive 我觉得你非常有吸引力 wǒ juéde nǐ fēicháng yǒu xīyǐnlì [wo jue-duh nee fay-chang yoh shee-yin-lee]

August 八月 bā yuè [ba yue]

▸ we're arriving on August 29th 我们将于八月二十九日到达 wǒmen jiāng yú bā yuè èrshíjiǔ rì dàodá [wo-meun jyang yoo ba yue er-shir-jew rir dow-da]

automatic 自动的 zìdòng de [zir-dong duh] ♦ (car) 自动挡汽车 zìdòngdǎng qìchē [zir-dong-dang chee-chuh]

▸ I want a car with automatic transmission 我想要一辆有自动变速器的汽车 wǒ xiǎng yào yī liàng yǒu zìdòng biànsùqì de qìchē [wo shyang yow yee lyang yoh zir-dong byen-soo-chee duh chee-chuh]

▸ is it a manual or an automatic? 是手动挡的车还是自动挡的车？ shì shǒudòngdǎng de chē háishi zìdòngdǎng de chē? [shir show-dong-dang duh chuh high-shir zir-dong-dang duh chuh]

available 可得到的 kě dédào de [kuh duh-dow duh]

▸ you don't have a table available before then? 再早点儿没有桌位了吗？ zài zǎo diǎnr méiyou zhuōwèi le ma? [zigh zow dyenr may-yoh jwore-way luh ma]

average 平均的 píngjūn de [ping-jun duh]

▸ what's the average price of a meal there? 那里平均一顿饭要多少钱？ nàli píngjūn yī dùn fàn yào duōshao qián? [na-lee ping-jun yee dun fan yow dwore-show chyen]

avoid 避开 bìkāi [bee-kigh]

▸ is there a route that would help us avoid the traffic? 是否有路线可以避开拥挤的交通？ shìfǒu yǒu lùxiàn kěyǐ bìkāi yōngjǐ de jiāotōng? [shir-foh yoh loo-shyen kuh-yee bee-kigh yong-jee duh jeow-tong]

away *(indicating movement)* 向远处 xiàng yuǎnchù [shyang ywan-choo]; *(indicating position)* 在离某距离处 zài lí mǒ jùlí chù [zigh lee mo joo-lee choo]

◆ **away from** 远离 yuǎnlí [ywan-lee]

▸ the village is 10 miles away 村庄在十英里外 cūnzhuāng zài shí yīnglǐ wài [tsun-jwung zigh shir ying-lee wigh]

▸ we're looking for a cottage far away from the town 我们在找一间远离城市的乡间小屋 wǒmen zài zhǎo yī jiān yuǎnlí chéngshì de xiāngjiān xiǎo wū [wo-meun zigh jow yee jyen ywan-lee chung-shir duh shyang-jyen shyow-woo]

▸ do you have any rooms away from the main road? 你有远离主干道的房间吗？ nǐ yǒu yuǎnlí zhǔgàndào de fángjiān ma? [nee yoh ywan-lee joo-gan-dow duh fang-jyen ma]

b

baby bottle 奶瓶 nǎipíng [nigh-ping]
▶ I need to sterilize a baby bottle 我得把奶瓶消毒一下 wǒ děi bǎ nǎipíng xiāodú yī xià [wo day ba nigh-ping shyow-doo yee shya]

back 往后 wǎnghòu [wang-hoh] ◆ *(part of body)* 背部 bèibù [bay-boo]; *(of room)* 后面 hòumian [hoh-myen]
▶ I'll be back in 5 minutes 我五分钟后回来 wǒ wǔ fēnzhōng hòu huílai [wo woo feun-jong hoh hway-ligh]
▶ I've got a bad back 我背不好 wǒ bèi bù hǎo [wo bay boo how]
▶ I prefer to sit at the back 我宁愿坐在后面 wǒ nìngyuàn zuò zài hòumian [wo ning-ywan zwore zigh hoh-myen]

backache 背疼 bèi téng [bay-tung]
▶ I've got a backache 我背疼 wǒ bèi téng [wo bay-tung]

backpack 背包 bēibāo [bay-bow]
▶ my passport's in my backpack 我的护照在我的背包里 wǒ de hùzhào zài wǒ de bēibāo li [wo duh hoo-jow zigh wo duh bay-bow lee]

back up 后退 hòutuì [hoh-tway]
▶ I think we have to back up and turn right 我想我们得后退，然后向右转 wǒ xiǎng wǒmen děi hòutuì, ránhòu xiàng yòu zhuǎn [wo shyang wo-meun day hoh-tway ran-hoh shyang yoh jwan]

bad 坏的 huài de [hwigh duh]
▶ the weather's bad today 今天天气不好 jīntiān tiānqì bù hǎo [jin-tyen tyen-chee boo how]

bag 包 bāo [bow]; *(suitcase)* 行李 xíngli [shing-lee]; *(purse)* 皮夹 píjiā [pee-jya]
▶ are these the bags from flight 502? 这些是502航班的行李吗？ zhèxiē shì wǔ líng èr hángbān de xíngli ma? [jir-shyeah shir woo ling er hang-ban duh shing-lee ma]
▶ can someone take our bags up to the room, please? 请问能有人把我们的行李拿到房间吗？ qǐng wèn néng yǒu rén bǎ wǒmen de xíngli nádào fángjiān ma? [ching weun nung yoh reun ba wo-meun duh shing-lee na-dow fang-jyen ma]

baggage 行李 xíngli [shing-lee]
▶ my baggage hasn't arrived 我的行李还没有到 wǒ de xíngli hái méiyou dào [wo duh shing-lee high may-yoh dow]
▶ I'd like to report the loss of my baggage 我的行李丢了，要报失 wǒ de xíngli diū le, yào bàoshī [wo duh shing-lee dew luh yow bow-shir]

baggage cart 行李手推车 xíngli shǒutuīchē [shing-lee show-tway chuh]
- I'm looking for a baggage cart 我在找行李手推车 wǒ zài zhǎo xíngli shǒutuīchē [wo zigh jow shing-lee show-tway chuh]

bakery 面包房 miànbāofáng [myen-bow-fang]
- is there a bakery nearby? 附近有面包房吗? fùjìn yǒu miànbāofáng ma? [foo-jin yoh myen-bow-fang ma]

balcony 阳台 yángtái [yang-tigh]
- do you have any rooms with a balcony? 你有带阳台的房间吗? nǐ yǒu dài yángtái de fángjiān ma? [nee yoh digh yang-tigh duh fang-jyen ma]

banana 香蕉 xiāngjiāo [shyang-jeow]
- a kilo of bananas, please 请来一公斤香蕉 qǐng lái yī gōngjīn xiāngjiāo [ching ligh yee gong-jin shyang-jeow]

bandage 绷带 bēngdài [bung-digh]
- I need a bandage for my ankle 我需要绷带包扎我的踝关节 wǒ xūyào bēngdài bāozhā wǒ de huái guānjié [wo shoo-yow bung-digh bow-ja wo duh hwigh gwan-jyeah]

Band-Aid® 创可贴 chuāngkětiē [chwung-kuh-tyeah]
- can I have a Band-Aid® for my cut? 我能要一个创可贴包扎伤口吗? wǒ néng yào yī gè chuāngkětiē bāozhā shāngkǒu ma? [wo nung yow yee guh chwung-kuh-tyeah bow-ja shang-koh ma]

bank *(finance)* 银行 yínháng [yin-hang]
- is there a bank nearby? 附近有银行吗? fùjìn yǒu yínháng ma? [foo-jin yoh yin-hang ma]

---

at the bank

- I'd like to change 200 dollars into yuan 我想把200美元兑换成人民币 wǒ xiǎng bǎ èrbǎi měiyuán duìhuànchéng rénmínbì [wo shyang ba er-bigh may-ywan dway-hwan-chung reun-min-bee]
- in small bills, please 请给我小面值的货币 qǐng gěi wǒ xiǎo miànzhí de huòbì [ching gay wo shyow myen-jir duh hwore-bee]
- what is the exchange rate for the dollar? 美元的汇率是多少? měiyuán de huìlǜ shì duōshao? [may-ywan duh hway-looh shir dwore-show]
- how much is that in dollars? 用美元付款是多少钱? yòng měiyuán fù kuǎn shì duōshao qian? [yong may-ywan foo-kwan shir dwore-show chyen]
- do you take traveler's checks? 你收旅行支票吗? nǐ shōu lǚxíng zhīpiào ma? [nee shoh looh-shing jir-peow ma]
- do you charge a commission? 要收手续费吗? yào shōu shǒuxùfèi ma? [yow shoh shoh-shoo-fay ma]

are banks open on Saturdays? 星期六银行开门吗？ **xīngqīliù yínháng kāimén ma?** [shing-chee-lew yin-hang kigh-meun ma]

bank card 银行卡 **yínhángkǎ** [yin-hang-ka]

▸ I've lost my bank card 我的银行卡丢了 **wǒ de yínhángkǎ diū le** [wo duh yin-hang-ka dew luh]

bar *(establishment serving alcohol)* 酒吧 **jiǔbā** [jew-ba]; *(counter)* 柜台 **guìtái** [gway-tigh]; *(of soap)* 条 **tiáo** [tyow]

▸ are there any good bars around here? 这附近有什么好的酒吧？ **zhè fùjìn yǒu shénme hǎo de jiǔbā?** [jir foo-jin yoh sheun-muh how duh jew-ba]

base *(bottom)* 底座 **dǐzuò** [dee-zwore]; *(starting point)* 基地 **jīdì** [jee-dee]

▸ the base of the lamp got broken 灯的底座坏了 **dēng de dǐzuò huài le** [dung duh dee-zwore hwigh luh]

▸ we're going to use the village as our base to explore the area 我们把这个村庄作为探索该地区的基地 **wǒmen bǎ zhège cūnzhuāng zuòwéi tànsuǒ gāi dìqū de jīdì** [wo-meun ba jir-guh tsun-jwung zwore-way tan-swore gigh dee-choo duh jee-dee]

basic 基本的 **jīběn de** [jee-beun duh]　◆ **basics** 基本的东西 **jīběn de dōngxi** [jee-beun duh dong-shee]

▸ do the staff all have a basic knowledge of English? 是不是所有的员工都会说一些基本的英语？ **shìbùshì suǒyǒu de yuángōng dōu huì shuō yīxiē jīběn de yīngyǔ?** [shir-boo-shir swore-yoh duh ywan-gong doh hway shwore yee-shyeah jee-beun duh ying-yoo]

▸ I know the basics, but no more than that 我知道基本的东西，但仅此而已 **wǒ zhīdao jīběn de dōngxi, dàn jǐn cǐ ěryǐ** [wo jir-dow jee-beun duh dong-shee dan jin tsir er-yee]

basis 基础 **jīchǔ** [jee-choo]

▸ the price per night is on a double-occupancy basis 每晚的价格是以两人入住为基准计算的 **měi wǎn de jiàgé shì yǐ liǎng rén rùzhù wéi jīzhǔn jìsuàn de** [may wan duh jya-guh shir yee lyang reun roo-joo way jee-jun jee-swan duh]

bat *(for table tennis)* 球拍 **qiúpāi** [chew-pigh]

▸ can you rent bats? 能租到球拍吗？ **néng zūdào qiúpāi ma?** [nung zoo-dow chew-pigh ma]

bath 洗澡 **xǐzǎo** [shee-zow]

▸ to take a bath 洗澡 **xǐzǎo** [shee-zow]

bathroom *(with toilet and bathtub or shower)* 浴室 **yùshì** [yoo-shir]; *(with toilet)* 卫生间 **wèishēngjiān** [way-shung-jyen]

▸ where's the bathroom? *(with bathtub)* 浴室在哪里？ **yùshì zài nǎli?** [yoo-shir zigh na-lee]; *(toilet)* 卫生间在哪里？ **wèishēngjiān zài nǎli?** [way-shung-jyen zigh na-lee]

bathtub 浴缸 yùgāng [yoo-gang]
- there's no plug for the bathtub 没有塞浴缸的塞子 méiyou sāi yùgāng de sāizi [may-yoh sigh yoo-gang duh sigh-zir]

battery *(for radio, flashlight)* 电池 diànchí [dyen-chir]; *(in car)* 蓄电池 xùdiànchí [shoo-dyen-chir]
- I need new batteries 我需要新的电池 wǒ xūyào xīn de diànchí [wo shoo-yow shin duh dyen-chir]
- the battery needs to be recharged 电池需要充电了 diànchí xūyào chōngdiàn le [dyen-chir shoo-yow chong-dyen luh]
- the battery's dead 电池没电了 diànchí méi diàn le [dyen-chir may dyen luh]

be
- where are you from? 你从哪里来？ nǐ cóng nǎli lái? [nee tsong na-lee ligh]
- I'm a teacher 我是个老师 wǒ shì gè lǎoshī [wo shir guh low-shir]
- I'm happy 我感到快乐 wǒ gǎndào kuàilè [wo gan-dow kwigh-luh]
- how are you? 你身体怎么样？ nǐ shēntǐ zěnmeyàng? [nee sheun-tee zeun-muh-yang]
- I'm fine 我很好 wǒ hěn hǎo [wo heun how]
- where is terminal 1? 一号航站楼在哪里？ yī hào hángzhànlóu zài nǎli? [yee how hang-jan-loh zigh na-lee]
- could you show me where I am on the map? 你能在地图上指出我在哪里吗？ nǐ néng zài dìtú shang zhǐchū wǒ zài nǎli ma? [nee nung zigh dee-too shang jir-choo wo zigh na-lee ma]
- have you ever been to the United States? 你曾经去过美国吗？ nǐ céngjīng qùguo měiguó ma? [nee tsung-jing choo-gwore may-gwore ma]
- it's the first time I've been here 这是我第一次到这里 zhè shì wǒ dì yī cì dào zhèlǐ [jir shir wo dee yee tsir dow juh-lee]
- how old are you? 你多大了？ nǐ duō dà le? [nee dwore da luh]
- I'm 18 (years old) 我18岁了 wǒ shíbā suì le [wo shir-ba sway luh]
- it was over 35 degrees 气温超过35度 qìwēn chāoguò sānshíwǔ dù [chee-weun chow-gwore san-shir doo]
- it's cold in the evenings 晚上挺冷的 wǎnshang tǐng lěng de [wan-shang ting lung duh]
- how much is it? 多少钱？ duōshao qián? [dwore-show chyen]
- I'm 1.68 meters tall 我身高1米68 wǒ shēn gāo yī mǐ liù bā [wo shen gow yee mee lew ba]

beach 海滩 hǎitān [high-tan]
- it's a sandy beach 这是个沙质海滩 zhè shì gè shā zhì de hǎitān [jir shir guh sha jir duh high-tan]
- is it a quiet beach? 是个宁静的海滩吗？ shì gè níngjìng de hǎitān ma? [shir guh ning-jing duh high-tan ma]

beach umbrella 遮阳伞 **zhēyángsăn** [juh-yang-san]
▸ can you rent beach umbrellas? 能租到遮阳伞吗？ **néng zūdào zhēyáng-săn ma?** [nung woo-doz juh-yang-san ma]

beautiful 漂亮的 **piàoliang de** [peow-lyang]
▸ isn't the weather beautiful today? 今天的天气真美，不是吗？ **jīntiān de tiānqì zhēn měi, bù shì ma?** [jin-tyen duh tyen-chee jeun may boo shir ma]

bed 床 **chuáng** [chwung]
▸ is it possible to add an extra bed? 能否加张床？ **néngfǒu jiā zhāng chuáng?** [nung-foh jya jang chwung]
▸ do you have a children's bed? 你们有给小孩睡的床吗？ **nǐmen yǒu gěi xiǎohái shuì de chuáng ma?** [nee-meun yoh gay sheow-high shway duh chwung ma]
▸ to go to bed 睡觉 **shuìjiào** [shway-jeow]
▸ I went to bed late 我睡晚了 **wǒ shuì wǎn le** [wo shway wan luh]
▸ I need to put my children to bed now 我现在得让孩子们上床睡觉了 **wǒ xiànzài děi ràng háizimen shàng chuáng shuìjiào le** [wo shyen-zigh day rang high-zir-meun shang chwung shway-jeow luh]

bedroom 卧室 **wòshì** [wo-shir]
▸ how many bedrooms does the apartment have? 这套公寓有几间卧室？ **zhè tào gōngyù yǒu jǐ jiān wòshì?** [jir tow gong-yoo yoh jee jyen wo-shir]

bedside lamp 床头灯 **chuángtóudēng** [chwung-toh-dung]
▸ the bedside lamp doesn't work 床头灯坏了 **chuángtóudēng huài le** [chwung-toh-dung hwigh luh]

beef 牛肉 **niúròu** [new-roh]
▸ I don't eat beef 我不吃牛肉 **wǒ bù chī niúròu** [wo boo chir new-roh]

beer 啤酒 **píjiǔ** [pee-jew]
▸ two beers, please 请来两杯啤酒 **qǐng lái liǎng bēi píjiǔ** [ching ligh lyang bay pee-jew]

begin *(start)* 开始 kāishǐ [kigh-shir]
> ▸ when does the performance begin? 表演什么时候开始？ biǎoyǎn shénme shíhou kāishǐ? [byow-yan sheun-muh shir-hoh kigh-shir]

beginner 新手 xīnshǒu [shin-shoh]
> ▸ I'm a complete beginner 我完全是一个新手 wǒ wánquán shì yī gè xīnshǒu [wo wan-chwan shir yeeguh shin-shoh]

behind 在后面 zài hòumian [zigh hoh-myen]
> ▸ from behind 从后面 cóng hòumian [tsong hoh-myen]
> ▸ the rest of the family was in the car behind 家里的其他成员在后面的那辆车里 jiā li de qítā chéngyuán zài hòumian de nà liàng chē li [jya lee duh chee-ta chung-ywan zigh hoh-myen duh na lyang chuh lee]

berth *(on ship)* 卧铺 wòpù [wo-poo]
> ▸ I'd prefer the upper berth 我宁愿要上铺 wǒ nìngyuàn yào shàngpù [wo ning-ywan yow shang-poo]

beside 在......旁边 zài...pángbiān [zigh...pang-byen]
> ▸ is there anyone sitting beside you? 你旁边有人坐吗？ nǐ pángbiān yǒu rén zuò ma? [nee pang-byen yoh reun zwore ma]

best 最好的 zuì hǎo de [zway how duh]
> ▸ what's the best restaurant in town? 城里最好的餐馆是哪一家？ chéng li zuì hǎo de cānguǎn shì nǎ yī jiā? [chung lee zway how duh tsan-gwan shir na yee jya]

better 更好的 gèng hǎo de [gung how duh]
> ▸ I've been on antibiotics for a week and I'm not any better 我服用抗生素已有一周了，没有感觉好一些 wǒ fúyòng kàngshēngsù yī yǒu yī zhōu le, méiyou gǎnjué hǎo yīxiē [wo foo-yong kang-shung-soo yee yoh yee joh luh may-yoh gan-jue how yee-shyeah]
> ▸ the better situated of the two hotels 两家旅馆中位置较好的那一家 liǎng jiā lǚguǎn zhōng wèizhi jiào hǎo de nà yī jiā [lyang jya looh-gwan jong way-jir jeow how duh na yee jya]

between 在......之间 zài...zhī jiān [zigh...jir-jyen]
> ▸ a bus runs between the airport and the hotel 往返于机场和旅馆之间的公共汽车 wǎngfǎn yú jīchǎng hé lǚguǎn zhī jiān de gōnggòng qìchē [wang-fan yoo jee-chang huh looh-gwan jir jyen duh gong-gong chee-chuh]

bicycle 自行车 zìxíngchē [zir-shing-chuh]
> ▸ is there a place to leave bicycles? 有停放自行车的地方吗？ yǒu tíngfàng zìxíngché de dìfang ma? [yoh ting-fang-chuh duh dee-fang ma]

bicycle lane 自行车道 zìxíngchēdào [zir-shing-chuh dow]
> ▸ are there any bicycle lanes? 有自行车道吗？ yǒu zìxíngchēdào ma? [yoh zir-shing-chuh dow ma]

bicycle pump 自行车打气筒 zìxíngchē dǎqìtǒng [zir-shing-chuh da-chee-tong]

▸ do you have a bicycle pump? 你有自行车打气筒吗？ nǐ yǒu zìxíngchē dǎqìtǒng ma? [nee yoh zir-shing-chuh da-chee-tong]

big 大的 dà de [da de]

▸ do you have it in a bigger size? 你有大一点的尺码吗？ nǐ yǒu dà yìdiǎn de chǐmǎ ma? [nee yoh da yee-dyen duh chir-ma ma]

▸ it's too big 太大了 tài dà le [tigh da luh]

bike 自行车 zìxíngchē [zir-shing-chuh]

▸ I'd like to rent a bike for an hour 我想租一小时的自行车 wǒ xiǎng zū yī xiǎoshí de zìxíngchē [wo shyang zoo yee shyao-shir de zir-shing-chuh]

▸ I'd like to do a bike tour 我想参加自行车游 wǒ xiǎng cānjiā zìxíngchē yóu [wo shyang tsan-jya zir-shing-chuh yoh]

bill 账单 zhàngdān [jang-dan]; (paper money) 钞票 chāopiào [chow-peow]

▸ I think there's a mistake with the bill 我想账算错了 wǒ xiǎng zhàng suàn cuò le [wo shyang jang swan tswore luh]

▸ put it on my bill 记在我的账上 jì zài wǒ de zhàng shang [jee zigh wo duh jang shang]

▸ can you write up my bill, please? 请结账好吗？ qǐng jiézhàng hǎo ma? [ching jyeah-jang how ma]

birthday 生日 shēngrì [shung-rir]

▸ happy birthday! 生日快乐！ shēngrì kuàilè! [shung-rir kwigh luh]

bite (animal) 咬 yǎo [yow]; (insect) 叮 dīng [ding]

▸ do you have a cream for mosquito bites? 你有擦蚊子叮咬的药膏吗？ nǐ yǒu cā wénzi dīngyǎo de yàogāo ma? [nee yoh tsa wen-zir ding-yow duh yow-gow ma]

▸ I've been bitten by a mosquito 我被蚊子叮了 wǒ bèi wénzi dīng le [wo bay wen-zir ding luh]

black 黑色的 hēisè de [hay-suh duh]; (coffee, tea) 不加奶的 bù jiā nǎi de [boo jya nigh duh]

▸ I'm looking for a little black dress 我想要一件黑色的小连衣裙 wǒ xiǎng yào yī jiàn hēisè de xiǎo liányīqún [wo shyang yow yee jyen hay-suh duh shyow lyen-yee-chun]

black-and-white 黑白的 hēibái de [hay-bigh duh]

▸ I like black-and-white movies 我喜欢看黑白电影 wǒ xǐhuan kàn hēibái diànyǐng [wo shee-hwan kan hay-bigh jyen-ying]

black ice 看不见的薄冰 kàn bù jiàn de báobīng [kan boo jyen duh bow-bing]

▸ there's black ice 有看不见的薄冰 yǒu kàn bù jiàn de báobīng [yoh kan boo jyen duh bow-bing]

blanket 毯子 tǎnzi [tan-zir]
▸ I'd like an extra blanket 我想再要一条毯子 wǒ xiǎng zài yào yī tiáo tǎnzi [wo shyang zigh yow teow yee teow tan-zir]

bleed 流血 liú xuè [lew shue]
▸ it won't stop bleeding 血流个不停 xuè liú gè bù tíng [shue lew guh boo ting]

blind *(on window)* 百叶窗 bǎiyèchuāng [bigh-yuh-chwung]
▸ can we pull down the blinds? 我们能把百叶窗拉上吗? wǒmen néng bǎ bǎiyèchuāng lāshang ma? [wo-meun nung bigh-yuh-chwung la-shang ma]

blister 水泡 shuǐpào [shway-pow]
▸ I got a blister 我长了个水泡 wǒ zhǎngle gè shuǐpào [wo jang-luh guh shway-pow]

block *(pipe, sink)* 堵塞 dǔsè [doo-suh]; *(road)* 堵住 dǔzhù [doo-joo]
▸ the toilet's blocked 厕所堵住了 cèsuǒ dǔzhù le [tsuh-swore doo-joo luh]
▸ my ears are completely blocked 我的耳朵完全被塞住了 wǒ de ěrduo wánquán bèi sāizhù le [wo duh er-dwore wan-chwan bay sigh-joo luh]

blond 金色的 jīnsè de [jin-suh duh]
▸ I have blond hair 我的头发是金色的 wǒ de tóufa shì jīnsè de [wo duh toh-fa shir jin-suh duh]

blood 血 xuè [shue]
▸ traces of blood 血迹 xuèjì [shue-jee]

blood pressure 血压 xuèyā [shue-ya]
▸ I have high blood pressure 我有高血压 wǒ yǒu gāoxuèyā [wo yoh gow-shue-ya]

blood type 血型 xuèxíng [shue-shing]
▸ my blood type is A positive 我的血型是A型 wǒ de xuèxíng shì a xíng [wo duh shue-shing shir a shing]

blue 蓝色的 lánsè de [lan-suh duh]
▸ the blue one 蓝色的那个 lánsè de nàge [lan-suh duh na-guh]

board *(plane)* 上 shàng [shang] ♦ 登机 dēngjī [dung-jee]
▸ what time will the plane be boarding? 飞机几点开始登机? fēijī jǐ diǎn kāishǐ dēngjī? [fay-jee jee dyen kigh-shir dung-jee]
▸ where is the flight to Beijing boarding? 去北京的飞机在哪里登机? qù běijīng de fēijī zài nǎli dēngjī? [choo bay-jing duh fay-jee zigh na-lee dung-jee]

boarding pass 登机牌 dēngjīpái [dung-jee-pigh]
▸ I can't find my boarding pass 我找不到我的登机牌了 wǒ zhǎo bù dào wǒ de dēngjīpái le [wo jow boo dow wo duh dung-jee-pigh luh]

boat 船 chuán [chwan]
▸ can we get there by boat? 我们能坐船去那里吗? wǒmen néng zuò chuán qù nàli ma? [wo-meun nung zwore chwan choo na-lee ma]

boat trip 乘船游玩 chéng chuán yóuwán [chung chwan yoh-wan]
▸ are there boat trips on the river? 河上有乘船游玩的吗？ hé shang yǒu chéng chuán yóuwán de ma? [huh shang yoh chung chwan yoh-wan duh ma]

book *(for reading)* 书 shū [shoo]; *(of tickets, stamps, matches)* 沓 dá [da]
♦ *(ticket, room)* 预定 yùdìng [yoo-ding]
▸ do you sell English-language books? 你们卖英文书吗？ nǐmen mài yīngwén shū ma? [nee-meun migh ying-weun shoo ma]
▸ is it more economical to buy a book of tickets? 买一沓票是否更合算？ mǎi yī dá piào shìfǒu gèng hésuàn? [migh yee da peow shir-foh gung huh-swan]
▸ I'd like to book a ticket 我想预定一张票 wǒ xiǎng yùdìng yī zhāng piào [wo shyang yoo-ding yee jang peow]
▸ do you need to book in advance? 需要事先预定吗？ xūyào shìxiān yùdìng ma? [shoo-yow shir-shyen yoo-ding ma]

born
▸ to be born 出生 chūshēng [choo-sheng]
▸ I was born on March 3rd, 1985 我出生于1985年3月3日 wǒ chūshēng yú yī jiǔ bā wǔ nián sān yuè sān rì [wo choo-sheng yoo jew ba woo nyen san yue san-rir]

bottle 瓶 píng [ping]
▸ a bottle of red wine, please 请来一瓶红葡萄酒 qǐng lái yī píng hóng pútaojiǔ [ching ligh yee ping hong poo-tow-jew]

bottle opener 开瓶器 kāipíngqì [kigh-ping-chee]
▸ can you pass me the bottle opener? 你能把开瓶器递给我吗？ nǐ néng bǎ kāipíngqì dì gěi wǒ ma? [nee nung ba kigh-ping-chee dee gay wo ma]

bottom *(of a well, of a box)* 底部 dǐbù [dee-boo]
▸ my passport's at the bottom of my suitcase 我的护照在我的手提箱的箱底 wǒ de hùzhào zài wǒ de shǒutíxiāng de xiāngdǐ [wo duh hoo-jow zigh wo duh show-tee-shyang duh shyang-dee]

box 盒 hé [huh]
▸ could I have a box of matches, please? 请给我一盒火柴好吗？ qǐng gěi wǒ yī hé huǒchái hǎo ma? [ching gay wo yee huh hwore-chigh how ma]

boy *(young male)* 男孩 nánhái [nan-high]; *(son)* 儿子 érzi [er-zir]
▸ he seems like a nice boy 他似乎是个好孩子 tā sìhū shì gè hǎo háizi [ta sir-hoo shir guh how high-zir]
▸ she has two boys 她有两个儿子 tā yǒu liǎng gè érzi [ta yoh lyang guh er-zir]

boyfriend 男朋友 nánpéngyou [nan-pung-yoh]
▸ my boyfriend is a biologist 我的男朋友是个生物学家 wǒ de nánpéngyou shì gè shēngwùxuéjiā [wo duh nan-pung-yoh shir guh shung-woo-shue-jya]

brake 刹车 shāchē [sha-chuh]
▸ the brakes aren't working properly 刹车坏了 shāchē huài le [sha-chuh hwigh luh]

bread

Although bread is not a traditional Chinese food, it is available in bakeries and pastry shops and many supermarkets sell their own bread. A lot of foods in China are made with flour, including a variety of noodles and also 包子 bāozi [bow-zir], little steamed rolls stuffed with meat or vegetables.

brake fluid 刹车油 shāchēyóu [sha-chuh-yoh]
- could you check the brake fluid? 你能检查一下刹车油吗？ nǐ néng jiǎnchá yī xià shāchēyóu ma? [nee nung jyen-cha yee shya-chuh-yoh ma]

branch *(of bank)* 分行 fēnháng [fen-hang]
- which branch should I visit to get the replacement traveler's checks? 我应该去哪个支行补办旅行支票？ wǒ yīnggāi qù nǎge zhīháng bǔbàn lǚxíng zhīpiào? [wo ying-gigh choo na-guh jir-hang boo-ban looh-shing jir-peow]

bread 面包 miànbāo [myen-bow]
- do you have any bread? 你有面包吗？ nǐ yǒu miànbāo ma? [nee yoh myen-bow ma]
- could we have some more bread? 我们能再要点儿面包吗？ wǒmen néng zài yào diǎnr miànbāo ma? [wo-meun nung yow dyenr myen-bow ma]

break *(pause)* 中止 zhōngzhǐ [jong-jir] ♦ 把......弄破 bǎ......nòngpò [ba......nong-po]
- should we take a break? 我们能休息一下吗？ wǒmen néng xiūxi yī xià ma? [wo-meun nung shew-shee yee shya ma]
- be careful you don't break it 小心别把它弄破了 xiǎoxīn bié bǎ tā nòngpò le [shyow-shin byeah ba ta nong-po luh]
- I think I've broken my ankle 我想我的踝关节骨折了 wǒ xiǎng wǒ de huái guā njié gǔzhé le [wo shyang wo duh hwigh gwan-jee goo-jir luh]

break down 出故障 chū gùzhàng [choo goo-jang]
- my car has broken down 我的车抛锚了 wǒ de chē pāomáo le [wo duh chuh pow-mow luh]

breakdown 故障 gùzhàng [goo-jang]
- we had a breakdown on the freeway 我们在高速公路上抛锚了 wǒmen zài gāosù gōnglù shang pāomáo le [wo-meun zigh gow-soo gong-loo shang pow-mow luh]

breakfast 早餐 zǎocān [zow-tsan]
- to have breakfast 吃早餐 chī zǎocān [chir zow-tsan]
- what time is breakfast served? 几点开始供应早餐？ jǐ diǎn kāishǐ gōngyìng zǎocān? [jee dyen kigh-shir gong-ying zow-tsan]

bridge *(over river)* 桥 qiáo [cheow]; *(on ship)* 驾驶台桥 jiàshǐtáiqiáo [jya-shir-tigh-cheow]

▸ do you have to pay a toll to use the bridge? 过桥需要付费吗？ guò qiáo xūyào fù fèi ma? [gwore cheow shoo-yow foo fay ma]

bring 带来 dàilai [digh-ligh]

▸ what should we bring to drink? 我们要带饮料来吗？ wǒmen yào dài yǐnliào lái ma? [wo-meun yow digh yin-leow ligh ma]

bring down *(bags, luggage)* 把......拿下来 bǎ......náxialai [ba...na-shya-ligh]

▸ could you get someone to bring down our luggage, please? 请你叫人把我们的行李拿下来好吗？ qǐng nǐ jiào rén bǎ wǒmen de xíngli náxialai hǎo ma? [ching nee jeow reun ba wo-meun duh shing-lee na-shya-ligh how ma]

bring in *(bags, luggage)* 把......拿进来 bǎ......nájinlai [ba...na-jin-ligh]

▸ can you bring in my bags, please? 请你把我的行李拿进来好吗？ qǐng nǐ bǎ wǒ de xíngli nájinlai hǎo ma? [ching nee ba wo duh shing-lee na-jin-ligh how ma]

broken *(equipment)* 损坏了的 sǔnhuàile de [sun-hwigh-luh duh]; *(part of the body)* 折断了的 héduànle de [huh-dwan-luh duh]

▸ the lock is broken 锁坏了 suǒ huài le [swore hwigh luh]

▸ I think I've got a broken leg 我想我的一条腿断了 wǒ xiǎng wǒ de yī tiáo tuǐ duàn le [wo shyang wo duh yee teow tway dwan luh]

bronchitis 支气管炎 zhīqìguǎnyán [jir-chee-gwan-yan]

▸ do you have anything for bronchitis? 你有治疗支气管炎的药吗？ nǐ yǒu zhìliáo zhīqìguǎnyán de yào ma? [nee yoh jir-leow jir-chee-gwan-yan duh yow ma]

brother 兄弟 xiōngdi [shyong-dee]

▸ I don't have any brothers or sisters 我没有兄弟姐妹 wǒ méiyou xiōngdi jiěmèi [wo may-yoh shyong-dee jyeah-may]

brown 棕色的 zōngsè de [zong-suh duh]

▸ he has brown hair 他的头发是棕色的 tā de tóufa shì zōngsè de [ta duh toh-fa shir zong-suh duh]

▸ I'm looking for a brown leather belt 我在找一条棕色的皮带 wǒ zài zhǎo yī tiáo zōngsè de pídài [wo zigh jow yee teow zong-suh duh pee-digh]

brush *(for hair, clothes, with short handle)* 刷子 shuāzi [shwa-zir]; *(broom)* 扫帚 sàozhou [sow-joh] ◆ *(hair)* 刷 shuā [shwa]

▸ where are the brush and dustpan? 扫帚和簸箕在哪儿？ sàozhou hé bòji zài nǎr? [sow-joh huh bo-jee zigh nar]

▸ to brush one's teeth 刷牙 shuā yá [shwa ya]

bulb *(light)* 灯泡 dēngpào [dung-pow]

▸ the bulb's out in the bathroom 浴室的灯坏了 yùshì de dēngpào huài le [yoo-shir duh dung-pow hwigh luh]

bus

Bus networks are highly developed in all the major cities. Unfortunately buses are often completely packed in the rush hour. You buy your ticket on the bus, from a conductor. The price depends on how far you are traveling and how comfortable the bus is (it costs more if the bus has air-conditioning) but it is usually about 1 to 3 yuan. Buses usually stop at every stop on the route, but as there's no 'stop request' button, you sometimes have to signal to the conductor to tell him when you want to get off. Bus destinations are usually given in Chinese with no *pinyin* transcription, so you may need to ask for help.

bunk beds 双层床 shuāngcéngchuáng [shwung-tsung-chwung]
 ▸ are there bunk beds for the children? 这个双层床是给孩子用的吗？ zhège shuāngcéngchuáng shì gěi háizi yòng de ma? [jir-guh shwung-tsung-chwung shir gay high-zir yong duh ma]

burn 烧毁 shāohuǐ [show-hway]
 ▸ the food's completely burnt 食物全烧焦了 shíwù quán shāojiāo le [shir-woo chwan show-jeow luh]
 ▸ I've burned my hand 我烧伤了自己的手 wǒ shāoshāng le zìjǐ de shǒu [wo show-shang luh zir-jee duh shoh]

burst *(tire)* 爆裂 bàoliè [bow-lyeah]
 ▸ one of my tires burst 我的一个轮胎爆裂了 wǒ de yī gè lúntāi bào le [wo duh yee guh lun-tigh bow luh]

bus 公共汽车 gōnggòng qìchē [gong-gong chee-chuh]
 ▸ does this bus go downtown? 这辆公共汽车到市区吗？ zhè liǎng gōnggòng qìchē dào shìqū ma? [jir lyang gong-gong chee-chuh dow shir-choo ma]
 ▸ which bus do I have to take to go to…? 到……去我该乘坐哪辆公共汽车？ dào……qù wǒ gāi chéngzuò nǎ liǎng gōnggòng qìchē? [dow…choo wo gigh chung-zwore na lyang gong-gong chee-chuh]

bus driver 公共汽车驾驶员 gōnggòng qìchē jiàshǐyuán [gong-gong chee-chuh jya-shir-yuwan]
 ▸ does the bus driver speak English? 公共汽车驾驶员会说英语吗？ gōnggòng qìchē jiàshǐyuán huì shuō yīngyǔ ma? [gong-gong chee-chuh jya-shir-ywan hway shwore ying-yoo ma]

business *(commerce)* 商业 shāngyè [shang-yuh]; *(company)* 公司 gōngsī [gong-sir]; *(concern)* 关心的事 guānxīn de shì [gwan-shin duh shir]; *(affair, matter)* 事务 shìwù [shir-woo]
 ▸ it's none of your business 这不干你的事 zhè bù gān nǐ de shì [jir boo gan nee duh shir]

business cards

These are extremely important when you meet someone through business as they show the position of the person you are talking to as well as their contact details. Business cards are exchanged with great respect. You should present and receive the card holding the corners in both hands. You should look at the card for a while to show your respect for the person who has given you the card, especially if she or he has a high position. Meetings usually begin with an exchange of business cards. You should present yours to the person with the highest status first. People who work in an international business environment will often have bilingual business cards (English on one side and Chinese on the other). This means that as a foreigner you will need to have your name translated into Chinese, and that as a Chinese person you will need to take an English first name.

business card 名片 míngpiàn [ming-pyen]
  ▸ here's my business card 这是我的名片 zhè shì wǒ de míngpiàn [jir shir wo duh ming-pyen]

business class 商务舱 shāngwùcāng [shang-woo-tsang] ◆ 乘坐商务舱 chéngzuò shāngwùcāng [chung-zwore shang-woo-tsang]
  ▸ are there any seats in business class? 商务舱还有座位吗？ shāngwùcāng hái yǒu zuòwèi ma? [shang-woo-tsang high yoh zwore-way ma]
  ▸ I prefer to travel business class 我外出旅行比较喜欢乘坐商务舱 wǒ wàichū lǚxíng bǐjiào xǐhuan chéngzuò shāngwùcāng [wo wigh-choo looh-shing bee-jeow shee-hwan chung-zwore shang-woo-tsang]

bus station 公共汽车总站 gōnggòng qìchē zǒngzhàn [gong-gong chee-chuh jong-jan]
  ▸ I'm looking for the bus station 我在找公共汽车总站 wǒ zài zhǎo gōnggòng qìchē zǒngzhàn [wo zigh jow gong-gong chee-chuh zong-jan]

bus stop 公共汽车站 gōnggòng qìchēzhàn [gong-gong chee-chuhjan]
  ▸ where's the nearest bus stop? 最近的公共汽车站在哪儿？ zuì jìn de gōnggòng qìchēzhàn zài nǎr? [zway jin duh gong-gong chee-chuh-jan zigh nar]

busy (person, period) 忙的 máng de [mang duh]; (town, beach, street) 繁忙的 fánmáng de [fan-mang duh]; (phone line) 正被占用的 zhèng bèi zhànyòng de [jung bay jan-yong duh]
  ▸ I'm afraid I'm busy tomorrow 恐怕我明天忙 kǒngpà wǒ míngtiān máng [kong-pa wo ming-tyen mang]
  ▸ the line's busy 正在占线 zhèngzài zhànxiàn [jung-zigh jan-shyen]

butter 黄油 huángyóu [hwung-yoh]
  ▸ could you pass the butter, please? 请您把黄油递给我好吗？ qǐng nín bǎ huángyóu dì gěi wǒ hǎo ma? [ching neen ba hwung-yoh dee gay wo how ma]

buy 买 **mǎi** [migh]

▶ where can I buy tickets? 我可以在哪里买票？ **wǒ kěyǐ zài nǎli mǎi piào?** [wo kuh-yee zigh na-lee migh peow]

▶ can I buy you a drink? 我能请你喝一杯吗？ **wǒ néng qǐng nǐ hē yī bēi ma?** [wo nung ching nee huh bay ma]

bye 再见 **zàijiàn** [zigh-jyen]

▶ bye, see you tomorrow! 再见，明天见！ **zàijiàn, míngtiān jiàn!** [zigh-jyen ming-tyen jyen]

C

cab 出租车 **chūzūchē** [choo-zoo-chuh]

▶ can you order me a cab to the airport? 你能帮我叫一辆出租车去飞机场吗？ **nǐ néng bāng wǒ jiào yī liàng chūzūchē qù fēijīchǎng ma?** [nee nung bang wo jyow yee lyang choo-zoo-chuh choo fay-jee-chang ma]

cab driver 出租车司机 **chūzūchē sījī** [choo-zoo-chuh sir-jee]

▶ does the cab driver speak English? 出租车司机说英文吗？ **chūzūchē sījī shuō yīngwén ma?** [choo-zoo-chuh sir-jee shwore ying-weun ma]

cabin *(on boat)* 船舱 **chuáncāng** [chwan-tsang]; *(on plane)* 机舱 **jīcāng** [jee-tsang]

▶ can I have breakfast in my cabin? 我能在我的舱位里用早餐吗？ **wǒ néng zài wǒ de cāngwèi li yòng zǎocān ma?** [wo nung zigh wo duh tsang-way lee yong zow-tsan ma]

cable 有线电视 **yǒuxiàn diànshì** [yoh-shyen dyen-shir]

▶ does the hotel have cable? 饭店里有有线电视吗？ **fàndiàn li yǒu yǒuxiàn diànshì ma?** [fan-dyen lee yoh yoh-shyen dyen-shir ma]

café 小餐馆 **xiǎo cānguǎn** [shyow tsan-gwan]

▶ is there a café near here? 附近有小餐馆吗？ **fùjìn yǒu xiǎo cānguǎn ma?** [foo-jin yoh shyow tsan-gwan ma]

---

in a café

▶ is this table/seat free? 这张桌子/这个座位有人吗？ **zhè zhāng zhuōzi/zhège zuòwèi yǒu rén ma?** [jir jang jwore-zir/juh-guh zwore-way yoh reun ma]

▶ excuse me! 劳驾！ **láojià!** [low-jya]

▶ can I have another beer, please? 请再来一杯啤酒好吗？ **qǐng zài lái yī bēi píjiǔ hǎo ma?** [ching zigh ligh yee bay pee-jew how ma]

cake 蛋糕 dàngāo [dan-gow]
> ‣ a piece of that cake, please 请来一块蛋糕 qǐng lái yī kuài dàngāo [ching ligh yee kwigh dan-gow]

call *(on phone)* 打电话 dǎ diànhuà [da dyen-hwa] ♦ *(name)* 叫 jiào [jeow]
> ‣ I have to make a call 我得打个电话 wǒ děi dǎ gè diànhuà [wo day da guh dyen-hwa]
> ‣ what is this called? 这个叫什么? zhège jiào shénme? [jir-guh jeow sheun-muh]
> ‣ who's calling? 你是哪位? nǐ shì nǎ wèi? [nee shir nay way]

call back 给......回电话 gěi......huí diànhuà [gay...hway dyen-hwa] ♦ 打回电话 dǎ huí diànhuà [da...hway dyen-hwa]
> ‣ could you ask her to call me back? 你能叫她给我回电话吗? nǐ néng jiào tā gěi wǒ huí diànhuà ma? [nee nung jeow ta gay wo hway dyen-hwa ma]
> ‣ I'll call back (later) 我（一会儿）会打回电话的 wǒ (yīhuìr) huì dǎ huí diànhuà de [wo (yee-hwayr) hway da hway dyen-hwa duh]

calm 镇定的 zhèndìng de [jeun-ding duh]
> ‣ keep calm! 保持镇定! bǎochí zhèndìng! [bow-chir jeun-ding]

camera *(for taking photos)* 照相机 zhàoxiàngjī [jow-shyang-jee]; *(for filming)* 摄像机 shèxiàngjī [shuh-shyang-jee]
> ‣ can I use the camera here? 我能在这里拍照吗? wǒ néng zài zhèli pāizhào ma? [wo nung zigh juh-lee pigh-jow ma]

camper 野营车 yěyíngchē [yuh-ying-chuh]
> ‣ do you have a space left for a camper? 你有没有停放野营车的空位? nǐ yǒuméiyǒu tíngfàng yěyíngchē de kòngwèi? [nee yoh-may-yoh ting-fang yuh-ying-chuh duh kong-way]
> ‣ I'd like to book space for a camper for the night of August 15th 我想在8月15日的晚上预定一个停放野营车的位置 wǒ xiǎng zài bā yuè shíwǔ rì de wǎnshang yùdìng yī gè tíngfàng yěyíngchē de wèizhi [wo shyang zigh ba yue shir-woo rir duh wan-shang yoo-ding yee guh ting-fang yuh-ying-chuh duh dee-fang]

campground 野营地 yěyíngdì [yuh-ying-dee]
> ‣ I'm looking for a campground 我在找野营地 wǒ zài zhǎo yěyíngdì [wo zigh jow yuh-ying-dee]

camping 露营度假 lùyíng dùjià [loo-ying doo-jya]
> ‣ I love going camping 我喜欢露营度假 wǒ xǐhuan lùyíng dùjià [wo shee-hwan loo-ying doo-jya]

can *(of food, drink)* 罐 guàn [gwan]; *(of oil, paint)* 桶 tǒng [tong]
> ‣ a can of oil, please 请来一桶油 qǐng lái yī tǒng yóu [ching ligh yee-tong yoh]

can *(be able to)* 能 néng [nung]; *(know how to)* 会 huì [hway]
> ‣ can I help you? 我能帮你吗? wǒ néng bāng nǐ ma? [wo nung bang nee ma]

▸ can you understand English? 你懂英语吗？ **nǐ dǒng yīngyǔ ma?** [nee dong ying-yoo ma]

Canada 加拿大 jiānádà [jya-na-da]

▸ I'm from Canada 我来自加拿大 **wǒ láizì jiānádà** [wo ligh-zir jya-na-da]
▸ I live in Canada 我住在加拿大 **wǒ zhù zài jiānádà** [wo joo zigh jya-na-da]
▸ have you ever been to Canada? 你去过加拿大吗？ **nǐ qùguo jiānádà ma?** [nee choo-gwore jya-na-da ma]

Canadian 加拿大的 jiānádà de [jya-na-da duh] ♦ 加拿大人 jiānádàrén [jya-na-da-reun]

▸ I'm Canadian 我是加拿大人 **wǒ shì jiānádàrén** [wo shir jya-na-da-reun]
▸ we're Canadians 我们是加拿大人 **wǒmen shì jiānádàrén** [wo-meun shir jya-na-da-reun]

cancel 取消 qǔxiāo [choo-shyow]

▸ is it possible to cancel a reservation? 是否可以取消预定？ **shìfǒu kěyǐ qǔxiāo yùdìng?** [shir-foh kuh-yee choo-shyow yoo-ding]

canoeing 划独木舟 huá dúmùzhōu [hwa doo-moo-joh]

▸ I was told we could go canoeing 我听说我们可以去划独木舟 **wǒ tīngshuō wǒmen kěyǐ qù huá dúmùzhōu** [wo ting-shwore wo-meun kuh-yee choo hwa doo-moo-joh]

car *(automobile)* 汽车 qìchē [chee-chuh]; *(on train)* 车厢 chēxiāng [chuh-shyang]

▸ I'd like to rent a car for a week 我想租一个星期的车 **wǒ xiǎng zū yī gè xīngqī de chē** [wo shyang zoo yee guh shing-chee duh chuh]
▸ I've just crashed my car 我刚把我的车撞坏了 **wǒ gāng bǎ wǒ de chē zhuànghuài le** [wo gang ba wo duh chuh jwung-hwigh luh]
▸ can you help us push the car? 你能帮我推一下车吗？ **nǐ néng bāng wǒ tuī yī xià chē ma?** [nee nung bang wo tway yee shya chuh ma]
▸ my car's been towed away 我的车被拖走了 **wǒ de chē bēi tuōzǒu le** [wo duh chuh bay twore-zoh luh]

---

renting a car

▸ with comprehensive insurance 带有全程保险 **dàiyǒu quánchéng bǎoxiǎn** [digh-yoh chwan-cheng bow-shyen]
▸ can I leave the car at the airport? 我能把车留在机场吗？ **wǒ néng bǎ chē liú zài jīchǎng ma?** [wo nung ba chuh lew zigh jee-chang ma]
▸ can I see your driver's license, please? 请让我看一下你的驾照好吗？ **qǐng ràng wǒ kàn yī xià nǐ de jiàzhào hǎo ma?** [ching rang wo kan yee shya nee duh jya-jow how ma]

▸ my car's broken down 我的车出故障了 wǒ de chē chū gùzhàng le [wo duh chuh choo goo-jang luh]

carafe 玻璃瓶 bōlípíng [bo-lee-ping]
▸ a large carafe of water, please 请来一大瓶水 qǐng lái yī dà píng shuǐ [ching ligh yee da ping shway]

car crash 车祸 chēhuò [chuh-hwore]
▸ he's been killed in a car crash 他在一次车祸中丧生了 tā zài yī cì chēhuò zhōng sàngshēng le [ta zigh zay tsir chuh-hwore jong sang-sheng luh]

card *(finance)* 卡片 kǎpiàn [ka-pyen]; *(greeting card)* 贺卡 hèkǎ [huh-ka]; *(business card)* 名片 míngpiàn [ming-pyen]
▸ the waiter hasn't brought my card back 服务员还没有把我的信用卡还给我 fúwùyuán hái méiyou bǎ wǒ de xìnyòngkǎ huán gěi wǒ [foo-woo-ywan high may-yoh ba wo duh shin-yong-ka hwan gay wo]
▸ can I give you my card? 我给你一张名片好吗？ wǒ gěi nǐ yī zhāng míngpiàn hǎo ma? [wo gay nee yee jang ming-pyen how ma]

cardigan 毛线衣 máoxiànyī [mow-shyen-yee]
▸ should I take a cardigan for the evening? 晚上我需要带件毛线衣吗？ wǎnshang wǒ xūyào dài jiàn máoxiànyī ma? [wan-shang wo shoo-yow da jyen mow-shyen-yee ma]

carpet 地毯 dìtǎn [dee-tan]
▸ the carpet hasn't been vacuumed 地毯还没有用吸尘器清理过 dìtǎn hái méiyou yòng xīchénqì qīnglǐguo [dee-tan high may-yoh yong shee-chen-chee ching-lee-gwore]

car rental 租车 zūchē [zoo-chuh]
▸ is car rental expensive? 租车贵吗？ zūchē guì ma? [zoo-chuh gway ma]

car rental agency 租车公司 zūchē gōngsī [zoo-chuh gong-sir]
▸ do you know any car rental agencies? 你知道什么租车公司吗？ nǐ zhīdao shénme zūchē gōngsī ma? [nee jir-dow sheun-muh zoo-chuh gong-sir ma]

carry *(baggage)* 携带 xiédài [shyeah-digh] ◆ *(sound)* 能达到远处 néng dádào yuǎnchù [nung da-dow ywan-choo]
▸ could you help me carry something? 你能帮我拿点东西吗？ nǐ néng bāng wǒ ná diǎn dōngxi ma? [nee nung bang wo na dyen dong-shee ma]

carry-on bag 手提行李 shǒutí xínglǐ [shoh-tee shing-lee]
▸ am I only allowed one carry-on bag? 我是否只许带一件手提行李？ wǒ shìfǒu zhǐ xǔ dài yī jiàn shǒutí xínglǐ? [wo shir-foh jir shoo da yee jyen shoh-tee shing-lee]

cart *(for luggage)* 手推车 shǒutuīchē [show-tway-chuh]; *(in supermarket)* 购物车 gòuwùchē [goh-woo-chuh]

cash

People still tend to use cash rather than checks or credit cards in China. In fact, a lot of organizations still pay their staff's salaries in cash. Many transactions are made in cash, even large purchases such as those for televisions or domestic appliances, so it isn't at all uncommon to carry a lot of cash on you in China. Checks are virtually unused outside the world of big business. Credit cards are used more widely, but are still not accepted in many stores and restaurants. However, they are accepted in most big hotels and some department stores.

▸ where can I get a cart? 我在哪里可以找到手推车？ **wǒ zài nǎli kěyǐ zhǎodào shǒutuīchē?** [wo zigh na-lee kuh-yee jow-dow show-tway-chuh]

carton *(of cigarettes)* 盒 hé [huh]
▸ I'd like a carton of cigarettes 我要一盒香烟 **wǒ yào yī hé xiāngyān** [wo yow yee huh shyang-yan]

cash *(notes and coins)* 现金 xiànjīn [shyen-jin] ◆ *(check)* 把...... 兑现 bǎ...... duìxiàn [ba...dway-shyen]
▸ I'll pay cash 我用现金支付 **wǒ yòng xiànjīn zhīfù** [wo yong shyen-jin jir-foo]
▸ I want to cash this traveler's check 我想把这张旅行支票兑现 **wǒ xiǎng bǎ zhè zhāng lǚxíng zhīpiào duìxiàn** [wo shyang ba juh jang looh-shing jir-peow dway-shyen]

castle 城堡 chéngbǎo [chung-bow]
▸ is the castle open to the public? 这座城堡对公众开放吗？ **zhé zuò chéngbǎo duì gōngzhòng kāifàng ma?** [juh zwore chung-bow dway gong-jong kigh-fang ma]

catalog 目录 mùlù [moo-loo]
▸ do you have a catalog? 你有目录吗？ **nǐ yǒu mùlù ma?** [nee yoh moo-loo ma]

catch *(with hands)* 接住 jiēzhù [jyeah-joo]; *(cold)* 感染上 gǎnrǎnshang [gan-ran-shang]; *(hear clearly)* 听见 tīngjian [ting-jyen]
▸ I've caught a cold 我感冒了 **wǒ gǎnmào le** [wo gan-mow luh]
▸ I'm sorry, I didn't quite catch your name 对不起，我没听清你的名字 **duìbuqǐ, wǒ méi tīngqīng nǐ de míngzì** [dway-boo-chee wo may ting-ching nee duh ming-zir]

Catholic 天主教的 tiānzhǔjiào de [tyen-joo-jeow duh] ◆ 天主教 tiānzhǔjiào [tyen-joo-jeow duh]
▸ where is there a Catholic church? 哪里有天主教堂？ **nǎli yǒu tiānzhǔjiào-táng?** [na-lee yoh tyen-joo-jeow-tang]

CD CD [cd]

- how much does this CD cost? 这张CD多少钱? zhè zhāng cd duōshao qián? [juh jung cd dwore-show chyen]

cellphone 手机 shǒujī [shoh-jee]

- is there an outlet so I can recharge my cellphone? 有没有电源插座我可以给我的手机充电? yǒuméiyǒu diànyuán chāzuò wǒ kěyǐ gěi wǒ de shǒujī chōngdiàn? [yoh-may-yoh dyen-ywan cha-zwore wo kuh-yee gay wo duh shoh-jee chong-dyen]
- what's your cellphone number? 你的手机号码是多少? nǐ de shǒujī hàomǎ shì duōshao? [nee duh shoh-jee how-ma shir dwore-show]

center 中心 zhōngxīn [jong-shin]

- we want to be based near the center of the region 我们想住在这个区的中心的附近 wǒmen xiǎng zhù zài zhège qū de zhōngxīn de fùjìn [wo-meun shyang joo zigh juh-guh choo duh jong-shin duh foo-jin]

chair 椅子 yǐzi [yee-zir]

- could we have another chair in our room? 能不能再给我们房间一把椅子? néngbùnéng zài gěi wǒmen fángjiān yī bǎ yǐzi? [nung-boo-nung zigh gay wo-meun fang-jyen yee ba yee-zir]

change 改变 gǎibiàn [gigh-byen]; (money) 零钱 língqián [ling-chyen] ♦ (baby) 给......换尿布 gěi......huàn niàobù [gay...hwan neow-boo] ♦ (clothes) 更衣 gēngyī [gung-yee]

- do you have any change? 你有零钱吗? nǐ yǒu língqián ma? [nee yoh ling-chyen ma]
- keep the change 不用找了 bùyòng zhǎo le [boo-yong jow luh]
- I don't have exact change 我没有刚好的零钱 wǒ méiyou gānghǎo de língqián [wo may-yoh gang-how duh ling-chyen]
- is it possible to change a reservation? 是否可以更改预定? shìfou kěyǐ gēnggǎi yùdìng? [shir-foh kuh-yee gung-gigh yoo-ding]
- I'd like to change 200 dollars into yuan 我想把两百美元换成人民币 wǒ xiǎng bǎ liǎngbǎi měiyuán huànchéng rénmínbì [wo shyang ba lyang-bigh may-ywan hwan-chung reun-min-bee]
- I'd like to change these traveler's checks 我想把这些旅行支票兑现 wǒ xiǎng bǎ zhèxiē lǚxíng zhīpiào duìxiàn [wo shyang ba juh-shyeah loo-shing jir-peow dway-shyen]
- can you help me change the tire? 你能帮我换胎吗? nǐ néng bāng wǒ huàn tāi ma? [nee nung bang wo hwan tigh ma]
- the oil needs to be changed 得换油了 děi huàn yóu le [day hwan yoh luh]

changing table (for baby) 婴儿台 yīng'értái [ying-er-tigh]

- is there a changing table? 有婴儿台吗? yǒu yīng'értái ma? [yoh ying-er-tigh ma]

the check

The usual term for this is 结账 jiézhàng [jyeah-jang] but you often also hear 买单 mǎidān [migh-dan], especially in the South.

charge *(cost)* 费用 fèiyòng [fay-yong]

▸ is there a charge for the parking lot? 停车场收费吗? tíngchēchǎng shōu fèi ma? [ting-chuh-chang shoh fay ma]
▸ is there a charge for using the facilities? 使用这些设施要收费吗? shǐyòng zhèxiē shèshī yào shōu fèi ma? [shir-yong juh-shyeah shuh-shir yow shoh fay ma]
▸ is there a charge for cancellations? 取消要收费吗? qǔxiāo yào shōu fèi ma? [choo-sheow yow shoh fay ma]
▸ I'd like to speak to the person in charge 我想和负责的人说话 wǒ xiǎng hé fùzé de rén shuōhuà [wo shyang huh foo-zuh duh reun shwore-hwa]

charter flight 包机航班 bāojī hángbān [bow-jee hang-ban]

▸ where do we board the charter flight to Beijing? 前往北京的包机航班在哪里登机? qiánwǎng běijīng de bāojī hángbān zài nǎli dēngjī? [chyen-wang bay-jing duh bow-jee hang-ban zigh na-lee dung-jee]

cheap *(goods)* 廉价的 liánjià de [lyen-jya duh]; *(ticket)* 便宜的 piányi de [pyen-yee duh]

▸ I'm trying to find a cheap flight home 我正在找便宜的航班回家 wǒ zhèngzài zhǎo piányi de hángbān huí jiā [wo jung-zigh jow pyen-yee duh hang-ban hway jya]

check *(in restaurant)* 结账 jiézhàng [jyeah-jang]; *(for paying)* 支票 zhīpiào [jir-peow] ◆ *(test, verify)* 检查 jiǎnchá [jyen-cha]

checking

▸ is it right and then left? 是先向右再向左吗? shì xiān xiàng yòu zài xiàng zuǒ ma? [shir shyen shyang yoh zigh shyang zwore ma]
▸ is this the train for Shanghai? 这是开往上海的火车吗? zhè shì kāiwǎng shànghǎi de huǒchē ma? [juh shir kigh-wang shang-high duh hwore-chuh ma]
▸ could you tell me where to get off, please? 请你告诉我在哪几下好吗? qǐng nǐ gàosu wǒ zài nǎr xià hǎo ma? [ching nee gow-soo wo zigh nar shya how ma]
▸ is this the right stop for...? 到......是在这一站下吗? dào......shì zài zhè yī zhàn xià ma? [dow...shir zigh juh yee jan shya ma]
▸ are you sure that he'll be able to come? 你确定他能来? nǐ quèdìng tā néng lái? [nee chue-ding ta nung ligh]

▸ the check, please! 请结账! qǐng jiézhàng! [ching jyeah-jang]

▸ can I pay by check? 我能用支票付款吗? wǒ néng yòng zhīpiào fù kuǎn ma? [wo nung yong jir-peow foo kwan ma]

▸ can you check the oil? 你能检查一下油吗? nǐ néng jiǎnchá yī xià yóu ma? [nee nung jyen-cha yee shya yoh ma]

checkbook 支票本 zhīpiàoběn [jir-peow-ben]

▸ my checkbook's been stolen 我的支票本被偷了 wǒ de zhīpiàoběn bèi tōu le [wo duh jir-peow-ben bay toh luh]

check in *(baggage)* 托运 tuōyùn [toh-yun] ♦ *(at airport)* 办理登机手续 bànlǐ dēngjī shǒuxù [ban-lee dung-jee shoh-shu]; *(at hotel)* 办理入住手续 bànlǐ rùzhù shǒuxù [ban-lee roo-joo shoh-shoo]

▸ I'd like to check in both these bags, please 我想把这两件行李都托运掉 wǒ xiǎng bǎ zhè liàng jiàn xínglǐ dōu tuōyùndiào [wo shyang ba juh lyang jyen shing-lee doh twore-yun-deow]

▸ what time do you have to be at the airport to check in? 在机场什么时候你必须得办理登机手续? zài jīchǎng shénme shíhou nǐ bìxū děi bànlǐ dēngjī shǒuxù [zigh jee-chang sheun-muh shir-hoh nee bee-shoo day ban-lee dung-jee shoh-shoo]

check-in desk *(at airport)* 办票柜台 bànpiào guìtái [ban-peow gway-tigh]

▸ where is the United Airlines check-in desk? 美国联合航空公司的办票柜台在哪里? měiguó liánhé hángkōng gōngsī de bànpiào guìtái zài nǎli? [may-gwore lyen-huh hang-kong gong-sir duh ban-peow gway-tigh zigh na-lee]

check out *(from hotel)* 办理退房手续 bànlǐ tuìfáng shǒuxù [ban-lee tway-fang shwore-shoo]

▸ what time do you have to check out by? 几点必须得退房? jǐdiǎn bìxū děi tuìfáng? [jee-dyen bee-shoo day tway-fang]

cheers 干杯 gānbēi [gan-bay]

▸ cheers and all the best! 干杯，祝一切顺利 ! gānbēi, zhù yīqiè shùnlì! [gan-bay joo yee-chyeah shun-lee]

cheese 奶酪 nǎilào [nigh-low]

▸ what are the best local cheeses? 当地的奶酪哪种最好? dāngdì de nǎilào nǎ zhǒng zuì hǎo? [dang-dee duh nigh-low na jong zway how]

chicken 鸡肉 jīròu [jee-roh]

▸ half a roast chicken, please 请来半只烤鸡 qǐng lái bàn zhī kǎojī [ching ligh ban jir kow-jee]

▸ a chicken sandwich and fries 鸡肉三明治和炸薯条 jīròu sānmíngzhì hé zhá shǔtiáo [jee-roh san-ming-jir huh ja shoo-teow]

child 孩子 háizi [high-zir]

▸ do you have children? 你有孩子吗? nǐ yǒu háizi ma? [nee yoh high-zir ma]

▸ two adults and two children, please 两个大人和两个小孩儿 **liǎng gè dàrén hé liǎng gè xiǎoháir** [lyang guh da-reun huh lyang guh shyow-highr]

▸ do you have discounts for children? 小孩儿是否有折扣？ **xiǎoháir shìfǒu yǒu zhékòu** [sheow-highr shir-foh yoh juh-koh]

chilled *(wine)* 冰镇的 **bīngzhèn de** [bing-jeun duh]

▸ this wine isn't chilled enough 这葡萄酒不够冰 **zhè pútaojiǔ bù gòu gīng** [juh poo-tow-jew boo goh bing]

chocolate 巧克力 **qiǎokèlì** [cheow-kuh-lee]

▸ I'd like a bar of chocolate 我想要一块巧克力 **wǒ xiǎng yào yī kuài qiǎokèlì** [wo shyang yow yee kwigh cheow-kuh-lee]

choose 选择 **xuǎnzé** [shwan-zuh]

▸ I don't know which one to choose 我不知道选哪个 **wǒ bù zhīdao xuǎn nǎge** [wo boo jir-dow shwan na-guh]

chopsticks 筷子 **kuàizi** [kwigh-zir]

▸ I can't use chopsticks; could I have a spoon, please 我不会用筷子，请给我一个勺子好吗？ **wǒ bù huì yòng kuàizi, qǐng gěi wǒ yī gè sháozi hǎo ma?** [wo boo hway yong kwigh-zir ching gay wo yee guh show-zir how ma]

Christmas *(day)* 圣诞日 **shèngdàn rì** [shung-dan rir]; *(period)* 圣诞节 **shèngdàn jié** [shung-dan jyeah]

▸ Merry Christmas! 圣诞节快乐！ **shèngdàn jié kuàilè!** [shung-dan jyeah kwigh-luh]

▸ I wish you a very merry Christmas 祝你圣诞节快乐 **zhù nǐ shèngdàn jié kuàilè** [joo nee shung-dan jyeah kwigh-luh]

Christmas Day 圣诞日 **shèngdàn rì** [shung-dan rir]

▸ we're closed on Christmas Day 我们圣诞日关门 **wǒmen shèngdàn rì guānmén** [wo-meun shung-dan rir gwan-meun]

church 教堂 **jiàotáng** [jeow-tang]

▸ how old is the church? 这个教堂有多古老了？ **zhège jiàotáng yǒu duō gǔlǎo le?** [juh guh jeow-tang yoh dwore goo-low luh]

▸ where can we find a Protestant church? 我们在哪里可以找到新教教堂？ **wǒmen zài nǎlǐ kěyǐ zhǎodào xīnjiào jiàotáng?** [wo-meun zigh na-lee kuh-yee jow-dow shin-jeow jeow-tang]

▸ where is there a Catholic church? 哪里有天主教教堂？ **nǎli yǒu tiānzhǔjiào jiàotáng?** [na-lee yoh tyen-joo-jeow jeow-tang]

cigarette 香烟 **xiāngyān** [shyang-yen]

▸ can I ask you for a cigarette? 你有香烟吗？ **nǐ yǒu xiāngyān ma?** [nee yoh shyang-yan ma]

▸ where can I buy cigarettes? 我在哪里可以买到香烟？ **wǒ zài nǎli kěyǐ mǎidào xiāngyān?** [wo zigh na-lee kuh-yee migh-dow shyang-yan]

cigarette lighter 打火机 dǎhuǒjī [da-hwore-jee]

▸ do you have a cigarette lighter? 你有打火机吗？ nǐ yǒu dǎhuǒjī ma? [nee yoh da-hwore-jee ma]

city 城市 chéngshì [chung-shir]

▸ what's the nearest big city? 最近的大城市是什么？ zuì jìn de dà chéngshì shì shénme? [zway jin duh da-chung-shir shir sheun-muh]

class *(on train, plane)* 等级 děngjí [dung-jee]

▸ which class are your seats in? 你们的座位在哪一等级？ nǐmen de zuòwei zài nǎ yī děngjí? [nee-meun duh zwore-way zigh na yee dung-jee]

clean 干净的 gānjìng de [gan-jing duh] ◆ 把......扫干净 bǎ......dǎsǎo gānjìng [ba...da-sow gan-jing]

▸ the sheets aren't clean 床单不干净 chuángdān bù gānjìng [chwung-dan boo gan-jing]

▸ do we have to clean the apartment before leaving? 走之前我们必须把公寓打扫干净吗？ zǒu zhīqián wǒmen bìxū bǎ gōngyù dǎsǎo gānjìng ma? [zoh jir-chyen wo-meun bee-sho ba gong-yoo da-sow gan-jing ma]

▸ could you clean the windshield? 你能把挡风玻璃擦干净吗？ nǐ néng bǎ dǎngfēng bōli cā gānjìng ma? [nee nung ba dang-gung bo-lee tsa gan-jing ma]

cleaning 打扫卫生 dǎsǎo wèishēng [da-sow way-sheng]

▸ who does the cleaning? 谁打扫卫生？ shéi dǎsǎo wèishēng? [shay da-sow way-shung]

clear *(easily understood)* 清晰的 qīngxī de [ching-shee duh]; *(way)* 通畅的 tōngchàng de [tong-chang duh] ◆ *(road, path)* 使......通畅 shǐ.....tōngchàng [shir...tong-chang]

▸ is that clear? 清楚了吗？ qīngchu le ma? [ching-choo luh ma]

▸ is the road ahead clear? 前面的道路通畅吗？ qiánmian de dàolù tōngchàng ma? [chyen-myen duh dow-loo tong-chang ma]

▸ when will the road be cleared? 道路什么时候能够通畅？ dàolù shénme shíhou nénggòu tōngchàng? [dow-loo sheun-muh shir-hoh nung-goh tong-chang]

climb *(mountaineer)* 攀登 pāndēng [pan-dung]; *(plane)* 上升 shàngshēng [shang-shung]; *(road)* 向上延伸出去 xiàng shàng yánshēn chūqu [shyang shang yan-sheun choo-choo]

▸ the road climbs steadily after you leave the village 离开村庄后，道路一直向上延伸出去 líkāi cūnzhuāng hòu, dàolù yīzhí xiàng shàng yánshēn chūqu [lee-kigh tsun-jwang hoh dow-loo yee-jir shyang shang yan-sheun choo-choo]

climbing 登山 dēngshān [dung-shan]

▸ can you go climbing here? 可以在这里登山吗？ kěyǐ zài zhèli dēngshān ma? [kuh-yee zigh juh-lee dung-shan ma]

cloakroom *(in a museum, a theater)* 衣帽间 yīmàojiān [yee-mow-jyen]

- is there a charge for the cloakroom? 衣帽间要收费吗？ yīmàojiān yào shōu fèi ma? [yee-mow-jyen yow shoh fay ma]
- I'd like to leave my things in the cloakroom 我想把东西留在衣帽间 wǒ xiǎng bǎ dōngxi liú zài yīmàojiān [wo shyang ba dong-shee lew zigh yee-mow-jyen]

close *(door, window)* 关 guān [gwan] ◆ *(store)* 关门 guānmén [gwan-meun]; *(door, window)* 关上 guānshang [gwan-shang]

- what time do the stores close? 商店几点关门？ shāngdiàn jǐ diǎn guānmén? [shang-dyen jee dyen gwan-meun]
- what time do you close? 你们几点关门？ nǐmen jǐ diǎn guānmén? [nee-meun jee dyen gwan-meun]
- the door won't close 门不会关上的 mén bù huì guānshang de [meun boo hway gwan-shang duh]

closed 关门的 guānmén de [gwan-meun duh]

- are the stores closed on Sundays? 商店星期天关门吗？ shāngdiàn xīngqītiān guānmén ma? [shang-dyen shing-chee-tyen gwan-meun ma]

clothes 衣服 yīfu [yee-foo]

- where can we wash our clothes? 我们可以在哪里洗衣服？ wǒmen kěyǐ zài nǎli xǐ yīfu? [wo-meun kuh-yee zigh na-lee shee yee-foo]

club *(nightclub)* 夜总会 yèzǒnghuì [yeh-zong-hway]

- we could go to a club afterwards 之后我们可以去夜总会 zhīhòu wǒmen kěyǐ qù yèzǒnghuì [jir-hoh wo-meun kuh-yee choo yeh-zong-hway]

coach 长途汽车 chángtú qìchē [chang-too chee-chuh]

- what time does the coach leave? 长途汽车几点出发？ chángtú qìchē jǐ diǎn chūfā? [chang-too chee-chuh jee dyen choo-fa]

coffee *(drink, beans)* 咖啡 kāfēi [ka-fay]

- coffee with milk or cream 加奶的咖啡 jiā nǎi de kāfēi [jya nigh duh ka-fay]
- black coffee 不加奶的咖啡 bù jiā nǎi de kāfēi [boo jya nigh duh ka-fay]
- I'd like a coffee 我想要杯咖啡 wǒ xiǎng yào bēi kāfēi [wo shyang yow bay ka-fay]
- would you like some coffee? 你要来点咖啡吗？ nǐ yào lái diǎn kāfēi ma? [nee yow ligh dyen ka-fay ma]

coin 硬币 yìngbì [ying-bee]

- the machine only takes coins 这台机子只收硬币 zhè tái jīzi zhǐ shōu yìngbì [juh tigh jee-zir jir shoh ying-bee]

cold 冷的 lěng de [lung duh] ◆ *(illness)* 感冒 gǎnmào [gan-mow]; *(low temperature)* 冷 lěng [lung]

- it's cold today 今天天气冷 jīntiān tiānqì lěng [jin-tyen tyen-chee lung]

- I'm very cold 我感到很冷 wǒ gǎndào hěn lěng [wo gan-dow lung]
- to have a cold 感冒 gǎnmào [gan-mow]
- I've caught a cold 我感冒了 wǒ gǎnmào le [wo gan-mow luh]

collect 用对方付费的方式 yòng duìfāng fù fèi de fāngshì [yong dway-fang foo fay duh fang-shir]

- I have to call my parents collect 我只能用对方付费的方式打电话给我的父母 wǒ zhǐ néng yòng duìfāng fù fèi de fāngshì dǎ diànhuà gěi wǒ de fùmǔ [wo jir nung yong dway-fang foo fay duh fang-shir da dyen-hwa gay wo duh foo-moo]

collect call 对方付费的电话 duìfāng fù fèi de diànhuà [dway-fang foo fay duh dyen-hwa]

- to make a collect call 拨打对方付费的电话 bōdǎ duìfāng fù fèi de diànhuà [bo-da dway-fang foo fay duh dyen-hwa]

color 颜色 yánsè [yan-suh]

- do you have it in another color? 你有没有其他的颜色？ nǐ yǒuméiyǒu qítā de yánsè？ [nee yoh-may-yoh chee-ta duh yan-suh]

color film 彩色胶卷 cǎisè jiāojuǎn [tsigh-suh jeow-jwan]

- I'd like a roll of color film 我要一卷彩色胶卷 wǒ yào yī juǎn cǎisè jiāojuǎn [wo yow yee jwan tsigh-suh jeow-jwan]

come *(move here)* 来 lái [ligh]; *(arrive)* 来到 láidào [ligh-dow]

- come here! 过来！ guòlai! [gwore-ligh]
- coming! 马上就来！ mǎshàng jiù lái! [ma-shang jew ligh]
- when does the bus come? 公共汽车几点来？ gōnggòng qìchē jǐ diǎn lái? [gong-gong chee-chuh jee dyen ligh]

come from 来自 láizì [ligh-zir]

- where do you come from? 你从哪里来？ nǐ cóng nǎli lái? [nee tsong na-lee ligh]

come in *(enter)* 进入 jìnrù [jin-roo]; *(train)* 到达终点 dàodá zhōngdiǎn [dow-da jong-dyen]; *(tide)* 涨 zhǎng [jang]

- may I come in? 我可以进来吗？ wǒ kěyǐ jìnlai ma? [wo kuh-yee jin-ligh ma]
- come in! 进来！ jìnlai! [jin-ligh]
- what time does the Beijing train come in? 北京方向开来的火车几点到站？ běijīng fāngxiàng kāilái de huǒchē jǐ diǎn dào zhàn? [bay-jing fang-shyang kigh-ligh duh hwore-chuh jee dyen dow jan]
- the tide's coming in 涨潮了 zhǎng cháo le [jang chow luh]

come on *(light, heating)* 开始 kāishǐ [kigh-shir]

- the heating hasn't come on 还没有开始供暖 hái méiyou kāishǐ gōng nuǎn [high may-yoh kigh-shir gong nwan]
- come on! 快点！ kuài diǎn! [kwigh dyen]

come with *(go with)* 陪......去 péi......qù [pay...choo]; *(be served with)* 和......配在一起 hé......pèi zài yīqǐ [huh...pay zigh yee-chee]

▸ could you come with me to...? 你能陪我去......吗？ nǐ néng péi wǒ qù......ma? [nee nung pay wo choo...ma]

▸ what does it come with? 这个和什么配在一起？ zhège hé shénme pèi zài yīqǐ [juh-guh huh sheun-muh pay zigh yee-chee]

comfortable *(person)* 舒服的 shūfu de [shoo-foo duh]

▸ we're very comfortable here 我们在这里很舒服 wǒmen zài zhèlǐ hěn shūfu [wo-meun zigh juh-lee heun shoo-foo]

commission 手续费 shǒuxùfèi [shoh-shoo-fay]

▸ what commission do you charge? 你收多少手续费？ nǐ shōu duōshao shǒuxùfèi? [nee shoh dwore-show shoh-shoo-fay]

company *(firm)* 公司 gōngsī [gong-sir]

▸ is it a big company? 那是家大公司吗？ nà shì jiā dà gōngsī ma? [na shir jya da gong-sir ma]

compartment 车厢 chēxiāng [chuh-shyang]

▸ which compartment are our seats in? 我们的座位在哪个车厢？ wǒmen de zuòwei zài něige chēxiāng? [wo-meun duh zwore-way zigh nay-guh chuh-shyang]

complain 投诉 tóusù [toh-soo]

▸ I will be writing to your headquarters to complain 我会给你们总部写信投诉的 wǒ huì gěi nǐmen zǒngbù xiě xìn tóusù de [wo hway gay nee-meun zong-boo shyeah shin toh-soo duh]

complaint *(protest)* 不满 bùmǎn [boo-man]; *(in store)* 投诉 tóusù [toh-soo]

▸ I'd like to make a complaint *(protest, in store)* 我要投诉 wǒ yào tóusù [wo yow toh-soo]

---

complaints

▸ I'd like to see the manager, please 请让我见经理 qǐng ràng wǒ jiàn jīnglǐ [ching rang wo jyen jing-lee]

▸ I have a complaint 我要投诉 wǒ yào tóusù [wo yow toh-soo]

▸ there's a problem with the heating 暖气有问题 nuǎnqì yǒu wèntí [nwan-chee yoh weun-tee]

▸ I am relying on you to sort this problem out 我就指望你解决这问题了 wǒ jiù zhīwang nǐ jiějué zhè wèntí le [wo jew jir-wang nee jyeah-jue juh weun-tee luh]

▸ I expect the cost of the camera to be fully reimbursed 我要求按照照相机的价格全额退款 wǒ yāoqiú ànzhào zhàoxiàngjī de jiàgé quán é tuì kuǎn [wo yow-chew an-jow jow-shyang-jee duh jya-guh chwan-uh tway-kwan]

complete *(form)* 填 tián [tyen]
- here's the completed form 这是填好的表格 zhè shì tiánhǎo de biǎogé [juh-shir tyen-how duh byow-guh]

comprehensive insurance 综合险 zōnghéxiǎn [jong-huh-shyen]
- how much extra is the comprehensive insurance coverage? 要保综合险，我们要再付多少钱？ yào bǎo zōnghéxiǎn, wǒmen yào zài fù duōshao qián? [yow bow zong-huh-shyen wo-meun yow zigh foo dwore-show chyen]

computer 计算机 jìsuànjī, 电脑 diànnǎo [jee-swan-jee dyen-now]
- is there a computer I could use? 有没有计算机我可以用？ yǒuméiyǒu jìsuànjī wǒ kěyǐ yòng? [yoh-may-yoh jee-swan-jee wo kuh-yee yong]

concert 音乐会 yīnyuèhuì [yin-yue-hway]
- did you like the concert? 你喜欢那场音乐会吗？ nǐ xǐhuan nà chǎng yīnyuèhuì ma? [nee shee-hwan na chang yin-yue-hway ma]

condom 避孕套 bìyùntào [bee-yun-tow]
- do you have any condoms? 你有避孕套吗？ nǐ yǒu bìyùntào ma? [nee yoh bee-yun-tow ma]

confirm 确认 quèrèn [chue-reun]
- I confirmed my reservation by phone 我用电话确认过预定了 wǒ yòng diànhuà quèrènguo yùdìng le [wo yong dyen-hwa chue-reun–gwore yoo-ding luh]
- I'd like to confirm my return flight 我想确认一下回程的机票 wǒ xiǎng quèrèn yī xià huíchéng de jīpiào [wo shyang chue-reun yee shya hway-chung duh jee-peow]

congratulations 恭喜 gōngxǐ [gong-shee]
- congratulations! 恭喜！ gōngxǐ! [gong-shee]

connecting flight 转机 zhuǎnjī [jwan-jee]
- does the connecting flight leave from the same terminal? 转乘的飞机是从同一个航站楼起飞吗？ zhuǎnchéng de fēijī shì cóng tóngyī gè hángzhànlóu qǐfēi ma? [jwan-chung duh fay-jee shir tsong tong-yee guh hang-jan-loh chee-fay ma]

connection *(on phone)* 线路 xiànlù [shyen-loo]; *(transportation)* 联运 liányùn [lyen-yun]
- the connection is very bad: I can't hear very well 线路很差，我听得不是很清楚 xiànlù hěn chà, wǒ tīng de bù shì hěn qīngchu [shyen-loo heun cha wo ting duh boo shir heun ching-choo]
- I've missed my connection 我误了联运 wǒ wùle liányùn [wo woo-luh lyen-yun]

consulate 领事馆 lǐngshìguǎn [ling-shir-gwan]
- where is the American consulate? 美国领事馆在哪儿？ měiguó lǐngshìguǎn zài nǎli? [may-gwore ling-shir-gwan zigh na-lee]

cooking

Chinese cuisine is traditionally divided into four major groups. These are the cooking in the North and Shandong: 鲁菜 lǔcài [loo-tsigh], in the Shanghai and Jiangsu regions: 淮扬菜 huáiyángcài [hwigh-yang-tsigh], in Sichuan (spicy): 川菜 chuāncài [chwan-tsigh], and in Canton: 粤菜 yuècài [yue-tsigh]. There are also many other local cuisines.

contact *(communication)* 联系 liánxì [lyen-shee]
▸ I need to contact my family in the States 我需要联系在美国的家人 wǒ xūyào liánxì zài měiguó de jiārén [wo shoo-yow lyen-shee zigh may-gwore duh jya-reun]
▸ do you know how to get in contact with him? 你知道怎样联系他吗？ nǐ zhīdao zěnme liánxì tā ma？ [nee jir-dow zeun-muh lyen-shee ta ma]

contact lens 隐形眼镜 yǐnxíng yǎnjìng [yin-shing yan-jing]
▸ I've lost a contact (lens) 我的隐形眼镜丢了 wǒ de yǐnxíng yǎnjìng diū le [wo duh yin-shing yan-jing dew luh]

cookie *(food)* 饼干 bǐnggān [bing-gan]
▸ a box of cookies, please 请来一盒饼干 qǐng lái yī hé bǐnggān [ching ligh yee huh bing-gan]

cooking *(activity)* 烹饪 pēngrèn [pung-reun]; *(type of food)* 饭菜 fàncài [fan-tsigh]
▸ we prefer to do our own cooking 我们更喜欢自己做饭菜 wǒmen gèng xǐhuan zìjǐ zuò fàncài [wo-meun gung shee-hwan zir-jee zwore fan-tsigh]
▸ do you like Chinese cooking? 你喜欢中国菜吗？ nǐ xǐhuan zhōngguócài ma？ [nee shee-hwan jong-gwore-tsigh ma]

cork *(for a bottle)* 软木塞 ruǎnmùsāi [rwang-moo-sigh]
▸ where's the cork for the bottle? 这个瓶子的软木塞在哪里？ zhège píngzi de ruǎnmùsāi zài nǎli? [jir-guh ping-zir duh rwan-moo-sigh zigh na-lee]

corked 用软木塞塞住的 yòng ruǎnmùsāi sāizhù de [yong rwan-moo-sigh sigh-joo duh]
▸ this wine is corked 这瓶酒用软木塞塞住了 zhè píng jiǔ yòng ruǎnmùsāi sāizhù le [juh ping jew yong rwan-moo-sigh sigh-joo luh]

corner *(of street, table)* 拐角处 guǎijiǎochù [gwigh-jeow-choo]; *(spot)* 角落 jiǎoluò [jeow-lwore]
▸ stop at the corner 在拐角处停下来 zài guǎijiǎochù tíngxialai [zigh gwigh-jeow-choo ting-shya-ligh]

coronary 心脏病发作 xīnzàngbìng fāzuò [shin-zang-bing fa-zwore]
▸ he's had a coronary 他心脏病发作了 tā xīnzàngbìng fāzuò le [ta shin-zang-bing fa-zwore luh]

correct *(check)* 正确的 zhèngquè de [jung-chue duh]
- that's correct 是的 shì de [shir duh]

cost 花费 huāfèi [hwa-fay]
- how much will it cost to go to the airport? 去机场需要花多少钱? qù jīchǎng xūyào huā duōshao qián? [choo jee-chang shoo-yow hwa dwore-show chyen]

cot *(single bed)* 简易单人床 jiǎnyì dānrénchuáng [jyen-yee dan-reun-chwung]
- we can put a cot in the room for you 我们可以为你在房间里加一张简易单人床 wǒmen kěyǐ wèi nǐ zài fángjiān li jiā yī zhāng jiǎnyì dānrénchuáng [wo-meun kuh-yee way nee zigh fang-jyen lee jya yee jang jyen-yee dan-reun-chwung]

cough 咳嗽 késou [kuh-soh]
- I've got a cough 我咳嗽了 wǒ késou le [wo kuh-soh luh]
- I need something for a cough 我需要治咳嗽的药 wǒ xūyào zhì késou de yào [wo shooh-yow jir-kuh-soh duh yow]

could 能 néng [nung]; *(in polite requests and suggestions)* 可以 kěyǐ [kuh-yee]
- could you help me? 你能帮我吗? nǐ néng bāng wǒ ma? [nee nung bang wo ma]

counter *(in store, bank)* 柜台 guìtái [gway-tigh]
- which counter do I have to go to? 我该去哪个柜台? wǒ gāi qù nǎge guìtái? [wo gigh chooh na-guh gway-tigh]
- do you sell this medication over the counter? 这药无需处方就可以购买吗? zhè yào wúxū chǔfāng jiù kěyǐ gòumǎi ma? [juh yow woo-shooh choo-fang jew kuh-yee goh-migh ma]

country 国家 guójiā [gwore-jya]
- what country do you come from? 你来自哪个国家? nǐ láizì nǎge guójiā? [nee ligh zir na-guh gwore-jya]

couple 夫妻 fūqī [foo-chee]
- we need a room for a couple and two children 我们需要一间给一对夫妻和两个孩子的房间 wǒmen xūyào yī jiān gěi yī duì fūqī hé liǎng gè háizi de fángjiān [wo-meun shoo-yow yee jyen gay yee dway foo-chee huh lyang guh high-zir duh fang-jyen]

course *(of a meal)* 道 dào [dow]; *(of a ship, a plane)* 航线 hángxiàn [hang-shyen]; *(for a race)* 赛道 sàidào [sigh-dow]; *(in yoga, sailing)* 课程 kèchéng [kuh-chung] ◆ **of course** 当然 dāngrán [dang-ran]
- is the set meal three courses? 套餐包括三道菜吗? tàocān bāokuò sān dào cài ma? [tow-tsan bow-kwore san-dow tsigh ma?]
- how much does the sailing course cost? 上帆船课要多少钱? shàng fānchuánkè yào duōshao qián? [shang fan-chwan-kuh yow dwore-show chyen]
- of course he'll come 他当然会来 tā dāngrán huì lái [ta dang-ran hway ligh]

cream *(for the skin)* 乳霜 rǔshuāng [roo-shwang]
> I need some cream for my sunburn 我晒伤了，需要些乳霜 wǒ shàishāng le, xūyào xiē rǔshuāng [wo shigh-shang luh , shooh-yow shyeah roo-shwang]

credit card 信用卡 xìnyòngkǎ [shin-yong-ka]
> do you take credit cards? 你们收信用卡吗？ nǐmen shōu xìnyòngkǎ ma? [nee-muen show shin-yong ka ma]

cross *(street, river)* 穿过 chuānguo [chwan-gwore]; *(border)* 越过 yuèguo [yue-gwore]
> how do we cross this street? 我们怎么过马路？ wǒmen zěnme guò mǎlù? [wo-muen zeun-muh gwore ma-loo]

cross-country skiing 越野滑雪 yuèyě huáxuě [yue-ye hwa-shue]
> where can I go cross-country skiing around here? 在这附近我可以去哪里越野滑雪？ zài zhè fùjìn wǒ kěyǐ qù nǎli yuèyě huáxuě? [zigh juh foo-jin wo kuh-yee choo na-lee yue-yuh hwa-shue]

crosswalk 人行横道 rénxíng héngdào [reun-shing hung-dow]
> always cross at the crosswalk 一定要走人行横道 yīdìng yào zǒu rénxíng héngdào [yee-ding yow zoh reun-shing hung-dow]

cry 哭 kū [koo]
> don't cry 别哭了 bié kū le [byeah-koo luh]

cup 杯 bēi [bay]
> I'd like a cup of tea 我想要一杯茶 wǒ xiǎng yào yī bēi chá [wo shyang-yow yee bay cha]
> a coffee cup 一只咖啡杯 yī zhī kāfēibēi [yee jir ka-fay bay]
> could we have an extra cup? 能再给我们一个杯子吗？ néng zài gěi wǒmen yī gè bēizi ma? [nung zigh gay wo-muen yee guh bay-zir ma]

currency *(money)* 货币 huòbì [hwore-bee]
> how much local currency do you have? 你有多少当地的货币？ nǐ yǒu duōshao dāngdì de huòbì? [nee yoh dwore-show dang-dee hwore-bee]

cut 切割 qiēgē [chyeah-guh]
> I cut my finger 我把手指割破了 wǒ bǎ shǒuzhǐ gēpò le [wo ba shoh-jir guh-po luh]

d

daily 每天的 měi tiān de [may-tyen duh] ◆ 日报 rìbào [rir-bow]
- what's the name of the local daily newspaper? 当地日报的名字是什么？ dāngdì rìbào de míngzi shì shénme? [dang-dee rir-bow ming-zir shir sheun-muh]

damage 损坏 sǔnhuài [sun-hwigh]
- my suitcase was damaged in transit 我的行李箱在运送过程中被损坏了 wǒ de xínglixiāng zài yùnsòng guòchéng zhōng bèi sǔnhuài le [wo-duh shing-lee-shyang zigh yun-song gwore-chung jong bay sun-hwigh luh]

damp 潮湿的 cháoshī de [chow-shir]
- it's damp today 今天挺潮湿 jīntiān tǐng cháoshī [jin-tyen ting chow-shir]

dance 跳舞 tiàowǔ [teow-woo] ◆ 跳 tiào [teow]
- shall we dance? 我们跳舞好吗？ wǒmen tiàowǔ hǎo ma? [wo-meun teow-woo how ma]
- I can't dance 我不会跳舞 wǒ bù huì tiàowǔ [wo bu hway teow-woo]

dancing 跳舞 tiàowǔ [teow-wu]
- will there be dancing? 会有跳舞吗？ huì yǒu tiàowǔ ma? [hway yoh teow-woo ma]
- where can we go dancing? 我们可以去哪里跳舞？ wǒmen kěyǐ qù nǎli tiàowǔ? [wo-meun kuh-yee chooh na-lee teow-woo]

dandruff 头皮屑 tóupíxiè [toh-pee-shyeah]
- I have bad dandruff 我的头皮屑很厉害 wǒ de tóupíxiè hěn lìhai [wo-duh toh-pee-shyeah heun lee-high]

danger 危险 wēixiǎn [way-shyen]
- hurry! she's in danger! 快点！她有危险！ kuàidiǎn! tā yǒu wēixiǎn! [kwigh dyen ta yoh way-shyen]

dangerous 危险的 wēixiǎn de [way-shyen duh]
- this stretch of the river is quite dangerous 这段河流相当危险 zhè duàn héliú xiāngdāng wēixiǎn [juh dwan huh-lew shyang-dang way-shyen]

dark (room, night) 黑暗的 hēi'àn de [hay-an duh]; (hair) 黑色的 hēisè de [hay-suh duh]
- it's very dark outside 外面很黑 wàimian hěn hēi [wigh-myen heun hay]
- she has dark hair 她的头发是黑色的 tā de tóufa shì hēisè de [ta-duh toh-fa shir hay-sir duh]

dark chocolate 黑巧克力 hēiqiǎokèlì [hay-cheow-kuh-lee]
- I prefer dark chocolate 我更喜欢黑巧克力 wǒ gèng xǐhuan hēiqiǎokèlì [wo gung shee-hwan hay-cheow-kuh-lee]

days of the week

The days of the week are shown by using the word 'week': 星期 xīngqī [shing-chee] or 周 zhōu [joh] together with a figure to mark the day: 'one' 一 yī [yee] for 'Monday', 'two' 二 èr [er] for 'Tuesday' and so on up to Saturday. Sunday is 星期日 xīngqīrì [shing-chee-rir] or 星期天 xīngqītiān [shing-chee-tyen].

date *(in time)* 日期 rìqī [rir-chee]; *(appointment)* 约会 yuēhuì [yue-hway]
- I've got a date tonight 今晚我有个约会 jīnwǎn wǒ yǒu gè yuēhuì [jin-wan wo yoh guh yue-hway]

date-stamp 在......盖邮戳 zài......gài yóuchuō [zigh...gigh yoh-chwore]
- do I have to date-stamp this receipt? 我必须在这张发票上盖上日期吗？wǒ bìxū zài zhè zhāng fāpiào shang gàishang rìqī ma? [wo bee-shooh zigh juh jang fa-peow shang gigh-shang rir-chee ma]

daughter 女儿 nǚ'ér [nooh-er]
- this is my daughter 这是我的女儿 zhè shì wǒ de nǚ'ér [juh shir wo-duh nooh-er]

day 日 rì [rir]; *(expressing duration)* 天 tiān [tyen]
- what day is it? 今天星期几？jīntiān xīngqī jǐ? [jin-tyen shing-chee jee]
- I arrived three days ago 我三天前到的 wǒ sān tiān qián dào de [wo san-tyen chyen dow duh]
- I'd like to do a round trip in a day 我想当天往返 wǒ xiǎng dāngtiān wǎngfǎn [wo shyang dang-tyen wang-fan]
- how much is it per day? 每天多少钱？měi tiān duōshao qián? [may-tyen dwore-show chyen]

dead 死的 sǐ de [sir-duh]
- he was pronounced dead at the scene 他当场被宣告死亡 tā dāngchǎng bèi xuāngào sǐwáng [ta dang-chang bay shwan-gow sir-wang]
- the battery's dead 电池没电了 diànchí méi diàn le [dyen-chir may dyen luh]

dead end 死胡同 sǐ hútong [sir hoo-tong]
- it's a dead end 是个死胡同 shì gè sǐ hútong [shir-guh sir hoo-tong]

deal *(business agreement)* 交易 jiāoyì [jeow-yee]
- I got a good deal on the room 我拿到的房间价格不错 wǒ nádào de fángjiān jiàgé bùcuò [wo na-dow duh fang-jyen jya-guh boo-tswore]

death *(state)* 死亡 sǐwáng [sir-wang]; *(person)* 死人 sǐrén [sir-reun]
- there were two deaths 有两个死人 yǒu liǎng gè sǐrén [yoh lyang-guh sir-reun]

decaf, decaffeinated 不含咖啡因的咖啡 bù hán kāfēiyīn de kāfēi [boo-han ka-fay-yin duh ka-fay] ◆ 不含咖啡因的 bù hán kāfēiyīn de [boo-han ka-fay-yin duh]

▸ a decaf/decaffeinated coffee, please 请来一杯不含咖啡因的咖啡 qǐng lái yī bēi bù hán kāfēiyīn de kāfēi [ching ligh yee-bei boo-han ka-fay-yin duh ka-fay]

December 十二月 shí'èr yuè [shir-er yue]

▸ December 10th 十二月十日 shí'èr yuè shí rì [shir-er yue shir rir]

decide 决定 juédìng [jue-ding]

▸ we haven't decided yet 我们还没有决定 wǒmen hái méiyǒu juédìng [wo-meun high may-yoh jue-ding]

deck (of ship) 甲板 jiǎbǎn [jya-ban]; (of cards) 副 fù [foo]

▸ how do I get to the upper deck? 我怎么去上层甲板? wǒ zěnme qù shàngcéng jiǎbǎn? [wo zeun-muh choo shang-tsung jya-ban]

deckchair 折叠式躺椅 zhédiéshì tǎngyǐ [juh-dyeah-shir tang-yee]

▸ I'd like to rent a deckchair 我想租一把折叠式躺椅 wǒ xiǎng zū yī bǎ zhédiéshì tǎngyǐ [wo shyang zoo yee-ba juh-dyeah-shir tang-yee]

declare 申报 shēnbào [sheun-bow]

▸ I have nothing to declare 我没有东西要申报 wǒ méiyǒu dōngxi yào shēnbào [wo may-yoh dong-shee yow sheun-bow]

▸ I have a bottle of spirits to declare 我有一瓶烈酒要申报 wǒ yǒu yī píng lièjiǔ yào shēnbào [wo yoh yee-ping lyeah-jew yow sheun-bow]

definitely 一定 yīdìng [yee-ding]

▸ we'll definitely come back here 我们一定回到这里 wǒmen yīdìng huídào zhèli [wo-meun yee-ding hway-dow juh-lee]

degree 度 dù [doo]

▸ 5 degrees below freezing 零下5度 líng xià wǔ dù [ling-shya woo-doo]

delay 延误 yánwù [yan-woo]

▸ is there a delay for this flight? 这个航班是否有延误? zhège hángbān shìfǒu yǒu yánwù? [juh-guh hang-ban shir-fo yoh yan-woo]

delayed 延误的 yánwù de [yan-woo duh]

▸ how long will the flight be delayed? 这个航班将延误多久? zhège hángbān jiāng yánwù duō jiǔ? [juh-guh hang-ban jyang yan-woo dwore jew]

delighted 高兴的 gāoxìng de [gow-shing duh]

▸ we're delighted you could make it 你能来我们真高兴 nǐ néng lái wǒmen zhēn gāoxìng [nee nung ligh wo-meun jeun gow-shing]

dentist 牙医 yáyī [ya-yee]

▸ I need to see a dentist urgently 我急需见牙医 wǒ jíxū jiàn yáyī [wo jee-shoo jyen ya-yee]

department (in store) 部 bù [boo]

dessert

This does not necessarily form part of a meal, as there is no starter – main course – dessert structure in Chinese cuisine. At the beginning of a meal you should order hot and cold dishes, which are usually brought to the table together. At the end of the meal, you might eat fruit (watermelon, apples, oranges) to freshen the palate. There may be a few small sweet dishes, however, made from flour or cereals.

▸ I'm looking for the menswear department 我在找男装部 wǒ zài zhǎo nánzhuāngbù [wo zigh jow nan-jwang-boo]

department store 百货商店 bǎihuò shāngdiàn [bigh-hwore shang-dyen]

▸ where are the department stores? 哪里有百货商店？ nǎli yǒu bǎihuò shāngdiàn? [na-lee yoh bigh-hwore shang-dyen]

departure 离开 líkāi [lee-kigh]

▸ 'departures' (in airport) '出发' 'chūfā' [choo-fa]

departure lounge 候机室 hòujīshì [hoh-jee-shir]

▸ where's the departure lounge? 候机室在哪里？ hòujīshì zài nǎli? [hoh-jee-shir zigh na-lee]

deposit (against loss or damage) 押金 yājīn [ya-jin]; (down payment) 定金 dìngjīn [ding-jin]

▸ is there a deposit to pay for using the equipment? 用这个设备要付押金吗？ yòng zhège shèbèi yào fù yājīn ma? [yong juh-guh shuh-bay yow foo ya-jin ma]

▸ how much is the deposit? 定金是多少？ dìngjīn shì duōshao? [ding-jin shir dwore-show]

desk (in office, home) 桌子 zhuōzi [jwore-zir]; (at hotel) 服务台 fúwùtái [foo-woo-tigh]; (for cashier or airport) 柜台 guìtái [gway-tigh]

▸ where can I find the American Airlines desk? 我可以在哪里找到美国航空的柜台？ wǒ kěyǐ zài nǎli zhǎodào měiguó hángkōng de guìtái? [wo kuh-yee zigh na-lee jow-dow may-gwore hang-kong duh gway-tigh]

dessert 甜点 tiándiǎn [tyen-dyen]

▸ what desserts do you have? 你有什么甜点？ nǐ yǒu shénme tiándiǎn? [nee yoh sheun-muh tyen-dyen]

dessert wine 餐后甜酒 cān hòu tiánjiǔ [tsan-hoh tyen-jew]

▸ can you recommend a good dessert wine? 你能推荐一种好一点的餐后甜酒吗？ nǐ néng tuījiàn yī zhǒng hǎo yīdiǎn de cān hòu tiánjiǔ ma? [nee nung tway-jyen yee-jong how-yee-dyen duh tsan-hoh-jew ma]

detour 绕行路线 ràoxíng lùxiàn [row-shing loo-shyen]
 ▸ is there a detour ahead? 前面有绕道吗？ qiánmian yǒu ràodào ma? [chyen-myen yoh row-dow ma]

develop 冲洗 chōngxǐ [chong-shee]
 ▸ how much does it cost to develop a roll of 36 photos? 冲洗一卷36张照片的胶卷要多少钱？ chōngxǐ yī juǎn sānshíliù zhāng zhàopiàn de jiāojuǎn yào duōshao qián? [chong-shee yee jwan san-shir-lew jang jow-pyen duh jeow-jwan yow dwore-show chyen]

diabetic 糖尿病的 tángniàobìng de [tang-neow-bing duh] ◆ 糖尿病患者 tángniàobìng huànzhě [tang-neow-bing duh hwan-juh]
 ▸ I'm diabetic and I need a prescription for insulin 我有糖尿病，要开一张胰岛素的处方 wǒ yǒu tángniàobìng, yào kāi yī zhāng yídǎosù de chǔfāng [wo yoh tang-neow-bing yow kigh yee-jang yee-dow-soo duh choo-fang]

diarrhea 腹泻 fùxiè [foo-shyeah]
 ▸ I'd like something for diarrhea 我要止腹泻的药 wǒ yào zhǐ fùxiè de yào [wo yow jir foo-shyeah duh yow]

difference (in price, cost) 差价 chājià [cha-jya]
 ▸ will you pay the difference? 你能付差价吗？ nǐ néng fù chājià ma? [nee nung foo cha-jya ma]

difficult 难的 nán de [nan-duh]
 ▸ I find some sounds difficult to pronounce 我发现有些音很难发 wǒ fāxiàn yǒuxiē yīn hěn nán fā [wo fa-shyen yoh-shyeah yin heun nan-fa]

difficulty 困难 kùnnan [kun-nan]
 ▸ I'm having difficulty finding the place 我找不到那个地方 wǒ zhǎo bù dào nàge dìfang [wo jow boo dow na-guh dee-fang]

digital camera 数码相机 shùmǎ xiàngjī [shoo-ma jow-shyang-jee]
 ▸ my digital camera's been stolen 我的数码相机被偷了 wǒ de shùmǎ xiàngjī bèi tōu le [wo-duh shoo-ma jow-shyang-jee bay-toh-luh]

dining room 餐厅 cāntīng [tsan-ting]
 ▸ do you have to have breakfast in the dining room? 必须得去餐厅吃早饭吗？ bìxū děi qù cāntīng chī zǎofàn ma? [bee-shoo day-choo tsan-ting chir zow-fan ma]

dinner 晚餐 wǎncān [wan-tsan]
 ▸ up to what time do they serve dinner? 晚餐供应到几点？ wǎncān gōngyìng dào jǐ diǎn? [wan-tsan gong-ying dow jee-dyen]

direct 直达的 zhídá de [jir-da duh]
 ▸ is that train direct? 那辆火车是直达的吗？ ná liàng huǒchē shì zhídá de ma? [na lyang hwore-chuh shir jir-da duh ma]

directions

In the North of China, directions are usually given by referring to the four points of the compass. So you need to make sure you know which way is North! In Beijing, the main streets make up a grid pattern, with the *Forbidden City* in the center. Many streets take their names from their geographical position: 北路 běi lù [bay-loo] (North Street) or 东大街 dōng dàjiē [dong da-jyeah] (Eastern Avenue). Beijing's subway stations are usually located at major junctions, so there'll be exits with the names North-East, North-West, etc. In the South of China, it's more common to say 'right', 'left', 'straight ahead', etc. when giving directions.

direction 方向 fāngxiàng [fang-shyang]

▸ am I going in the right direction for the train station? 去火车站朝这个方向走对吗？ qù huǒchēzhàn cháo zhège fāngxiàng zǒu duì ma? [choo hwore-chuh jan juh-guh fang-shyan zwore dway ma]

directory assistance 电话号码查询服务 diànhuà hàomǎ cháxún fúwù [dyen-hwa-how cha-shun foo-woo]

▸ what's the number for directory assistance? 电话号码查询服务的号码是多少？ diànhuà hàomǎ cháxún fúwù de hàomǎ shì duōshao? [dyen-hwa-how cha-shun foo-woo duh how-ma shir dwore-show]

dirty *(room, tablecloth)* 脏的 zāng de [zang duh]

▸ the sheets are dirty 被单脏了 bèidān zāng le [bay-dan zang luh]

disability 残疾 cánjí [tsan-jee]

▸ do you have facilities for people with disabilities? 你们是否有供残疾人使用的设施？ nǐmen shìfǒu yǒu gōng cánjírén shǐyòng de shèshī? [nee-meun shir-fo yoh gong tsan-jee-reun shir-yong duh shuh-shir]

disabled 有残疾的 yǒu cánjí de [yoh tsan-jee duh]

▸ where's the nearest disabled parking spot? 最近的残疾人停车点在哪里？ zuì jìn de cánjírén tíngchēdiǎn zài nǎli? [zway-jin duh tsan-jee-reun ting-chuh-dyen zigh na-lee]

disco *(club)* 迪斯科 dísīkē [dee-sir-kuh]

▸ are there any discos around here? 这附近有迪斯科舞厅吗？ zhè fùjìn yǒu dísīkē wǔtīng ma? [juh foo-jin yoh dee-sir-kuh woo-ting ma]

discount 打折 dǎzhé [da-juh]

▸ is there any chance of a discount? 有可能打折吗？ yǒu kěnéng dǎzhé ma? [yoh kuh-nung da-juh ma]

dish *(plate)* 盘子 pánzi [pan-zir]; *(food)* 菜肴 càiyáo [tsigh-yow] ◆ **dishes** 餐具 cānjù [tsan-joo]

- what's the dish of the day? 今天的推荐菜是什么? jīntiān de tuījiàncài shì shénme? [jin-tyen duh tway-jyen tsigh shir sheun-muh]
- can I help you with the dishes? 你洗碗要我帮忙吗? nǐ xǐwǎn yào wǒ bāngmáng ma? [nee shee-wan yow wo bang-mang ma]

disposable 一次性的 yīcìxìng de [yee-tsir-shing duh]

- I need some disposable razors 我需要一些一次性剃须刀 wǒ xūyào yīxiē yīcìxìng de tìxūdāo [wo shoo-yow yee-shyeah yee-tsir-shing duh tee-shoo-dow]
- do you sell disposable cameras? 你有售一次性的照相机吗? nǐ yǒu shòu yīcìxìng de zhàoxiàngjī ma? [nee yoh shoh yee-tsir-shing duh jow-shyang-jee ma]

distance 距离 jùlí [joo-lee]

- the hotel is only a short distance from here 饭店离这儿不远 fàndiàn lí zhèr bù yuǎn [fan-dyen lee jer boo-ywan]

district (of town) 区 qū [choo]

- which district do you live in? 你住在哪个区? nǐ zhù zài nǎge qū? [nee joo zigh na-guh choo]

dive 潜水 qiánshuǐ [teow-shway]

- can we do a night dive? (scuba diving) 我们可以晚上去潜水吗? wǒmen kěyǐ wǎnshang qù qiánshuǐ ma? [wo-meun kuh-yee wan-shang choo chyen-shway ma]

diving (scuba diving) 潜水 qiánshuǐ [chyen-shway]

- I'd like to take diving lessons 我想上潜水课 wǒ xiǎng shàng qiánshuǐ kè [wo shyang shang chyen-shway-kuh]
- do you rent out diving equipment? 你们出租潜水设备吗? nǐmen chūzū qiánshuǐ shèbèi ma? [nee-meun choo-zoo chyen-shway shuh-bay ma]

diving board 跳水板 tiàoshuǐbǎn [teow-shway-ban]

- is there a diving board? 有跳水板吗? yǒu tiàoshuǐbǎn ma? [yoh teow-shway-ban ma]

dizzy spell 一阵头晕 yī zhèn tóuyūn [yee-jeun toh-yun]

- I've been having dizzy spells 我感到一阵阵头晕 wǒ gǎndào yīzhènzhèn tóuyūn [wo gan-dow yee-jeun-jeun toh-yun]

do (perform action) 做 zuò [zwore]; (cover distance) 走过 zǒuguo [zwore-gwore]

- what do you do for a living? 你以什么为生? nǐ yǐ shénme wéishēng? [nee yee sheun-muh way-shung]
- is there anything I can do (to help)? 我能（帮忙）做点儿什么吗? wǒ néng (bāngmáng)zuò diǎnr shénme ma? [wo nung (bang-mang) zwore-dyen sheun-ma]
- what are you doing tonight? 今晚你干什么? jīnwǎn nǐ gàn shénme? [ji-wan nee gan sheun-muh]

▸ what is there to do here on Sundays? 星期天都可以干些什么？ xīngqītiān dōu kěyǐ gàn xiē shénme? [shing-chee-tyen doh kuh-yee gan shyeah sheun-muh]

doctor 医生 yīshēng [yee-shung]

▸ I have to see a doctor 我得去看医生 wǒ děi qù kàn yīshēng [wo day choo kan yee-shung]

dollar 美元 měiyuán [may-ywan]

▸ I'd like to change 200 dollars into yuan 我想把200美元兑换成人民币 wǒ xiǎng bǎ èrbǎi měiyuán duìhuànchéng rénmínbì [wo shyang ba er-bigh may-ywan dway-hwan-chung reun-min-bee]

door 门 mén [meun]

▸ do you want me to answer the door? 你要我去开门吗？ nǐ yào wǒ qù kāi mén ma? [nee yow wo choo kigh-meun ma]

dormitory *(in youth hostel; for students)* 宿舍 sùshè [soo-shuh]

▸ are you staying in the dormitory? 你住在宿舍吗？ nǐ zhù zài sùshè ma? [nee joo zigh soo-shuh ma]

double 两倍的 liǎng bèi de [lyang-bay duh] ◆ 增加一倍 zēngjiā yī bèi [zung yee-bay]

▸ it's spelled with a double 'l' 双写'l' shuāng xiě 'l' [shwan-shyeah l]

▸ prices have doubled since last year 自去年以来，价格增长了一倍 zì qùnián yǐlái, jiàgé zēngzhǎngle yī bèi [zir choo-nyen yee-ligh jya-guh zung-jang luh yee-bay]

double bed 双人床 shuāngrénchuáng [shwang-reun-chwung]

▸ does the room have a double bed? 房间里有双人床吗？ fángjiān li yǒu shuāngrénchuáng ma? [fang-jyen yoh shwang-reun-chwung ma]

double room 双人房 shuāngrénfáng [shwang-reun-fang]

▸ I'd like a double room for five nights, please 请给我一间双人房，住五个晚上 qǐng gěi wǒ yī jiān shuāngrénfáng, zhù wǔ gè wǎnshang [ching gay wo yee jyen shwang-reun-fang joo woo guh wan-shang]

downtown 市中心的 shì zhōngxīn de [shir jong-shin duh] ◆ 去市中心 qù shì zhōngxīn [choo shir jong-shin] ◆ 市中心 shì zhōngxīn [shir jong-shin]

▸ we're looking for a good downtown hotel 我们在找位于市中心的好一点儿的宾馆 wǒmen zài zhǎo wèiyú shì zhōngxīn de hǎo yīdiǎnr de bīnguǎn [wo-meun zigh jow way-yoo shir jong-shin duh bee-jeow how duh fan-dyen]

▸ does this bus go downtown? 这辆公共汽车去市中心吗？ zhè liàng gōnggòng qìchē qù shì zhōngxīn ma? [juh lyang gong-gong-chee-chuh choo shir jong-shin ma]

draft beer 生啤 shēngpí [shung-pee]

▸ a draft beer, please 请来一杯生啤 qǐng lái yī bēi shēngpí [ching ligh yee-bay shung-pee]

driver's license

You can't drive in China without a Chinese driver's license. Foreign or international driver's licenses aren't accepted. In practice, you have to be resident of China to take the Chinese driving test.

dream 梦 mèng [mung] ♦ 梦到 mèngdao [mung-dow] ♦ 做梦 zuòmèng [zwore-mung]

- ▶ to have a dream 有梦想 yǒu mèngxiǎng [yoh mung-shyang]
- ▶ I dreamt (that)...... 我梦到...... wǒ mèngdao...... [wo mung-dow]

drink 饮料 yǐnliào [yin-leow] ♦ 喝 hē [huh]

- ▶ I'll have a cold drink 我要喝一杯冷饮 wǒ yào hē yī bēi lěngyǐn [wo yow huh yee-bay lung-yin]
- ▶ I could do with a drink 我很想喝一杯饮料 wǒ hěn xiǎng hē yī bēi yǐnliào [wo heun shyang huh yee-bay yin-leow]
- ▶ what kind of hot drinks do you have? 你们有什么饮料？ nǐmen yǒu shénme yǐnliào? [nee-meun yoh sheun-muh yin-leow]
- ▶ shall we go for a drink? 我们出去喝一杯好吗？ wǒmen chūqu hē yī bēi hǎo ma? [wo-meun choo-choo huh yee bay how ma]
- ▶ can I buy you a drink? 能让我给你买杯喝的吗？ néng ràng wǒ gěi nǐ mǎi bēi hē de ma? [nung rang wo gay nee migh bay huh-duh ma]

drinking water 饮用水 yǐnyòngshuǐ [yin-yong-shway]

- ▶ I'm looking for bottled drinking water 我在找瓶装饮用水 wǒ zài zhǎo píngzhuāng yǐnyòngshuǐ [wo zigh jow ping-jwung yin-yongshway]

drive *(in vehicle)* 开车 kāichē [kigh-chuh] ♦ *(vehicle)* 驾驶 jiàshǐ [jya-shir]

- ▶ is it a long drive? 要开很久的车吗？ yào kāi hěn jiǔ de chē ma? [yow kigh heun-jew duh chuh ma]
- ▶ could you drive me home? 你能开车送我回家吗？ nǐ néng kāichē sòng wǒ huí jiā ma? [nee nung kigh chuh song wo hway-jya ma]
- ▶ she was driving too close to the car in front 她开车时离前面的车太近了 tā kāichē shí lí qiánmiàn de chē tài jìn le [ta kigh-chuh shir lee chyen-myen duh chuh tigh jin luh]

driver 驾驶员，司机 jiàshǐyuán，sījī [jya-shir-ywan，sir-jee]

- ▶ the other driver wasn't looking where he was going 另一个司机没有注意他在往哪儿开 lìng yī gè sījī méiyǒu zhùyì tā zài wǎng nǎr kāi [ling yee guh sir-jee may-yoh joo-yee ta zigh nar kigh]

driver's license 驾照 jiàzhào [jya-jow]

- ▶ can I see your driver's license? 我能看一下你的驾照吗？ wǒ néng kàn yī xià nǐ de jiàzhào ma? [wo nung kan yee-shya nee duh jya-jow ma]

drugstores

All the major towns have drugstores where you can buy medicines similar to those found in the US. Some of them can be bought over the counter without a prescription. If you struggle with the Chinese language, it is best to know the main ingredient of any medicine you are looking for, rather than its name. The main difference from a Western pharmacy is the wide range of Chinese traditional medicines on offer. These are often based on plants and are particularly effective for treating minor ailments (headaches, colds, digestive problems, etc.).

---

drop *(of liquid)* 滴 dī [dee]; *(small amount)* 点滴 diǎndī [dyen-dee] ◆ *(let fall)* 使......落下 shǐ......luòxià [shir...lwore-shya]; *(let out of vehicle)* 让.....下车 ràng.....xià chē [rang...shya]

▸ could I just have a drop of milk? 我能不能就要一点点的牛奶？ wǒ néngbùnéng jiù yào yīdiǎndiǎn de niúnǎi? [wo nung-boo-nung jew yow yee-dyen-dyen duh new-nigh]

▸ I dropped my scarf 我的围巾掉了 wǒ de wéijīn diào le [wo-duh way-jin deow luh]

drop off *(let out of vehicle)* 让......下车 ràng......xià chē [rang...shya]

▸ could you drop me off here? 你能让我在这儿下车吗？ nǐ néng ràng wǒ zài zhèr xià chē ma? [nee nung rang wo zigh jer shya-chuh ma]

drown 淹死 yānsǐ [yan-sir]

▸ he's drowning: somebody call for help 他要淹死了，快去找人帮忙 tā yào yānsǐ le, kuài qù zhǎo rén bāngmáng [ta yow yan-sir le, kwigh choo jow reun bang-mang]

drugstore 药店 yàodiàn [yow-dyen]

▸ where is the nearest drugstore? 最近的药店在哪里？ zuì jìn de yàodiàn zài nǎlǐ? [zway jin duh yow-dyen zigh na-lee]

---

at the drugstore

▸ I'd like something for a headache/a sore throat/diarrhea 我要治头疼/喉咙疼/腹泻的药 wǒ yào zhì tóu téng/hóulong téng/fùxiè de yào [wo yow dyen jir toh-tun/hoh-long-tun/foo-shyeah duh yow]

▸ I'd like some aspirin/some Band-Aids® 我要一些阿司匹林/创可贴 wǒ yào yīxiē āsīpǐlín/chuāngkětiē [wo yow dyen a-sir-pee-lin/chwung-tyeah]

▸ could you recommend a doctor? 你能推荐一名医生吗？ nǐ néng tuījiàn yī míng yīshēng ma? [nee nung tway-jyen yee-ming yee-shung ma]

drunk 喝醉的 hēzuì de [huh-zway duh]

▸ he's very drunk 他醉得厉害 tā zuì de lìhai [ta zway-duh heun lee-high]

dry *(clothing, wine)* 干的 gān de [gan-duh]; *(skin, day)* 干燥的 gānzào de [gan-zow-duh]; *(climate)* 少雨的 shǎo yǔ de [show-yoo duh] ◆ *(gen)* 使......干 shǐ......gān [shir...gan]; *(with a cloth, a towel)* 把......擦干 bǎ......cāgān [ba...tsa-gan] ◆ 弄干 nònggān [nong-gan]

▸ a small glass of dry white wine 一小杯干白葡萄酒 yī xiǎo bēi gān bái pútaojiǔ [yee-shyeow-bay gan bigh poo-tow-jew]

▸ where can I put my towel to dry? 我可以把毛巾放在哪里让它干？ wǒ kěyǐ bǎ máojīn fàng zài nǎli ràng tā gān? [wo kuh-yee ba mow-jin fang-zigh na-lee rang ta gan]

dry cleaner's 干洗店 gānxǐdiàn [gan-shee-dyen]

▸ is there a dry cleaner's nearby? 附近有干洗店吗？ fùjìn yǒu gānxǐdiàn ma? [foo-jin yoh gan-shee-dyen ma]

dryer *(for laundry)* 烘干机 hōnggānjī [hong-gan-jee]

▸ is there a dryer? 有烘干机吗？ yǒu hōnggānjī ma? [yoh hong-gan-jee ma]

dub *(movie)* 给......配音 gěi......pèiyīn [gay...pay-yin]

▸ do they always dub English-language movies? 英文电影常有配音吗？ yīngwén diànyǐng cháng yǒu pèiyīn ma? [ying-weun dyen-ying chang yoh pay-yin ma]

during 在......的期间 zài......de qījiān [zigh...duh chee-jyen]

▸ is there restricted parking during the festival? 在节日期间停车是否有限制？ zài jiérì qījiān tíngchē shìfǒu yǒu xiànzhì? [zigh jyeah-rir chee-jyen ting-chuh shir-foh yoh shyen-jir]

duty *(tax)* 税 shuì [shway]

▸ do I have to pay duty on this? 买这个要付税吗？ mǎi zhège yào fù shuì ma? [migh juh-guh yow foo shway ma]

duty-free shop 免税店 miǎnshuìdiàn [myen-shway-dyen]

▸ where are the duty-free shops? 免税店在哪里？ miǎnshuìdiàn zài nǎli? [myen-shway-dyen zigh na-lee]

DVD DVD [dvd]

▸ can I play this DVD in the States? 这张DVD在美国能放吗？ zhè zhāng dvd zài měiguó néng fàng ma? [juh jang dvd zigh may-gwore nung fang ma]

ear 耳朵 ěrduo [er-dwore]
- I have a ringing in my ears 我耳朵里嗡嗡作响 wǒ ěrduo li wēngwēng zuò xiǎng [wo-duh er-dwore wung-wung zwore-shyang]

earache 耳朵疼 ěrduo téng [er-dwore tung]
- he has an earache 他耳朵疼 tā ěrduo téng [ta er-dwore tung]

ear infection 耳朵感染 ěrduo gǎnrǎn [er-dwore gan-ran]
- I think I have an ear infection 我想我耳朵感染了 wǒ xiǎng wǒ ěrduo gǎnrǎn le [wo shywang wo er-dwore gan-ran luh]

early *(before the expected time)* 提前的 tíqián de [tee-chyen duh]; *(in the day)* 早的 zǎo de [zow-duh]; *(at the beginning)* 早期的 zǎoqī de [zow-chee duh] ♦ *(before the expected time)* 提前地 tíqián de [tee-chyen duh]; *(in the day)* 早早地 zǎozǎo de [zow-zow duh]; *(at the beginning)* 在早期 zài zǎoqī [zigh zow-chee]
- is there an earlier flight? 有早一点儿的航班吗? yǒu zǎo yīdiǎnr de hángbān ma? [yoh yee-dyen zow yee-dyen duh hang-ban]
- we arrived early 我们提前到了 wǒmen tíqián dào le [wo-meun tee-chyen dow luh]
- I'll be leaving early in the morning 早上我会早早地出发 zǎoshang wǒ huì zǎozǎo de chūfā [zow-shang wo hway zow-zow duh choo-fa]

Easter 复活节 fùhuó jié [foo-hwore-jyeah]
- Happy Easter! 复活节快乐! fùhuó jié kuàilè! [foo-hwore-jyeah kwigh-luh]

easy 简单的 jiǎndān de [jyen-dan duh]
- is it easy to use? 是否易于使用? shìfǒu yìyú shǐyòng? [shir-foh yee-yoo shir-yong]
- I'd like something easy to carry 我想要易于携带的东西 wǒ xiǎng yào yìyú xiédài de dōngxi [wo shyang yow yee-yoo shyeah-digh duh dong-shee]

eat 吃 chī [chir]
- I'm afraid I don't eat meat 抱歉我不吃肉 bàoqiàn wǒ bù chī ròu [bow-chyen wo boo chir-roh]

---

eating

Chinese cuisine and gastronomy are world famous. Most Chinese people are interested in food not only in terms of gastronomy but also for its benefits to their health. Food is the basis of life, health and longevity. In Northern China and Beijing, you can greet your friends by saying 你吃饭了吗? nǐ chīfàn le ma? [nee chir-fan luh ma], which literally means 'have you eaten?.'

‣ where can we get something to eat? 我们到哪里去可以吃点东西？ wǒmen dào nǎli qù kěyǐ chī diǎn dōngxi [wo-meun dow na-lee choo kuh-yee chir dong-shee]

economy (class) 经济舱 jīngjìcāng [jing-jee-tsang] ◆ 坐经济舱 zuò jīngjìcāng [zwore jing-jee-tsang]

‣ are there any seats in economy class? 经济舱有座位吗？ jīngjìcāng yǒu zuòwei ma? [jing-jee-tsang yoh zwore-way ma]

‣ I'd prefer to go economy 我宁愿坐经济舱去 wǒ nìngyuàn zuò jīngjìcāng qù [wo ning-ywan zwore jing-jee-tsang choo]

egg 鸡蛋 jīdàn [jee-dan]

‣ I'd like my eggs sunny side up, please 请给我来单面煎的鸡蛋 qǐng gěi wǒ lái dān miàn jiàn de jīdàn [ching gay wo ligh dan-myen jyen duh jee-dan]

eight 八 bā [ba]

‣ there are eight of us 我们有八个人 wǒmen yǒu bā gè rén [wo-meun yoh ba guh reun]

electric heater 电暖器 diànnuǎnqì [dyen-nwan-chee]

‣ do you have an electric heater? 你有电暖器吗？ nǐ yǒu diànnuǎnqì ma? [nee yoh dyen-nwan-chee ma]

electricity 电 diàn [dyen]

‣ there's no electricity in the room 房间里没电 fángjiān li méi diàn [fang-jyen-lee may dyen]

electric razor, electric shaver 电动剃须刀 diàndòng tìxūdāo [dyen-dong tee-shoo-dow]

‣ where can I plug in my electric razor? 我可以把我的电动剃须刀插在哪里？ wǒ kěyǐ bǎ wǒ de diàndòng tìxūdāo chā zài nǎli? [na-lee wo kuh-yee cha wo duh dyen-dong tee-shoo-dow]

elevator 电梯 diàntī [dyen-tee]

‣ is there an elevator? 有电梯吗？ yǒu diàntī ma? [yoh dyen-tee ma]

‣ the elevator is out of order 电梯坏了 diàntī huài le [dyen-tee hwigh-luh]

eleven 十一 shíyī [shir-yee]

‣ there are eleven of us 我们有十一个人 wǒmen yǒu shíyī gè rén [wo-meun yoh shir-yee guh reun]

e-mail 电子邮件 diànzǐ yóujiàn [dyen-zir yoh-jyen]

‣ I'd like to send an e-mail 我想发电子邮件 wǒ xiǎng fā diànzǐ yóujiàn [wo shyang fa dyen-zir yoh-jyen]

‣ where can I check my e-mail? 我可以在哪里查我的电子邮件？ wǒ kěyǐ zài nǎli chá wǒ de diànzǐ yóujiàn? [wo ku-yee zigh na-lee cha wo duh dyen-zir yoh-jyen]

emergencies

The first emergency number to remember is the police: 110. If they are needed, the police are obliged to respond, in person, within 15 minutes of an emergency call being placed. In the event of fire, call the fire department on 119. For medical emergencies, call 120. Note that even though there are ambulance services operating in large cities, these are often slow to respond, so it's usually better to go to a hospital if possible.

e-mail address 电子邮件地址 diànzǐ yóujiàn dìzhǐ [dyen-zir yoh-jyen dee-jir]
  ▸ do you have an e-mail address? 你有电子邮件地址吗？ nǐ yǒu diànzǐ yóujàn dìzhǐ ma? [nee yoh dyen-zir yoh-jyen dee-jir ma]

emergency 紧急情况 jǐnjí qíngkuàng [jin-jee ching-kwung]
  ▸ it's an emergency! 是紧急情况！ shì jǐnjí qíngkuàng! [shir jin-jee ching-kwung]
  ▸ what number do you call in an emergency? 发生紧急情况时该打哪个号码？ fāshēng jǐnjí qíngkuàng shí gāi dǎ nǎge hàomǎ? [fa-shung jin-jee ching-kwung gigh da na-guh dyen-hwa]

emergency cord 紧急刹车索 jǐnjí shāchēsuǒ [jin-jee sha-chuh-swore]
  ▸ someone's pulled the emergency cord 有人拉了紧急刹车索 yǒu rén lāle jǐnjí shāchēsuǒ [yoh reun la-luh jin-jee sha-chuh-swore]

emergency exit 紧急出口 jǐnjí chūkǒu [jin-jee choo-koh]
  ▸ remember that the nearest emergency exit may be behind you (on plane) 记住，最近的紧急出口可能就在您的身后 jìzhù, zuì jìn de jǐnjí chūkǒu kěnéng jiù zài nín de shēnhòu [jee-joo zway-jin duh jin-jee choo-koh kuh-nung jew zigh nin duh sheun-hoh]

emergency room 急诊室 jízhěnshì [jee-jeun-shir]
  ▸ I need to go to the emergency room right away 我得立即去急诊室 wǒ děi lìjí qù jízhěnshì [wo day lee-jee choo jee-jeun-shir]

emergency services 应急服务机构 yìngjí fúwù jīgòu [ying-jee foo-woo jee-goh]
  ▸ do you a have a listing of emergency services numbers? 你有应急服务机构的电话名单吗？ nǐ yǒu yìngjí fúwù jīgòu de diànhuà míngdān ma? [nee yoh ying-jee foo-woo jee-goh duh dyen-hwa ming-dan ma]

end (conclusion, finish) 末端 mòduān [mo-dwan]
  ▸ at the end of July 在7月底 zài qī yuè dǐ [zigh chee yue dee]

engine 发动机 fādòngjī [fa-dong-jee]
  ▸ the engine is making a funny noise 发动机发出奇怪的声音 fādòngjī fāchū qíguài de shēngyīn [fa-dong-jee duh shung-yin gwigh-gwigh duh]

English

English is used as an international language in China. Signs, notices at tourist attractions, and museum descriptions are usually translated into English, but the English used is not always correct. You may notice that a lot of street signs or English menus contain poor or broken English. This has become known as *Chinglish*. The Beijing authorities are clamping down on *Chinglish* in preparation for the 2008 Olympic Games, and replacing signs such as 'Oil Gate' with real English equivalents ('Gas Station,' in this example).

English 英格兰的 yīnggélán de [ying-guh-lan duh] ◆ *(language)* 英语 yīngyǔ [ying-yoo]

▸ I'm English 我是英格兰人 wǒ shì yīnggélánrén [wo shir ying-guh-lan-reun]

▸ how do you say that in English? 那个用英语怎么说？ nàge yòng yīngyǔ zěnme shuō? [na-guh yong ying-yoo zeun-muh shwore]

▸ do you understand English? 你懂英语吗？ nǐ dǒng yīngyǔ ma? [nee dong ying-yoo ma]

enjoy 从......中获得乐趣 cōng......zhōng huòdé lèqù [tsong...jong hwore-duh luh-choo]

▸ to enjoy oneself 感到开心 gǎndào kāixīn [gan-dow kigh-shin]

▸ enjoy your meal! 吃得开心！ chī de kāixīn! [chir duh kigh-shin]

▸ did you enjoy your meal? 你吃得开心吗？ nǐ chī de kāixīn ma? [nee chir duh kigh-shin ma]

enough 足够得 zúgòu de [zoo-goh duh] ◆ 足够 zúgòu [zoo-goh]

▸ I don't have enough money 我没有足够得钱 wǒ méiyou zúgòu de qián [wo may-yoh zoo-goh duh chyen]

▸ that's enough! 够了！ gòu le! [goh-luh]

▸ no thanks, I've had quite enough 不，谢谢。我够了 bù, xièxie. wǒ gòu le [boo, shyeah-shyeah wo goh-luh]

enter *(type in)* 键入 jiànrù [jyen-roo]

▸ do I enter my PIN number now? 我现在要键入密码吗？ wǒ xiànzài yào jiànrù mìmǎ ma? [wo shyen-zigh yow jyen-roo mee-ma ma]

entrance 入口 rùkǒu [roo-koh]

▸ where's the entrance to the subway? 地铁的入口在哪里？ dìtiě de rùkǒu zài nǎli? [dee-tyeah duh roo-koh zigh na-lee]

entry *(to place)* 进入 jìnrù [jin-roo]

▸ entry to the exhibit is free 参观展览是免费的 cānguān zhǎnlǎn shì miǎnfèi de [tsan-gwan jan-lan shir myen-fay duh]

envelope 信封 xìnfēng [shin-fung]
  ▸ I'd like a pack of envelopes 我想要一包信封 wǒ xiǎng yào yī bāo xìnfēng [wo shyang yow yee-bow shin-fung]

equipment 设备 shèbèi [shuh-bay]
  ▸ do you provide the equipment? 你们提供设备吗? nǐmen tígōng shèbèi ma? [nee tee-gong shuh-bay ma]

escalator 自动扶梯 zìdòng fútī [zir-dong foo-tee]
  ▸ is there an escalator? 有自动扶梯吗? yǒu zìdòng fútī ma? [yoh zir-dong foo-tee ma]

evening 晚上 wǎnshang [wan-shang]; *(expressing duration)* 晚间 wǎnjiān [wan-jyen]
  ▸ why don't we meet up this evening? 我们为什么不今晚见面呢? wǒmen wèi shénme bù jīnwǎn jiànmiàn ne? [wo-meun way-sheun-muh boo jin-wan jyen-myen nuh]
  ▸ in the evening *(of every day)* 在晚上 zài wǎnshang [zigh wan-shang]

event *(cultural)* 活动 huódòng [hwore-dong]
  ▸ what's the program of events? 活动是怎么安排的? huódòng shì zěnme ānpái de? [hwore-dong shir zeun-muh an-pigh duh]

ever *(at any time)* 从来 cónglái [tsong-ligh]; *(before now)* 曾经 céngjīng [tsung-jing]
  ▸ have you ever been to Boston? 你曾去过波士顿吗? nǐ céng qùguo bōshìdùn ma? [nee tsung-jing choo-gwore bo-shir-dun ma]

everything 一切事物 yīqiè shìwù [yee-chyeah shir-woo]
  ▸ that's everything, thanks 就这些, 谢谢 jiù zhèxiē, xièxie [jew juh-shyeah shyeah-shyeah]
  ▸ we didn't have time to see everything 我们没有时间去看所有的东西 wǒmen méiyou shíjiān qù kàn suǒyǒu de dōngxi [wo-meun may-yoh shir-jyen choo kan swore-yoh duh dong-shee]

excess baggage 超重行李 chāozhòng xíngli [chow-jong shing-lee]
  ▸ what's your policy on excess baggage? 你们对超重的行李有何规定? nǐmen duì chāozhòng de xíngli yǒu hé guīdìng? [nee-meun dway chow-jong duh shing-lee yoh huh gway-ding]

exchange 调换 diàohuàn [deow-hwan]
  ▸ I'd like to exchange this T-shirt 我想调换这件短袖圆领衫 wǒ xiǎng diàohuàn zhè jiàn duǎn xiù yuán lǐng shān [wo shyang deow-hwan juh-jyen tee-shoo-shan]

exchange rate 汇率 huìlǜ [hway-looh]
  ▸ what is today's exchange rate? 今天的汇率是多少? jīntiān de huìlǜ shì duōshao? [jin-tyen duh hway-looh shir dwore-show]

exhibits

China is 'the workshop of the world,' so it holds many exhibits and fairs to display products made in China and to forge business contacts. One of the most famous of these is the China Export Commodities Fair 广交会 guǎngjiāohuì [gwang-jeow-hway] in Canton, which is held twice a year in spring and fall.

excursion 短途旅行 duǎntú lǚxíng [dwan-too looh-shing]

▸ I'd like to sign up for the excursion on Saturday 我想参加星期六的短途旅行 wǒ xiǎng cānjiā xīngqīliù de duǎntú lǚxíng [wo shyang tsan-jya shing-chee-lew duh dwan-too looh-shing]

excuse *(behavior, person)* 原谅 yuánliàng [ywan-lyang]

▸ excuse me? *(asking for repetition)* 请再说一遍 qǐng zài shuō yī biàn [ching zigh shwore yee-byen]

▸ excuse me! *(to get attention; to get by)* 劳驾 láojià [low-jya]; *(when interrupting, apologizing, leaving)* 对不起 duìbuqǐ [dway-boo-chee]; *(expressing disagreement)* 抱歉 bàoqiàn [bow-chyen]

▸ you'll have to excuse my (poor) Chinese 请你原谅，我中文说得不好 qǐng nǐ yuánliàng, wǒ zhōngwén shuō de bù hǎo [ching nee ywan-lyang wo jong-weun shwore duh boo-how]

exhaust 排气管 páiqìguǎn [pigh-chee-gwan]

▸ the exhaust is making a strange noise 排气管发出奇怪的声音 páiqìguǎn fāchū qíguài de shēngyīn [pigh-chee-gwan fa-choo chee-gwigh duh shung-yin]

exhausted *(tired)* 精疲力尽的 jīng pí lì jìn de [jing pee lee jin duh]

▸ I'm exhausted 我累死了 wǒ lèisǐ le [wo lay-sir luh]

exhibit 展览 zhǎnlǎn [jan-lan]

▸ I'd like a ticket for the temporary exhibit 我要一张参观常规展览的票 wǒ yào yī zhāng cānguān chángguī zhǎnlǎn de piào [wo yow yee jang tsan-gwan chang-gway jan-lan duh peow]

▸ is this ticket valid for the exhibit too? 这张票也可以用于餐馆展览吗？ zhè zhāng piào yě kěyǐ yòngyú cānguān zhǎnlǎn ma? [juh jang peow yuh kuh-yee yong-yoo tsan-gwan jan-lan ma]

exit 出口 chūkǒu [choo-koh]

▸ where's the exit? 出口在哪里？ chūkǒu zài nǎli? [choo-koh zigh na-lee]

▸ is it far to the next exit? 下一个出口远吗？ xià yī gè chūkǒu yuǎn ma? [shya yee guh choo-koh ywan ma]

expect *(baby, letter)* 期待 qīdài [chee-digh]

▸ I'll be expecting you at eight o'clock at... 我8点钟在......等你 wǒ bā diǎnzhōng zài......děng nǐ [wo ba dyen-jong zigh...dung nee]

‣ when do you expect it to be ready? 你认为它什么时候能好？ nǐ rènwéi tā shénme shíhou néng hǎo? [nee reun-way ta sheun-muh shir-hoh nung how]

expensive 贵的 guì de [gway duh]

‣ do you have anything less expensive? 你有什么东西不那么贵吗？ nǐ yǒu shénme dōngxi bù nàme guì ma? [nee yoh sheun-muh boo na-muh gway ma]

expire *(visa)* 过期 guòqī [gwore-chee]

‣ my passport has expired 我的护照过期了 wǒ de hùzhào guòqī le [wo duh hoo-jow gwore-chee luh]

explain 说明 shuōmíng [shwore-ming]

‣ please explain how to get to the airport 请说一下怎么去机场？ qǐng shuō yī xià zěnme qù jīchǎng? [ching shwore yee shya zeun-muh choo jee-chang]

‣ can you explain what this means? 你能解释一下这是什么意思吗？ nǐ néng jiěshì yī xià zhè shì shénme yisi ma? [nee nung jyeah-shir yee shya juh shir sheun-muh yee-sir ma]

express *(train)* 快车 kuàichē [kwigh-chuh]

‣ how long does it take by express train? 乘快车要多久？ chéng kuàichē yào duō jiǔ? [chung kwigh-chuh yow dwore jew]

extension *(phone line)* 分机 fēnjī [feun-jee]

‣ could I have extension 358, please? 请转分机358 qǐng zhuǎn fēnjī sān wǔ bā [ching jwan feun-jee san woo ba]

extra 额外的 éwài de [uh-wigh duh]

‣ is it possible to add an extra bed? 是否可以另加一张床？ shìfǒu kěyǐ lìng jiā yī zhāng chuáng? [shir-foh kuh-yee ling jya yee jang chwung]

‣ would it be possible to stay an extra night? 是否可以再住一个晚上？ shìfǒu kěyǐ zài zhù yī gè wǎnshang? [shir-foh kuh-yee zigh joo yee guh wan-shang]

extra charge 额外收费 éwài shōufèi [uh-wigh shoh-fay]

‣ what would the extra charge be for this service? 该服务是否要另外付费？ gāi fúwù shìfǒu yào lìngwài fù fèi? [gigh foo-woo shir-foh yow ling-wigh foo-fay]

‣ at no extra charge 没有额外的收费 méiyou éwài de shōu fèi [may-yoh uh-wigh duh shoh-fay]

eye 眼睛 yǎnjīng [yan-jing]

‣ she has blue eyes 她的眼睛是蓝色的 tā de yǎnjīng shì lánsè de [ta duh yan-jing shir lan-suh duh]

‣ can you keep an eye on my bag for a few minutes? 你能帮我照看几分钟行李吗？ nǐ néng bāng wǒ zhàokàn jǐ fēnzhōng xínglǐ ma? [nee nung bang wo jow-kan jee feun-jong shing-lee ma]

eye drops 眼药水 yǎnyàoshuǐ [yan-yow-shway]

‣ do you have any eye drops? 你有眼药水吗？ nǐ yǒu yǎnyàoshuǐ ma? [nee yoh yan-yow-shway ma]

eye shadow 眼罩 yǎnzhào [yan-jow]

▸ is this the only eye shadow you've got? 你只有这种眼罩吗？ nǐ zhǐ yǒu zhè zhǒng yǎnzhào ma? [nee jir yoh juh jong yan-jow ma]

eyesight 视力 shìlì [shir-lee]

▸ I don't have very good eyesight 我的视力不大好 wǒ de shìlì bù dà hǎo [wo duh shir-lee boo da how]

face *(of person)* 脸 liǎn [lyen]

▸ the attacker had a broad face 攻击者的脸挺宽 gōngjīzhě de liǎn tǐng kuān [gong-jee-juh duh lyen ting kwan]

facilities 设施 shèshī [shuh-shir]

▸ what kind of exercise facilities do you have here? 你这里有什么样的运动设施? nǐ zhèlǐ yǒu shénme yàng de yùndòng shèshī? [nee juh-lee yoh sheun-muh yang duh yun-dong shuh-shir]

▸ do you have facilities for people with disabilities? 你们是否有供残疾人使用的设施? nǐmen shìfǒu yǒu gōng cánjírén shǐyòng de shèshī? [nee-meun shi-foh yoh gong tsan-jee-reun shir-yong duh shuh-shir]

▸ are there facilities for children? 有供孩子用的设施吗? yǒu gōng háizi yòng de shèshī ma? [yoh gong high-zir yong duh shuh-shir ma]

faint 晕倒 yūndǎo [yun-dow]

▸ I fainted twice last week 我上星期晕倒了两次 wǒ shàng xīngqī yūndǎole liǎng cì [wo shang shing-chee yun-dow luh lyang tsir]

fair *(person, situation)* 公平的 gōngpíng de [gong-ping duh]; *(price)* 合理的 hélǐ de [huh-lee duh]; *(hair)* 金色的 jīnsè de [jin-suh duh]; *(skin, complexion)* 白皙的 báixī de [bigh-shee duh]

'face'

In China, a smile isn't always an indication that everything is well. It can contain other meanings – it can hide shame, embarrassment or suppressed anger. In general, you should always avoid getting annoyed, and try to keep your cool. In social situations it is second nature to the Chinese to 'save face' which is a sort of 'keen awareness of honor.' You must try to compromise and not get into direct confrontation.

family

This is the basic group of Chinese society, and also an important element in terms of language and culture. It is quite common for a family to all work together, or for several generations of the same family to live under one roof. When Chinese people want to get to know you, they won't hesitate to ask about your family situation, whether you are married or if you have children. With people from an older generation, it is common to show respect and affection by calling a man 叔叔 shūshu [shoo-shoo] (uncle) and a woman 阿姨 āyí [a-yee] (aunt).

▸ this isn't a fair price 这价格不合理 zhè jiàgé bù hélǐ [juh jya-guh boo huh-lee]
▸ it's not fair! 不公平！ bù gōngpíng! [boo gong-ping]

fall 倒下 dǎoxia [dow-shya]
▸ I fell on my back 我仰面倒下 wǒ yǎngmiàn dǎoxia [wo yang-myen dow-shya]

family 家人 jiārén [jya-reun]
▸ do you have any family in the area? 在这个地方你有家人吗？ zài zhège dìfang nǐ yǒu jiārén ma? [zigh juh-guh dee-fang nee yoh jya-reun ma]

fan 电扇 diànshàn [dyen-shan]
▸ how does the fan work? 这个电扇怎么用？ zhège diànshàn zěnme yòng? [juh-guh dyen-shan zeun-muh yong]

far *(in distance, time)* 远 yuǎn [ywan]
▸ am I far from the village? 我离村庄远吗？ wǒ lí cūnzhuāng yuǎn ma? [wo lee tsun-jwung ywan ma]
▸ is it far to walk? 步行去远吗？ bùxíng qù yuǎn ma? [boo-shing choo ywan ma]
▸ is it far by car? 开车去远吗？ kāichē qù yuǎn ma? [kigh-chuh choo ywan ma]
▸ how far is the market from here? 市场离这儿有多远？ shìchǎng lí zhèr yǒu duōyuǎn? [shir-chang lee juh yoh dwore-ywan]
▸ far away/off *(in distance, time)* 遥远 yáoyuǎn [yow-ywan]
▸ so far 至今 zhìjīn [jir-jin]

fast 快的 kuài de [kwigh duh] ◆ 迅速地 xùnsù de [shun-soo duh]
▸ please don't drive so fast 请别把车开得那么快 qǐng bié bǎ chē kāi de nàme kuài [ching byeah ba chuh kigh duh na-muh kwigh]
▸ to be fast *(watch, clock)* 快 kuài [kwigh]
▸ my watch is five minutes fast 我的表快了五分钟 wǒ de biǎo kuài le wǔ fēnzhōng [wo duh beow kwigh luh woo feun-jong]

fat *(in diet)* 脂肪 zhīfáng [jir-fang]
▸ it's low in fat 这是低脂的 zhè shì dīzhī de [juh-shir dee-jir duh]

father 父亲 fùqin [foo-chin], 爸爸 bàba [ba-ba]
- this is my father 这是我的父亲 zhèshì wǒ de fùqin [juh shir wo duh foo-chin], 这是我的爸爸 zhè shì wǒ de bàba [juh shir wo duh ba-ba]

fault (responsibility) 错误 cuòwù [tsore-woo]
- it was my fault 是我的错 shì wǒ de cuò [shir wo duh tsore]

favor (kind act) 恩惠 ēnhuì [eun-hway]
- can I ask you a favor? 我能请你帮个忙吗? wǒ néng qǐng nǐ bāng gè máng ma? [wo nung ching nee bang guh mang ma]

favorite 最喜欢的 zuì xǐhuan de [zway shee-hwan duh] ♦ 最喜欢的事物 zuì xǐhuan de shìwù [zway shee-hwan duh shir-woo]
- it's my favorite book 这是我最喜欢的书 zhèshì wǒ zuì xǐhuan de shū [juh-shir wo zway shee-hwan duh shoo]

feather 羽毛 yǔmáo [yoo-mow]
- are these feather pillows? 这些是羽绒枕头吗? zhèxiē shì yǔróng zhěntou ma? [juh-shyeah shir yoo-rong jeun-toh ma]

February 二月 èr yuè [er yue]
- February 8th 二月八日 èr yuè bā rì [er yue ba rir]

feed 给......喂食 gěi......wèishí [gay...way-shir]
- where can I feed the baby? 我可以在哪里给孩子喂食? wǒ kěyǐ zài nǎli gěi háizi wèishí? [wo zigh na-lee kuh-yee gay high-zir way-shir]

feel (touch) 摸上去 mōshangqu [mo-shang-choo]; (sense, physically) 感觉 gǎnjué [gan-jue]
- I can't feel my feet 我的脚没感觉了 wǒ de jiǎo méi gǎnjué le [wo duh jeow may gan-jue luh]
- I don't feel well 我感觉不舒服 wǒ gǎnjué bù shūfu [wo gan-jue boo shoo-foo]

ferry 渡船 dùchuán [doo-chwan]
- when does the next ferry leave? 下一班渡船几点离开? xià yī bān dùchuán jǐ diǎn líkāi? [shya yee-ban doo-chwan jee dyen lee-kigh]

ferry terminal 渡船码头 dùchuán mǎtou [doo-chwan ma-toh]
- which way is the ferry terminal? 去渡船码头往哪里走? qù dùchuán mǎtou wǎng nǎli zǒu? [choo doo-chwan ma-toh wang na-lee zoh]

fever 发烧 fāshāo [fa-show]
- the baby's got a fever 宝宝发烧了 bǎobao fāshāo le [bow-bow fa-show luh]

few 不多的 bù duō de [boo-dwore duh] ♦ **a few** 一些 yīxiē [yee-shyeah]
- there are few sights worth seeing around here 这附近值得看的景点不多 zhè fùjìn zhíde kàn de jǐngdiǎn bù duō [juh foo-jin jir-duh kan duh jing-dyen boo dwore]
- we're thinking of staying a few more days 我们在考虑再住几天 wǒmen zài kǎolǜ zài zhù jǐ tiān [wo-meun zigh kow-looh zigh joo jee tyen]

fifth 第五的 dì–wǔ de [dee woo duh] ♦ *(gear)* 五挡 wǔdǎng [woo-dang]

▸ I can't get it into fifth 我挂不进五挡 wǒ guà bù jìn wǔdǎng [wo gwa boo jin woo-dang]

filling *(in a tooth)* 补牙 bǔ yá [boo-ya]

▸ one of my fillings has come out 我补的一颗牙掉了 wǒ bǔ de yī kē yá diào le [wo boo duh yee kuh ya deow luh]

fill up 给......加满油 gěi......jiāmǎn yóu [gay...jya-man yoh] ♦ 加满油 jiāmǎn yóu [jya-man yoh]

▸ fill it up, please 请把汽油加满 qǐng bǎ qìyóu jiāmǎn [ching ba chee-yoh jya-man]

film *(for camera)* 胶卷 jiāojuǎn [jeow-jwan] ♦ 用摄像机拍摄 yòng shèxiàngjī pāishè [yong shuh-shyang-jee pigh-shuh]

▸ I'd like to have this film developed 我想把这卷胶卷冲出来 wǒ xiǎng bǎ zhè juǎn jiāojuǎn chōngchulai [wo shyang ba juh jwan jeow-jwan chong-choo-ligh]

▸ do you have black-and-white film? 你有黑白胶卷吗? nǐ yǒu hēibái jiāojuǎn ma? [nee yoh hay-bigh jeow-jwan ma]

▸ is filming allowed in the museum? 在博物馆里可以使用摄像机吗? zài bówùguǎn li kěyǐ shǐyòng shèxiàngjī ma? [zigh bo-woo-gwan lee kuh-yee shir-yong shuh-shyang-jee ma]

find 发现 fāxiàn [fa-shyen]; *(lost object)* 找到 zhǎodào [jow-dow]

▸ has anyone found a watch? 有人捡到过一块手表吗? yǒu rén jiǎndàoguo yī kuài shǒubiǎo ma? [yoh-reun jyen-dow-gwore yee-kwigh shoh-beow ma]

▸ where can I find a doctor on a Sunday? 星期天我可以去哪儿看病? xīngqītiān wǒ kěyǐ qù nǎr kànbìng? [shing-chee-tyen wo kuh-yee choo nar kan-bing]

find out 找出 zhǎochū [jow-choo]

▸ I need to find out the times of trains to Shanghai 我得弄清楚开往上海的火车时间 wǒ děi nòng qīngchu kāiwǎng shànghǎi de huǒchē shíjiān [wo day nong ching-choo kigh-wang shang-high duh hwore-chuh shir-jyen]

fine *(in health etc.)* 健康的 jiànkāng de [jyen-kang de] ♦ 罚金 fájīn [fa-jin]

▸ fine thanks, and you? 很好，谢谢。你呢? hěn hǎo, xièxie. nǐ ne? [heun-how shyeah-shyeah nee-nuh]

▸ how much is the fine? 罚金是多少? fájīn shì duōshao? [fa-jin shir dwore-show]

finger 手指 shǒuzhǐ [shoh-jir]

▸ I've cut my finger 我把我的手指割破了 wǒ bǎ wǒ de shǒuzhǐ gēpò le [wo ba wo duh shoh-jir guh-po luh]

finish 结束 jiéshù [jyeah-shoo]

▸ can we leave as soon as we've finished our meal? 我们一吃完饭就走好

吗？ wǒmen yī chīwán fàn jiù zǒu hǎo ma? [wo-meun yee chir-wan fan jew zoh how-ma]

fire 火 huǒ [hwore]; *(out of control)* 火灾 huǒzāi [hwore-zigh]
> ▸ to make a fire 生火 shēng huǒ [shung-hwore]
> ▸ on fire *(forest, house)* 着火 zháohuǒ [toh-dung]

fire department 消防队 xiāofángduì [sheow-fang-dway]
> ▸ call the fire department! 快叫消防队！ kuài jiào xiāofángduì! [kwigh jeow sheow-fang-dway]

fireworks 烟火 yānhuǒ [yan-hwore]
> ▸ what time do the fireworks start? 烟火什么时候开始放？ yānhuǒ shénme shíhou kāishǐ fàng? [yan-hwore sheun-muh shir-hoh kigh-shir fang]

first 第一的 dì–yī de [dee-yee duh] ◆ *(before all others)* 第一 dì–yī [dee-yee]; *(gear)* 一挡 yīdǎng [yee-dang]; *(class)* 头等 tóudǎng [toh-dung]
> ▸ it's the first time I've been here 这是我第一次来这里 zhè shì wǒ dì–yī cì lái zhèlǐ [juh-shir wo dee-yee-tsir ligh juh-lee]
> ▸ you have to take the first left after the lights 你得在过了红绿灯后的第一个拐弯处向左拐 nǐ děi zài guòle hónglǜdēng hòu de dì–yī gè guǎiwānchù xiàng zuǒ guǎi [nee day zigh gwore luh hong-looh-dung hoh duh dee-yee-guh gwigh-wan-choo shyang xwore gwigh]
> ▸ put it into first 挂一挡 guà yīdǎng [gwa yee-dang]

first-aid kit 急救箱 jíjiùxiāng [jee-jew-shyang]
> ▸ do you have a first-aid kit? 你有急救箱吗？ nǐ yǒu jíjiùxiāng ma? [nee yoh jee-jew-shyang-ma]

first class 头等舱 tóuděngcāng [toh-dung-tsang] ◆ 在头等舱 zài tóuděngcāng [zigh toh-dung-tsang]
> ▸ are there any seats in first class? 头等舱还有座位吗？ tóuděngcāng hái yǒu zuòwei ma? [toh-dung-tsang high-yoh zwore-way ma]
> ▸ I prefer to travel first class 我外出旅行更爱坐头等舱 wǒ wàichū lǚxíng gèng ài zuò tóuděngcāng [wo wigh-choo looh-shing gung igh zwore woh-dung-tsang]

fish 鱼 yú [yoo]
> ▸ I don't eat fish 我不吃鱼 wǒ bù chī yú [wo boo chir yoo]

fishing permit 钓鱼许可证 diào yú xǔkězhèng [deow-yoo shoo-kuh-jung]
> ▸ do you need a fishing permit to fish here? 是否要有钓鱼许可证才可以在这里钓鱼？ shìfǒu yào yǒu diào yú xǔkězhèng cái kěyǐ zài zhèlǐ diào yú? [shir-foh yow yoh deow-yoo shoo-kuh-jung tsigh kuh-yee zigh juh-lee deow-yoo]

fit *(of laughter, tears)* 一阵发作 yī zhèn fāzuò [yee-jeun fa-zwore] ◆ *(be correct size for)* 合适 héshì [huh-shir] ◆ *(be correct size)* 合身 héshēn [huh-sheun]
> ▸ I think she's having some kind of fit 我想她正大发雷霆 wǒ xiǎng tā zhèng

fish and seafood

The Chinese like their fish and seafood to be so fresh that most fish restaurants have their own aquariums where fish are kept alive. This is so that you can choose the fish and seafood you like the look of, and then discuss how it should be cooked. Before it is cooked, you may sometimes be brought the freshly-caught fish in a bag or a net, to show you just how fresh it is. This means that it can also be weighed to see how much it will cost. The approximate weight is measured in 斤 jīn [jin], which is roughly equivalent to a pound.

dà fā léitíng [wo shyang ta jung da fa lay-ting]

▸ those pants fit you better 那条裤子更合你的身 nà tiáo kùzi gèng hé nǐ de shēn [na teow koo-zir gung huh nee duh sheun]

▸ the key doesn't fit in the lock 这把钥匙打不开这把锁 zhè bǎ yàoshi dǎ bù kāi zhè bǎ suǒ [juh ba yow-shir da boo kigh juh ba swore]

▸ we won't all fit around one table 我们一张桌子坐不下 wǒmen yī zhāng zhuōzi zuò bù xià [wo-meun yee-jang jwore-zir zwore boo shya]

fit in *(go in)* 放得进 fàng de jìn [fang duh jin] ◆ *(put in)* 放入 fàngrù [fang-roo]

▸ I can't get everything to fit in my suitcase 我没法把所有的东西都放进我的手提箱 wǒ méifǎ bǎ suǒyǒu de dōngxi dōu fàngjìn wǒ de shǒutíxiāng [wo may-fa ba swore-yoh duh dong-shee doh fang-jin wo duh shoh-tee-shyang]

▸ how many people can you fit in this car? 你的车可以坐下多少人？ nǐ de chē kěyǐ zuòxià duōshao rén? [nee duh chuh kuh-yee zwore-shya dwore-show reun]

fitting room 试衣间 shìyījiān [shir-yee-jyen]

▸ where are the fitting rooms? 试衣间在哪里？ shìyījiān zài nǎlǐ? [shir-yee-jyen zigh na-lee]

five 五 wǔ [woo]

▸ there are five of us 我们有五个人 wǒmen yǒu wǔ gè rén [wo-meun yoh woo guh reun]

fix 修理 xiūlǐ [shew-lee]

▸ where can I find someone to fix my bike? 我去哪里可以找人修理我的自行车？ wǒ qù nǎli kěyǐ zhǎo rén xiūlǐ wǒ de zìxíngchē? [wo choo na-lee kuh-yee jow reun shew-lee wo duh zir-shing-chuh]

fixed price 固定的价格 gùdìng de jiàgé [goo-ding duh jya-guh]

▸ do taxis to the airport charge a fixed price? 乘坐出租车去机场收费是固定的吗？ chéngzuò chūzūchē qù jīchǎng shōu fèi shì gùdìng de ma? [chung-zwore choo-zoo-chuh choo jee-chang shoh-fay shir goo-ding duh ma]

flash 闪光灯 shǎnguāngdēng [shang-gwang-dung]

▸ I'd like some batteries for my flash 我要一些用在闪光灯上的电池 wǒ yào yīxiē yòng zài shǎnguāngdēng shang de diànchí [wo yow yee-shyeah yong zigh shang-gwang-dung shang duh dyen-chir]

flash photography 使用闪光灯拍摄照片 shǐyòng shǎnguāngdēng pāishè zhàopiān [shir-yong shang-gwang-dung pigh-shuh jow-pyen]

▸ is flash photography allowed here? 在这里拍照是否可以用闪光灯？ zài zhèlǐ pāizhào shìfǒu yěyǐ yòng shǎnguāngdēng? [zigh juh-lee pigh-jow shir-foh yuh-yee yong shir-yong shang-gwang-dung]

flat (tire) 没气的 méi qì de [may chee duh]

▸ the tire's flat 轮胎没气了 lúntāi méi qì le [lun-tigh may chee luh]

flavor (of food) 味道 wèidao [way-dow]; (of ice cream, yogurt) 口味 kǒuwèi [koh-way]

▸ I'd like to try a different flavor of ice cream 我想试一试另一种口味的冰激淋 wǒ xiǎng shì yī shì lìng yī zhǒng kǒuwèi de bīngjīlín [wo shyang shir yee shir ling yee-jong koh-way duh bing-jee-lin]

flight 航班 hángbān [hang-ban]

▸ how many flights a day are there? 每天有多少个航班？ měi tiān yǒu duōshao gè hángbān? [may-tyen yoh dwore-show guh hang-ban]

▸ what time is the flight? 这个航班是几点钟的？ zhège hángbān shì jǐ diǎnzhōng de? [juh-guh hang-ban shir jee dyen-jong duh]

flight of stairs 楼梯 lóutī [loh-tee]

▸ your room's up that flight of stairs 你的房间在那个楼梯上 nǐ de fángjiān zài nàge lóutī shang [nee duh fang-jyen zigh na-guh loh-tee-shang]

floor (story) 层 céng [tsung]

▸ which floor is it on? 在几层？ zài jǐ céng? [zigh jee tsung]

▸ it's on the top floor 在顶层 zài dǐngcéng [zigh ding-tsung]

flower 花 huā [hwa]

▸ do you sell flowers? 你们卖花吗？ nǐmen mài huā ma? [nee-meun migh hwa ma]

flower tea 花茶 huāchá [hwa-cha]

▸ I'd like a flower tea 我想要杯花茶 wǒ xiǎng yào bēi huāchá [wo shyang yow bay hwa-cha]

flu 流感 liú-gǎn [lew-gan]

▸ I'd like something for the flu 我要治流感的药 wǒ yào zhì liú-gǎn de yào [wo yow jir lew-gan duh yow]

flush 脸红 liǎnhóng [lyen-hong] ♦ (toilet) 冲 chōng [chong] ♦ (person) 脸红 liánhóng [lyen-hong]; (toilet) 冲厕所 chōng cèsuǒ [chong tsuh-swore]

‣ the toilet won't flush 厕所冲不了了 cèsuǒ chōng bù liǎo le [tsuh-swore chong boo leow luh]

fog 雾 wù [woo]

‣ is there a lot of fog today? 今天雾大吗? jīntiān wù dà ma? [jin-tyen woo da ma]

food 食物 shíwù [shir-woo]

‣ is there someplace to buy food nearby? 这附近有地方买吃的吗? zhè fùjìn yǒu dìfang mǎi chī de ma? [juh foo-jin yoh dee-fang migh chir duh ma]

‣ the food here is excellent 这里的食品很棒 zhèli de shípǐng hěn bàng [juh-lee duh shir-ping heun bang]

food cart (on train, plane) 手推餐车 shǒutuī cānchē [shoh-tway tsan-chuh]

‣ is there a food cart service on this train? 这辆火车上有手推餐车服务吗? zhè liàng huǒchē shang yǒu shǒutuī cānchē fúwù ma? [juh lyang hwore-chuh shang yoh shoh-tway tsan-chuh foo-woo ma]

food section (in store) 食品区 shípǐngqū [shir-ping-choo]

‣ where's the food section? 食品区在什么地方? shípǐngqū zài shénme dìfang? [shir-ping-choo zigh sheun-muh dee-fang]

foot 脚 jiǎo [jeow]

‣ on foot 步行 bùxíng [boo-shing]

for (expressing purpose, function) 为了 wèile [way-luh]; (indicating direction, destination) 前往 qiánwǎng [chyen-wang]; (indicating duration) 达 dá [da]; (since) 因为 yīnwei [yin-way]

‣ what's that for? 那是干什么用的? nà shì gàn shénme yòng de? [na-shir gan sheun-muh yong duh]

‣ the flight for Xi'an 前往西安的航班 qiánwǎng xī'ān de hángbān [chyen-wang shee-an duh hang-ban]

‣ is this the right train for Beijing? 这是开往北京的火车吗? zhè shì kāiwǎng běijīng de huǒchē ma? [juh-shir kigh-wang bay-jing duh hwore-chuh ma]

‣ I'm staying for two months 我会呆两个月 wǒ huì dāi liǎng gè yuè [wo hway digh-lyang guh yue]

‣ I've been here for a week 我来这儿一周了 wǒ lái zhèr yī zhōu le [wo ligh juhr yee-joh luh]

‣ I need something for a cough 我需要治疗咳嗽的药 wǒ xūyào zhìliáo késou de yào [wo shoo-yow jir-leow kuh-soh duh yow]

foreign (country, language) 外国的 wàiguó de [wigh-gwore duh]

‣ I don't speak any foreign languages 我不会说任何外语 wǒ bù huì shuō rènhé wàiyǔ [wo boo-hway shwore reun-huh wigh-yoo]

exchanging foreign currency

The Chinese currency is the 人民币 rénmínbì [reun-min-bee] or *RMB*, in other words 'the people's money,' which is often known by its unit the 元 yuán [ywan]. You can exchange money at the big banks (such as the Bank of China), the airport, or the reception desk in large hotels. The best rates of exchange are usually to be found in banks. Cash advances are available on most common credit/debit cards e.g. American Express®/Visa®/Master-Card®. A fee of 3-4% will apply. Note that you cannot exchange the *yuan* outside China, so try to spend all your cash, or change it before leaving the country.

foreign currency 外币 wàibì [wigh-bee]
▸ do you change foreign currency? 你们兑换外币吗? nǐmen duìhuàn wàibì ma? [nee-meun dway-hwan wigh-bee ma]

foreigner 外国人 wàiguórén [wigh-gwore-reun]
▸ as a foreigner, this custom seems a bit strange to me 作为外国人，这种风俗我觉得有点儿奇怪 zuòwéi wàiguórén, zhè zhǒng fēngsú wǒ juéde yǒu diǎnr qíguài [zwore-way wigh-gwore-reun juh-jong fung-soo wo jue-duh yoh dyen chee-gwigh]

forever 永远 yǒngyuǎn [yong-ywan]
▸ our money won't last forever 我们不会永远都有钱的 wǒmen bù huì yǒngyuǎn dōu yǒu qián de [wo-meun boo-hway yong-ywan doh yoh chyen duh]

fork 叉子 chāzi [cha-zir]
▸ could I have a fork? 能给我一个叉子吗? néng gěi wǒ yī gè chāzi ma? [nung gay wo yee-guh cha-zir ma]

forward 转发 zhuǎnfā [jwan-fa]
▸ can you forward my mail? 你能把我的邮件转发给我吗? nǐ néng bǎ wǒ de yóujiàn zhuǎnfā gěi wǒ ma? [nee nung ba wo duh yoh-jyen jwan-fa gay wo ma]

four 四 sì [sir]
▸ there are four of us 我们有四个人 wǒmen yǒu sì gè rén [wo-meun yoh sir guh reun]

fourth 第四的 dì-sì de [dee-sir duh] ◆ *(gear)* 四挡 sìdǎng [sir-dang]
▸ it's hard to get it into fourth 四挡很难挂 sìdǎng hěn nán guà [sir-dang heun nan gwa]

four-wheel drive 四轮驱动的车 sì lún qūdòng de chē [sir lun choo-dong duh chuh]
▸ I'd like a four-wheel drive 我想要一辆四轮驱动的车 wǒ xiǎng yào yī liàng sì lún qūdòng de chē [wo shyang yow yee lyang sir lun choo-dong duh chuh]

four

The Chinese don't like the figure 4 because of the similarity of its pronunciation to the character 死 sǐ [sir], meaning 'death.' Superstitious people avoid it and you might notice that some elevators and buildings don't have a 4th floor. On the other hand, the number 8 is highly thought of because it sounds similar to 发 fā [fa], meaning 'to prosper.' It's considered good luck to have an 8 in your telephone number.

fracture 裂缝 lièfèng [lyeah-fung]

▸ is it a hairline fracture? 是个很细的裂缝吗? shì gè hěn xì de lièfèng ma? [shir guh heun shee duh lyeah-fung ma]

free *(offered at no charge)* 免费的 miǎnfèi de [myen-fay duh]; *(not occupied)* 没人的 méi rén de [may reun duh]; *(available)* 有空的 yǒu kòng de [yoh-kong duh]

▸ is it free? 是免费的吗? shì miǎnfèi de ma? [shir myen-fay duh ma]

▸ is this seat free? 这个座位有人吗? zhège zuòwei yǒu rén ma? [juh-guh zwore-way yoh reun ma]

▸ are you free on Thursday evening? 星期四晚上你有空吗? xīngqīsì wǎnshang nǐ yǒu kòng ma? [shing-chee-sir wan-shang nee yoh kong ma]

freeway 高速公路 gāosù gōnglù [gow-soo gong-loo]

▸ what is the speed limit on freeways? 高速公路上的时速限制是多少? gāosù gōnglù shang de shísù xiànzhì shì duōshao? [gow-soo gong-loo shang duh shir-soo shyen-jir shir dwore-show]

▸ how do I get onto the freeway? 我该怎么上高速公路? wǒ gāi zěnme shàng gāosù gōnglù? [wo gigh zeun-muh shang gow-soo gong-loo]

freezing (cold) *(room, day)* 极冷的 jí lěng de [jee lung duh]

▸ I'm freezing (cold) 我感到冷极了 wǒ gǎndào lěngjí le [wo gan-dow lung-jee luh]

frequent 频繁的 pínfán de [pin-fan duh]

▸ how frequent are the trains to the city? 开往那个城市的火车多久有一班? kāiwǎng nàge chéngshì de huǒchē duō jiǔ yǒu yī bān? [kigh-wang na-guh chung-shir duh hwore-chuh dwore-jew yoh yee-ban]

fresh *(food)* 新鲜的 xīnxiān de [shin-shyen duh]

▸ I'd like some fresh orange juice 我要一些新鲜的橙汁 wǒ yào yīxiē xīnxiān de chéngzhī [wo yow yee-shyeah shin-shyen duh chung-jir]

freshly 刚刚 gānggāng [gang-gang]

▸ freshly squeezed orange juice 刚刚榨的橙汁 gānggāng zhà de chéngzhī [gang-gang ja duh chung-jir]

friendship stores

Many Chinese cities still have 'friendship stores,' 友谊商店 yǒuyì shāngdiàn [yoh-yee shang-dyen]. Until the 1990s these were the almost exclusive preserve of foreign shoppers, using a special currency known as FEC (Foreign Exchange Certificate). Today they are regular department stores with well-stocked gift and souvenir sections. A tip: friendship stores can offer special services such as international shipping of bulky purchases.

Friday 星期五 xīqīwǔ [shing-chee-woo]

> we're arriving/leaving on Friday 我们星期五到/离开 wǒmen xīngqīwǔ dào/líkāi [wo-meun shing-chee-woo dow/lee-kigh]

fried egg 煎鸡蛋 jiān jīdàn [jyen jee-dan]

> I'd like a fried egg 我要一个煎鸡蛋 wǒ yào yī gè jiān jīdàn [wo yow yee guh jyen jee-dan]

friend 朋友 péngyou [pung-yoh]

> are you with friends? 你和朋友们在一起吗? nǐ hé péngyoumen zài yīqǐ ma? [nee huh pung-yoh-meun zigh yee-chee ma]

> I've come with a friend 我和一个朋友一起来 wǒ hé yī gè péngyou yīqǐ lái [wo huh yee-guh pung-yoh-yee-chee ligh]

> I'm meeting some friends 我要去见几个朋友 wǒ yào qù jiàn jǐ gè péngyou [wo yow choo jyen jee-guh pung-yoh]

from *(expressing origin)* 来自 láizì [ligh-zir]; *(leaving from)* 从 cóng [tsong]

> I'm from the United States 我来自美国 wǒ láizì měiguó [wo ligh-zir may-gwore]

> how many flights a day are there from Beijing to Shanghai? 每天有多少次航班从北京飞往上海? měi tiān yǒu duōshao cì hángbān cóng běijīng fēiwǎng shànghǎi? [may-tyen yoh dwore-show tsir hang-ban tsong bay-jing fay-wang shang-high]

front *(of train)* 车头 chētóu [chuh-toh] ◆ **in front** 在前 zài qián [zigh-chyen]
◆ **in front of** 在……的前面 zài……de qiánmiàn [zigh…chyen-myen]

> I'd like a seat toward the front of the train 我想要一个朝车头方向的位置 wǒ xiǎng yào yī gè cháo chētóu fāngxiàng de wèizhi [wo shyang yow yee guh chow chuh-toh fang-shyang duh way-jir]

> the car in front braked suddenly 前面的车突然刹车 qiánmiàn de chē tūrán shāchē [chyen-myen duh chuh too-ran sha-chuh]

> I'll meet you in front of the museum 我在博物馆前与你会面 wǒ zài bówùguǎn qián yǔ nǐ huìmiàn [wo zigh bo-woo-gwan chyen yoo nee hway-myen]

front door 前门 qiánmén [chyen-meun]

▸ which is the key to the front door? 哪一把是开前门的钥匙？ nǎ yī bǎ shì kāi qiánmén de yàoshi? [na yee ba shir kigh chyen-meun duh yow-shir]

▸ the front door is closed 前门关了 qiánmén guān le [chyen-meun gwan luh]

frozen *(person)* 极冷的 jí lěng de [jee lung duh]; *(pipes)* 冻结的 dòngjié de [dong-jyeah duh]

▸ I'm absolutely frozen 我冻死了 wǒ dòngsǐ le [wo dong-sir luh]

▸ the lock is frozen 锁被冻住了 suǒ bèi dòngzhù le [swore bay dong-joo luh]

frozen food 冷冻食品 lěngdòng shípǐn [lung-dong shir-ping]

▸ is that all the frozen food you have? 你所有的冷冻食品都在那儿了吗？ nǐ suǒyǒu de lěngdòng shípǐn dōu zài nàr le ma? [nee swore-yoh duh lung-dong shir-pin doh zigh nar luh ma]

fruit juice 果汁 guǒzhī [gwore-jir]

▸ what types of fruit juice do you have? 你有什么果汁？ nǐ yǒu shénme guǒzhī? [nee yoh sheun-muh gwore-jir]

full *(hotel, restaurant, train)* 满的 mǎn de [man duh]; *(with food)* 吃饱的 chībǎo de [chir-bow duh]

▸ is it full? 满了吗？ mǎn le ma? [man luh ma]

▸ I'm quite full, thank you 我吃饱了，谢谢 wǒ chībǎo le, xièxie [wo chir-bow luh shyeah-shyeah]

full up *(with food)* 吃饱的 chībǎo de [chir-bow duh]

▸ I'm full up 我吃饱了 wǒ chībǎo le [wo chir-bow luh]

fun *(pleasure, amusement)* 快乐 kuàilè [kwigh-luh]

▸ we had a lot of fun 我们很开心 wǒmen hěn kāixīn [wo-meun heun kigh-shin]

g

gallery *(for art)* 展览馆 zhǎnlǎnguǎn [jan-lan-gwan]

▸ what time does the gallery open? 展览馆几点开门？ zhǎnlǎnguǎn jǐ diǎn kāimén? [jan-lan-gwan jee dyen kigh-meun]

game *(fun activity)* 游戏 yóuxì [yoh-shee]; *(of sports)* 运动 yùndòng [yun-dong]

▸ do you want to play a game of tennis tomorrow? 明天你想打一场网球吗？ míngtiān nǐ xiǎng dǎ yī chǎng wǎngqiú ma? [ming-tyen nee shyang da yee-chang wang-chew ma]

garage *(for car repair)* 修车场 xiūchēchǎng [shew-chuh-chang]

▸ is there a garage near here? 这里有修车场吗？ zhèlǐ yǒu xiūchēchǎng ma? [juh-lee yoh shew-chuh-chang ma]

▸ could you tow me to a garage? 你能把我的车拖到修车场吗？ nǐ néng bǎ wǒ de chē tuōdào xiūchēchǎng ma? [nee nung ba wo duh chuh twore dow shew-chuh-chang ma]

garbage can 垃圾桶 lājītǒng [la-jee-tong]

▸ where is the garbage can? 垃圾桶在哪里? lājītǒng zài nǎli? [la-jee-tong zigh na-lee]

gas *(for vehicle)* 汽油 qìyóu [chee-yoh]; *(for domestic use)* 煤气 méiqì [may-chee]; *(for medical use)* 麻醉气体 mázuì qìtǐ [ma-zway chee-tee]

▸ where can I get gas? 我可以去哪里加油? wǒ kěyǐ qù nǎli jiā yóu? [wo kuh-yee choo na-lee jya-yoh]

▸ I've run out of gas 我没汽油了 wǒ méi qìyóu le [wo may chee-yoh luh]

gas pump 气泵 qìbèng [chee-bung]

▸ how do you use this gas pump? 该怎么用这个气泵? gāi zěnme yòng zhège qìbèng? [gigh zeun-muh yong juh-guh chee-bung]

gas station 加油站 jiāyóuzhàn [jya-yoh-jan]

▸ where can I find a gas station? 我在哪里可以找到加油站? wǒ zài nǎli kěyǐ zhǎodào jiāyóuzhàn? [wo zigh na-lee kuh-yee jow-dow jya-yoh-jan]

gas stove 煤气炉 méiqìlú [may-chee-loo]

▸ do you have a gas stove we could borrow? 你能借给我们一个煤气炉吗? nǐ néng jiè gěi wǒmen yī gè méiqìlú ma? [nee nung jyeah gay wo-meun yee guh may-chee-loo ma]

gas tank 油箱 yóuxiāng [yoh-shyang]

▸ the gas tank is leaking 油箱漏了 yóuxiāng lòu le [yoh-shyang loh luh]

gate *(of a garden, a town)* 门 mén [meun]; *(at an airport)* 登机口 dēngjīkǒu [dung-jee-koh]

▸ where is Gate 2? 二号登机口在哪里? èr hào dēngjīkǒu zài nǎli? [er how dung-jee-koh zigh na-lee]

gear *(of a car, a bike)* 挡 dǎng [dang]

▸ how many gears does the bike have? 这辆自行车有几个挡? zhè liàng zìxíngchē yǒu jǐ gè dǎng? [juh lyang zir-shing-chuh yoh jee-guh dang]

get *(obtain)* 得到 dédào [duh-dow]; *(understand)* 明白 míngbai [ming-bigh]
◆ *(make one's way)* 到 dào [dow]

▸ where can we get something to eat this time of night? 晚上这个时候我们可以去哪里买吃的? wǎnshang zhège shíhou wǒmen kěyǐ qù nǎli mǎi chī de? [wan-shang juh-guh shir-hoh wo-meun kuh-yee choo na-lee migh chir duh]

▸ I can't get it into reverse 我挂不进倒车挡 wǒ guà bù jìn dàochēdǎng [wo gwa boo jin dow-chuh-dang]

▸ now I get it 我现在知道了 wǒ xiànzài zhīdao le [wo shyen-zigh jir-dow luh]

▸ I got here a month ago 我一个月前到了这里 wǒ yī gè yuè qián dàole zhèli [wo yee-guh yue chyen dow-luh juh-lee]

- can you get there by car? 可以开车去那里吗？ kěyǐ kāichē qù nàli ma? [kuh-yee kigh-chuh choo na-lee ma]
- how can I get to... 去……我该怎么走？ qù......wǒ gāi zěnme zǒu? [choo...wo gigh zeun-muh zoh]
- could you tell me the best way to get to the Forbidden City? 您是否能告诉我去故宫最近的一条路该怎么走？ nín shìfǒu néng gàosu wǒ qù gùgōng zuì jìn de yī tiáo lù gāi zěnme zǒu? [neen shir-foh nung gow-soo wo choo goo-gong zway-jin duh yee-teow loo gigh zeun-muh zoh]
- how do we get to Terminal 2? 去二号登机口我们该怎么走？ qù èr hào dēngjīkǒu wǒmen gāi zěnme zǒu? [choo er-how dung-jee-koh wo-meun gigh zuen–muh zoh]

get back (money) 拿回 náhuí [na-hway]
- I just want to get my money back 我只想退货还钱 wǒ zhǐ xiǎng tuì huò huán qián [wo jir shyang tway hwore hwan chyen]

get back onto (road) 返回到 fǎnhuídào [fan-hway dow]
- how can I get back onto the freeway? 我怎样才能返回到高速公路？ wǒ zěnyàng cái néng fǎnhuídào gāosù gōnglù? [wo zeun-yang tsigh-nung fan-hway dow gow-soo gong-loo]

get in (arrive) 到达目的地 dàodá mùdìdì [dow-da moo-dee]; (gain entry) 进入 jìnrù [jin-roo] ◆ (car) 上 shàng [shang]
- what time does the train get in to Beijing? 火车几点钟到达北京？ huǒchē jǐ diǎnzhōng dàodá běijīng? [hwore-chuh jee dyen-jong dow-da bay-jing]
- what time does the flight get in? 航班几点到达目的地？ hángbān jǐ diǎn dàodá mùdìdì? [hang-ban jee dyen dow-da moo-dee-dee]
- do you have to pay to get in? 进去是否要付钱？ jìnqù shìfǒu yào fù qián? [jin-choo shir-foh yow foo-chyen]

get off (bus, train, bike) 下 xià [shya]; (road) 离开 líkāi [lee-kigh] ◆ 离开 líkāi [lee-kigh]
- where do we get off the bus? 我们在哪里下车？ wǒmen zài nǎli xià chē? [wo-meun zigh na-lee shya-chuh]
- where do I get off the freeway? 我该在哪里下高速公路？ wǒ gāi zài nǎli xià gāosù gōnglù? [wo gigh zigh na-lee shya gow-soo gong-loo]

get on (train, bus, plane) 上 shàng [shang]
- which bus should we get on to go downtown? 去市区我们该上哪辆公共汽车？ qù shìqū wǒmen gāi shàng nǎ liàng gōnggòng qìchē? [choo shir-choo wo-meun gigh shang na lyang gong-gong chee-chuh]

get past 通过 tōngguò [tong-gwore]
- sorry, can I get past, please? 对不起，请让我过一下好吗？ duìbuqǐ, qǐng ràng wǒ guò yī xià hǎo ma? [dway-boo-chee ching rang wo gwore yee-shya how ma]

get up *(in morning)* 起床 qǐchuáng [chee-chwung]

> I got up very early 我起得很早 wǒ qǐ de hěn zǎo [wo chee duh heun-zow]

gift-wrap 把...... 包装成礼品 bǎ......bāozhuāngchéng lǐpǐn [ba...bow-jwang chung lee-ping]

> could you gift-wrap it for me? 你能帮我把这个包装成礼品吗? nǐ néng bāng wǒ bǎ zhège bāozhuāngchéng lǐpǐn ma? [nee nung bang wo ba juh-guh bow-jwang chung lee-ping ma]

girl *(young female)* 女孩 nǚhái [nooh-high]; *(daughter)* 女儿 nǚ'ér [nooh-er]

> who is that girl? 那个女孩是谁? nàge nǚhái shì shéi? [na-guh nooh-high shir shay]

> I've got two girls 我有两个女儿 wǒ yǒu liǎng gè nǚ'ér [wo yoh lyang guh nooh-er]

girlfriend 女朋友 nǚpéngyou [nooh-pung-yoh]

> is she your girlfriend? 她是你的女朋友吗? tā shì nǐ de nǚpéngyou ma? [ta shir nee duh nooh-pung-yoh ma]

give 给 gěi [gay]

> I can give you my e-mail address 我可以给你我的电子邮箱地址 wǒ kěyǐ gěi nǐ wǒ de diànzǐ yóuxiāng dìzhǐ [wo kuh-yee gay nee wo duh dyen-zir yoh-shyang dee-jir]

> can you give me a hand? 你能帮我吗? nǐ néng bāng wǒ ma? [nee nung bang wo ma]

glass *(material)* 玻璃 bōli [bo-lee]; *(for drinking)* 玻璃杯 bōlibēi [bo-lee-bay]

♦ **glasses** 眼镜 yǎnjìng [yan-jing]

> can I have a clean glass? 我能要一个干净的玻璃杯吗? wǒ néng yào yī gè gānjìng de bōlibēi ma? [wo nung yow yee-guh gan-jing duh bo-lee-bay ma]

> would you like a glass of champagne? 你要一杯香槟酒吗? nǐ yào yī bēi xiāngbīnjiǔ ma? [nee yow yee bay shyang-bin-jew ma]

> I've lost my glasses 我的眼镜丢了 wǒ de yǎnjìng diū le [wo duh yan-jing dway luh]

glove 手套 shǒutào [shoh-tow]

> I've lost a brown glove 我丢了一只棕色的手套 wǒ diū le yī zhī zōngsè de shǒutào [wo dway luh yee-jir zong-duh duh shoh-tow]

go *(move, vehicle, travel)* 去 qù [choo]; *(depart)* 离去 líqù [lee-choo]; *(lead)* 通往 tōngwǎng [tong-wang]

> let's go to the beach 我们去海滩吧 wǒmen qù hǎitān ba [wo-meun choo high-tan ba]

> where can we go for breakfast? 我们可以去哪里吃早餐? wǒmen kěyǐ qù nǎli chī zǎocān? [wo-meun kuh-yee choo na-lee chir zow-tsan]

> where does this path go? 这条路通往哪里? zhè tiáo lù tōngwǎng nǎli? [juh teow loo tong-wang na-lee]

- I must be going 我一定得走了 wǒ yīdìng děi zǒu le [wo yee-ding day zoh luh]
- we're going home tomorrow 我们明天回家 wǒmen míngtiān huí jiā [wo-meun ming-tyen hway-jya] ▸ see box on p. 76

go away *(person)* 走开 zǒukāi [zoh-kigh]; *(pain)* 消失 xiāoshī [shyow-shir]

- go away and leave me alone! 走开，别烦我！zǒukāi, bié fán wǒ! [soh-kigh byeah fan wo]

go back *(return)* 回 huí [hway]

- we're going back home tomorrow 我们明天回家 wǒmen míngtiān huí jiā [wo-meun ming-tyen hway-jya]

go down *(stairs)* 走下 zǒuxià [zwore-shya]; *(street)* 沿着......往下走 yánzhe......wǎng xià zǒu [yen-juh...wang shya zoh]

- go down that street and turn left at the bottom 沿着那条街往下走，到底 的时候往左拐 yánzhe nà tiáo jiē wǎng xià zǒu, dào dǐ de shíhou wǎng zuǒ guǎi [yan-juh na teow yeah wang shya zoh dow-dee duh shir-hoh wang zwore gwigh]

gold *(metal)* 金子 jīnzi [jin-zir]

- is it made of gold? 它是金子做的吗？tā shì jīnzi zuò de ma? [ta shir jin-zir zwore duh ma]

golf 高尔夫球 gāo'ěrfūqiú [gow-er-foo-chew]

- I play golf 我打高尔夫球 wǒ dǎ gāo'ěrfūqiú [wo da gow-er-foo-chew]

golf club 高尔夫球杆 gāo'ěrfūqiúgān [gow-er-foo-chew-gan]

- where can I rent golf clubs? 我去哪里可以租到高尔夫球杆？wǒ qù nǎli kěyǐ zūdào gāo'ěrfūqiúgān? [woo choo na-lee kuh-yee zoo-dow gow-er-foo-chew-gan]

golf course 高尔夫球场 gāo'ěrfūqiúchǎng [gow-er-foo-chew-chew-chang]

- is there a golf course nearby? 附近有高尔夫球场吗？fùjìn yǒu gāo'ěrfū- qiúchǎng ma? [foo-jin yoh gow-er-foo-chew-chang ma]

good 好的 hǎo de [how duh]; *(high-quality)* 优质的 yōuzhì de [yoh-jir duh]

- this isn't a very good restaurant 这家餐馆不是很好 zhè jiā cānguǎn bù shì hěn hǎo [juh jya tsan-gwan boo-shir heun how]
- you're really good at cooking! 你做饭做得真好啊！nǐ zuò fàn zuò de zhēn hǎo a! [nee zwore-fan zwore duh jeun how a]
- we had a good time 我们玩的很开心 wǒmen wán de hěn kāixīn [wo-meun wan duh heun kigh-shin]

good afternoon 下午好 xiàwǔ hǎo [shya-woo how]

- good afternoon! isn't it a beautiful day? 下午好！天气真好，不是吗？ xiàwǔ hǎo! tiānqì zhēn hǎo, bù shì ma? [shya-woo how tyen-chee jeun how boo-shir ma]

goodbye 再见 zàijiàn [zigh-jyen]

- I'd better say goodbye now 我现在最好说再见了 wǒ xiànzài zuìhǎo shuō zàijiàn le [wo shyen-zigh zway-how shwore zigh-jyen luh]

going out

For the most up-to-date information on where to go, get hold of one of the free (English) magazines that are published by expatriates in Beijing and Shanghai: *Time Out*, *That's*, *City Weekend*, etc. A favorite evening out for the Chinese is going to a karaoke bar. This is often written with the *OK* in English, 卡拉 OK kǎlā ok [ka-la-o-kay]. People tend to go to karaoke with friends, or after work with colleagues or business contacts. Karaoke bars can be found in hotels and special karaoke centers. These are sometimes as big as hotels, and they can be luxurious, with individual lounges offering light refreshment services.

good evening 晚上好 wǎnshang hǎo [wan-shang how]

▸ good evening! how are you tonight? 晚上好！今天晚上你怎么样？ wǎnshang hǎo! jīntiān wǎnshang nǐ zěnmeyàng? [wan-shang how! jin-tyen wan-shang nee zeun-muh-yang]

good morning 早上好 zǎoshang hǎo [zow-shang how]

▸ good morning! how are you today? 早上好！今天你怎么样？ zǎoshang hǎo! jīntiān nǐ zěnmeyàng? [zow-shang how! jin-tyen nee zeun-muh-yang]

good night *(when leaving)* 再见 zàijiàn [zigh-jyen]; *(when going to bed)* 晚安 wǎn'ān [wan-an]

▸ I'll say good night, then 那我就道晚安了 nà wǒ jiù dào wǎn'ān le [na wo jew dow wan-an luh]

go out *(leave house)* 外出 wàichū [wigh-choo]; *(socially)* 参加社交活动 cānjiā shèjiāo huódòng [tsan-jya shuh-jeow hwore-dong]; *(on date)* 约会 yuēhuì [yue-hway]; *(tide)* 退潮 tuìcháo [tway-chow]

▸ what's a good place to go out for a drink? 外出喝一杯去哪里比较好？ wàichū hē yī bēi qù nǎli bǐjiào hǎo? [wigh-choo huh yee-bay choo na-lee bee-jeow how]

▸ the tide's going out 潮水退了 cháoshuǐ tuì le [chow-shway tway luh]

grapefruit 柚子 yòuzi [yoh-zir]

▸ I'll just have the grapefruit 我只要柚子就行了 wǒ zhǐ yào yòuzi jiù xíng le [wo jir-yow yoh-zir jew shing luh]

great *(very good)* 很好的 hěn hǎo de [heun how duh]

▸ that's great! 太好了 tài hǎo le [tigh how luh]

▸ it was really great! 那真是太好了！ nà zhēn shì tài hǎo le! [na jeun-shir tigh how luh]

green 绿色的 lǜsè de [looh-suh duh]

▸ the green one 绿色的那个 lǜsè de nàge [looh-suh duh na-guh]

grocery store 杂货店 záhuòdiàn [za-hwore-dyen]
- is there a grocery store around here? 这附近有杂货店吗？ zhè fùjìn yǒu záhuòdiàn ma? [juh foo-jin yoh za-hwore-dyen ma]

group 组 zǔ [zoo]
- there's a group of twelve of us 我们组有12个人 wǒmen zǔ yǒu shí'èr gè rén [wo-meun zoo yoh shir-er guh reun]
- are there reductions for groups? 团队是否有折扣？ tuánduì shìfǒu yǒu zhékòu? [tan-dway shir-foh yoh juh-koh]

group rate 团队价 tuánduìjià [twan-dway-jya]
- are there special group rates? 是否有团队特价？ shìfǒu yǒu tuánduì tè jià? [shir-foh yoh twan-dway tuh jya]

guarantee *(for purchased product)* 保修 bǎoxiū [bow-shew]
- it's still under guarantee 是否还在保修期内 shìfǒu hái zài bǎoxiūqī nèi [shir-foh high zigh bow-shew-chee nay]

guesthouse 宾馆 bīnguǎn [bin-gwan]
- we're looking for a guesthouse for the night 我们在找宾馆住一个晚上 wǒmen zài zhǎo bīnguǎn zhù yī gè wǎnshang [wo-meun zigh jow bin-gwan joo yee guh wan-shang]

guide *(person)* 导游 dǎoyóu [dow-yoh]; *(book)* 指南 zhǐnán [jir-nan]
- does the guide speak English? 导游会说英语吗？ dǎoyóu huì shuō yīngyǔ ma? [dow-yoh hway shwore ying-yoo ma]

guidebook 旅游指南 lǚyóu zhǐnán [looh-yoh jir-nan]
- do you have a guidebook in English? 你有英文版的旅游指南吗？ nǐ yǒu yīngwén bǎn de lǚyóu zhǐnán ma? [nee yoh ying-weun-ban duh looh-yoh jir-nan ma]

guided tour 有讲解的参观 yǒu jiǎngjiě de cānguān [yoh jyang-jyeah duh tsan-gwan]
- what time does the guided tour begin? 有讲解的参观几点开始？ yǒu jiǎngjiě de cānguān jǐ diǎn kāishǐ? [yoh jyang-jyeah duh tsan-gwan jee dyen kigh-shir]
- is there a guided tour in English? 是否有用英语进行解说的参观？ shì fǒu yǒu yòng yīngyǔ jìnxíng jiěshuō de cānguān? [shir foh yoh yong ying-yoo jin-shing jyeah-shwore duh tsan-gwan]
- are there guided tours of the museum? 在博物馆是否有有人解说的参观？ zài bówùguǎn shìfǒu yǒu yǒu rén jiěshuō de cānguān? [zigh bo-woo-gwan shir-foh yoh reun jyeah-shwore duh tsan-gwan]

h

hair 头发 tóufa [toh-fa]
- she has short hair 她是短头发 tā shì duǎn tóufa [ta shir dwan toh-fa]
- he has red hair 他是红头发 tā shì hóng tóufa [ta shir hong toh-fa]

hairbrush 发刷 fàshuā [fa-shwa]
- do you sell hairbrushes? 你们卖发刷吗？ nǐmen mài fàshuā ma? [nee-meun migh fa-shwa ma]

hairdryer 吹风机 chuīfēngjī [chway-fung-jee]
- do the rooms have hairdryers? 房间里有吹风机吗？ fángjiān li yǒu chuīfēngjī ma? [fang-jyen lee yoh chway-fung-jee ma]

hair salon 发廊 fàláng [fa-lang]
- does the hotel have a hair salon? 旅馆里有美发室吗？ lǚguǎn li yǒu měifàshì ma? [looh-gwan lee yoh may-fa-shir ma]

half 一半的 yībàn de [yee-ban duh] ◆ 一半 yībàn [yee-ban]
- shall we meet in half an hour? 我们半小时后见面好吗？ wǒmen bàn xiǎoshí hòu jiànmiàn hǎo ma? [wo-meun ban shyow-shir hoh jyen-myen how ma]
- it's half past eight 现在是8点半 xiànzài shì bā diǎn bàn [shyen-zigh shir ba dyen ban]

ham 火腿 huǒtuǐ [hwore-tway]
- I'd like five slices of ham 我想要五片火腿 wǒ xiǎng yào wǔ piàn huǒtuǐ [wo shyang yow woo-pyen hwore-tway]

hand 手 shǒu [shoh]
- where can I wash my hands? 我可以去哪里洗手？ wǒ kěyǐ qù nǎli xǐ shǒu? [wo kuh-yee choo na-lee shee-shoh]

handbag 手提包 shǒutíbāo [shoh-tee-bow]
- someone's stolen my handbag 有人偷了我的手提包 yǒu rén tōule wǒ de shǒutíbāo [yoh reun toh-luh wo duh shoh-tee-bow]

---

hair salons

Besides haircuts, Chinese hair salons often offer relaxing head and shoulder massages that last about twenty minutes. These can be requested separately from a haircut, or in conjunction with a hair wash.

hand baggage 手提行李 shǒutí xíngli [shoh-tee shing-lee]

▸ I have one suitcase and one piece of hand baggage 我有一个手提箱和一件手提行李 wǒ yǒu yī gè shǒutíxiāng hé yī jiàn shǒutí xíngli [wo yoh yee-guh shoh-tee-shyang huh yee jyen shoh-tee shing-li]

handkerchief 手帕 shǒupà [shoh-pa]

▸ do you have a spare handkerchief? 你有一块多余的手帕吗？ nǐ yǒu yī kuài duōyú de shǒupà ma? [nee yoh yee-kwigh doh-yoo duh shoh-pa ma]

handle 把手 bǎshou [ba-shoh]

▸ the handle's broken 把手断了 bǎshou duàn le [ba-shoh dwan luh]

handmade 手工制作的 shǒugōng zhìzuò de [shoh-gong jir-zwore duh]

▸ is this handmade? 这是手工制作的吗？ zhè shì shǒugōng zhìzuò de ma? [juh-shir shoh-gong jir-zwore duh ma]

happen 发生 fāshēng [fa-shung]

▸ what happened? 发生了什么？ fāshēng le shénme? [fa-shung luh sheun-muh]

▸ these things happen 没有办法 méiyou bànfǎ [may-yoh ban-fa]

happy (not sad) 开心的 kāixīn de [kigh-shin duh]; (satisfied) 令人满意的 lìng rén mǎnyì de [ling reun man-yee duh]

▸ I'd be happy to help 乐意效劳 lèyì xiàoláo [luh-yee sheow-low]

▸ Happy Birthday! 生日快乐！ shēngrì kuàilè! [shung-rir kwigh-luh]

▸ Happy New Year! 新年快乐！ xīnnián kuàilè! [shin-nyen kwigh-luh]

hat 帽子 màozi [mow-zir]

▸ I think I left my hat here 我想我把帽子落在这里了 wǒ xiǎng wǒ bǎ màozi là zài zhèli le [wo shyang wo ba mow-zir la zigh juh-lee luh]

hate 讨厌 tǎoyàn [tow-yan]

▸ I hate golf 我讨厌高尔夫 wǒ tǎoyàn gāo'ěrfū [wo tow-yan gow-er-foo]

have (possess, meal, drink) 有 yǒu [yoh]; (as characteristic) 具有 jùyǒu [joo-yoh] ◆ (be obliged) 必须 bìxū [bee-shoo]

▸ do you have any bread? 你有面包吗？ nǐ yǒu miànbāo ma? [nee yoh myen-bow ma]

▸ do you have them in red? 你有红色的吗？ nǐ yǒu hóngsè de ma? [nee yoh hong-suh duh ma]

▸ he has brown hair 他的头发是棕色的 tā de tóufa shì zōngsè de [ta duh tohfa shir zong-suh duh]

▸ where should we go to have a drink? 我们上哪儿去喝一杯？ wǒmen shàng nǎr qù hē yī bēi? [wo-meun shang nar choo huh yee bay]

▸ I have to be at the airport by six (o'clock) 我必须在6点前到达机场 wǒ bìxū zài liù diǎn qián dàodá jīchǎng [wo bee-shoo zigh lew-dyen chyen dow-da jee-chang]

▸ we have to go 我们必须得走了 wǒmen bìxū děi zǒu le [wo-meun bee-shoo day zwore luh]

head *(of a person)* 头 tóu [toh]; *(of a shower)* 喷头 pēntóu [peun-toh]
  ▸ I hit my head when I fell 我摔倒时撞到了头 wǒ shuāidǎo shí zhuàngdao le tóu [wo shwigh-dow shir jwang-dow luh toh]
  ▸ the shower head is broken 淋浴的喷头坏了 línyù de pēntóu huài le [lin-yoo duh pen-toh hwigh luh]

headache 头疼 tóu téng [toh tung]
  ▸ I've got a headache 我头疼 wǒ tóu téng [wo toh tung]
  ▸ do you have anything for a headache? 你有治头疼的药吗? nǐ yǒu zhì tóu téng de yào ma? [nee yoh jir toh tung duh yow ma]

headlight 车头灯 chētóudēng [chuh-toh-dung]
  ▸ one of my headlights got smashed 我的一个车头灯被撞碎了 wǒ de yī gè chētóudēng bèi zhuàngsuì le [wo duh yee guh chuh-toh-dung bay jwang-sway luh]

headphones 耳机 ěrjī [er-jee]
  ▸ did you find my headphones? 你找到了我的耳机吗? nǐ zhǎodàole wǒ de ěrjī ma? [nee jow-dow-luh wo duh er-jee ma]

health 健康 jiànkāng [jyen-kang]
  ▸ in good/poor health 身体健康/身体不好 shēntǐ jiànkāng/shēntǐ bù hǎo [sheun-tee jyen-kang/sheun-tee boo-how]

hear 听到 tīngdào [ting-dow]; *(learn of)* 得知 dézhī [duh-jir]
  ▸ I've heard a lot about you 我听说了很多关于你的事 wǒ tīngshuōle hěn duō guānyú nǐ de shì [wo ting-shwore-luh heun dwore gwan-yoo nee duh shir]

heart 心脏 xīnzàng [shin-zang]
  ▸ he's got a weak heart 他心脏不好 tā xīnzàng bù hǎo [ta shin-zang boo how]

heart attack 心脏病发作 xīnzàngbìng fāzuò [shin-zang-bing fa-zwore]
  ▸ he had a heart attack 他心脏病发作了 tā xīnzàngbìng fāzuò le [ta shin-zang-bing fa-zwore luh]
  ▸ I nearly had a heart attack! 我差点儿心脏病发作! wǒ chàdiǎnr xīnzàngbìng fāzuò! [wo cha-dyenr shin-zang-bing fa-zwore]

heart condition 心脏不好 xīnzàng bù hǎo [shin-zang boo how]
  ▸ to have a heart condition 心脏有问题 xīnzàng yǒu wèntí [shin-zang yoh weun-tee]

heat *(hot quality)* 热 rè [ruh]; *(weather)* 酷暑 kùshǔ [koo-shoo]; *(for cooking)* 热度 rèdù [ruh-doo]
  ▸ there's no heat from the radiator in my room 我房间里的暖气片不制热了 wǒ fángjiān li de nuǎnqìpiàn bù zhì rè le [wo fang-jyen lee duh nwan-chee-pyen boo jir ruh luh]

heating 供暖系统 gōngnuǎn xìtǒng [gong-nwan shee-tong]
  ▸ how does the heating work? 供暖系统该怎么使用? gōngnuǎn xìtǒng gāi zěnme shǐyòng? [gong-nwan shee-tong gigh zeun-muh shir-yong]

---

saying hello

If you want to say hello to someone, say 你好 nǐ hǎo [nee-how] which uses the personal pronoun 你 nǐ [nee] (to one person). If you are speaking to a number of people, use the plural pronoun 你们好 nǐmen hǎo [nee-meun how] or 大家好 dàjiā hǎo [da-jya how] for 'everybody.'

---

heavy 重的 zhòng de [jong duh]

▸ my bags are very heavy 我的行李非常重 wǒ de xínglǐ fēicháng zhòng [wo duh shing-lee fay-chang jong]

heel (of a foot) 脚跟 jiǎogēn [jeow-geun]; (of a shoe) 鞋跟 xiégēn [shyeah-geun]

▸ can you put new heels on these shoes? 你能把这些鞋子的跟换成新的吗？nǐ néng bǎ zhèxiē xiézi de gēn huànchéng xīn de ma? [nee nung ba jir-shyeah shyeah-zir duh geun hwan-chung shin duh ma]

hello (as a greeting) 你好 nǐ hǎo [nee how]; (on the phone) 喂 wèi [way]

▸ hello, is this...? 你好，这是……吗？nǐ hǎo, zhè shì……ma? [nee how juh shir...ma]

helmet 头盔 tóukuī [toh-kway]

▸ do you have a helmet you could lend me? 你有能借给我的头盔吗？nǐ yǒu néng jiè gěi wǒ de tóukuī ma? [nee yoh nung jyeah gay wo duh toh-kway ma]

help (assistance) 帮助 bāngzhù [bang-joo]; (emergency aid) 救命 jiùmìn [jew-min] ♦ 帮助 bāngzhù [bang-joo]

▸ help! 救命啊！jiùmìn à! [jew-min a]

▸ go and get help quickly! 快去找人来帮忙！kuài qù zhǎo rén lái bāngmáng! [kwigh choo jow reun ligh bang-mang]

▸ thank you for your help 谢谢你的帮助 xièxie nǐ de bāngzhù [shyeah nee duh bang-joo]

▸ could you help me? 你能帮我吗？nǐ néng bāng wǒ ma? [nee nung bang wo ma]

▸ could you help us push the car? 你能帮我们推车吗？nǐ néng bāng wǒmen tuī chē ma? [nee nung bang wo-meun tway chuh ma]

▸ let me help you with that 让我来帮你吧 ràng wǒ lái bāng nǐ ba [rang wo ligh bang nee ba]

▸ could you help me with my bags? 你能帮我拿行李吗？nǐ néng bāng wǒ ná xínglǐ ma? [nee nung bang wo na shing-lee ma]

here (in this place) 在这里 zài zhèlǐ [zigh juh-lee]; (to this place) 来这里 lái zhèlǐ [ligh juh-lee] ♦ (giving) 这儿 zhèr [juhr]

▸ I've been here two days 我在这里两天了 wǒ zài zhèli liǎng tiān le [wo zigh juh-lee lyang tyen luh]

▸ I came here three years ago 我三年前来到这里 wǒ sān nián qián láidào zhèli [wo san nyen chyen ligh-dow zigh-lee]

▸ are you from around here? 你住在这附近吗？ nǐ zhù zài zhè fùjìn ma? [nee joo zigh juh foo-jin ma]

▸ I'm afraid I'm a stranger here myself 恐怕我自己对这里也不熟悉 kǒngpà wǒ zìjǐ duì zhèli yě bù shúxī [kong-pa wo zir-jee dway juh-lee yuh boo shoo-shee]

▸ it's five minutes from here 从这里过去五分钟 cóng zhèli guòqu wǔ fēnzhōng [tsong juh-lee gwore-choo woo feun-jong]

▸ here is/are... 给你...... gěi nǐ...... [gay nee]

▸ here are my passport and ticket 这是我的护照和票 zhè shì wǒ de hùzhào hé piào [juh shir wo duh hoo-jow huh peow]

hi 嘿 hèi [hay]

▸ hi, I'm Julia 嘿，我是茱莉亚 hèi, wǒ shì zhūlìyà [hay wo shir joo-lee-ya]

high beam 远光灯 yuǎnguāngdēng [ywan-gwung-dung]

▸ put your lights on high beam 打开远光灯 dǎkāi yuǎnguāngdēng [da kigh ywan-gwung-dung]

high chair 高脚椅 gāojiǎoyǐ [gow-jeow-yee]

▸ could we have a high chair for the baby? 能给我们一把婴儿坐的高脚椅吗？ néng gěi wǒmen yī bǎ yīng'ér zuò de gāojiǎoyǐ ma? [nung gay wo-meun yee ba ying-er zwore duh gow-jeow-yee ma]

high season 旺季 wàngjì [wang-jee]

▸ is it very expensive in the high season? 在旺季贵吗？ zài wàngjì guì ma? [zigh wang-jee gway ma]

high tide 高潮 gāocháo [gow-chow]

▸ what time is high tide? 高潮什么时候来？ gāocháo shénme shíhou lái? [gow-chow sheun-muh shir-hoh ligh]

hike 徒步旅行 túbù lǚxíng [too-boo looh-shing]

▸ are there any good hikes around here? 这附近有什么好的徒步旅行路线？ zhè fùjìn yǒu shénme hǎo de túbù lǚxíng lùxiàn? [juh foo-jin yoh sheun-muh how duh too-boo looh-shing loo-shyen]

hiking 徒步旅行 túbù lǚxíng [too-boo looh-shing]

▸ to go hiking 去徒步旅行 qù túbù lǚxíng [choo too-boo looh-shing]

▸ are there any hiking trails? 有徒步旅行的路线吗？ yǒu túbù lǚxíng de lùxiàn ma? [yoh too-boo looh-shing duh loo-shyen ma]

hiking boot 登山鞋 dēngshānxié [dung-shan-shyeah]

▸ do you need to wear hiking boots? 需要穿登山鞋吗？ xūyào chuān dēngshānxié ma? [shoo-yoe chwan dung-shan-shyeah ma]

holidays

China enjoys a lot of national holidays but the most important festival is the *Chinese New Year* or *Spring Festival* , 春节 chūn jié [chun-jyeah]. This corresponds to the first day of the lunar calendar year, so its date changes from the end of January to the beginning of February each year. It's a time of family celebration and for many families may be the only time in the whole year when they can get together. Many companies and stores close over Chinese New Year to allow staff to return to their parents' homes for one to three weeks' vacation. It's a tradition for families to make ravioli 饺子 jiǎozi [jeow-zir] together at this time of year. Chinese people also celebrate *Labor Day* 劳动节 láodòng jié [low-dong-jyeah] on May 1st and *National Day* 国庆节 guóqìng jié [gwore-ching-jyeah] on October 1st, both of which are usually celebrated over a seven-day period known as 'golden week.'

hitchhike 搭顺风车 dā shùnfēngchē [da shun-fung-chuh]
- we hitchhiked here 我们是搭顺风车到这里的 wǒmen shì dā shùnfēngchē dào zhèli de [wo-meun shir da shun-fung-chuh dow juh-lee duh]

holiday 假日 jiàrì [jya-rir]
- is tomorrow a holiday? 明天是假日吗? míngtiān shì jiàrì ma? [ming-tyen shir jya-rir ma]

home *(house)* 家 jiā [jya] ◆ 在家 zài jiā [zigh jya]
- to stay at home 呆在家里 dāi zài jiā li [digh zigh jya lee]
- we're going home tomorrow 我们明天回家 wǒmen míngtiān huí jiā [wo-meun ming-tyen hway jya]

homemade 自己做的 zìjǐ zuò de [zir-jee zwore-duh]
- is it homemade? 是自己做的吗? shì zìjǐ zuò de ma? [shir zir-jee zwore duh ma]

hood *(of car)* 引擎盖 yǐnqínggài [yin-ching-gigh]
- I've dented the hood 我把引擎盖撞出了一个凹痕 wǒ bǎ yǐnqínggài zhuàngchūle yī gè āohén [wo ba yin-ching-gigh jwung-choo-luh yee guh ow-heun]

horrible *(weather, day)* 糟糕的 zāogāo de [zow-gow duh]; *(person)* 讨厌的 tǎoyàn de [tow-yan duh]
- what horrible weather! 天气真糟! tiānqì zhēn zāo! [tyen-chee jeun zow]

horseback riding 骑马 qí mǎ [chee ma]
- can we go horseback riding? 我们能去骑马吗? wǒmen néng qù qí mǎ ma? [wo-meun nung choo chee ma ma]

hospitals

The major Chinese cities have medical and hospital systems that easily meet international standards for performance. Hospitals are the most important part of the medical infrastructure as there are no private doctors, apart from dentists and cosmetic surgeons, or those in international hospitals. Consultations with doctors are made at the hospital and there is no need to make an appointment. As this results in very long lines, large hospitals offer a special service for foreigners which is quicker but more expensive.

hospital 医院 yīyuàn [yee-ywan]

▸ where is the nearest hospital? 最近的医院在哪里? zuì jìn de yīyuàn zài nǎli? [zway jyen duh yee-ywan zigh na-lee]

hot *(in temperature)* 热的 rè de [ruh duh]; *(spicy)* 辣的 là de [la duh]

▸ I'm too hot 我太热了 wǒ tài rè le [wo tigh ruh luh]

▸ this dish is really hot 这菜真的很辣 zhè cài zhēn de hěn là [juh tsigh jeun duh heun la]

▸ there's no hot water 没有热水 méiyou rèshuǐ [may-yoh ruh-shway]

hotel 饭店 fàndiàn [fan-dyen]

▸ do you have a list of hotels in this area? 你有这个地区饭店的名单吗? nǐ yǒu zhège dìqū fàndiàn de míngdán ma? [nee yoh juh-guh fan-dyen duh ming-dan ma]

at the hotel

▸ we'd like a double room/two single rooms 我们要一间双人房/两间单人房 wǒmen yào yī jiān shuāngrénfáng/liǎng jiān dānrénfáng [wo-meun yow yee jyen shwung-reun-fang/lyang jyen dan-reun-fang]

▸ I have a reservation in the name of Jones 我用琼斯的名字预定过了 wǒ yòng qióngsī de míngzi yùdìngguo le [wo yong chyong-sir duh ming-zir yoo-ding-gwore luh]

▸ what time is breakfast/dinner served? 几点提供早餐/晚餐? jǐ diǎn tígōng zǎocān/wǎncān? [jee dyen tee-gong zow-tsan/wan-tsan]

▸ could I have a wake-up call at 7 a.m.? 能在早上7点的时候给我一个叫醒电话吗? néng zài zǎoshang qī diǎn de shíhou gěi wǒ yī gè jiàoxǐng diànhuà ma? [nung zigh zow-shang chee dyen duh shir-hoh gay wo yee guh jeow-shing dyen-hwa ma]

hotels

Note that the prices posted at hotel entrances are usually negotiable. You can often get a reduced rate by bargaining a little or by booking your room through a travel agent.

▸ are there any reasonably priced hotels near here? 这附近有什么价格合理的饭店吗? zhè fùjìn yǒu shénme jiàgé hélǐ de fàndiàn ma? [juh foo-jyen yoh sheun-muh jya-guh huh-lee duh fan-dyen ma]

▸ is the hotel downtown? 饭店在市区吗? fàndiàn zài shìqū ma? [fan-dyen zigh shir-choo ma]

▸ could you recommend another hotel? 你能再推荐一家饭店吗? nǐ néng zài tuījiàn yī jiā fàndiàn ma? [nee nung zigh tway-jyen yee jya fan-dyen ma]

hour 小时 xiǎoshí [sheow-shir]

▸ I'll be back in an hour 我一小时后回来 wǒ yī xiǎoshí hòu huílai [wo yee sheow-shir hoh hway-ligh]

▸ the flight takes three hours 飞机航行需要三小时 fēijī hángxíng xūyào sān xiǎoshí [fay-jee hang-shing shoo-yow san shao-shir]

house 房子 fángzi [fang-zir]

▸ is this your house? 这是你的房子吗? zhè shì nǐ de fángzi ma? [juh shir nee duh fang-zir ma]

house wine 餐厅招牌酒 cāntīng zhāopáijiǔ [tsan-ting jow-pigh-jew]

▸ a bottle of house wine, please 请来一瓶餐厅招牌酒 qǐng lái yī píng cāntīng zhāopáijiǔ [ching ligh yee ping tsan-ting jow-pigh-jew]

how 怎样 zěnme [zeun-muh]

▸ how are you? 你好吗? nǐ hǎo ma? [nee how ma]

▸ how do you spell it? 怎么拼写? zěnme pīnxiě? [zeun-muh pin-shyeah]

▸ how about a drink? 喝一杯好吗? hē yī bēi hǎo ma? [huh yee bay how ma]

humid 潮湿的 cháoshī de [thow-shir duh]

▸ it's very humid today 今天很潮湿 jīntiān hěn cháoshī [jin-tyen heun thow-shir]

hungry

▸ to be hungry 饿 è [uh]

▸ I'm starting to get hungry 我开始感到饿了 wǒ kāishǐ gǎndào è le [wo kigh-shir gan-dow uh luh]

hurry

▸ to be in a hurry 匆忙 cōngmáng [tsong-mang]

hurry up 加快做 jiākuài zuò [jya-kwigh zwore]

▸ hurry up! 快点儿! kuài diǎnr! [kwigh-dyenr]

hurt *(to cause physical pain)* 使......疼 shǐ......téng [shir...tung] ◆ 引起疼痛 yǐnqǐ téngtòng [yin-chee tung-tong]

▸ you're hurting me! 你弄疼我了！ nǐ nòngténg wǒ le! [nee nong-tung wo luh]
▸ to hurt oneself 弄疼了自己 nòngshāngle zìjǐ [nong-shang luh zir-jee]
▸ I hurt myself 我伤到了自己 wǒ shāngdàole zìjǐ [wo shang-dow-luh zir-jee]
▸ I hurt my hand 我伤到了手 wǒ shāngdàole shǒu [wo shang-dow-luh shoh]
▸ it hurts 那儿疼 nàr téng [na tung]

ice *(frozen water)* 冰 bīng [bing]; *(cubes)* 冰块 bīngkuài [bing-kwigh]
▸ the car skidded on the ice 汽车在冰上打滑了 qìchē zài bīng shang dǎhuá le [chee-chuh zigh bing shang da-hwa]
▸ a Diet Coke® without ice, please 请来一杯不加冰的健宜可乐 qǐng lái yī bēi bù jiā bīng de jiànyí kělè [ching ligh yee bay boo jya bing duh jyen-yee kuh-luh]

ice cream 冰激淋 bīngjīlín [bing-jee-lee-lin]
▸ I'd like some ice cream 我想要一些冰激淋 wǒ xiǎng yào yīxiē bīngjīlín [wo shyang yow yee-shyeah bing-jee-lin]

ice cube 冰块 bīngkuài [bing-kwigh]
▸ could I have a carafe of water with no ice cubes in it? 能给我来一大瓶不加冰块的水吗？ néng gěi wǒ lái yī dà píng bù jiā bīngkuài de shuǐ ma? [nung gay wo ligh yee da ping boo jya bing-kwigh duh shway ma]

iced coffee 冰咖啡 bīng kāfēi [bing ka-fay]
▸ I'd like an iced coffee 我要一杯冰咖啡 wǒ yào yī bēi bīng kāfēi [wo yow yee bay bing ka-fay]

ice rink 冰场 bīngchǎng [bing-chang]
▸ is there an ice rink nearby? 附近有冰场吗？ fùjìn yǒu bīngchǎng ma? [foo-jin yoh bing-chang ma]

ice skate 冰鞋 bīngxié [bing-shyeah]
▸ I'd like to rent some ice skates 我要租冰鞋 wǒ yào zū bīngxié [wo yow zoo bing-shyeah]

ice-skating 溜冰 liūbīng [lew-bing]
▸ would you like to go ice-skating tomorrow? 明天你想去溜冰吗？ míngtiān nǐ xiǎng qù liūbīng ma? [ming-tyen nee shyang choo lew-bing ma]

ID card 身份证 shēnfènzhèng [sheun-feun-jung]
▸ I don't have an ID card: will a passport work? 我没有身份证，护照可以吗？ wǒ méiyou shēnfènzhèng, hùzhào kěyǐ ma? [wo may-yoh sheun-feun-jung hoo-jow kuh-yee ma]

if 如果 rúguǒ [roo-gwore]
- we'll go if you want 如果你想，我们就去 rúguǒ nǐ xiǎng, wǒmen jiù qù [roo-gwore nee shyang wo-meun jew choo]

ill 生病的 shēngbìng de [shung-bing duh]
- my son is ill 我的儿子生病了 wǒ de érzi shēngbìng le [wo duh er-zir shung-bing luh]

immediately 马上 mǎshàng [ma-shang]
- can you do it immediately? 你能马上办吗? nǐ néng mǎshàng bàn ma? [nee nung ma-shang ban ma]

improve 提高 tígāo [tee-gow]
- I'm hoping to improve my Chinese while I'm here 希望我在这里的时候能提高我的中文水平 xīwàng wǒ zài zhèli de shíhou néng tígāo wǒ de zhōngwén shuǐpíng [shee-wang wo zigh juh-lee duh shir-hoh nung tee-gow wo duh jong-weun shway-ping]

in 在 zài [zigh]
- our bags are still in the room 我们的行李还在房间里 wǒmen de xíngli hái zài fángjiān li [wo-meun duh shing-lee high zigh fang-jyen lee]
- do you live in Beijing? 你住在北京吗? nǐ zhù zài běijīng ma? [nee joo zigh bay-jing ma]

in case 万一 wànyī [wan-yee]
- just in case 以防万一 yǐ fáng wànyī [yee fang wan-yee]

included 包括在内的 bāokuò zàinèi de [bow-kwore zigh-nay duh]
- is breakfast included? 早餐包括在内吗? zǎocān bāokuò zàinèi ma? [zow-tsan bow-kwore zigh-nay ma]
- is sales tax included? 增值税包括在内吗? zēngzhíshuì bāokuò zàinèi ma? [zeung-jir-shway bow-kwore zigh-nay ma]
- is the tip included? 包含了小费吗? bāohán le xiǎofèi ma? [bow-han luh sheow-fay ma]

indoor 室内的 shìnèi de [shir-nay duh]
- is there an indoor pool? 有室内游泳池吗? yǒu shìnèi yóuyǒngchí ma? [yoh shir-nay yoh-yong-chir ma]

infection 感染 gǎnrǎn [gan-ran]
- I have an eye infection 我的眼睛感染了 wǒ de yǎnjīng gǎnrǎn le [wo duh yan-jing gan-ran luh]

information (facts) 消息 xiāoxi [sheow-shee]; (service, department) 通知 tōngzhī [tong-jir]
- a piece of information 一则消息 yī zé xiāoxi [yee zuh sheow-shee]
- may I ask you for some information? 我能问你一些情况吗? wǒ néng wèn nǐ yīxiē qíngkuàng ma? [wo nung weun nee yee-shyeah ching-kwung ma]

the Internet

China has more people connected to the Internet than any other country in the world – there are over 110 million users. All urban centers have Internet cafés, 网吧 wǎngbā [wang-ba], and you will usually be able to access the Internet directly via cable modem from your hotel room or the hotel's business center. Many restaurants and cafes are wirelessly connected, so if your laptop has Wi-Fi connectivity you should be able to access the Internet from a wide variety of public places.

- where can I find information on...? 我在哪里可以找到有关......的资料？ wǒ zài nǎli kěyǐ zhǎodào yǒuguān......de zīliào? [wo zigh na-lee kuh-yee jow-dow yoh-gwan...duh zir-leow]

injection *(medicine)* 注射 zhùshè [joo-shuh]

- am I going to need an injection? 我需要打针吗？ wǒ xūyào dǎzhēn ma? [wo shoo-yow da-jeun ma]

injure 使......受伤 shǐ......shòushāng [shir...shoh-shang]

- to injure oneself 伤了自己 shāngle zìjǐ [shang-luh zir-jee]
- I injured myself 我伤了自己 wǒ shāngle zìjǐ [wo shang luh zir-jee]

inside 在......的里面 zài......de lǐmian [zigh...duh lee-myen] ◆ 在里面 zài lǐmian [zigh lee-myen]

- are you allowed inside the castle? 允许进入城堡吗？ yǔnxǔ jìnrù chéngbǎo ma? [yun-shoo jin-roo chung-bow ma]
- we'd prefer a table inside 我们想要一个里面的桌子 wǒmen xiǎng yào yī gè lǐmian de zhuōzi [wo-meun shyang yow yee guh lee-myen duh jwore-zir]

insurance 保险 bǎoxiǎn [bow-shyen]

- what does the insurance cover? 保险都保些什么？ bǎoxiǎn dōu bǎo xiē shénme? [bow-shyen doh bow shyeah sheun-muh]

insure *(house, car)* 为......投保 wèi......tóubǎo [way...toh-bow]

- yes, I'm insured 是的，我上了保险 shì de, wǒ shàngle bǎoxiǎn [shir duh wo shang-luh bow-shyen]

interesting 有趣的 yǒuqù de [yoh-choo duh]

- it's not a very interesting place 不是一个非常有趣的地方 bù shì yi gè fēicháng yǒuqù de dìfang [boo shir yee-guh fay-chang yoh-choo duh dee-fang]

international call 国际长途电话 guójì chángtú diànhuà [gwore-jee chang-too dyen-hwa]

- I'd like to make an international call 我想打国际长途电话 wǒ xiǎng dǎ guójì chángtú diànhuà [wo shyang da gwore-jee chang-too dyen-hwa]

introductions

China is a country that is very densely populated, so many local and public services are overwhelmed with work. Getting to know an influential person who might be able to help you or point you in the right direction, or even procure you special favors by 'greasing the administrative wheels,' is something the Chinese are always trying to arrange through their 'connections.' These mutual aid networks, with their reciprocal exchange of services, are called 关系 guānxi [gwan-shee].

Internet 因特网 yīntèwǎng [yin-tuh-wang]

▸ where can I connect to the Internet? 我去哪里可以上网？ wǒ qù nǎli kěyǐ shàngwǎng? [wo chew na-lee kuh-yee shang-wang]

introduce *(present)* 介绍 jièshào [jyeah-show]

▸ to introduce oneself 进行自我介绍 jìnxíng zìwǒ jièshào [jin-shing zir-wo jyeah-show]

▸ allow me to introduce myself: I'm Michael 请允许我自我介绍，我是迈克尔 qǐng yǔnxǔ wǒ zìwǒ jièshào, wǒ shì màikè'ěr [ching yun-shoo wo zir-wo jyeah-show wo shir migh-kuh-er]

invite 邀请 yāoqǐng [yow-ching]

▸ I'd like to invite you to dinner next weekend 下个周末我想邀请你吃晚饭 xià gè zhōumò wǒ xiǎng yāoqǐng nǐ chī wǎnfàn [shya guh joh-mo wo shyang yow-ching nee chir wan-fan]

iron *(for ironing)* 熨斗 yùndǒu [yun-doh] ◆ 熨烫 yùntàng [yun-tang]

▸ I need an iron 我需要一个熨斗 wǒ xūyào yī gè yùndǒu [wo shoo-yow yee guh yun-doh]

itch 痒 yǎng [yang]

▸ I've got an itch on my left leg 我左腿痒 wǒ zuǒ tuǐ yǎng [wo zwore tway yang]

itinerary 旅行计划 lǚxíng jìhuà [looh-shing jee-hwa]

▸ is it possible to modify the planned itinerary? 是否有可能更改已经定下来的旅行计划？ shìfǒu yǒu kěnéng gēnggǎi yǐjīng dìngxialai de lǚxíng jìhuà? [shir-foh yoh kuh-nung gung-gigh yee-jing ding-shya-ligh duh looh-shing jee-hwa]

j

January 一月 yī yué [yee yue]
- January 4th 一月四日 yī yuè sì rì [yee yue sir rir]

Jet Ski® 水上摩托艇 shuǐshàng mótuōtǐng [shway-shang mo-twore-ting]
- I'd like to rent a Jet Ski® 我想租一辆水上摩托艇 wǒ xiǎng zū yī liàng shuǐshàng mótuōtǐng [wo shyang zoo yee lyang shway-shang mo-twore-ting]

job (employment) 工作 gōngzuò [gong-zwore]
- I'm looking for a summer job in the area 我在这个地区寻找暑期工作 wǒ zài zhège dìqū xúnzhǎo shǔqī gōngzuò [wo zigh juh-guh dee-choo shun-jow shoo-chee gong-zwore]

joke 玩笑 wánxiào [wan-sheow] ◆ 开玩笑 kāi wánxiào [kigh wan-sheow]
- it's beyond a joke! 这不是闹着玩的 zhè bù shì nàozhewán de [juh boo shir now-juh-wan duh]
- I was just joking 我只是开玩笑 wǒ zhǐshì kāi wánxiào [wo jir-shir kigh wan-sheow]

journey 旅程 lǚchéng [looh-chung]
- how long does the journey take? 旅程要多久？ lǚchéng yào duō jiǔ? [loo-chung yow dwore jew]

juice (from fruit) 果汁 guǒzhī [gwore-jir]
- what types of juice do you have? 你有什么果汁？ nǐ yǒu shénme guǒzhī? [nee yoh sheun-muh gwore-jir]

July 七月 qī yuè [chee yue]
- July 4th 七月四日 qī yuè sì rì [chee yue sir rir]

June 六月 liù yuè [lew yue]
- June 2nd 六月二日 liù yuè èr rì [lew yue er rir]

just (recently) 刚刚 gānggāng [gang-gang]; (at that moment) 正 zhèng [jung]; (only, simply) 仅 jǐn [jin]
- he just left 他刚离开 tā gāng líkāi [ta gang lee-kigh]
- I'll just have one 我只要一个 wǒ zhǐ yào yī gè [wo jir yow yee guh]

k

karaoke 卡拉OK kǎlā ok [ka-la ok]

▸ where is the nearest karaoke bar? 最近的卡拉OK厅在哪里？ zuì jìn de kǎlā ok tīng zài nǎli? [zway jin duh ka-la ok ting zigh na-lee]

kayak 小艇 xiǎotǐng [sheow-ting]

▸ can we rent kayaks? 我们能租小艇吗？ wǒmen néng zū xiǎotǐng ma? [wo-meun nung zoo sheow-ting ma]

keep *(retain)* 保留 bǎoliú [bow-lew]; *(promise, appointment)* 遵守 zūnshǒu [zun-shoh]

▸ I'm sorry, I won't be able to keep the appointment 对不起，我无法赴约了 duìbuqǐ, wǒ wúfǎ fùyuē le [dway-boo-chee wo woo-fa foo-yue luh]

▸ keep the change 零钱不用找了 língqián bù yòng zhǎo le [ling-chyen boo yong jow luh]

key *(for a door, a container)* 钥匙 yàoshi [yow-shir]; *(on a keyboard)* 键 jiàn [jyen]; *(of a phone)* 按键 ànjiàn [an-jyen]

▸ which is the key to the front door? 开前门的钥匙是哪一把？ kāi qiánmén de yàoshi shì nǎ yī bǎ? [kigh chyen-meun duh yow-shir na yee ba]

kilometer 公里 gōnglǐ [gong-lee]

▸ how much is it per kilometer? 每公里多少钱？ měi gōnglǐ duōshao qián? [may gong-lee dwore-show chyen]

kind *(nice)* 亲切的 qīnqiè de [chin-chyeah duh] ◆ *(sort, type)* 种类 zhǒnglèi [jong-lay]

▸ that's very kind of you 你真是太好了 nǐ zhēn shì tài hǎo le [nee jeun shir tigh how luh]

▸ what's your favorite kind of music? 你喜欢哪种类型的音乐？ nǐ xǐhuan nǎ zhǒng lèixíng de yīnyuè? [nee shee-hwan na jong lay-shing duh yin-yue]

kitchen 厨房 chúfáng [choo-fang]

▸ is the kitchen shared? 厨房是公用的吗？ chúfáng shì gōngyòng de ma? [choo-fang shir gong-yong duh ma]

Kleenex® 面巾纸 miànjīnzhǐ [myen-jin-jir]

▸ do you have any Kleenex®? 你有面巾纸吗？ nǐ yǒu miànjīnzhǐ ma? [nee yoh myen-jin-jir ma]

knife 刀 dāo [dow]

▸ could I have a knife? 能给我把刀吗？ néng gěi wǒ bǎ dāo ma? [nung gay wo ba dow ma]

know *(fact)* 知道 zhīdao [jir-dow]; *(person)* 认识 rènshi [reun-shir]; *(place)* 熟悉 shúxí [shoo-shee]

▸ I know this town very well 我不是很熟悉这个城市 wǒ bù shì hěn shúxí zhège chéngshì [wo boo shir heun shoo-shee juh-guh chung-shir]

▸ I know the basics but no more than that 我知道基本的东西，但仅此而已 wǒ zhīdao jīběn de dōngxi, dàn jǐn cǐ éryǐ [wo jir-dow jee-beun duh dong-shee dan jin tsir er-yee]

▸ do you know each other? 你们相互认识吗？ nǐmen xiānghù rènshi ma? [nee-meun shyang-hoo reun-shir ma]

knowledge 知识 zhīshi [jir-shir]

▸ without my knowledge 在我不知道的情况下 zài wǒ bù zhīdao de qíngkuàng xià [zigh wo boo jir-dow duh ching-kwang shya]

ladies' room 女厕所 nǚ cèsuǒ [nooh tsuh-swore]

▸ where's the ladies' room? 女厕所在哪里？ nǚ cèsuǒ zài nǎli? [nooh tsuh-swore zigh na-lee]

lake 湖 hú [hoo]

▸ can you go swimming in the lake? 能在湖里游泳吗？ néng zài hú li yóuyǒng ma? [nung zigh hoo lee yoh-yong ma]

lamp 灯 dēng [dung]

▸ the lamp doesn't work 灯坏了 dēng huài le [dung hwigh luh]

land *(plane)* 着陆 zhuólù [jwore-loo]

▸ what time is the plane scheduled to land? 按规定飞机几点着陆？ àn guīdìng fēijī jǐ diǎn zhuólù? [an gway-ding fay-jee jee dyen jwore-loo]

landmark 路标 lùbiāo [loo-beow]

▸ do you recognize any landmarks? 你认出什么路标了吗？ nǐ rènchū shénme lùbiāo le ma? [nee reun-choo sheun-muh loo-beow luh ma]

lane 车道 chēdào [chuh-dow]

▸ a four-lane highway 四车道高速公路 sì chēdào gāosù gōnglù [sir chuh-dow gow-soo gong-loo]

laptop 手提电脑 shǒutí diànnǎo [shoh-tee dyen-now]

▸ my laptop's been stolen 我的手提电脑被偷了 wǒ de shǒutí diànnǎo bèi tōu le [wo duh shoh-tee dyen-now bay toh luh]

last 最后的 zuìhòu de [zway-hoh duh] ◆ 持续 chíxù [chir-shoo]

▸ when does the last bus go? 最后一班公共汽车什么时候开？ zuìhòu yī

bān gōnggòng qìchē shénme shíhou kāi? [zway-hoh yee ban gong-gong chee-chuh sheun-muh shir-hoh kigh]

- when is the last subway train? 最后一班地铁是几点？ zuìhòu yī bān dìtiě shì jǐ diǎn? [zway-hoh yee ban dee-tyeah shir jee dyen]

last name 姓 xìng [shing]

- could I have your last name? 能告诉我你姓什么吗？ néng gàosu wǒ nǐ xìng shénme ma? [nee nung gow-soo wo nee shing sheun-muh ma]

late 晚的 wǎn de [wan duh] ◆ 晚 wǎn [wan]

- the plane was two hours late 飞机晚点了两个小时 fēijī wǎndiǎnle liǎng gè xiǎoshí [fay-jee wan-dyen-luh lyang guh sheow-shir]
- could you tell me if the train to Lanzhou is running late? 你能否告诉我开往兰州的火车是不是晚点了？ nǐ néng fǒu gàosu wo kāiwǎng lánzhōu de huǒchē shìbùshì wǎndiǎn le? [nee nung foh gow-soo wo kai-wang lan-joh duh hwore-chuh shir-boo-shir wan-dyen luh]

later 更晚的 gèng wǎn de [gung wan duh] ◆ 稍后 shāo hòu [show hoh]

- is there a later train? 是否有更晚的火车？ shìfǒu yǒu gèng wǎn de huǒchē? [shir-foh chuh gung wan duh hwore-chuh]
- see you later! 一会儿见! yīhuìr jiàn! [yee-hwayr jyen]

latest (most recent) 最新的 zuì xīn de [zway shin duh]; (very last) 最后的 zuìhòu de [zway-hoh duh]

- what's the latest time we can check out? 我们最晚要在几点办理退房手续？ wǒmen zuì wǎn yào zài jǐ diǎn bànlǐ tuìfáng shǒuxù? [wo-meun zway-wan yow zigh jen ban-lee tway-fang shoh-shoo]

laugh 笑 xiào [sheow]

- I just did it for a laugh 我只是开玩笑而已 wǒ zhǐshì kāi wánxiào éryǐ [wo jir-shir kigh wan-sheow er-yee]

Laundromat® 自助洗衣店 zìzhù xǐyīdiàn [zir-joo shee-yee-dyen]

- is there a Laundromat® nearby? 附近有自助洗衣店吗？ fùjìn yǒu zìzhù xǐyīdiàn ma? [foo-jin yoh jir-joo shee-yee-dyen ma]

laundry (washed clothes) 洗好的衣服 xǐ hǎo de yīfu [shee-how duh yee-foo]; (unwashed clothes) 待洗的衣服 dài xǐ de yīfu [digh shee duh yee-foo]; (business) 洗衣店 xǐyīdiàn [shee-yee-dyen]; (room) 洗衣房 xǐyīfáng [shee-yee-fang]

- where can we do our laundry? 我们在哪里可以洗衣服？ wǒmen zài nǎli kěyǐ xǐ yīfu? [wo-meun zigh na-lee kuh-yee shee yee-foo]
- where's the nearest laundry? 最近的洗衣店在哪里？ zuìjìn de xǐyīdiàn zài nǎli? [zway-jin duh shee-yee-dyen zigh na-lee]

lawyer 律师 lǜshī [looh-shir]

- I'm a lawyer 我是一名律师 wǒ shì yī míng lǜshī [wo shir yee ming looh-shir]
- I need a lawyer 我需要一位律师 wǒ xūyào yī wèi lǜshī [wo shoo-yow yee-way looh-shir]

leaflet 小册子 xiǎocèzi [sheow-tsuh-zir]

▸ do you have any leaflets in English? 你们有英文版的小册子吗 nǐmen yǒu yīngwén bǎn de xiǎocèzi ma? [nee-meun yoh ying-weun ban duh sheow-tsuh-zir ma]

learn 学 xué [shue]

▸ I've just learned a few words from a book 我刚从一本书上学了几个词 wǒ gāng cóng yī běn shū shang xué le jǐ gè cí [wo gang tsong yee beun shoo shang shue luh jee guh tsir]

least 最少的 zuì shǎo de [zway show duh] ♦ 最少 zuì shǎo [zway show] ♦ 最少 zuì shǎo [zway show] ♦ **at least** 至少 zhìshǎo [jir-show]

▸ it's the least I can do 这是我能做的最起码的事 zhè shì wǒ néng zuò de zuì qǐmǎ de shì [juh shir wo nung zwore duh zway chee-ma duh shir]

▸ not in the least 一点也不 yīdiǎn yě bù [yee-dyen yuh boo]

▸ to say the least 至少可以说 zhìshǎo kěyǐ shuō [jir-show kuh-yee shwore]

▸ it's at least a three-hour drive 至少三个小时的车程 zhìshǎo sān gè xiǎoshí de chēchéng [jir-show san guh sheow-shir duh chuh-chung]

leave *(go away from)* 离开 líkāi [lee-kigh]; *(let stay)* 把......留下 bǎ......liúxia [ba......lew-shya]; *(forget to take)* 落下 làxia [la-shya] ♦ *(go away)* 离开 líkāi [lee-kigh]

▸ can I leave my backpack at the reception desk? 我能把背包留在接待处吗？ wǒ néng bǎ bēibāo liú zài jiēdàichù ma? [wo nung ba bay-bow lew zigh jyeah-digh-choo ma]

▸ can I leave the car at the airport? 我能把汽车留在机场吗？ wǒ néng bǎ qìchē liú zài jīchǎng ma? [wo nung ba chee-chuh lew zigh jee-chang ma]

▸ leave us alone! 别打扰我们！ bié dǎrǎo wǒmen! [byeah da-row wo-meun]

▸ I've left something on the plane 我把东西落在飞机上了 wǒ bǎ dōngxi là zài fēijī shang le [wo ba dong-shee la zigh fay-jee shang luh]

▸ I'll be leaving at nine o'clock tomorrow morning 我明天早晨9点出发 wǒ míngtiān zǎochén jiǔ diǎn chūfā [ming-tyen zow-cheun jew dyen choo-fa]

▸ what platform does the train for Beijing leave from? 开往北京的火车从哪个站台出发？ kāiwǎng běijīng de huǒchē cóng nǎge zhàntái chūfā? [kigh-wang bay-jing duh hwore-chuh tsong na guh jan-tigh choo-fa]

left *(not right)* 左的 zuǒ de [zwore duh] ♦ 左边 zuǒbian [zwore-byen]

▸ to be left 留 liú [lew]

▸ are there any tickets left for...? 有为......留的票吗？ yǒu wèi......liú de piào ma? [yoh way...lew duh peow ma]

▸ to the left (of) 在（......的）左边 zài (......de) zuǒbian [zigh (...duh) zwore-byen]

left-hand 左手边的 zuǒshǒubiān de [zwore-shoh-byen duh]

▸ on your left-hand side 在你的左边 zài nǐ de zuǒbian [zigh nee duh zwore-byen]

leg 腿 tuǐ [tway]

▸ I have a pain in my left leg 我左腿疼 wǒ zuǒ tuǐ téng [wo zwore tway tung]

▸ I can't move my leg 我的腿动不了了 wǒ de tuǐ dòng bù liǎo le [wo duh tway dong boo leow luh]

lemon 柠檬 níngméng [ning-mung]

▸ can I have half a kilo of lemons? 能给我来半公斤的柠檬吗? néng gěi wǒ lái bàn gōngjīn de níngméng ma? [nung gay wo ligh ban gong-jin duh ming-mung ma]

lend 借 jiè [jyeah]

▸ could you lend us your car? 你能把车借给我们吗? nǐ néng bǎ chē jiè gěi wǒmen ma? [nee nung ba chuh jyeah gay wo-meun ma]

lens (of camera) 镜头 jìngtóu [jing-toh]; (contact lens) 隐形眼镜 yǐnxíng yǎnjìng [yin-shing yan-jing]

▸ there's something on the lens 镜头上有东西 jìngtóu shang yǒu dōngxi [jing-toh shang yoh dong-shee]

▸ I have hard lenses 我用硬性隐形眼镜 wǒ yòng yìngxíng yǐnxíng yǎnjìng [wo yong ying-shing yin-shing-yan-jing]

▸ I have soft lenses 我用软性隐形眼镜 wǒ yòng ruǎnxíng yǐnxíng yǎnjìng [wo yong rwan-shing yin-shing yan-jing]

less 更少的 gèng shǎo de [gung show duh] ◆ 较少的东西 jiào shǎo de dōngxi [jeow show duh dong-shee] ◆ 较少地 jiào shǎo de [jeow show dun]

▸ less and less 越来越少 yuè lái yuè shǎo [yue ligh yue show]

▸ a little less 少一点 shǎo yìdiǎn [show yee-dyen]

lesson 课 kè [kuh]

▸ how much do lessons cost? 上课要花多少钱? shàngkè yào huā duōshao qián? [shang-kuh yow hwa dwore-show chyen]

▸ can we take lessons? 我们能上课吗? wǒmen néng shàngkè ma? [wo-meun nung shang-kuh ma]

let off (allow to disembark) 下 xià [shya]

▸ could you let me off here, please? 请你让我在这里下好吗? qǐng nǐ ràng wǒ zài zhèlǐ xià hǎo ma? [ching nee rang wo zigh juh-lee shya how ma]

letter 信 xìn [shyen]

▸ I would like to send this letter to the States 我想把这封信寄往美国 wǒ xiǎng bǎ zhè fēng xìn jìwǎng měiguó [wo shyang ba juh fung shin jee-wang may-gwore]

letters

When you are writing the address on an envelope remember that the Chinese go 'from the general to the particular.' In other words, they start with the name of the country, the town, then the address and the name of the recipient. If you are sending a letter abroad, you might want to write the name of the country in Chinese as well as English. Note that as the sender you should put your name and address on the right bottom corner of the envelope, and the addressee's name and address in the center.

▸ I confirmed my reservation by letter 我用信函的方式确定了我的预定 wǒ yòng xìnhán de fāngshì quèdìngle wǒ de yùdìng [wo yong shin-han duh fang-shir chue-ding-luh wo duh yoo-ding]

level *(amount)* 程度 chéngdù [chung-doo]; *(of a building, a ship)* 层 céng [tsung]
▸ do you know if cabin 27 is on this level? 请问27号船舱是否在这一层？ qǐng wèn èrshíqī hào chuáncāng shìfǒu zài zhè yī céng? [ching weun er-shir-chee how chwan-tsung shir-foh zigh juh yee tseng]

license 许可证 xǔkězhèng [shoo-kuh-jung]; *(for driving)* 执照 zhízhào [jir-jow]
▸ do you need a license to hunt here? 在这里打猎是否需要许可证？ zài zhèli dǎliè shìfǒu xūyào xǔkězhèng [zigh juh-lee da-lyeah shir-foh shoo-yow shoo-kuh-jung]
▸ I left my driver's license in my hotel room 我把我的驾驶执照落在旅馆的房间里了 wǒ bǎ wǒ de jiàshǐ zhízhào là zài lǚguǎn de fángjiān li le [wo ba wo duh jya-shir jir-jow la zigh looh-gwan duh fang-jyen lee luh]

license number 车牌号码 chēpái hàomǎ [chuh-pigh how-ma]
▸ I got the license number 我有车牌号码了 wǒ yǒu chēpái hàomǎ le [wo yoh chuh-pigh how-ma luh]

license plate 车号牌 chēhàopái [chuh-how-pigh]
▸ the car had an expired license plate 这辆汽车的车号牌过期了 zhè liàng qìchē de chēhàopái guòqī le [juh lyang chee-chuh duh chuh-how-pigh gwore-chee luh]

lifebelt 救生圈 jiùshēngquān [jew-shung-gwan]
▸ throw me a lifebelt! 把救生圈扔给我！ bǎ jiùshēngquān rēng gěi wǒ! [ba jew-shung-chwan rung gay wo]

lifeboat 救生艇 jiùshēngtǐng [jew-shung-ting]
▸ how many lifeboats are there? 有多少艘救生艇？ yǒu duōshao sōu jiùshēngtǐng? [yoh dwore-show teow jew-shung-ting]

lifejacket 救生衣 jiùshēngyī [jew-shung-yee]
▸ are there any lifejackets? 有救生衣吗？ yǒu jiùshēngyī ma? [yoh jew-shung-yee ma]

likes

▶ I really love that painting 我真的很喜欢那幅画 wǒ zhēn de hěn xǐhuan nà fú huà [wo jeun shee-hwan na foo hwa]

▶ I like your younger brother 我喜欢你的弟弟 wǒ xǐhuan nǐ de dìdi [wo shee-hwan nee duh dee-dee]

▶ I've got a soft spot for her 我挺喜欢她的 wǒ tǐng xǐhuan tā de [wo ting shee-hwan ta duh]

▶ I think she's very nice 我认为她非常好 wǒ rènwéi tā fēicháng hǎo [wo reun-way ta fay-chang how]

light *(brightness)* 光 guāng [gwang]; *(on a car)* 车灯 chē dēng [chuh dung]; *(regulating traffic)* 红绿灯 hónglǜdēng [hong-looh-dung]; *(for a cigarette)* 点火物 diǎnhuǒwù [dyen-hwore-woo]; *(in a lamp)* 灯泡 dēngpào [dung-pow]

▸ the light doesn't work 灯坏了 dēng huài le [dung hwigh luh]

▸ could you check the lights? 你能检查一下车灯吗? nǐ néng jiǎnchá yī xià chē dēng ma? [nee nung jyen-cha yee shya chuh dung ma]

▸ stop at the next light 在下一个红绿灯处停下 zài xià yī gè hónglǜdēng chù tíngxia [zigh shya yee guh hong-looh-dung choo ting-shya]

▸ do you have a light? 能借个火儿吗? néng jiè gè huǒr ma? [nung jyeah guh hwore ma]

lighter 打火机 dǎhuǒjī [da-hwore-jee]

▸ can I borrow your lighter? 我能借一下你的打火机吗? wǒ néng jiè yī xià nǐ de dǎhuǒjī ma? [wo nung jyeah yee shya nee duh da-hwore-jee ma]

lighthouse 灯塔 dēngtǎ [dung-ta]

▸ are there boat trips to the lighthouse? 是否能乘船去灯塔? shìfǒu néng chéng chuán qù dēngtǎ? [shir-foh nung chung-chwan choo dung-ta]

like *(similar to)* 像 xiàng [shyang]; *(such as)* 例如 lìrú [lee-roo] ♦ 喜欢 xǐhuan [shee-hwan]

dislikes

▶ I hate football 我讨厌足球 wǒ tǎoyàn zúqiú [wo tow-ywan zoo-chew]

▶ I can't stand him 我受不了他 wǒ shòu bù liǎo tā [wo shoh boo leow ta]

▶ I don't really like him/her 我并不怎么喜欢他/她 wǒ bìng bù zěnme xǐhuan tā/tā [wo bing boo zeun-muh shee-hwan ta/ta]

▶ I'm not really into walking 我不怎么喜欢散步 wǒ bù zěnme xǐhuan sànbù [wo boo zeun-muh shee-hwan san-boo]

- it's quite like English 和英语挺像的 hé yīngyǔ tǐng xiàng de [huh ying-yoo ting shyang duh]
- I like it 我喜欢它 wǒ xǐhuan tā [wo shee-hwan ta]
- I don't like it 我不喜欢它 wǒ bù xǐhuan tā [wo boo shee-hwan ta]
- do you like it here? 你喜欢这儿吗? nǐ xǐhuan zhèr ma? [nee shee-hwan jer ma]
- I like Chinese food very much 我非常喜欢中国菜 wǒ fēicháng xǐhuan zhōngguó cài [wo fay-chang shee-hwan jong-gwore tsigh]
- do you like the movies? 你喜欢这部电影吗? nǐ xǐhuan zhè bù diànyǐng ma? [nee shee-hwan jeh boo dyen-ying ma]
- would you like a drink? – yes, I'd love one 你想喝一杯吗? 是的, 我很乐意。 nǐ xiǎng hē yī bēi ma? – shì de, wǒ hěn lèyì [nee shyang huh yee bay ma shir duh wo heun luh-yee]
- I'd like to speak to the manager 我想和经理说话 wǒ xiǎng hé jīnglǐ shuōhuà [wo shyang huh jing-lee shwore-hwa]

lime 青柠檬 qīng níngméng [ching ning-mung]
- can I have half a kilo of limes? 能给我来半公斤的青柠檬吗? néng gěiwǒ lái bàn gōngjīn de qīng níngméng ma? [nung gay wi ligh ban gong-jin duh ching ning-mung ma]

limit 界限 jièxiàn [jyeah-shin] ◆ 限制 xiànzhì [shyen-jir]
- is that area off limits? 那个地方不允许去吗? nàge dìfang bù yǔnxǔ qù ma? [na-guh dee-fang boo yun-shoo choo ma]

line *(phone connection)* 线 xiàn [shyen]; *(of people waiting)* 队 duì [dway]; *(of a railroad)* 铁轨 tiěguǐ [tyeah-gway]; *(on a subway)* 线 xiàn [shyen]; *(bus service)* 路线 lùxiàn [loo-shyen]
- the line was busy 电话占线 diànhuà zhànxiàn [dyen-hwa jan-shyen]
- we had to stand in line for 15 minutes 我们不得不排了15分钟的队 wǒmen bùdébù páile shíwǔ fēnzhōng de duì [wo-meun boo-duh-boo pigh-luh shir-woo feun-jong duh dway]
- which line do I take to get to...? 去......我该坐哪条线? qù......wǒ gāi zuò nǎ tiáo xiàn? [choo...wo gigh zwore na teow shyen]

lipstick 口红 kǒuhóng [koh-hong]
- I need to buy some lipstick 我要买口红 wǒ yào mǎi kǒuhóng [wo yow migh koh-hong]

listen 听 tīng [ting]
- listen, I really need to see a doctor 听着, 我真的需要看医生 tīngzhe, wǒ zhēn de xūyào kàn yīshēng [ting-juh wo jeun duh shoo-yow kan yee-shung]
- listen to me carefully 仔细听我说说 zǐxì tīng wǒ shuō [zir-shee ting wo shwore]

liter 公升 gōngshēng [gong-shung]
- a two-liter bottle of soda 一瓶两公升的苏打水 yī píng liǎng gōngshēng de sūdǎshuǐ [yee ping lyang gong-shung duh soo-da-shway]

little *(small)* 小的 xiǎo de [sheow duh]; *(young)* 幼小的 yòuxiǎo de [yoh-sheow duh] ♦ 些许 xiēxǔ [shyeah-shoo] ♦ **a little** 少量 shǎoliàng [show-lyang] ♦ 有些 yǒuxiē [yoh-shyean]

> it's for a little girl 是给小女孩儿的 shì gěi xiǎo nǚháir de [shir gay sheow nooh-highr duh]

> as little as possible 尽可能少 jǐn kěnéng shǎo [jin kuh-nung show]

> I speak a little Chinese 我会说一点点的中文 wǒ huì shuō yī diǎndiǎn de zhōngwén [wo hway shwore yee dyen-dyen duh jong-weun]

> we've only got a little money left 我们只剩一点钱了 wǒmen zhǐ shèng yīdiǎn qián le [wo-meun jir shung yee-dyen chyen luh]

> a little bit 一点儿 yīdiǎnr [yee-dyenr]

> a little less 少一点儿 shǎo yīdiǎnr [show yee-dyenr]

> a little more 多一点儿 duō yīdiǎnr [dwore yee-dyenr]

live 住 zhù [joo]

> do you live around here? 你住在这附近吗? nǐ zhù zài zhè fùjìn ma? [nee joo zigh juh foo-jin ma]

> I live in Shanghai 我住在上海 wǒ zhù zài shànghǎi [wo joo zigh shang-high]

live music 现场音乐表演 xiànchǎng yīnyuè biǎoyǎn [shyen-chang yin-yue beow-yan]

> I'd like to go to a bar with live music 我想去有现场音乐表演的酒吧 wǒ xiǎng qù yǒu xiànchǎng yīnyuè biǎoyǎn de jiǔbā [wo shyang choo yoh shyen-chang yin-yue beow-yan duh jew-ba]

living room 客厅 kètīng [kuh-ting]

> I can sleep in the living room 我可以睡在客厅 wǒ kěyǐ shuì zài kètīng [wo kuh-yee shway zigh kuh-ting]

loaf (of bread) 长面包 cháng miànbāo [chang myen-bow]

> I'd like one of those large loaves 我想要那些长面包中的一个 wǒ xiǎng yào nàxiē cháng miànbāo zhōng de yī gè [wo shyang na-shyeah chang myen-bow jong duh yee guh]

local 当地的 dāngdì de [dang-dee duh]

> what's the local specialty? 当地的特色菜是什么? dāngdì de tèsècài shì shénme? [dang-dee duh tuh-suh-tsigh shir sheun-muh]

lock 锁 suǒ [swore] ♦ 把......锁上 bǎ......suǒshang [ba...swore-shang]

> the lock's broken 锁坏了 suǒ huài le [swore hwigh luh]

> I locked the door 我把门锁上了 wǒ bǎ mén suǒshang le [wo ba meun swore-shang luh]

lock out

> to lock oneself out 把自己关在外面 bǎ zìjǐ guān zài wàimian [ba zir-jee gwan zigh wigh-myen]

▸ I've locked myself out 我把自己关在外面了 wǒ bǎ zìjǐ guān zài wàimian le [wo zir-jee gwan zigh wigh-myen luh]

long *(in space)* 长的 cháng de [chang duh]; *(in time)* 久的 jiǔ de [jew duh] ◆ 长久 chángjiǔ [chang-jew]

▸ it's ten feet long 它长十英尺 tā cháng shí yīngchǐ [ta chang shir ying-chir]

▸ I waited for a long time 我等了很久 wǒ děngle hěn jiǔ [wo dung-luh heun jew]

▸ how long? 多久？ duō jiǔ? [dwore jew]

▸ how long will it take? 需要多久？ xūyào duō jiǔ? [shoo-yow dwore jew]

▸ we're not sure how long we're going to stay 我们不确定我们会呆多久 wǒmen bù quèdìng wǒmen huì dāi duō jiǔ [wo-meun boo chue-ding wo-meun hway digh dwore jew]

look *(with eyes)* 看 kàn [kan]; *(appearance)* 外表 wàibiāo [wigh-beow] ◆ *(seem)* 看上去 kànshangqu [kan-shang-choo]

▸ could you have a look at my car? 你能看一下我的汽车吗？ nǐ néng kàn yī xià wǒ de qìchē ma? [nee nung kan yee shya wo duh chee-chuh ma]

▸ no, thanks, I'm just looking 不，谢谢。我只是看看 bù, xièxie. wǒ zhǐshì kànkan [boo shyeah-shyeah wo jir-shir kan-kan]

▸ what does she look like? 她长得什么样？ tā zhǎng de shénmeyàng? [ta jang duh sheun-muh-yang]

▸ you look like your brother 你长得像你的兄弟 nǐ zhǎng de xiàng nǐ de xiōngdì [nee jang duh shyang nee duh shyong-dee]

▸ it looks like it's going to rain 看上去好像要下雨 kànshangqu hàoxiàng yào xià yǔ [kan-shang-choo how-shyang yow shya yoo]

look after *(child, ill person)* 照顾 zhàogù [jow-goo]; *(luggage)* 照看 zhào kàn [jow-kan]

▸ can someone look after the children for us? 谁能为我们照顾孩子？ shéi néng wèi wǒmen zhàogù háizi? [shay nung w/we wo-meun jow-goo high-zir]

▸ can you look after my things for a minute? 你能照看一下我的行李吗？ nǐ néng zhàokàn yī xià wǒ de xínglǐ ma? [nee nung jow-kan yee shya wo duh shing-lee ma]

look for 寻找 xúnzhǎo [shun-jow]

▸ I'm looking for a good restaurant that serves regional cuisine 我在找一家好一些的提供当地菜肴的餐馆 wǒ zài zhǎo yī jiā hǎo yīxiē de tígōng dāngdì càiyáo de cānguǎn [wo zigh jow jya how yee-shyeah duh tee-gong dang-dee tsigh-yow duh tsan-gwan]

lose *(be unable to find)* 丢失 diūshī [dew-shir]

▸ I've lost the key to my room 我丢了我房间的钥匙 wǒ diūle wǒ fángjiān de yàoshi [wo dew-luh wo fang-jyen duh yow-shir]

▸ I've lost my way 我迷路了 wǒ mílù le [wo mee-loo luh]

lost 丢失的 diūshī de [dew-shir duh]

- who do you have to see about lost luggage? 丢了行李要找谁？ diūle xíngli yào zhǎo shéi? [dew-luh shing-lee yow jow shay]
- could you help me? I seem to be lost 你能帮助我吗？我好像迷路了 nǐ néng bāngzhù wǒ ma? wǒ hǎoxiàng mílù le [nee nung bang-ju wo ma wo how-shyang mee-loo luh]
- to get lost 迷路 mílù [mee-loo]
- get lost! 走开！ zǒukāi! [zoh kigh]

lost-and-found 失物招领处 shīwù zhāolǐngchù [shir-woo jow-ling-choo]

- where's the lost-and-found? 失物招领处在哪里？ shīwù zhāolǐngchù zài nǎlí? [shir-woo jow-ling-choo zigh na-lee]

lot ◆ a lot 非常 fēicháng [fay-chang]

- a lot of ... 许多 ...... xǔduō...... [shoo-dwore]
- are there a lot of things to see around here? 这附近有许多东西值得看吗？ zhè fùjìn yǒu xǔduō dōngxi zhíde kàn ma? [juh foo-jin yoh shoo-dwore dong-shee jir-duh kan ma]
- will there be a lot of other people there? 那里有许多其他人吗？ nàli yǒu xǔduō qítārén ma? [na-lee yoh shoo-dwore chee-ta-reun ma]
- thanks a lot 非常感谢 fēicháng gǎnxiè [fay-chang gan-shyeah]

loud *(noise)* 大的 dà de [da duh]; *(voice)* 响亮的 xiǎngliàng de [shyang-lyang duh]; *(music)* 喧闹的 xuānnào de [shwan-now duh]

- the television is too loud 电视的声音太吵了 diànshì de shēngyīn tài chǎo le [dyen-shir duh shung-yin tigh chow luh]

loudly *(speak)* 大声地 dàshēng de [da-sheun duh]

- can you speak a little more loudly? 你能说得再大声点儿吗？ nǐ néng shuō de zài dàshēng diǎnr ma? [nee nung shwore duh zigh da-shung dyenr ma]

love 爱 ài [igh]

- I love you 我爱你 wǒ ài nǐ [wo igh nee]
- I love the movies 我爱看电影 wǒ ài kàn diànyǐng [wo igh kan dyen-ying]
- I love cooking 我爱烹饪 wǒ ài pēngrèn [wo igh pung-reun]

lovely 可爱的 kě'ài de [kuh-igh duh]

- what a lovely room! 这个房间太好了！ zhège fángjiān tài hǎo le! [juh-guh fang-jyen tigh how luh]
- it's lovely today 今天天气真好 jīntiān tiānqì zhēn hǎo! [jin-tyen tyen-chee jeun how]

low *(temperature)* 低的 dī de [dee duh]; *(speed)* 慢的 màn de [man duh]

- temperatures are in the low twenties 温度为二十几度 wēndù wéi èrshí jǐ dù [weun-doo way er-shir jee doo]

low beam 近光灯 jìnguāngdēng [jin gwung-dung]

▸ keep your lights on low beam 保持近光灯 bǎochí jìnguāngdēng [bow-chir jin-gwung-dung]

lower 降低 jiàngdī [jyang-dee] ◆ 更低的 gèng dī de [gung dee duh]

▸ is it OK if I lower the blind a little? 我可以把百叶窗拉低点儿吗? wǒ kěyǐ bǎ bǎiyèchuāng lā dī diǎnr ma? [wo kuh-yee ba bigh-yuh-chwung la dee dyanr ma]

▸ how do we get to the lower level? 我们如何去下一层? wǒmen rúhé qù xià yī céng? [wo-meun roo–huh choo shya yee-tsung]

low-fat (yogurt) 低脂的 dīzhī de [dee-jir duh]

▸ do you have any low-fat yogurt? 你有低脂酸奶吗? nǐ yǒu dīzhī suānnǎi ma? [nee yoh dee-jir swan-nigh ma]

low season 淡季 dànjì [dan-jee]

▸ what are prices like in the low season? 淡季的价格怎么样? dànjì de jiàgé zěnmeyàng? [dan-jee duh jya-guh zeun-muh yang]

low tide 低潮 dīcháo [dee-chow]

▸ what time is low tide today? 今天的低潮是什么时候? jīntiān de dīcháo shì shénme shíhou? [jin-tyen duh dee-chow shir sheun-muh shir-hoh]

luck 运气 yùnqì [yun-chee]

▸ good luck! 祝你好运! zhù nǐ hǎoyùn! [joo nee how yun]

luggage 行李 xíngli [shing-lee]

▸ my luggage hasn't arrived 我的行李还没有到 wǒ de xíngli hái méiyou dào [wo-duh shing-lee high may-yoh dow]

▸ I'd like to report the loss of my luggage 我的行李丢了，来报失 wǒ de xíngli diū le, lái bàoshī [wo duh shing-lee dew luh ligh bow-shir]

luggage cart 行李手推车 xíngli shǒutuīchē [shing-lee tway-chuh]

▸ I'm looking for a luggage cart 我在找行李手推车 wǒ zài zhǎo xíngli shǒutuīchē [wo zigh jow shing-lee-shoh-tway-chuh]

lunch 午餐 wǔcān [woo-tsan]

▸ to have lunch 吃午餐 chī wǔcān [chir woo-tsan]

▸ what time is lunch served? 几点供应午餐? jǐ diǎn gōngyìng wǔcān? [jee dyen gong–ying woo-tsan]

m

machine-washable 可以用洗衣机洗的 kěyǐ yòng xǐyījī xǐ de [kuh–yee yong shee-yee-jee shee duh]
- is it machine-washable? 可以用洗衣机洗吗？ kěyǐ yòng xǐyījī xǐ ma? [kuh-yee yong shee-yee-jee shee ma]

maid 保姆 bǎomǔ [bow-moo]
- what time does the maid come? 保姆什么时候过来？ bǎomǔ shénme shíhou guòlai? [bow-moo sheun-muh shir-hoh gwore-ligh]

maid service 保姆服务 bǎomǔ fúwù [bow-moo foo-woo]
- is there maid service? 是否有保姆服务？ shìfǒu yǒu bǎomǔ fúwù? [shir-foh yoh bow-moo foo-woo]

mailbox (for getting mail) 收件箱 shōujiànxiāng [shoh-jyen-shyang]; (for sending mail) 发件箱 fājiànxiāng [fa-jyen-shyang]
- where's the nearest mailbox? 最近的邮箱在哪里？ zuì jìn de yóuxiāng zài nǎli? [zway-jin duh yoh-shyang zigh nah-lee]

main course 主菜 zhǔcài [joo-tsigh]
- what are you having for your main course? 主菜你要什么？ zhǔcài nǐ yào shénme? [joo-tsigh nee yoh sheun-muh]

make (create, produce) 做 zuò [zwore]; (cause to become) 使......变成 shǐ......biànchéng [shir...byen-chung]
- how is this dish made? 这盘菜是怎么做的？ zhè pán cài shì zěnme zuò de? [juh pan tsigh shir zeun-muh zwore duh]
- I hope to make new friends here 我希望在这里结交新朋友 wǒ xīwàng zài zhèli jiéjiāo xīn péngyou [wo shee-wang zigh juh-lee jyeah-jeow shin pung-yoh]

make up (compensate for) 弥补 míbǔ [mee-boo]; (invent) 虚构 xūgòu [shoo-goh]
- will we be able to make up the time we've lost? 我们是否能把错过的时间补回来？ wǒmen shìfǒu néng bǎ cuòguo de shíjiān bǔhuílai? [wo-meun shir-foh nung ba tswore-gwore duh shir-jyen boo-hway-ligh]

man 男人 nánrén [nan-reun]
- that man is bothering me 那个男人真让我烦 nàge nánrén zhēn ràng wǒ fán [na-guh nan-reun jeun rang wo fan]

man-made 人造的 rénzào de [reun-zow duh]
- it's man-made 那是人造的 nà shì rénzào de [na shir reun-zow duh]

many 许多的 xǔduō de [shoo-dwore duh]

- there are many good restaurants here 这里有许多好的餐馆 zhèli yǒu xǔduō hǎo de cānguǎn [juh-lee yoh shoo-dwore how duh tsan-gwan]
- how many? 多少？ duōshao? [dwore-show]
- how many days will you be staying? 你将呆几天？ nǐ jiāng dāi jǐ tiān? [nee jyang digh jee tyen]

map *(of a country, town, network)* 地图 dìtú [dee-too]

- where can I buy a map of the area? 在哪里我可以买到这个地区的地图？ zài nǎli wǒ kěyǐ mǎidào zhège dìqū de dìtú? [zigh na-lee wo kuh-yee migh dow juh-guh dee-choo duh dee-too]
- can you show me where we are on the map? 你能在地图上指给我看我们的位置吗？ nǐ néng zài dìtú shang zhǐ gěi wǒ kàn wǒmen de wèizhi ma? [nee nung zigh dee-too shang jir gay wo-kan wo-meun duh way-jir ma]
- can I have a map of the subway? 能给我一份地铁图吗？ néng gěi wǒ yī fèn dìtiětú ma? [nung gay wo yee feun dee-tyeah-too ma]

March 三月 sān yuè [san yue]

- March 1st 三月一日 sān yuè yī rì [san yue yee rir]

market 集市 jíshì [jee-shir]

- is there a market in the square every day? 广场上每天都有集市吗？ guǎngchǎng shang měi tiān dōu yǒu jíshì ma? [gwung-chang shang may-tyen doh yoh jee-shir ma]

married 结婚的 jiéhūn de [jyeah-hun]

- are you married? 你结婚了吗？ nǐ jiéhūnle ma? [nee jyeah-hun luh ma]

mass *(religion)* 弥撒 mísa [mee-sa]

- what time is mass? 弥撒是什么时候？ mísa shì shénme shíhou? [mee-sa shir sheun-muh shir-hoh]

match *(for lighting)* 火柴 huǒchái [hwore-chigh]

- do you have any matches? 你有火柴吗？ nǐ yǒu huǒchái ma? [nee yoh hwore-chigh ma]

matter 有关系 yǒu guānxi [yoh gwan-shee]

- it doesn't matter 没关系 méi guānxi [may gwan-shee]

mattress 床垫 chuángdiàn [chwung-dyen]

- the mattresses are saggy 床垫太软了 chuángdiàn tài ruǎn le [chwung-dyen tigh rwan luh]

May 五月 wǔ yuè [woo yue]

- May 9th 五月九日 wǔ yuè jiǔ rì [woo yue jew rir]

maybe 可能 kěnéng [kuh-nung]

- maybe the weather will be better tomorrow 明天天气可能会好一些 míngtiān tiānqì kěnéng huì hǎo yīxiē [ming-tyen tyen-chee kuh-nung hway how yee shyeah]

meals

The Chinese particularly enjoy sharing meals with relatives, friends, work colleagues or business associates. They love having dinner with lots of people sitting together around a circular table. During the meal, you should not fiddle with your chopsticks, and you must never stick them in your bowl of rice. The Chinese eat early: lunch at about 12 o'clock and dinner from 6 p.m. If you're staying up late, you can have a snack 夜宵 yèxiāo [yuh-sheow] in the evening, after dinner, at about 10 p.m.

meal 餐 cān [tsan]
- are meals included? 包括吃饭吗? bāokuò chīfàn ma? [bow-kwore chir-fan ma]

mean *(signify)* 意思是 yìsi shì [yee-sir shir]; *(matter)* 意味 yìwèi [yee-way]; *(intend)* 打算 dǎsuan [da-swan]
- what does that word mean? 那个词是什么意思? nàge cí shì shénme yìsi? [na-guh tsir shir sheun-muh yee-sir]
- I mean it 我是认真的 wǒ shì rènzhēn de [wo shir reun-jeun duh]
- I didn't mean it 我不是有意的 wǒ bù shì yǒuyì de [wo boo-shir yoh-yee duh]

meat 肉 ròu [roh]
- I don't eat meat 我不吃肉 wǒ bù chī ròu [wo boo chir-roh]

mechanic 修理工 xiūlǐgōng [shew-lee-gong]
- what did the mechanic say was wrong with the car? 修理工说汽车有什么毛病? xiūlǐgōng shuō qìchē yǒu shénme máobìng? [shew-lee-gong shwore chee-chuh yoh sheun-muh mow-bing]

medication 药物 yàowù [yow-woo]
- I'm not taking any other medication at the moment 我目前没有在服其他药物 wǒ mùqián méiyou zài fú qítā de yàowù [wo moo-chyen may-yoh zigh foo chee-ta duh yow-woo]

medicine 药 yào [yow]
- how many times a day do I have to take the medicine? 这个药我一天得吃几次? zhège yào wǒ yī tiān děi chī jǐ cì? [jug-guh yow wo yee tyen day chir jee-tsir]

medium *(size)* 中号的 zhōnghào de [jong-how duh]; *(steak)* 半熟的 bàn shú de [ban-shoo duh]
- I'd like my steak medium, please 我点的牛排要半熟的 wǒ diǎn de niúpái yào bàn shú de [wo dyen duh new-pigh yow ban-shoo duh]
- do you have this shirt in a medium? 这件衬衫你有中号的吗? zhè jiàn chènshān nǐ yǒu zhōnghào de ma? [juh jyen cheun-shan nee yoh jong-how duh ma]

meeting people

The Chinese usually do not kiss each other on the cheek or go in for effusive welcomes when they meet, even with family members. They prefer to shake hands or nod.

meet *(by chance)* 碰见 pèngjian [pung-jyen]; *(by arrangement)* 约见 yuējiàn [yue-jyen]; *(make the acquaintance of)* 结识 jiéshí [jyeah-shir] ◆ *(by chance)* 相遇 xiāngyù [shyang-yoo]

- meet you at 9 o'clock in front of the town hall 九点在市政厅前和你见面 jiǔ diǎn zài shìzhèngtīng qián hé nǐ jiànmiàn [jew dyen zigh shir-jung-ting chyen huh nee jyen-myen]
- I have to meet my friend at 9 o'clock 我九点得去见我的朋友 wǒ jiǔ diǎn děi qù jiàn wǒ de péngyou [wo jew dyen day choo jyen wo duh pung-yoh]
- pleased to meet you/delighted to meet you/it was a pleasure meeting you 很高兴见到你 hěn gāoxìng jiàndào nǐ [heun gow-shing jyen-dow nee]
- goodbye! it was nice meeting you 再见！见到你很高兴 zàijiàn!jiàndào nǐ hěn gāoxìng [zigh-jyen jyen-dow nee heun gow-shing]
- Charles, I'd like you to meet Mr. Zhou 查尔斯，我想让你认识一下周先生 chá'ěrsī,wǒ xiǎng ràng nǐ rènshí yī xià zhōu xiānsheng [cha-er-sir wo shyang rang nee reun-shir yee shya joh shyen-shung]
- where shall we meet? 我们该在哪里见面呢？ wǒmen gāi zài nǎli jiànmiàn ne? [wo-meun gigh zigh na-lee jyen-myen nuh]
- what time are we meeting tomorrow? 明天我们什么时候见面？ míngtiān wǒmen shénme shíhou jiànmiàn? [ming-tyen sheun-muh shir-hoh jyen-myen]

member *(of a club)* 会员 huìyuán [hway-ywan]

- do you have to be a member? 必须得是会员吗？ bìxū děi shì huìyuán ma? [bee-shoo day shir hway-ywan ma]

men's room 男厕所 nán cèsuǒ [nan tsuh-swore]

- where's the men's room? 男厕所在哪里？ nán cèsuǒ zài nǎli? [nan-tsuh-swore zigh na-lee]

menu 菜单 càidān [tsigh-dan]

- can we see the menu? 我们能看一下菜单吗？ wǒmen néng kàn yī xià càidān ma? [wo-meun nung kan yee-shyeah tsigh-dan ma]
- do you have a menu in English? 你们有英文版的菜单吗？ nǐmen yǒu yīngwénbǎn de càidān ma? [nee-meun yoh ying-weun-ban duh tsigh-dan ma]
- do you have a children's menu? 你们有儿童菜单吗？ nǐmen yǒu értóng càidān ma? [nee-meun yoh er-tong tsigh-dan ma]

menu

Chinese restaurant menus are often very extensive, with a lot of dishes corresponding to each different way of preparing pork, beef, etc., and with a few changes according to the season or the produce available on the market. Sometimes you will come across menus that have been translated into English or the language of the place the specialties come from (Russian, Japanese, Korean, etc.). It's becoming more common for menus to include photographs of the dishes to give you an idea of what to expect. If you have problems ordering, ask what the restaurant's specialties are, look at what your neighbors are eating, or ask to look at the dishes in the kitchen.

message 信息 xìnxī [shin-shee]

 ▸ can you take a message? 你能捎个信吗? **nǐ néng shāo gè xìn ma?** [nee nung show guh shin ma]

 ▸ can I leave a message? 我能留个话吗? **wǒ néng liú gè huà ma?** [wo nung lew guh hwa ma]

 ▸ did you get my message? 你收到了我给你的留言吗? **nǐ shōudàole wǒ gěi nǐ de liúyán ma?** [nee shoh-dow-luh wo gay nee duh lew-yan ma]

meter *(measurement)* 米 mǐ [mee]; *(device)* 仪表 yíbiǎo [yee-beow]

 ▸ it's about 5 meters long 大约有五米长 **dàyuē yǒu wǔ mǐ cháng** [da-yue yoh woo mee chang]

midday 中午 zhōngwǔ [jong-woo]

 ▸ we have to be there by midday 我们中午前必须到那里 **wǒmen zhōngwǔ qián bìxū dào nàli** [wo-men jong-woo chyen bee-shoo dow na-lee ma]

midnight 半夜十二点 bànyè shí'èr diǎn [ban-yuh shir-er dyen]

 ▸ it's midnight 半夜十二点了 **bànyè shí'èr diǎn le** [ban-yuh shir-er dyen luh]

mileage *(distance)* 英里数 yīnglǐshù [ying-lee-shoo]

 ▸ is there unlimited mileage? 是否有里程数的限制 **shìfǒu yǒu lǐchéngshù de xiànzhì** [shir-foh yoh lee-chung-shoo duh shyen-jir]

milk 牛奶 niúnǎi [new-nigh]

 ▸ a gallon of milk 一加仑牛奶 **yī jiālún niúnǎi** [yee jya-lun new-nigh]

 ▸ tea with milk 加奶的茶 **jiā nǎi de chá** [jya-nigh duh cha]

milk chocolate 牛奶巧克力 niúnǎi qiǎokèlì [new-nigh cheow-kuh-lee]

 ▸ I prefer milk chocolate 我更喜欢牛奶巧克力 **wǒ gèng xǐhuan niúnǎi qiǎokèlì** [wo gung shee-hwan new-nigh cheow-kuh-lee]

mind *(object)* 介意 jièyì [jyeah-yee]

 ▸ I don't mind 我不介意 **wǒ bù jièyì** [wo boo jyeah-yee]

▸ do you mind if I smoke? 我抽烟你介意吗? **wǒ chōuyān nǐ jièyì ma** [wo choh-yan nee jyeah-yee ma]

▸ do you mind if I open the window? 我把窗户打开你介意吗? **wǒ bǎ chuānghu dǎkāi nǐ jièyì ma** [wo ba chwung-hoo da-kigh nee jyeah-yee ma]

▸ never mind 没关系 **méi guānxi** [may gwan-shee]

mineral water 矿泉水 **kuàngquánshuǐ** [kwung-chwan-shway]

▸ could I have a bottle of mineral water, please? 请给我一瓶矿泉水好吗? **qǐng gěi wǒ yī píng kuàngquánshuǐ hǎo ma?** [ching gay wo yee-ping kwung-chwan-shway how ma]

minus 低于 **dīyú** [dee-yoo]

▸ it's minus 2 degrees outside! 外面零下两度! **wàimian líng xià liǎng dù!** [wigh-myen ling-shya lyang doo]

minute 分钟 **fēnzhōng** [feun-jong]

▸ we'll go in a minute 我们马上就走 **wǒmen mǎshàng jiù zǒu** [wo-meun ma-shang jew zoh]

mirror 镜子 **jìngzi** [jing-zir]

▸ the mirror's cracked 镜子碎了 **jìngzi suì le** [jing-zir sway luh]

miss *(be too late for)* 错过 **cuòguò** [cwore-gwore duh]; *(regret the absence of)* 想念 **xiǎngniàn** [shyang-nyen]

▸ I've missed my connection 我错过了我的联运 **wǒ cuòguòle wǒ de liányùn** [wo cwore-gwore-luh wo duh lyang-yun]

▸ we're going to miss the train 我们要错过火车了 **wǒmen yào cuòguò huǒchē le** [wo-meun yow cwore-gwore hwore-chuh luh]

▸ I missed you 我想你 **wǒ xiǎng nǐ** [wo shyang nee]

missing 找不到的 **zhǎo bù dào de** [jow-boo-dow duh]

▸ one of my suitcases is missing 我的一个手提箱找不到了 **wǒ de yī gè shǒutíxiāng zhǎo bù dào le** [wo duh yee-guh shoh-tee-shyang jow-boo-dow luh]

mistake 错误 **cuòwù** [cwore-woo]

▸ I think there's a mistake with the bill 我想这个账单有误 **wǒ xiǎng zhège zhàngdān yǒu wù** [wo shyang juh-guh jang-dan yoh woo]

▸ you've made a mistake with my change 你给我的找零不对 **nǐ gěi wǒ de zhǎolíng bù duì** [nee gay wo duh jow-ling boo dway]

moment 目前 **mùqián** [moo-chyen]

▸ for the moment, we prefer staying in Beijing 目前我们更想呆在北京 **mùqián wǒmen gèng xiǎng dāi zài běijīng** [moo-chyen wo-meun gung shyang digh zigh bay-jing]

Monday 星期一 **xīngqīyī** [shing-chee-yee]

▸ we're arriving/leaving on Monday 我们星期一到/离开 **wǒmen xīngqīyī dào/líkāi** [wo-meun shing-chee-yee dow/lee-kigh]

morning

There are many words for morning, depending on the specific time. 早晨 zăochen [zow-chun] is the very early morning (just after sunrise), 早上 zăoshang [zow-shang] means the early morning, and 上午 shàngwǔ [shang-woo] means the morning (before noon). In the morning you can say hello by adding 好 hăo [how] to the end of one of these expressions (literally 'good morning').

money 钱 qián [chyen]

- where can I change money? 我去哪里可以换钱? wǒ qù nǎli kěyǐ huànqián? [wo choo na-lee kuh-yee hwan chyen]
- I want my money back 我想拿回我的钱 wǒ xiǎng náhui wǒ de qián [wo shyang na hway wo duh chyen]

money order 汇票 huìpiào [hway-peow]

- I'm waiting for a money order 我在等汇票 wǒ zài děng huìpiào [wo zigh dung hway-peow]

month 月 yuè [yue]

- I'm leaving in a month 我一个月后离开 wǒ yī gè yuè hòu líkāi [wo yee-guh yue hoh lee-kigh]

monument 纪念碑 jìniànbēi [jee-nyen-bay]

- what does this monument commemorate? 这个纪念杯是纪念什么的? zhège jìniànbēi shì jìniàn shénme de? [juh-guh jee-nyen-bay jee-nyen sheun-muh duh]

more 更 gèng [gung] ♦ 更多的 gèng duō de [gung-dwore duh] ♦ *(greater amount or number)* 更多 gèng duō [gung-dwore]; *(additional amount)* 额外 éwài [uh-wigh]

- can we have some more bread? 能再给我们一些面包吗? néng zài gěi wǒmen yīxiē miànbāo ma? [nung zigh gay wo-meun yee-shyeah myen-bow ma]
- a little more 再多一点儿 zài duō yīdiǎnr [zigh dwore yee-dyenr]
- could I have a little more wine? 能再给我来点儿葡萄酒吗? néng zài gěi wǒ lái diǎnr pútaojiǔ ma? [nung zigh gay wo ligh dyen poo-tow-jew ma]
- I don't want any more, thank you 我够了，谢谢 wǒ gòu le, xièxie [wo goh luh shyeah shyeah]
- I don't want to spend any more 我不想再花更多的钱了 wǒ bù xiǎng zài huā gèng duō de qián le [wo boo shyang zigh hwa gung dwore duh chyen]

morning 早上 zăoshang [zow-shang]; *(expressing duration)* 上午 shàngwǔ [shang-woo]

- the museum is open in the morning 博物馆上午开门 bówùguǎn shàngwǔ kāimén [bo-woo-gwan shang-woo kigh-meun]

morning-after pill 紧急避孕药 jǐnjí bìyùnyào [jin-jee bee-yun-yow]

▸ I need the morning-after pill 我需要紧急避孕药 wǒ xūyào jǐnjí bìyùnyào [wo shoo-yow jin-jee bee-yun-yow]

mosque 清真寺 qīngzhēnsì [ching-jeun-sir]

▸ where's the nearest mosque? 最近的清真寺在哪里? zuì jìn de qīngzhēnsì zài nǎli? [zway-jin duh ching-jeun-sir zigh na-lee]

most *(the majority of)* 大部分的 dàbùfen de [da-boo-fen duh]; *(the largest amount of)* 最多的 zuì duō de [zway dwore duh] ◆ *(the majority)* 大多数 dàduōshù [da-dwore-shoo]; *(the largest amount)* 最多 zuì duō [zway dwore] ◆ *(to the greatest extent)* 最 zuì [zway]; *(very)* 很 hěn [heun]

▸ are you here most days? 你大多数时候都在这里吗? nǐ dàduōshù shíhou dōu zài zhèli ma? [nee da dwore shoo shir-hoh doh zigh juh-lee]

▸ that's the most I can offer 那是我能给的最高价了 nà shì wǒ néng gěi de zuì gāo jià le [na shir wo nung gay duh zway-gow jya luh]

mother 母亲 mǔqin [moo-chin], 妈妈 māma [ma-ma]

▸ this is my mother 这是我的母亲 zhè shì wǒ de mǔqin [juh shir wo duh moo-chin], 这是我的妈妈 zhè shì wǒ de māma [juh shir wo duh ma-ma]

motorboat 摩托艇 mótuǒtǐng [mo-twore-ting]

▸ can we rent a motorboat? 我们能租摩托艇吗? wǒmen néng zū mótuǒtǐng ma? [wo-meun nung zoo mo-twore-ting ma]

motorcycle 摩托车 mótuǒchē [twore-chuh]

▸ I'd like to rent a motorcycle 我想租一辆摩托车 wǒ xiǎng zū yī liàng mótuǒchē [wo shyang zoo yee-lyang mo-twore-chuh]

mountain 山 shān [shan]

▸ in the mountains 在山上 zài shān shang [zigh shan shang]

mountain hut 山间小屋 shānjiān xiǎowū [shan-jyen sheow-woo]

▸ we slept in a mountain hut 我们睡在一个山间小屋里 wǒmen shuì zài yī gè shānjiān xiǎowū li [wo-meun shway zigh yee-guh shan-jyen sheow-woo lee]

mouth 嘴 zuǐ [zway]

▸ I've got a strange taste in my mouth 我嘴巴里有一种奇怪的味道 wǒ zuǐba li yǒu yī zhǒng qíguài de wèidao [wo zway-ba li yoh yee jong chee-gwigh duh way-dow]

move *(movement)* 变动 biàndòng [byen-dong]; *(step, measure)* 行动 xíngdòng [shing-dong] ◆ 移动 yídòng [yee-dong]

▸ I can't move my leg 我的腿动不了了 wǒ de tuǐ dòng bù liǎo le [wo duh tway dong boo leow luh]

▸ don't move him 不要移动他 bùyào yídòng tā [boo-yow yee-dong ta]

movie 电影 diànyǐng [dyen-ying]

▸ have you seen ...'s latest movie? 你看过......的最新的电影吗? nǐ

kànguo......de zuì xīn de diànyǐng ma? [nee kan gwore...duh zway-shin duh dyen-ying ma]

▸ it's a subtitled movie 这是一部带有字幕的电影 zhè shì yī bù dàiyǒu zìmù de diànyǐng [juh-shir yee-boo digh yoh zir-moo duh dyen-ying]

movie theater 电影院 diànyǐngyuàn [dyen-ying-ywan]

▸ where is there a movie theater? 电影院在哪里? diànyǐngyuàn zài nǎli? [dyen-ying-ywan zigh na-lee]

▸ what's on at the movie theater? 那个电影院在上映什么片子? nàge diànyǐngyuàn zài shàngyìng shénme piānzi? [na-guh dian-ying-ywan zigh shang-ying sheun-muh pyen-zir]

much 大量的 dàliàng de [da-lyang duh] ◆ 大量 dàliàng [da-lyang] ◆ *(considerably)* ......得多 ......de duō [duh dwore]; *(often)* 经常 jīngcháng [jing-chang]

▸ I don't have much money 我没有很多钱 wǒ méiyou hěn duō qián [wo may-yoh heun dwore chyen]

▸ how much is it? 这个多少钱? zhège duōshao qián? [juh-guh dwore-show chyen]

▸ how much is it for one night? 一个晚上多少钱? yī gè wǎnshang duōshao qián? [yee-guh wan-shang dwore-show chyen]

▸ how much is it per day and per person? 一个人一天多少钱? yī gè rén yī tiān duōshao qián? [yee-guh reun yee-tyen dwore-show]

▸ how much does it cost per hour? 一个小时多少钱? yī gè xiǎoshí duōshao qián? [yee-guh sheow-shir dwore-show chyen]

▸ how much is a ticket to Beijing? 去北京的票多少钱? qù běijīng de piào duōshao qián? [choo bay-jing duh peow dwore-show chyen]

museum 博物馆 bówùguǎn [bo-woo-gwan]

▸ what time does the museum open? 博物馆什么时候开门? bówùguǎn shénme shíhou kāimén? [bo-woo-gwan sheun-muh shir-hoh kigh-meun]

music 音乐 yīnyuè [yin-yue]

▸ what kind of music do they play in that club? 在那家夜总会里他们放什么样的音乐? zài nà jiā yèzǒnghuì li tāmen fàng shénmeyàng de yīnyuè? [zigh na jya yuh-zong-hway lee ta-meun fang sheun-muh-yang duh yin-yue]

must 一定 yīdìng [yee-ding]

▸ that must cost a lot 那一定很贵 nà yīdìng hěn guì [na yee-ding heun gway]

mustard 芥末 jièmo [jyeah-mo]

▸ is it strong mustard? 那是很辣的芥末吗? nà shì hěn là de jièmo ma? [na-shir heun la duh jyeah-mo ma]

n

nail *(on a finger, a toe)* 指甲 zhǐjia [jir-jya]

▸ I need to cut my nails 我该剪指甲了 wǒ gāi jiǎn zhǐjia le [wo gigh jyen jir-jya luh]

nail polish 指甲油 zhǐjiayóu [jir-jya-yoh]

▸ I'd like to find nail polish in a dark shade of red 我想要深红色的指甲油 wǒ xiǎng yào shēnhóngsè de zhǐjiayóu [wo shyang yow sheun-hong-suh duh jir-jya-yoh]

name 姓名 xìngmíng [shing-ming]

▸ what is your name? 你叫什么名字？ nǐ jiào shénme míngzi? [nee jeow sheun-muh ming-zir]

▸ my name is Patrick 我的名字叫帕特里克 wǒ de míngzi jiào pàtèlǐkè [wo duh ming-zir jeow pa-tuh-lee-kuh]

▸ hello, my name's John 你好，我叫约翰 nǐ hǎo, wǒ jiào yuēhàn [nee how wo jeow yue-han]

▸ I have a reservation in the name of Jackson 我用杰克逊的名字预定过 了 wǒ yòng jiékèxùn de míngzi yùdìngguo le [wo yong jyeah-kuh-shun duh ming-zir yoo-ding-gwore luh]

napkin 餐巾 cānjīn [tsan-jin]

▸ could I have a clean napkin, please? 请给我一块干净的餐巾好吗？ qǐng gěi wǒ yī kuài gānjìng de cānjīn hǎo ma? [ching gay wo yee-kwigh gan-jing duh tsan-jin how ma]

---

names

Generally, Chinese names are made up of a character for the family name (which comes first) followed by one or two characters for the given name. As Chinese characters are each a single syllable, it is easy to pronounce a whole name as it is often made up of only two or three syllables. Except with family and friends, it is polite to call someone by his or her family name followed by 'Mr.' 先生 xiānsheng [shyen-shung], 'Mrs.' 太太 tàitai [tigh-tigh] or 女士 nǚshì [nooh-shir], or 'Miss' 小姐 xiǎojie [sheow-jyeah]. It is also possible to use a title after the family name, such as 'Teacher' 老师 lǎoshī [low-shir], 'Manager' 经理 jīnglǐ [jing-lee], all of which have replaced the once-common 'comrade' 同志 tóngzhì [tong-jir]. You should avoid calling someone by their given name alone, as this is usually considered impolite.

national holiday 法定假日 fǎdìng jiàrì [fa-ding jya-rir]
- tomorrow is a national holiday 明天是法定假日 míngtiān shì fǎdìng jiàrì [ming-tyen shir fa-ding jya-rir]

nationality 国籍 guójí [gwore-jee]
- what nationality are you? 你的国籍是什么？ nǐ de guójí shì shénme? [nee duh gwore-jee shir sheun-muh]

nature (plants and animals) 大自然 dàzìrán [da zir-ran]; (essential qualities) 特点 tèdiǎn [tuh-dyen]; (character) 本性 běnxìng [beun-shing]
- I like to take long walks outdoors and enjoy nature 我想去户外走得久一些，享受大自然 wǒ xiǎng qù hùwài zǒu de jiǔ yīxiē,xiǎngshòu dàzìrán [wo shyang choo hoo-wigh zoh duh jew yee-shyeah shyang shoh da-zir-ran]

nausea 恶心 ěxīn [uh-shin]
- I've had nausea all day 我一整天都感到恶心 wǒ yī zhěng tiān dōu gǎndào ěxīn [wo yee jung tyen doh gan-dow uh-shin]

near (in space) 近的 jìn de [jin duh] ◆ (in space) 靠近 kàojìn [kow-jin]
- where's the nearest subway station? 最近的地铁站在哪里？ zuì jìn de dìtiězhàn zài nǎli? [zway-jin duh dee-tyeah-jan zigh na-lee]
- it's near the railway station 它在火车站附近 tā zài huǒchēzhàn fùjìn [ta zigh hwore-chuh-jan foo-jin]
- very near ... 离......很近 lí......hěn jìn [lee...heun jin]

nearby 在附近 zài fùjìn [zigh foo-jin]
- is there a supermarket nearby? 附近有超市吗？ fùjìn yǒu chāoshì ma? [foo-jin yoh chow-shir ma]

neck 脖子 bózi [bo-zir]
- I have a sore neck 我脖子疼 wǒ bózi téng [wo bo-zir tung]

need 需求 xūqiú [shoo-chew] ◆ 需要 xūyào [shoo-yow] ◆ 必须 bìxū [bee-shoo]
- I need something for a cough 我需要治咳嗽的药 wǒ xūyào zhì késou de yào [wo shoo-yow jir kuh-soh duh yow]
- I need to be at the airport by six (o'clock) 我得在六点前到机场 wǒ děi zài liù diǎn qián dào jīchǎng [wo duh zigh lew dyen chyen dow jee-chang]
- we need to go 我们得走了 wǒmen děi zǒu le [wo-meun bee-shoo day zoh luh]

neither 两者都不 liǎngzhě dōu bù [lyang-juh doh boo] ◆ 也不 yě bù [yuh-boo]
- neither of us 我们两人都不 wǒmen liǎng rén dōu bù [wo-meun lyang reun doh boo]
- me neither 我也不 wǒ yě bù [wo yuh boo]

neutral 空挡 kōngdǎng [kong-dang]
- make sure the car's in neutral 确保把排挡放在空挡的位置 quèbǎo bǎ páidǎng fàng zài kōngdǎng de wèizhi [chue-bow ba pigh-dang fang zigh kong-dang duh way-jir]

newspapers

Most of the big international newspapers can be bought in the luxury hotels but not from kiosks in the street. There are Chinese daily papers in English, such as the *China Daily*, 中国日报 zhōngguó rìbào [jong-gwore rir-bow]. This is often delivered free of charge to your hotel room.

never 从不 cóng bù [tsong-boo]
▸ I've never been to this part of China before 我过去从来没有来过中国的这个地方 wǒ guòqù cónglái méiyou láiguo zhōngguó de zhège difang [wo gwore-choo tsong-ligh may-yoh ligh-gwore jong-gwore duh juh-guh dee-fang]

new 新的 xīn de [shin duh]; *(recently arrived)* 刚到的 gāng dào de [gang dow duh]; *(unfamiliar)* 生疏的 shēngshū de [shung-shoo duh]
▸ could we have a new tablecloth, please? 请给我们一块新桌布好吗? qǐng gěi wǒmen yī kuài xīn zhuóbù hǎo ma? [ching gay wo-meun yee-kwigh shin jwore-boo how ma]

news *(information)* 消息 xiāoxi [sheow-shee]; *(on TV, radio)* 新闻 xīnwén [shin-weun]
▸ a piece of news 一则新闻 yī zé xīnwén [yee-zuh shin-weun]
▸ that's great news! 真是好消息! zhēn shì hǎo xiāoxi! [jeun shir how sheow-shee]
▸ I heard it on the news 我是从新闻中得知的 wǒ shì cóng xīnwén zhōng dézhī de [wo shir tsong shin-weun jong duh-jir duh]

newspaper 报纸 bàozhǐ [bow-jir]
▸ do you have any English-language newspapers? 你有英文报纸吗? nǐ yǒu yīngwén bàozhǐ ma? [nee yoh ying-weun bow-jir ma]

New Year 新年 xīnnián [shin-nyen]
▸ Happy New Year! 新年快乐! xīnnián kuàilè! [shin-nyen kwigh luh]

New Year's Day 元旦 yuándàn [ywan-dan]
▸ are stores open on New Year's Day? 商店在元旦那天开门吗? shāngdiàn zài yuándàn nà tiān kāimén ma? [shang-dyen zigh ywan-da na tyen kigh-meun ma]

next 下一个的 xià yī gè de [shya yee-guh duh] ◆ **next to** 在......的旁边 zài......de pángbiān [zigh...duh pang-byen]
▸ when is the next guided tour? 下一个有导游讲解的观光在什么时候? xia yī gè yǒu dǎoyóu jiǎngjiě de guānguāng zài shénme shíhou? [shya yee-guh yoh dow-yoh jyang-jyeah duh gwan-gwung zigh sheun-muh shir-hoh]
▸ when is the next train to Beijing? 下一趟去北京的火车是几点? xià yī tàng qù běijīng de huǒchē shì jǐ diǎn? [shya yee-tang choo bay-jing duh hwore-chuh shir jee dyen]

▸ what time is the next flight to London? 下一班去伦敦的飞机是几点？ xià yī bān qù lúndūn de fēijī shì jǐ diǎn? [shya yee ban choo lun-dun duh fay-jee shir jee-dyen]

▸ can we park next to the tent? 我们可以把车停在帐篷的旁边吗？ wǒmen kěyǐ bǎ chē tíng zài zhàngpeng de pángbiān ma? [wo-meun kuh-yee ba chuh ting zigh jang-peng duh pang-byen ma]

nice (vacation, food) 好的 hǎo de [how duh]; (kind) 友好的 yóuhǎo de [yoh-how duh]; (likable) 可爱的 kě'ài de [kuh-igh duh]

▸ have a nice vacation! 祝你假日快乐！ zhù nǐ jiàrì kuàilè! [joo nee jya-rir kwigh luh]

▸ we found a really nice little hotel 我们找到了一个非常棒的旅店 wǒmen zhǎodàole yī gè fēicháng bàng de lǚdiàn [wo-meun jow-dow luh yee-guh fay-chang bang duh looh-dyen]

▸ goodbye! it was nice meeting you 再见！见到你很高兴 zàijiàn!jiàndào nǐ hěn gāoxìng [zigh-jyen jyen-dow nee heun gow-shing]

night 晚上 wǎnshang [wan-shang]

▸ how much is it per night? 一个晚上多少钱？ yī gè wǎnshang duōshao qián? [yee-guh wan-shang dwore-show chyen]

▸ I'd like to stay an extra night 我想再多住一个晚上 wǒ xiǎng zài duō zhù yī gè wǎnshang [wo shyang zigh dwore joo yee-guh wan-shang]

nightclub 夜总会 yèzǒnghuì [yuh-zong-hway]

▸ are there any good nightclubs in this town? 这个城市里有什么不错的夜总会？ zhège chéngshì lǐ yǒu shénme bùcuò de yèzǒnghuì ma? [juh-guh chung-shir li yoh sheun-muh boo-cwore duh yuh-zong-hway ma]

nine 九 jiǔ [jew]

▸ there are nine of us 我们有九个人 wǒmen yǒu jiǔ gè rén [wo-meun yoh jew-guh reun]

▸ we have a reservation for nine (o'clock) 我们九点钟有个预约 wǒmen jiǔ diǎnzhōng yǒu gè yùyuē [wo-meun jew dyen-jong yoh guh yoo-yue]

no 不是的 bù shì de [boo-shir duh] ♦ 不 bù [boo]

▸ no thanks! 不，谢谢！ bù, xièxiè! [boo shyeah-shyeah]

▸ a cup of tea with no milk or sugar, please 请来一杯不加奶和糖的咖啡 qǐng lái yī bēi bù jiā nǎi hé táng de kāfēi [ching ligh yee-bay boo jya nigh huh tang duh ka-fay]

nobody 没有人 méiyou rén [may-yoh reun]

▸ there's nobody at the reception desk 接待处没有人 jiēdàichù méiyou rén [jyeah-digh-choo may-yoh reun]

noise 噪音 zàoyīn [zow-yin]

▸ to make a noise 制造噪音 zhìzào zàoyīn [jir-zow zow-yin]

noodles

Noodles are one of the cornerstones of Chinese cuisine. They are often eaten in the North of China (the 'China of wheat' rather than the 'China of rice' in the South). They can be made in different sizes, and either served in broth or fried. Try to find restaurants where experienced chefs will amaze you with their dexterity as they stretch the dough.

▸ I heard a funny noise 我听到奇怪的噪音声 wǒ tīngdào qíguài de zàoyīnshēng [wo ting-dow chee-gwigh duh zow-yin-shung]

noisy 吵闹的 chǎonào de [chow-now duh]

▸ I'd like another room: mine is too noisy 我想换一间房间，我的房间太吵了 wǒ xiǎng huàn yī jiān fángjiān, wǒ de fángjiān tài chǎo le [wo shyang hwan yee-jyen fang-jyen wo duh fang-jyen tigh chow luh]

nonsmoker 不吸烟的人 bù xīyān de rén [boo shee-yan duh reun]

▸ we're nonsmokers 我们不吸烟 wǒmen bù xīyān [wo-meun boo shee-yan]

nonsmoking 不吸烟的 bù xīyān de [boo shee-yan duh]

▸ is this restaurant nonsmoking? 这个餐馆禁烟吗？ zhège cānguǎn jìnyān ma? [juh-guh tsan-gwan jin-yan ma]

nonsmoking compartment 非吸烟车厢 fēixīyān chēxiāng [fay-shee-yan chuh-shyang]

▸ I'd like a seat in a nonsmoking compartment 我想要一个在非吸烟车厢里的座位 wǒ xiǎng yào yī gè zài fēixīyān chēxiāng li de zuòwei [wo shyang yow yee guh zigh fay shee-yan chuh-shyang lee duh zwore-way]

nonsmoking section 非吸烟区 fēixīyānqū [fay shee-yan choo]

▸ do you have a nonsmoking section? 你们有非吸烟区吗？ nǐmen yǒu fēixīyānqū ma? [nee-meun yoh fay-shee-yan-choo ma]

nonstop 直达的 zhídá de [jir-da duh] ♦ 不停地 bù tíng de [boo-ting duh]

▸ I'd like a nonstop flight from Beijing to Shanghai 我想要从北京到上海的直达航班 wǒ xiǎng yào cóng běijīng dào shànghǎi de zhídá hángbān [wo shyang yow tsong bay-jing dow shang-high jir-da duh hang-ban]

noodles 面条 miàntiáo [myen-teow]

▸ I'd like some noodles, please 我要面条 wǒ yào miàntiáo [wo yow myen-teow]

noon 中午 zhōngwǔ [jong-woo]

▸ we leave at noon 我们中午出发 wǒmen zhōngwǔ chūfā [wo-meun jong-woo choo-fa]

no one 没有人 méiyou rén [may-yoh reun]

▸ there's no one there 那里没有人 nàli méiyou rén [na-lee may-yoh reun]

telephone numbers

In China, when you give a telephone number you pronounce each figure separately, one by one. The number one, in this case, is pronounced [yow]. So, for example, the telephone number for the police is pronounced [yow-yow-ling] (110).

normal 正常的 zhèngcháng de [jung-chang duh] ◆ 正常 zhèngcháng [jung-chang]

▸ is it normal for it to rain as much as this? 下这么大的雨正常吗？ xià zhème dà de yǔ zhèngcháng ma? [shya juh-muh da duh yoo jung-chang ma]

not 不 bù [boo]

▸ I don't like spinach 我不喜欢菠菜 wǒ bù xǐhuan bōcài [wo boo shee-hwan bo-tsigh]

▸ I don't think so 我不这么认为 wǒ bù zhème rènwéi [wo boo jeun-muh reun-way]

▸ not at all 一点儿也不 yīdiǎnr yě bù [yee-dyen yuh boo]

note 便条 biàntiáo [byen-teow]

▸ could I leave a note for him? 我能给他留个便条吗？ wǒ néng gěi tā liú gè biàntiáo ma? [wo nung gay ta lew guh byen-teow ma]

nothing 没什么 méi shénme [may sheun-muh]

▸ there's nothing to do here in the evening 晚上这里没有任何事情可做 wǎnshang zhèli méiyou rènhé shìqing kě zuò [wan-shang shir-lee may-yoh reun-huh shir-ching kuh zwore]

▸ there's nothing I can do about it 我对此无能为力 wǒ duì cǐ wú néng wéi lì [wo dway tsir woo-nung-way-lee]

November 十一月 shíyī yuè [shir-yee yue]

▸ November 7th 十一月七日 shíyī yuè qī rì [shir yee yue chee rir]

now 现在 xiànzài [shyen-zigh]

▸ what should we do now? 我们现在该干什么？ wǒmen xiànzài gāi gàn shénme? [wo-meun shyen-zigh gigh gan sheun-muh]

number *(of a phone, a car, a room, an apartment)* 号 hào [how]; *(numeral)* 数字 shùzì [shoo-zir]; *(quantity)* 数量 shùliàng [shoo-lyang]

▸ my name is... and my number is... 我的名字是......，我的电话号码是...... wǒ de míngzi shì......wǒ de diànhuà hàomǎ shì...... [wo duh ming-zir shir...wo duh dyen-hwa how-ma shir]

occupied *(bathroom)* 有人的 yǒu rén de [yoh-reun duh]
- the restroom's occupied 洗手间有人 xǐshǒujiān yǒu rén [shee-shoh-jyen yoh reun]

ocean 海洋 hǎiyáng [high-yang]
- we'd like to see the ocean while we're here 我们想趁在这里的时候去看海 wǒmen xiǎng chèn zài zhèlǐ de shíhou qù kàn hǎi [wo-meun shyang cheun zigh juh-lee duh shir-hoh choo kan high]

o'clock
- it's eight o'clock 现在是8点钟 xiànzài shì bā diǎnzhōng [shyen-zigh shir ba dyen-jong]

October 十月 shí yuè [shir yue]
- October 12th 十月十二日 shí yuè shí'èr rì [shir yue shir-er rir]

of 属于 shǔyú [shoo-yoo]
- one of us 我们中的一个 wǒmen zhōng de yī gè [wo-meun jong duh yee-guh]

off *(indicating movement)* 离开 líkāi [lee-kigh] ♦ *(at a distance from)* 距 jù [joo]; *(deducted from)* 扣除 kòuchú [koh-choo]
- an island off the coast of Fujian 福建海岸边的一座岛屿 fújiàn hǎi'àn biān de yī zuò dǎoyǔ [foo-jyen high-an byen duh yee-zwore dow-yoo]
- this sweater is fifty percent off! 这件毛衣减价百分之五十 zhè jiàn máoyī jiǎnjià bǎifénzhī wǔshí [juh jyen mow-yee jyen-jya bigh-fen-jir woo-shir]

offer 给 gěi [gay]
- can I offer you a cigarette? 你要来根香烟吗? nǐ yào lái gēn xiāngyān ma? [nee yow ligh geun shyang-yan ma]

office 办公室 bàngōngshì [ban-gong-shir]
- where is the hotel office? 旅馆的办公室在哪里? lǚguǎn de bàngōngshì zài nǎli? [looh-gwan duh ban-gong-shir zigh na-lee]

often 经常 jīngcháng [jing-chang]
- how often does the ferry sail? 渡船多久有一班? dùchuán duō jiǔ yǒu yī bān? [doo-chwan dwore jew yoh yee-ban]

oil 汽油 qìyóu [chee-yoh]
- could you check the oil, please? 请你检查一下汽油好吗? qǐng nǐ jiǎnchá yī xià qìyóu hǎo ma? [ching nee jyen-cha yee-shya chee-yoh how ma]

OK 好的 hǎo de [how duh] ◆ 好 hǎo [how]

▸ that's OK 没关系 méi guānxi [may gwan-shee]

▸ do you think it's OK? 你认为那可以吗？ nǐ rènwéi nà kěyǐ ma? [nee reun-way na kuh-yee ma]

old (in discussing age) 年龄的 niánlíng de [nyen-ling duh]; (not young) 老的 lǎo de [low duh]; (not new) 旧的 jiù de [jew duh]

▸ how old are you? 你几岁了？ nǐ jǐ suì le? [nee jee sway luh]

▸ I'm 18 years old 我18岁 wǒ shíbā suì [wo shir-ba sway]

▸ have you visited the old town? 你参观过老城吗？ nǐ cānguānguo lǎochéng ma? [nee tsan-gwan-gwore low chung ma]

on (working) 打开的 dǎkāi de [da-kigh duh]; (happening) 进行的 jìnxíng de [jin-shing duh]

▸ how long is it on for? 它会持续多久？ tā huì chíxù duō jiǔ? [ta hway chir-shoo dwore jew]

once (on one occasion) 一次 yī cì [yee-tsir]; (previously) 曾经 céngjīng [tsung-jin] ◆ at once 立刻 lìkè [lee-kuh]

▸ I've been here once before 我曾经来过一次这里 wǒ céngjīng láiguo yī cì zhèli [wo tsung-jing ligh gwore yee-tsir juh-lee]

one 一 yī [yee]

▸ a table for one, please 请给一张一个人的桌子 qǐng gěi yī zhāng yī gè rén de zhuōzi [ching gay yee jang yee guh reun duh jwore-zir]

one-way (ticket) 单程（票） dānchéng(piào) [dan-chung peow]

▸ how much is a one-way ticket downtown? 去市区的单程票多少钱？ qù shìqū de dānchéngpiào duōshao qián? [choo shir-choo duh dan-chuh-peow dwore-chow chyen]

▸ a second-class one-way ticket to Beijing 一张去北京二等座位的单程票 yī zhāng qù běijīng èrděng zuòwei de dānchéngpiào [yee jang choo bay-jing er-dung zwore-way duh dan-chung-peow]

only 唯一的 wéiyī de [way-yee duh]

▸ that's the only one left 那是剩下的唯一的一个 nà shì shèngxia de wéiyī de yī gè [na-shir shung-shya duh way-yee duh yee guh]

open (door, window) 开着的 kāizhe de [kigh-juh duh]; (store) 营业的 yíngyè de [ying-yuh duh] ◆ (door, window) 打开 dǎkāi [da-kigh] ◆ (door, window) 开 kāi [kigh]; (store) 营业 yíngyè [ying-yuh]

▸ is the bank open at lunchtime? 银行午餐时间营业吗？ yínháng wǔcān shíjiān yíngyè ma? [yin-hang woo-tsan shir-jyen ying-yuh ma]

▸ is the museum open all day? 博物馆天天开放吗？ bówùguǎn quántiān kāifàng ma? [bo-woo-gwan chwan-tyen kigh-fang ma]

▸ at what time is ... open? ......什么时候开门？ ......shénme shíhou kāimén? [...sheun-muh shir-hoh kigh-meun]

▸ can I open the window? 我能把窗户打开吗? wǒ néng bǎ chuānghu dǎkāi ma? [wo mung bao chwung-hoo da-kigh ma]

▸ what time do you open? 你们几点钟开门? nǐmen jǐ diǎnzhōng kāimén? [nee-meun jee dyen-jong kigh-meun]

open-air 露天的 lùtiān de [loo-tyen duh]

▸ is there an open-air swimming pool? 有露天游泳池吗? yǒu lùtiān yóuyǒngchí ma? [yoh loo-tyen yoh-yong-chir ma]

operating room 手术室 shǒushùshì [shoh-shoo-shir]

▸ is she still in the operating room? 她还在手术室里吗? tā hái zài shǒushùshì li ma? [ta high zigh shoh-shoo-shir lee ma]

opinion 观点 guāndiǎn [gwan-dyen]

▸ in my opinion, … 依我看来,...... yī wǒ kàn lái,...... [yee wo kan ligh]

orange 橙色的 chéngsè de [chung-suh duh] ◆ (fruit) 橙子 chéngzi [chung-zir]

▸ I'd like a kilo of oranges 我要一公斤的橙子 wǒ yào yī gōngjīn de chéngzi [wo yow yee gong-jin duh chung-zir]

orange juice 橙汁 chéngzhī [chung-jir]

▸ I'll have a glass of orange juice 我要一杯橙汁 wǒ yào yī bēi chéngzhī [wo yow yee-bay chung-jir]

▸ I'd like a freshly squeezed orange juice 我要一杯现榨的橙汁 wǒ yào yī bēi xiànzhà de chéngzhī [wo yow yee-bay shyen-ja duh chung-jir]

order (in a restaurant, a café) 点菜 diǎn cài [dyen-tsigh]; (by mail) 定购 dìnggòu [ding-goh]

▸ this isn't what I ordered: I asked for… 这不是我点的菜, 我点的是...... zhè bù shì wǒ diǎn de cài, wǒ diǎn de shì...... [juh-guh boo-shir wo dyen de tsigh wo dyen duh shir]

▸ I ordered a coffee 我点了咖啡 wǒ diǎnle kāfēi [wo dyen-luh ka-fay]

---

opinions

▸ personally, I don't think it's fair 我个人认为那不公平 wǒ gèrén rènwéi nà bù gōngpíng [wo guh-reun reun-way na boo gong-ping]

▸ I think he's right 我想他是对的 wǒ xiǎng tā shì duì de [wo shyang ta shir dway duh]

▸ I don't want to say 我不想说 wǒ bù xiǎng shuō [wo boo shyang shwore]

▸ I'm not sure 我不确定 wǒ bù quèdìng [wo boo chue-ding]

▸ no idea! 不知道! bù zhīdao! [boo jir-dow]

▸ it depends 要看情况而定 yào kàn qíngkuàng ér dìng [yow kan ching-kwung er-ding]

> we'd like to order now 我们想现在点菜 wǒmen xiǎng xiànzài diǎn cài [wo shyang shyen-zigh dyen tsigh]

organize 安排 ānpái [an-pigh]

> can you organize the whole trip for us? 你能为我们安排整个行程吗？ nǐ néng wèi wǒmen ānpái zhěnggè xíngchéng ma? [nee nung way wo-meun an-pigh jeun-guh shing-chung ma]

other *(different)* 其他的 qítā de [chee-ta duh]; *(second of two)* 另一个的 lìng yī gè de [ling yee-guh] ◆ 另一个 lìng yī gè [ling yee-guh]

> I'll have the other one 我要另外的那一个 wǒ yào lìngwài de nà yī gè [wo yow ling-wigh duh na yee guh]

> on the other side of the street 在街道的另一边 zài jiēdào de lìng yībiān [zigh jyeah-dow duh ling yee-byen]

> go ahead; I'm going to wait for the others 你们往前走吧，我等剩下的人 nǐmen wǎng qián zǒu ba, wǒ děng shèngxia de rén [nee-meun wang chyen zoh ba wo dung sheung-shya duh reun]

out-of-date 过期的 guòqī de [gwore-chee duh]

> I think my passport is out-of-date 我想我的护照过期了 wǒ xiǎng wǒ de hùzhào guòqī le [wo shyang wo duh hoo-jow gwore-chee luh]

outside call 外线电话 wàixiàn diànhuà [da wigh-shyen dyen-hwa]

> I'd like to make an outside call 我想打外线 wǒ xiǎng dǎ wàixiàn [wo shyang da wigh-shyen]

outside line 外线 wàixiàn [wigh-shyen]

> how do you get an outside line? 如何打外线呢？ rúhé dǎ wàixiàn ne? [roo-huh da wigh-shyen nuh]

overheat 变得过热 biàn de guò rè [byen duh gwore ruh]

> the engine is overheating 发动机过热了 fādòngjī guò rè le [fa-dong-jee gwore ruh luh]

owner 物主 wùzhǔ [woo-joo]

> do you know who the owner is? 你知道谁是物主吗？ nǐ zhīdao shéi shì wùzhǔ ma? [nee jir-dow shay shir woo-joo ma]

p

pack *(of cigarettes, chewing gum)* 包 bāo [bow] ♦ *(for a trip)* 收拾行李 shōushi xíngli [show-shir shing-lee]

▸ how much is a pack of cigarettes? 一包香烟多少钱？ yī bāo xiāngyān duōshao qián? [yee bow shyang-yan dwore-show chyen]

▸ I need to pack 我得收拾行李了 wǒ děi shōushi xíngli le [wo day show-shir shing-lee luh]

package *(wrapped object)* 包裹 bāoguǒ [bow-gwore]; *(of butter)* 盒 hé [huh]; *(vacation deal)* 跟团旅游 gēn tuán lǚyóu [geun twan looh-yoh]

▸ I'd like to send this package to Boston by airmail 我想把这个包裹用航空邮件寄往波士顿 wǒ xiǎng bǎ zhège bāoguǒ yòng hángkōng yóujiàn jìwǎng bōshìdùn [wo shyang ban juh-guh bow-gwore yong hang-kong yoh-jyen jee-wang bo-shir-dun]

▸ do you have weekend packages? 你们有周末的团队旅游吗？ nǐmen yǒu zhōumò de tuánduì lǚyóu ma? [nee-meun yoh joh-moh twan-dway looh-yoh ma]

package tour 跟团旅行 gēn tuán lǚxíng [geun twan looh-shing]

▸ it's my first time on a package tour 这是我第一次跟团旅行 zhè shì wǒ dì-yī cì gēn tuán lǚxíng [juh shir wo dee-yee tsir geun twan looh-shing]

padlock 挂锁 guàsuǒ [gwa-swore]

▸ I'd like to buy a padlock for my bike 我想买一把挂锁锁我的自行车 wǒ xiǎng mǎi yī bǎ guàsuǒ suǒ wǒ de zìxíngchē [wo shyang migh yee ba gwa-swore swore wo duh zir-shing-chuh]

pain *(physical)* 疼 téng [teung]

▸ I'd like something for the pain 我想要一些止疼的东西 wǒ xiǎng yào yīxiē zhǐ téng de dōngxi [wo shyang yow yee-shyeah jir teung duh dong-shee]

▸ I have a pain here 我这儿疼 wǒ zhèr téng [wo jer teung]

painkiller 止痛药 zhǐtòngyào [jir-tong-yow]

▸ I have a really bad toothache: can you give me a painkiller, please? 我牙疼得厉害。请你给我一片止痛药好吗？ wǒ yá téng de lìhai. qǐng nǐ gěi wǒ yī piàn zhǐtòngyào hǎo ma? [wo ya teung duh lee-high ching nee gay wo yee pyen jir-tong-yow how ma]

pair *(of gloves, socks)* 副 fù [foo]

▸ a pair of shoes 一双鞋 yī shuāng xié [yee shwung shyeah]

▸ a pair of pants 一条裤子 yī tiáo kùzi [yee teow koo-zir]

▸ do you have a pair of scissors? 你有剪刀吗？ nǐ yǒu jiǎndāo ma? [ni yoh jyen-dow ma]

pants 裤子 kùzi [koo-zir]

> ▸ a pair of pants 一条裤子 yī tiáo kùzi [yee teow koo-zir]

> ▸ there is a hole in these pants 裤子上有个洞 kùzi shang yǒu gè dòng [koo-zir shang yoh guh dong]

pantyhose 连裤袜 liánkùwà [lyen-koo-wa]

> ▸ I got a run in my pantyhose 我的连裤袜抽丝了 wǒ de liánkùwà chōusī le [wo duh lyen-koo-wa choh-sir-luh]

paper (for writing on) 纸 zhǐ [jir]; (newspaper) 报纸 bàozhǐ [bow-jir] ◆ **papers** (official documents) 文件 wénjiàn [weun-jyen]

> ▸ a piece of paper 一张纸 yī zhāng zhǐ [yee jang jir]

> ▸ here are my papers 这是我的文件 zhè shì wǒ de wénjiàn [juh shir wo duh wen-jyen]

parasol 女式阳伞 nǚshì yángsǎn [nooh-shir yang-san]

> ▸ can you rent parasols? 能租到女式阳伞吗？ néng zūdào nǚshì yángsǎn ma? [nung zoo-dow nooh-shir yang-san ma]

pardon (forgiveness) 原谅 yuánliàng [ywan-lyang]

> ▸ I beg your pardon?/pardon me? (asking for repetition) 我没听清楚，请再 说一遍好吗？ wǒ méi tīng qīngchu, qǐng zài shuō yī biàn hǎo ma? [wo may ting ching-choo ching zigh shwore yee byen how ma]

> ▸ I beg your pardon!/pardon me! (to apologize) 对不起！ duìbuqǐ! [dway-boo-chee]; (showing disagreement) 什么！ shénme! [sheun-muh]

> ▸ pardon me! (to get past) 劳驾！ láojià! [low-jya]

park 停 tíng [ting] ◆ 停车 tíng chē [ting-chuh]

> ▸ can we park our trailer here? 我们可以把房式拖车停在这里吗？ wǒmen kěyǐ bǎ fáng shì tuōchē tíng zài zhèlǐ ma? [wo-meun kuh-yee ba fang shir twore-chuh ting zigh juh-lee ma]

> ▸ am I allowed to park here? 我可以在这儿停车吗？ wǒ kěyǐ zài zhèr tíng chē ma? [wo kuh-yee zigh jer ting chuh ma]

parking 停车的地方 tíng chē de dìfang [ting chuh duh dee-fang]

> ▸ is there any parking near the hostel? 招待所的附近有没有停车的地方？ zhāodàisuǒ de fùjìn yǒuméiyǒu tíng chē de dìfang? [jow-digh-swore duh foo-jin yoh-may-yoh ting chuh duh dee-fang]

parking lot 停车场 tíngchēchǎng [ting-chuh-chang]

> ▸ is there a parking lot nearby? 附近有停车场吗？ fùjìn yǒu tíngchēchǎng ma? [foo-jin yoh ting-chuh-chang ma]

parking space 停车位 tíngchēwèi [ting-chuh-way]

> ▸ is it easy to find a parking space in town? 在市区容易找到停车位吗？ zài shìqū róngyì zhǎodào tíngchēwèi ma? [zigh shir-choo rong-yee jow-dow ting-chuh-way ma]

part *(piece)* 部分 bùfen [boo-feun]; *(area)* 地区 dìqū [dee-choo]

- what part of China are you from? 你来自中国的哪个地区？ nǐ láizì zhōngguó de nǎge dìqū? [nee ligh-zir jong-gwore duh na-guh dee-choo]
- I've never been to this part of China before 我过去从来没有来过中国的这个地方 wǒ guòqù cónglái méiyou láiguo zhōngguó de zhège dìfang [wo gwore-choo tsong-ligh may-yoh ligh-gwore jong-gwore duh juh-guh dee-fang]

party 聚会 jùhuì [joo-hway] ◆ 尽情欢乐 jìnqíng huānlè [jin-ching hwan-luh]

- I'm planning a little party tomorrow 明天我要组织一个小型的聚会 míngtiān wǒ yào zǔzhī yī gè xiǎoxíng de jùhuì [ming-tyen wo yow zoo-jir yee guh sheow-shing duh joo-hway]

pass *(hand)* 递 dì [dee]; *(in a car)* 超过 chāoguo [chow-gwore] ◆ *(in a car)* 超车 chāochē [chow-chuh]

- can you pass me the salt? 你能把盐递给我吗？ nǐ néng bǎ yán dì gěi wǒ ma? [nee nung ba yan dee gay wo ma]
- can you pass on this road? 在这条街上你能超车吗？ zài zhè tiáo jiē shang nǐ néng chāochē ma? [zigh jur teow jyeah shang nee nung chow-chuh ma]

passage *(corridor)* 走廊 zǒuláng [zoh-lang]

- I heard someone outside in the passage 我听到有人在外面的走廊里 wǒ tīngdào yǒu rén zài wàimian de zǒuláng li [wo ting-dow yoh reun zigh wigh-myen duh zoh-lang]

passenger 旅客 lǚkè [looh-kuh]

- is this where the passengers from the New York flight arrive? 这是来自纽约的航班乘客下飞机的地方吗？ zhè shì láizì niǔyuē de hángbān chéngkè xià fēijī de dìfang ma? [juh shir ligh-zir new-yue duh hang-ban chung-kuh shya fay-jee duh dee-fang ma]

passport 护照 hùzhào [hoo-jow]

- I've lost my passport 我遗失了护照 wǒ yíshīle hùzhào [wo yee-shir-luh hoo-jow]
- I forgot my passport 我忘了带护照 wǒ wàngle dài hùzhào [wo wang-luh digh hoo-jow]
- my passport has been stolen 我的护照被偷了 wǒ de hùzhào bèi tōu le [wo duh hoo-jow bay toh luh]

past 在......之后 zài......zhī hòu [zigh...jir hoh]

- twenty past twelve 12点20分 shí'èr diǎn èrshí fēn [shir-er-dyen er-shir feun]

path *(track)* 小路 xiǎolù [sheow-loo]

- is the path well-marked? 这条小路标示清楚吗？ zhè tiáo xiǎolù biāoshì qīngchu ma? [juh teow sheow-loo beow-shir ching-choo ma]

pay *(check, bill)* 付 fù [foo]; *(waiter)* 付钱给 fù qián gěi [foo chyen gay]; *(money)* 支付 zhīfù [jir-foo] ◆ 付钱 fù qián [foo chyen]

▸ do I have to pay a deposit? 我得付定金吗？ wǒ děi fù dìngjīn ma? [wo day foo ding-jin ma]

▸ do you have to pay to get in? 进去要付费吗？ jìnqu yào fù fèi ma? [jin-choo yow foo fay ma]

▸ can you pay by credit card? 能用信用卡付钱吗？ néng yòng xìnyòngkǎ fù qián ma? [nung yong shin-yong-ka foo chyen ma]

▸ we're going to pay separately 我们分开付钱 wǒmen fēnkāi fù qián [wo-meun feun-kigh foo chyen]

pay-per-view channel 按次计费频道 àn cì jì fèi píndào [an tsir jee fay pin-dow]

▸ are there any pay-per-view channels? 有按次计费的频道吗？ yǒu àn cì jì fèi de píndào ma? [yoh an tsir jee fay duh pin-dow ma]

pay-per-view TV 按次计费的电视 àn cì jì fèi de diànshì [an tsir jee fay duh dyen-shir]

▸ is there pay-per-view TV in the room? 房间里有按次计费的电视吗？ fángjiān li yǒu àn cì jì fèi de diànshì ma? [fang-jyen lee yoh an tsir jee fay duh dyen-shir ma]

pedestrian 行人 xíngrén [shing-reun] ◆ 步行的 bùxíng de [boo-shing duh]

▸ is this just a pedestrian street? 这完全是一条步行街吗？ zhè wánquán shì yī tiáo bùxíngjiē ma? [juh wan-chwan shir yee teow boo-shing-jyeah ma]

pedestrian mall 步行区 bùxíngqū [boo-shing-choo]

▸ can you direct me to the pedestrian mall? 你能告诉我去步行区该怎么走吗？ nǐ néng gàosu wǒ qù bùxíngqū gāi zěnme zǒu ma? [nee nung gow-soo wo choo boo-shing-choo gigh zeun-muh zoh ma]

pen 钢笔 gāngbǐ [gang-bee]

▸ can you lend me a pen? 你能借给我一支钢笔吗？ nǐ néng jiè gěi wǒ yī zhī gāngbǐ ma? [nee nung jyeah gay wo yee jir gang-bee ma]

pencil 铅笔 qiānbǐ [chyen-bee]

▸ can you lend me a pencil? 你能借给我一支铅笔吗？ nǐ néng jiè gěi wǒ yī zhī qiānbǐ ma? [nee nung jyeah gay wo yee jir chyen-bee ma]

penicillin 青霉素 qīngméisù [ching-may-soo]

▸ I'm allergic to penicillin 我对青霉素过敏 wǒ duì qīngméisù guòmǐn [wo dway ching-may-soo gwore-min]

pepper 胡椒 hújiāo [hoo-jeow]

▸ pass the pepper, please 请递一下胡椒 qǐng dì yī xià hújiāo [ching dee yee shya hoo-jeow]

percent 百分之 bǎi fēn zhī [bigh feun jir]

▸ could you knock 10 percent off the price? 你能减价百分之十吗？ nǐ néng jiǎnjià bǎi fēn zhī shí ma? [nee nung jyen-jya bigh jir shir ma]

pets

Although you see more and more pet dogs on the sidewalks of Chinese cities these days (especially Pekinese!), birds are the traditional favorite pet of Chinese families. Older people often take their birds to the park and hang their cages up in trees to listen to them sing. There are some great bird markets in China, 鸟市 **niǎo shì** [neow shir].

performance *(show)* 演出 **yǎnchū** [yan-choo]; *(in a movie theater)* 放映 **fàngyìng** [fang-ying]

  ▸ what time does the performance begin? 演出什么时候开始？ **yǎnchū shénme shíhou kāishǐ?** [yan-choo sheun-muh shir-hoh kigh-shir]

perfume 香水 **xiāngshuǐ** [shyang-shway]

  ▸ how much is this perfume? 这香水多少钱？ **zhè xiāngshuǐ duōshao qián?** [juh shyang-shway dwore-show chyen]

perhaps 也许 **yěxǔ** [yuh-shoo]

  ▸ perhaps you can help me? 你也许可以帮助我？ **nǐ yěxǔ kěyǐ bāng wǒ?** [nee yuh-shoo ku-yee bang wo]

person 人 **rén** [reun]

  ▸ how much is it per person and per hour? 每人每小时多少钱？ **měi rén měi xiǎoshí duōshao qián?** [may reun may sheow-shir dwore-sheow chyen]

pet 宠物 **chǒngwù** [chong-woo]

  ▸ are pets allowed? 可以带宠物吗？ **kěyǐ dài chǒngwù ma?** [kuh-yee digh chong-woo ma]

phone 电话 **diànhuà** [dyen-hwa] ◆ 给......打电话 **gěi......dǎ diànhuà** [gay... da dyen-hwa] ◆ 打电话 **dǎ diànhuà** [da dyen-hwa]

  ▸ can I use the phone? 我能用电话吗？ **wǒ néng yòng diànhuà ma?** [wo nung yong dyen-hwa ma]

phone booth 电话亭 **diànhuàtíng** [dyen-hwa-ting]

  ▸ is there a phone booth near here? 这附近有电话亭吗？ **zhè fùjìn yǒu diànhuàtíng ma?** [juh foo-jin yoh dyen-hwa-ting ma]

phone call 电话 **diànhuà** [dyen-hwa]

  ▸ I'd like to make a phone call 我想打个电话 **wǒ xiǎng dǎ gè diànhuà** [wo shyang da guh dyen-hwa]

phonecard 电话卡 **diànhuàkǎ** [dyen-hwa-ka]

  ▸ where can I buy a phonecard? 我可以去哪里买电话卡？ **wǒ kěyǐ qù nǎlǐ mǎi diànhuàkǎ?** [wo kuh-yee choo na-lee migh dyen-hwa-ka]

photo 照片 zhàopiàn [jow-pyen]

- can I take photos in here? 我能在这里拍照吗? wǒ néng zài zhèli pāizhào ma? [wo mung zigh juh-lee pigh-jow ma]
- could you take a photo of us? 你能给我们拍张照片吗? nǐ néng gěi wǒmen pāi zhāng zhàopiàn ma? [nee nung gay wo-meun pigh jang jow-pyen ma]
- I'd like copies of some photos 一些照片我想再要一份. yīxiē zhàopiàn wǒ xiǎng zài yào yī fèn [yee shyeah jow-pyen wo shyang zigh yow yee feun]

photography 照片 zhàopiàn [jow-pyen]

- is photography allowed in the museum? 博物馆里允许拍照吗? bówù-guǎn li yǔnxǔ pāizhào ma? [bo-woo-gwan lee yun-shoo pigh-jow ma]

picnic 野餐 yěcān [yuh-tsan]

- could we go for a picnic by the river? 我们能去河边野餐吗? wǒmen néng qù hé biān yěcān ma? [wo-meun nung choo huh byen yuh-tsan ma]

piece *(of paper)* 张 zhāng [jang]; *(of chocolate, cake, wood)* 块 kuài [kwigh]; *(of apple)* 片 piàn [pyen]

- a piece of cake, please 请来一块蛋糕 qǐng lái yī kuài dàngāo [ching ligh yee kwigh dan-gow]
- a piece of advice 一条建议 yī tiáo jiànyì [yee teow jyen-yee]
- a piece of news 一则新闻 yī zé xīnwén [yee zuh shin-weun]

pill 药片 yàopiàn [yow-pyen]

- a bottle of pills 一瓶药片 yī píng yàopiàn [yee ping yow-pyen]
- the Pill *(contraceptive)* 避孕药 bìyùnyào [bee-yun-yow]

---

on the phone

- hello? 喂? wèi? [way]
- Joe Stewart speaking 这是乔·斯图亚特 zhè shì qiáo· sītúyàtè [juh shir cheow sir-too-ya-tuh]
- I'd like to speak to Jack Adams 我找杰克·亚当姆斯 wǒ zhǎo jiékè· yàdāngmǔsī [wo jow jyeah-kuh ya-dang-moo-sir]
- hold the line 别挂机 bié guàjī [byeah gwa-jee]
- can you call back in ten minutes? 你能十分钟后打回来吗? nǐ néng shí fēnzhōng hòu dǎ huílai ma? [nee nung shir feun-jong hoh da hway-ligh ma]
- would you like to leave a message? 你要留言吗? nǐ yào liúyán ma? [nee yow lew-yan ma]
- you have the wrong number 你拨错号码了 nǐ bō cuò hàomǎ le [nee bo tswore how-ma luh]

plates

You won't always be given a plate when you eat, and if you are, it'll be a small plate like a saucer. Dishes are served in the middle of the table, then everyone digs in with their chopsticks, using the little plate or a bowl of rice to eat from.

pillow 枕头 zhěntou [jeun-toh]

▸ could I have another pillow? 我能再要一个枕头吗？ wǒ néng zài yào yī gè zhěntou ma? [wo nung zigh yow yee-guh jeun-toh ma]

pizza 比萨饼 bǐsàbǐng [bee-sa-bing]

▸ I'd like a large mushroom pizza 我要一个大号的蘑菇比萨饼 wǒ yào yī gè dà hào de mógu bǐsàbǐng [wo yow yee guh da how duh mo-goo bee-sa-bing]

place *(area)* 地方 dìfang [dee-fang]; *(house)* 家 jiā [jya]; *(seat)* 座位 zuòwei [zwore-way]

▸ can you recommend a nice place to eat? 你能推荐一个吃饭的好地方吗？ nǐ néng tuījiàn yī gè chīfàn de hǎo dìfang ma? [nee nung tway-jyen yee guh chir-fan duh how dee-fang ma]

▸ do you want to change places with me? 你要和我换座位吗？ nǐ yào hé wǒ huàn zuòwei ma? [nee yow huh wo hwan zwore-way ma]

plain *(clear)* 清楚的 qīngchu de [ching-choo duh]; *(with nothing added)* 纯的 chún de [chun duh]

▸ do you have any plain yogurt? 你有纯的酸奶吗？ nǐ yǒu chún de suānnǎi ma? [nee yoh chun duh swan-new-nigh ma]

plan *(strategy)* 计划 jìhuà [jee-hwa]; *(intention, idea)* 打算 dǎsuan [da-swan] ◆ *(organize)* 为......制定计划 wèi......zhìdìng jìhuà [way...jir-ding jee-hwa]; *(intend)* 打算 dǎsuan [da-swan]

▸ do you have plans for tonight? 今晚你有什么打算吗？ jīnwǎn nǐ yǒu shénme dǎsuan ma? [jin-wan nee yoh sheun-muh da-swan ma]

▸ I'm planning to stay for just one night 我打算只住一个晚上 wǒ dǎsuan zhǐ zhù yī gè wǎnshang [wo da-swan jir joo yee guh wan-shang]

plane 飞机 fēijī [fay-jee]

▸ which gate does the plane depart from? 飞机从哪个登机口出发？ fēijī cóng nǎge dēngjīkǒu chūfā? [fay-jee tsong na-guh dung-jee-koh choo-fa]

plate 盘子 pánzi [pan-zir]

▸ this plate's got a crack in it 盘子上有条裂缝 pánzi shang yǒu tiáo lièfèng [pan-zir shang yoh teow lyeah-fung]

platform *(at a station)* 站台 zhàntái [jan-tigh]

- which platform does the train leave from? 火车从哪个站台出发？ huǒchē cóng nǎge zhàntái chūfā？ [hwore-chuh tsong na-guh jan-tigh choo-fa]

play *(at a theater)* 戏剧 xìjù [shee-joo] ◆ *(sport, game)* 参加比赛 cānjiā bǐsài [tsan-jya bee-sigh]; *(instrument, music)* 演奏 yǎnzòu [yan-zoh]

- do you play tennis? 你打网球吗？ nǐ dǎ wǎngqiú ma？ [nee da wang-chew ma]
- I play the cello 我拉大提琴 wǒ lā dàtíqín [wo la da tee-chin]

playroom 游戏室 yóuxìshì [yoh-shee-shir]

- is there a children's playroom here? 这里有儿童游戏室吗？ zhèlǐ yǒu yóuxìshì ma？ [juh-lee yoh yoh-shee-shir ma]

please 请 qǐng [ching]

- please sit down 请坐 qǐng zuò [ching zwore]
- can I come in? – please do 我能进来吗？ – 请进 wǒ néng jìnlai ma？ – qǐng jìn [wo nung jin-ligh ma – ching-jin]

pleased 高兴的 gāoxìng de [gow-shing duh]

- pleased to meet you 见到你很高兴 jiàndào nǐ hěn gāoxìng [jyen-dow nee heun gow-shing]

pleasure 高兴 gāoxìng [gow-shing]

- with pleasure! 非常乐意！ fēicháng lèyì！ [fay-chang luh-yee]
- it's a pleasure/my pleasure 不用谢 bù yòng xiè [boo-yong-shyeah]

plug *(on electrical equipment)* 插头 chātóu [cha-toh]

- where can I find an adaptor for the plug on my hairdryer? 我可以在哪里找到适配器用在我的电吹风的插头上？ wǒ kěyǐ zài nǎli zhǎodào shìpèiqì yòng zài wǒ de diànchuīfēng de chātóu shang？ [wo kuh-yee zigh na-lee jow-dow shir-pay-chee yong zigh wo duh dyen-chway-fung duh cha-toh shang]

plug in 把……插入电源 bǎ……chārù diànyuán [ba...cha-roo dyen-ywan]

- can I plug my cellphone in here to recharge it? 我能把插头插在这里充电吗？ wǒ néng bǎ chātóu chā zài zhèlǐ chōngdiàn ma？ [wo nung ba cha-toh cha zigh juh-lee chong-dyen ma]

---

platform

Access to station platforms is restricted. You have to keep your train ticket in hand. If you want to accompany someone onto a train, or meet your friends as they get off, you can buy a platform ticket 站台票 zhàntáipiào [jan-tigh-peow] which will get you through the barriers.

pork

The pig is the king of beasts on a Chinese farm. It's one of the traditional basic foods and is highly valued in all regions of China. It is still the most widely eaten meat in the country. Its importance in Chinese culture is such that the character meaning 'family' and 'home' 家 jiā [jya] shows, in symbolic form, a pig under a roof.

point *(moment)* 时刻 shíkè [shir-kuh]; *(spot, location)* 地点 dìdiǎn [dee-dyen]
- *(direct)* 指出 zhǐchū [jir-choo]
- points of the compass 方位 fāngwèi [fang-way]
- can you point me in the direction of the freeway? 你能给我指出高速公路的方向吗？ nǐ néng gěi wǒ zhǐchū gāosù gōnglù de fāngxiàng ma? [nee nung gay wo jir-choo gow-soo gong-loo duh fang-shyang ma]

police 警察 jǐngchá [jing-cha]
- call the police! 快叫警察！ kuài jiào jǐngchá! [kwigh jeow jing-cha]
- what's the number for the police? 报警的电话号码是多少？ bàojǐng de diànhuà hàomǎ shì duōshao? [bow-jing duh dyen-hwa how ma shir dwore-show]

police station 警察局 jǐngchájú [jing-cha-joo]
- where is the nearest police station? 最近的警察局在什么地方？ zuì jìn de jǐngchájú zài shénme dìfang? [zway jin duh jing-cha-joo zigh sheun-muh dee-fang]

pool *(for swimming)* 游泳池 yóuyǒngchí [yoh-yong-chir]
- main pool 主游泳池 zhǔ yóuyǒngchí [joo-yoh-yong-chir]
- kiddie pool 儿童游泳池 értóng yóuyǒngchí [er-tong-yoh-yong-chir]
- is the pool heated? 游泳池的水热吗？ yóuyǒngchí de shuǐ rè ma? [yoh-yong-chir duh shway ruh ma]
- is there an indoor pool? 有室内游泳池吗？ yǒu shìnèi yóuyǒngchí ma? [yoh shir-nay yoh-yong-chir ma]

pork 猪肉 zhūròu [joo-roh]
- I don't eat pork 我不吃猪肉 wǒ bù chī zhūròu [wo boo chir joo-roh]

portable 便携式的 biànxiéshì de [byen-shyeah-shir duh]
- do you have a portable heater we could borrow? 你是否有便携式暖风机可以借给我们？ nǐ shìfǒu yǒu biànxiéshì nuǎnfēngjī kěyǐ jiè gěi wǒmen? [nee shir-foh yoh byen-shyeah-shir nwan-fung-jee kuh-yee jyeah gay wo-meun]

portion 分量 fēnliang [feun-lyang]
- the portions at that restaurant are just right 餐馆饭菜的分量刚刚好 cānguǎn fàncài de fēnliang gānggāng hǎo [tsang-gwan fan-tsigh duh feun-lyang gang-gang how]

at the post office

International postage stamps cost about RMB 5 in China. You can mail letters and postcards in dark green mailboxes in the street or at large hotels. At the post office you can send packages up to a maximum weight of 30 kg. Most post offices offer their own packaging system. You have to leave the parcel open so that what is being sent can be inspected. It usually takes about ten days for a package or postcard to reach the US.

possible 可能的 kěnéng de [kuh-nung duh]
- without sauce, if possible 如有可能，不要加酱汁 rú yǒu kěnéng, bù yào jiā jiàngzhī [roo yoh kun-nung boo yow jya jyang-jir]

postcard 明信片 míngxìnpiàn [ming-shyen-pee-pyen]
- where can I buy postcards? 我在哪里可以买到明信片? wǒ zài nǎli kěyǐ mǎidào míngxìnpiàn? [wo zigh na-lee kuh-yee migh-dow ming-shing-pyen]
- how much are stamps for postcards to the States? 寄到美国去的明信片要贴多少钱的邮票? jìdào měiguó qù de míngxìnpiàn yào tiē duōshao qián de yóupiào? [jee-dow may-gwore choo duh ming-shing-pyen yow tyeah dwore-show chyen duh yoh-peow]

post office 邮局 yóujú [yoh-joo]
- where is the nearest post office? 最近的邮局在哪儿? zuì jìn de yóujú zài nǎr? [zway jin duh yoh-joo zigh nar]

power (electricity) 电 diàn [dyen]
- there's no power 没电了 méi diàn le [may dyen luh]

power failure 停电 tíng diàn [ting dyen]
- there's a power failure 停电了 tíng diàn le [ting dyen luh]
- how long is the power failure expected to last? 停电将持续多久? tíng diàn jiāng chíxù duō jiǔ? [ting dyen jyang dwore jew]

prawn 明虾 míngxiā [ming-shya]
- I'd like to try a dish with shrimp or prawns 我要试一试用小虾或明虾做的菜 wǒ yào shì yī shì yòng xiǎoxiā huò míngxiā zuò de cài [wo yow shir yee shir yong sheow-shya hwore ming-shya zwore duh tsigh]

prefer 更喜欢 gèng xǐhuan [gung shee-hwan]
- I'd prefer black tea 我更喜欢红茶 wǒ gèng xǐhuan hóngchá [wo gung shee-hwan hong-cha]
- I'd prefer you not smoke 我希望你不要吸烟 wǒ xīwàng nǐ bù yào xīyān [wo shee-wang nee boo yow shee-yan] ▶ see box on p. 132

prescription (medicine) 处方 chǔfāng [choo-fang]
- is it only available by prescription? 这个只能凭处方购买吗? zhège zhǐ néng píng chǔfāng gòumǎi ma? [juh-guh jir nung ping choo-fang goh-may ma]

expressing a preference

▸ I prefer red wine to white wine 我喜欢红葡萄酒胜于白葡萄酒 wǒ xǐhuan hóng pútaojiǔ shèng yú bái pútaojiǔ [wo shee-hwan hong poo-tow-jew shung yoo bigh poo-tow-jew]

▸ I'd rather fly than go by train 我宁愿坐飞机也不愿坐火车 wǒ nìngyuàn zuò fēijī yě bù yuàn zuò huǒchē [wo ning-ywan zwore fay-jee yuh boo ywan zwore hwore-chuh]

▸ Saturday would suit me better 星期六对我而言更合适 xīngqīliù duì wǒ ér yán gèng héshì [shing-shee-lew dway wo er yan gung huh-shir]

present 礼物 lǐwù [lee-woo]

▸ where can we buy presents around here? 这附近我们可以去什么地方买礼物？ zhè fùjìn wǒmen kěyǐ qù shénme dìfang mǎi lǐwù? [juh foo-jin wo-meun kuh-yee choo sheun-muh dee-fang migh lee-woo]

pretty 漂亮的 piàoliang de [peow-lyang duh]

▸ she's a very pretty girl 她是个非常漂亮的女孩 tā shì gè fēicháng piàoliang de nǚhái [ta shir guh fay-chang peow-lyang duh nooh-high]

price (cost) 价格 jiàgé [jya-guh]

▸ what's the price of gas today? 今天的汽油价格是多少？ jīntiān de qìyóu jiàgé shì duōshao? [jun-tyen duh chee-yoh jya-guh shir dwore-show]

▸ if the price is right 如果价格公道的话 rúguǒ jiàgé gōngdào dehuà [roo-gwore gong-dow duh hwa]

price list 价格表 jiàgébiǎo [jya-guh-beow]

▸ do you have a price list? 你有价格表吗？ nǐ yǒu jiàgébiǎo ma? [nee yoh jya-guh-beow ma]

presents (i)

Gift-giving is common as a means of strengthening relationships with friends and business associates, or if you are invited out for a meal. Wine or foreign alcoholic drinks are a good present for a man, and beauty products or perfume are suitable for a woman. Bear in mind that you should refuse a gift several times before eventually accepting it. When you give someone a present, do not be surprised if they put it away in a corner, as politeness also demands that it should only be opened later, and maybe not even in front of you.

print *(photograph)* 照片 zhàopiàn [jow-pyen]

▸ could I have another set of prints? 能给我再冲印一份照片吗? néng gěi wǒ zài chōngyìn yī fèn zhàopiàn ma? [nung gay wo zigh chong-yin yee feun jow-pyen]

problem 问题 wèntí [weun-tee]

▸ there's a problem with the central heating 中央暖气系统出问题了 zhōngyāng nuǎnqì xìtǒng chū wèntí le [jong-yang nwan-chee shee-tong choo weun-tee]

▸ no problem 没问题 méi wèntí [may weun-tee]

program *(for an event)* 节目单 jiémùdān [jyeah-moo-dan]

▸ could I see a program? 我能看节目单吗? wǒ néng kàn jiémùdān ma? [wo nung kan jyeah-moo-dan ma]

pronounce *(word)* 发......的音 fā......de yīn [fa...duh yin]

▸ how is that pronounced? 那个怎么发音? nàge zěnme fāyīn? [na-guh zeun-muh fa-yin]

public *(state)* 政府的 zhèngfǔ de [jung-foo duh]; *(open to all)* 公共的 gōnggòng de [gong-gong duh] ◆ 公众 gōngzhòng [gong-jong]

▸ let's go somewhere less public 我们去人少的地方吧 wǒmen qù rén shǎo de dìfang ba [wo-meun choo reun show duh dee-fang]

▸ is the castle open to the public? 这个城堡对公众开放吗? zhège chéngbǎo duì gōngzhòng kāifàng ma? [juh-guh chung-bow dway gong-jong kigh-fang ma]

public holiday 公共假期 gōnggòng jiàqī [gong-gong jya-chee]

▸ is tomorrow a public holiday? 明天是公共假期吗? míngtiān shì gōnggòng jiàqī ma? [ming-tyen shir gong-gong jya-chee ma]

public transportation 公共交通 gōnggòng jiāotōng [gong-gong jeow-tong]

▸ can you get there by public transportation? 坐公共交通能到那里吗? zuò gōnggòng jiāotōng néng dào nàli ma? [zwore gong-gong jeow-tong nung dow na-lee ma]

pull *(muscle)* 拉伤 lāshāng [la-shang]; *(tooth)* 拔 bá [ba]

▸ I've pulled a muscle 我拉伤了一块肌肉 wǒ lāshāngle yī kuài jīròu [wo la-shang-luh yee kwigh jee-roh]

puncture 刺孔 cìkǒng [tsir-kong]

▸ we've got a puncture 轮胎被刺破了 lúntāi bèi cìpò le [lun-tigh bay tsir-po luh]

purpose *(reason)* 原因 yuányīn [ywan-yin]; *(aim)* 目的 mùdì [moo-dee] ◆ **on purpose** 故意地 gùyì de [goo-yee duh]

▸ sorry, I didn't do it on purpose 对不起,我不是故意的 duìbuqǐ, wǒ bù shì gùyì de [dway-boo-chee wo boo shir goo-yee duh]

purse *(handbag)* 手提包 shǒutíbāo [shoh-tee-bow]; *(change purse)* 钱包 qiánbāo [chyen-bow]

▶ my purse was stolen 我的手提包被偷了 wǒ de shǒutíbāo bèi tōu le [wo duh shoh-tee-bow bay toh luh]

push 推 tuī [tway]

▶ can you help us push the car? 你能帮我们推车吗？ nǐ néng bāng wǒmen tuī chē ma? [nee nung bang wo-meun tway chuh ma]

put *(into place, position)* 放 fàng [fang]

▶ is there somewhere I can put my bags? 有可以让我放行李的地方吗？ yǒu kěyǐ ràng wǒ fàng xínglǐ de dìfang ma? [yoh kuh-yee rang wo fang shing-lee duh dee-fang ma]

put down *(set down)* 放下 fàngxia [fang-shya]

▶ can we put our things down in the corner? 我们可以把我们的东西放在角落里吗？ wǒmen kěyǐ bǎ wǒmen de dōngxi fàng zài jiǎoluò li ma? [wo-meun kuh-yee ba wo-meun duh gong-shee fang zigh jeow-lwore li ma]

put on *(clothes)* 穿上 chuānshang [chwan-shang]; *(TV, radio, heating)* 打开 dǎkāi [da-kigh]; *(on telephone)* 叫......接电话 jiào......jiē diànhuà [jeow... jyeah dyen-hwa]

▶ can you put the heat on? 你能把暖气打开吗？ nǐ néng bǎ nuǎnqì dǎkāi ma? [nee nung ba nwan-chee da-kigh ma]

▶ can you put Mrs. Martin on, please? 请叫马丁夫人接电话好吗？ qǐng jiào mǎdīng fūren jiē diànhuà hǎo ma? [ching jeow ma-ding foo-reun jyeah dyen-hwa how ma]

put out *(cigarette, fire)* 熄灭 xīmiè [shee-myeah]

▶ can you please put your cigarette out? 请你把香烟熄灭好吗？ qǐng nǐ bǎ xiāngyān xīmiè hǎo ma? [ching nee ba shyang-yan shee-myeah how ma]

put up *(erect)* 建造 jiànzào [jyen-zow]; *(provide accommodation for)* 为......提供住宿 wèi......tígòng zhùsù [way...tee-gon joo-soo]

▶ can we put up our tent here? 我们可以在这里搭帐篷吗？ wǒmen kěyǐ zài zhèlǐ dā zhàngpeng ma? [wo-meun kuh-yee zigh juh-lee da jang-pung ma]

q

quarter *(fourth)* 四分之一 sì fēn zhī yī [sir feun jir yee]

- I'll be back in a quarter of an hour 我15分钟后回来 wǒ shíwǔ fēnzhōng hòu huílai [wo shir-woo feun-jong hoh hway-ligh]
- a quarter past/after one 1点15分 yī diǎn shíwǔ fēn [yee dyen shir-woo feun]
- a quarter to/of one 12点45分 shí'èr diǎn sìshíwǔ fēn [shir-er dyen sir-shir-woo feun]

quay 码头 mǎtou [ma-toh]

- is the boat at the quay? 船停在码头吗? chuán tíng zài mǎtou ma? [chwan ting zigh ma-toh ma]

question 问题 wèntí [weun-tee]

- can I ask you a question? 我能问你一个问题吗? wǒ néng wèn nǐ yī gè wèntí ma? [wo nung weun nee yee guh weun-tee ma]

quickly 快地 kuài de [kwigh duh]

- everyone speaks so quickly 每个人说话都那么快 měi gè rén shuō huà dōu nàme kuài [may guh reun shwore hwa doh na-muh kwigh]

quiet 安静的 ānjìng de [an-jing duh]

- is it a quiet beach? 那是个安静的海滩吗? nà shì gè ānjìng de hǎitān ma? [na shir guh an-jing duh high-tan ma]
- do you have a quieter room? 你们有安静一点儿的房间吗? nǐmen yǒu ānjìng yīdiǎnr de fángjiān ma? [nee-meun yoh an-jing yee-dyenr fang-jyen ma]

quite *(rather)* 相当地 xiāngdāng de [shyang-dang duh]

- it's quite expensive around here 这附近相当贵 zhè fùjìn xiāngdāng guì [juh foo-jin shyang-dang gway]

r

racket *(for tennis)* 网球拍 wǎngqiúpāi [wang-chew-pigh]

- can you rent rackets? 能租到网球拍吗? néng zūdào wǎngqiúpāi ma? [nung zoo-dow wang-chew-pigh]

radiator 散热器 sànrèqì [san-reun-chee]

- the radiator's leaking 散热器漏水了 sànrèqì lòu shuǐ le [san-ruh-chee loh shway luh]

radio *(set)* 收音机 shōuyīnjī [shoh-yin-jee]

> the radio doesn't work 收音机坏了 shōuyīnjī huài le [shoh-yin-jee hway luh]

radio station 广播电台 guǎngbō diàntái [gwung-bo dyen-tigh]

> can you get any English-language radio stations here? 这里有英语广播电台吗？ zhèli yǒu yīngyǔ guǎngbō diàntái ma? [juh-lee yoh ying-yoo gwung-bo dyen-tigh ma]

railroad *(system)* 铁路系统 tiělù xìtǒng [tyeah-loo shee-tong]; *(organization)* 铁路公司 tiělù gōngsī [tyeah-loo gong-sir]; *(track)* 铁路 tiělù [tyeah-loo]

> what region does this railroad cover? 这个铁路通往哪里？ zhège tiělù tōngwǎng nǎlǐ? [juh-guh tyeah-loo tong-wang na-lee]

rain 下雨 xià yǔ [shya-yoo]

> it's raining 正在下雨 zhèng zài xià yǔ [jung zigh shya yoo]

random

> at random 任意的 rènyì de [reun-yee duh]

rare *(meat)* 半熟的 bàn shú de [ban-shoo duh]

> rare, please 请烧成半熟的 qǐng shāochéng bàn shú de [ching show-chung ban shoo duh]

rate *(price)* 价格 jiàgé [jya-guh]

> what's your daily rate? 一天的价格是多少？ yī tiān de jiàgé shì duōshao? [yee tyen duh jya-guh shir dwore-show]

rate of exchange 汇率 huìlǜ [hway-looh]

> they offer a good rate of exchange 他们给的汇率不错 tāmen gěi de huìlǜ bù cuò [ta-meun gay duh hway-looh boo tswore]

razor *(for wet shaving)* 剃刀 tìdāo [tee-dow]; *(electric)* 电动剃须刀 diàndòng tìxūdāo [dyen-dong tee-shoo-dow]

> where can I buy a new razor? 我可以去哪里买新的剃刀？ wǒ kěyǐ qù nǎli mǎi xīn de tìdāo? [wo ku-yee zigh na-lee migh shin duh tee-dow]

razor blade 剃刀刀片 tìdāo dāopiàn [tee-dow dow-pyen]

> I need to buy some razor blades 我需要买新的剃刀刀片 wǒ xūyào mǎi xīn de tìdāo dāopiàn [wo shoo-yow migh shin duh tee-dow dow-pyen]

ready *(prepared)* 准备好的 zhǔnbèi hǎo de [jun-bay how duh]; *(willing)* 决心做某事的 juéxīn zuò mǒu shì de [jue-shin zwore moh shir duh]

> when will it be ready? 什么时候能准备好？ shénme shíhou néng zhǔnbèi hǎo? [sheun-muh shir-hoh nung jun-bay how]

really *(actually)* 实际上 shíjìshang [shir-jee-shang]; *(very)* 非常 fēicháng [fay-chang]

> really? 真的？ zhēn de? [jeun duh]

rear *(of a train)* 后部 hòubù [hoh-boo]

> your seats are in the rear of the train 你们的座位在后面的车厢 nǐmen de

zuòwèi zài hòumian de chēxiāng [nee-meun duh zwore-way zigh hoh-myen duh chuh-shyang]

rec center, recreation center 娱乐中心 yúlè zhōngxīn [yoo-luh jong-shin]

 ▸ what kinds of activities does the recreation center offer? 这个娱乐中心有些什么娱乐活动？ zhège yúlè zhōngxīn yǒu xiē shénme yúlè huódòng? [juh-guh yoo-luh jong-shin yoh shyeah sheun-muh yoo-luh hwore-dong]

receipt *(for a purchase, meal, taxi)* 发票 fāpiào [fa-peow]; *(for rent)* 收据 shōujù [show-joo]

 ▸ can I have a receipt, please? 请给我一张发票好吗？ qǐng gěi wǒ yī zhāng fāpiào hǎo ma? [ching gay wo yee jang fa-peow how ma]

receive *(package, letter)* 收到 shōudào [show-dow]

 ▸ I should have received the package this morning 我早该在今天早晨收到包裹的 wǒ zǎo gāi zài jīntiān zǎochén shōudào bāoguǒ de [wo zow gigh jin-tyen zow-cheun show-dow bow-gwore duh]

reception *(party)* 接待 jiēdài [jyeah-digh]; *(for TV, radio, cell phone)* 信号 xìnhào [shin-how]

 ▸ there's no reception 没有信号 méiyou xìnhào [may yoh shin-how]

 ▸ I'm looking for the Mackenzie wedding reception 我在找麦肯希家的婚礼接待处 wǒ zài zhǎo màikěnxī jiā de hūnlǐ jiēdàichù [wo zigh jow migh-keun-shee jya duh hun-lee jyeah-digh-choo]

reception desk *(at hotel)* 服务台 fúwùtái [foo-woo-tigh]

 ▸ can I leave my backpack at the reception desk? 我可以把我的背包留在服务台吗？ wǒ kěyǐ bǎ wǒ de bēibāo liú zài fúwùtái ma? [wo kuh-yee ba wo duh bay-bow lew zigh foo-woo-tigh ma]

recline 把......向后躺 bǎ......xiàng hòu tǎng [ba...shyang hoh tang]

 ▸ do you mind if I recline my seat? 你介意我把我的座位向后倒吗？ nǐ jièyì wǒ bǎ wǒ de zuòwèi xiàng hòu dǎo ma? [nee jyeah-yee wo ba wo duh zwore-way shyang hoh dow ma]

recommend 推荐 tuījiàn [tway-jyen]

 ▸ could you recommend another hotel? 你能再推荐一家旅馆吗？ nǐ néng zài tuījiàn yī jiā lǚguǎn ma? [nee nung zigh tway-jyen yee jya looh-gwan ma]

 ▸ could you recommend a restaurant? 你能推荐一家饭馆吗？ nǐ néng tuījià yī jiā fàndiàn ma? [nee nung tway-jyen yee jya fan-dyen ma]

 ▸ what do you recommend? 你推荐什么呢？ nǐ tuījià shénme ne? [nee tway-jyen sheun-muh nuh]

record store 音像店 yīnxiàngdiàn [yin-shyang-dyen]

 ▸ I'm looking for a record store 我在找音像店 wǒ zài zhǎo yīnxiàngdiàn [wo zigh jow yen-shyang-dyen]

red

Red is the color of parties and of joy in China. It's also the traditional color of marriage. You will see a lot of red at Chinese New Year and during all of the traditional festivals. Red and gold are an especially common combination, particularly for written greetings.

red *(dress)* 红色的 **hóngsè de** [hong-suh duh]; *(hair)* 红褐色的 **hónghèsè de** [hong-huh-suh duh] ◆ *(color)* 红色 **hóngsè** [hong-suh]; *(wine)* 红 **hóng** [hong]

▸ dressed in red 身穿红色 **shēn chuān hóngsè** [sheun chwan hong-suh]

▸ what kinds of red wine do you have? 你有什么样的红葡萄酒？ **nǐ yǒu shénme yàng de hóng pútaojiǔ?** [nee yoh sheun-muh yang duh hong poo-tow-jew]

redhead 红褐色头发的女人 **hónghèsè tóufa de nǚrén** [hong-huh-suh toh-fa duh nooh-reun]

▸ a tall redhead wearing glasses 一个长着红褐色头发戴眼镜的高个儿女人 **yī gè zhǎngzhe hónghèsè tóufa dài yǎnjìng de gāo gèr nǚrén** [yee guh jang-juh hong-huh-suh toh-fa digh yan-jing duh gow guhr nooh-reun]

red light 红灯 **hóngdēng** [hong-dung]

▸ you failed to stop at a red light 你遇到红灯没有停 **nǐ yùdào hóngdēng méiyou tíng** [nee yoo-dow hong-dung may-yoh ting]

reduced *(price, rate)* 减价的 **jiǎnjià de** [jyen-jya duh]

▸ is there a reduced rate for students? 有给学生的折扣吗？ **yǒu gěi xuésheng de zhékòu ma?** [yoh gay shue-shung duh juh-koh ma]

reduced-price *(ticket)* 打折的 **dǎzhé de** [da-juh duh]

▸ two reduced-price tickets and one full-price 两张打折票和一张全价票 **liǎng zhāng dǎzhé piào hé yī zhāng quánjià piào** [lyang jang da-juh peow huh yee jang chwan-jya peow]

reduction 折扣 **zhékòu** [juh-koh]

▸ do you have reductions for groups? 给团队有折扣吗？ **gěi tuánduì yǒu zhékòu ma?** [gay twan-dway juh-koh ma]

reductions

Negotiations on price are often possible, and reductions can be agreed upon in many situations. Making a reduction or a discount is called 打折 **dǎzhé** [da-juh]. This term is used in an unusual way: you use numbers to show the percentage of the final price after discount, in relation to the original price. For example, 打7折 **dǎ qī zhé** [da chee-juh], using the number seven, doesn't mean you're getting a discount of 70% but that you're paying 70% of the original price (-30%).

red wine 红葡萄酒 hóng pútaojiǔ? [hong poo-tow-jew]
- a bottle of red wine 一瓶红葡萄酒 yī píng hóng pútaojiǔ [yee ping poo-tow-jew]

refresher course 进修课程 jìnxiū kèchéng [jin-shew kuh-chung]
- I need a refresher course 我需要参加进修课程 wǒ xūyào cānjiā jìnxiū kèchéng [wo shoo-yow tsan-jya jin-shew kuh-chung]

refuge (for animals) 收容所 shōuróngsuǒ [shoh-rong-swore]
- we'd like to visit the wildlife refuge 我们想参观野生动物收容所 wǒmen xiǎng cānguān yěshēng dòngwù shōuróngsuǒ [wo-meun shyang tsan-gwan yuh-shung dong-woo shoh-rong-swore]

refundable 可退还的 kě tuìhuán de [kuh tway-hwan du]
- are the tickets refundable? 这些票可以退吗? zhèxiē piào kěyǐ tuì ma? [juh shyeah peow kuh-yee tway ma]

regards 问候 wènhòu [weun-hoh] ◆ **with regard to** 对于 duìyú [dway-yoo]
- give my regards to your parents! 带我向你的父母问好! dài wǒ xiàng nǐ de fùmǔ wèn hǎo! [digh wo shyang nee duh foo-moo weun how]
- I'm calling you with regard to... 我给你打电话是因为...... wǒ gěi nǐ dǎ diànhuà shì yīnwei...... [wo gay nee da dyen-hwa shir yin-way]

region 在 zài [zigh]
- in the North East region of China 在中国的东北地区 zài zhōngguó de dōngběi dìqū [zigh jong-gwore duh dong-bay dee-choo]

registered mail 挂号邮寄 guàhào yóujiàn [gwa-how yoh-jyen]
- I would like to send a letter by registered mail 我想寄挂号信 wǒ xiǎng jì guàhàoxìn [wo shyang jee gwa-how-shin]

registration (of car) 牌照号码 páizhào hàomǎ [pigh-jow how-ma]
- here's the car's registration 这是汽车的牌照号码 zhè shì qìchē de páizhào hàomǎ [juh shir chee-chuh duh pigh-jow how-ma]

relative 亲戚 qīnqi [chin-chee]
- I have relatives in Beijing 我在北京有亲戚 wǒ zài běijīng yǒu qīnqi [wo zigh bay-jing yoh chin-chee]

remember 记得 jìde [jee-duh]
- do you remember me? 你记得我吗? nǐ jìde wǒ ma? [nee jee-duh wo ma]
- I can't remember his name 我记不起来他的名字 wǒ jì bù qǐlái tā de míngzi [wo jee boo chee-ligh ta duh ming-zir]

remote (control) 遥控器 yáokòngqì [yow-kong-chee]
- I can't find the remote for the TV 我找不到电视机的遥控器 wǒ zhǎo bù dào diànshìjī de yáokòngqì [wo jow boo dow dyen-shir-jee duh yow-kong-chee]

rent 租金 zūjīn [zoo-jin]; (for house) 房租 fángzū [fang-zoo] ◆ 租 zū [zoo]
- how much is the rent per week? 每个星期的租金是多少? měi gè xīngqī

de zūjīn shì duōshao? [may guh shing-chee duh zoo-jin shir dwore-show chyen]

▸ I'd like to rent a car for a week 我想租一个星期的车 wǒ xiǎng zū yī gè xīngqī de chē [wo shyang zoo yee guh shing-chee duh chuh]

▸ I'd like to rent a boat 我想租条船 wǒ xiǎng zū tiáo chuán [wo shyang zoo teow chwan]

▸ is it cheaper to rent the equipment by the week? 租一个星期的设备是不是会更便宜？ zū yī gè xīngqī de shèbèi shìbùshì huì gèng piányi? [zoo yee guh shing-shee-duh shuh-bay shir-boo-shir hway gung pyen-yee]

rental *(renting)* 租用 zūyòng [zoo-yong]; *(apartment, house or car)* 租金 zūjīn [zoo-jin]

▸ we have the rental for two weeks 我们租了两个星期 wǒmen zūle liǎng gè xīngqī [wo-meun zoo-luh lyang guh shing-chee]

repair 修理 xiūlǐ [shew-lee]

▸ will you be able to make the repairs today? 你今天能修好吗？ nǐ jīntiān néng xiūhǎo ma? [nee jin-tyen nung shew-how ma]

▸ how long will it take to repair? 修理需要多久？ xiūlǐ xūyào duō jiǔ? [shew-lee shoo-yow dwore jew]

repeat 重复 chóngfù [chong-foo]

▸ can you repeat that, please? 请你重复一遍好吗？ qǐng nǐ chóngfù yī biàn hǎo ma? [ching nee chong-foo yee byen how ma]

report *(theft)* 因......报案 yīn......bào'àn [yin...bow-an]

▸ I'd like to report something stolen 我要报案，我的东西被偷了 wǒ yào bào'àn, wǒ de dōngxi bèi tōu le [wo yow bow-an wo duh dong-shee bay toh luh]

▸ I'd like to report the loss of my credit cards 我的信用卡丢了，我要挂失 wo de xìnyòngkǎ diūle, wǒ yào guàshī [wo duh shin-yong-ka dew-luh wo yow gwa-shir]

reservation 预定 yùdìng [yoo-ding]

▸ do you have to make a reservation? 得预定吗？ děi yùdìng ma? [day yoo-ding ma]

▸ I have a reservation in the name of Jones 我用琼斯的名字预定过了 wǒ yòng qióngsī de míngzi yùdìngguo le [wo yong chyong-sir duh ming-zir yoo-ding-gwore luh]

reserve *(ticket, room)* 预定 yùdìng [yoo-ding]

▸ hello, I'd like to reserve a table for two for tomorrow night at 8 你好。 我想预定一张桌子，两个人，明天晚上八点钟 nǐ hǎo. wǒ xiǎng yùdìng yī zhāng zhuōzi, liǎng gè rén, míngtiān wǎnshang bā diǎnzhōng [nee how wo shyang yoo-ding yee jang jwore-zir lyang guh reun ming-tyen wan-shang ba dyen-jong]

reserved *(booked)* 预定的 yùdìng de [yoo-ding duh]

▸ is this table reserved? 这张桌子被预定了吗？ zhè zhāng zhuōzi bèi yùdìngle ma? [juh jang jwore-zir bay yoo-ding duh ma]

restaurants

These are usually very sociable places, with the emphasis on the quality of the food and speed of service rather than on the sophistication of the décor. People often go out to eat and prefer to invite friends and business colleagues to a restaurant to eat rather than to their home. If you're making business contacts, a meal out is often a prerequisite, and the Chinese will take a great interest in how and what you eat and drink. As a rule, people don't ask for separate checks. The person who invited you must pay for everything. There are many different types of restaurants, including small stalls 小吃店 xiǎochīdiàn [sheow-chir-dyen], which are a Chinese take on fast food, specializing in a few dishes that are often simple and delicious: ravioli, steamed rolls, noodles, kebobs, etc. It's quite common to ask for a 'doggy bag' to take leftovers home (except in formal situations, of course).

rest *(relax)* 休息 xiūxi [shew-shee]

▸ I've come here to get some rest 我到这里来稍事休息 wǒ dào zhèli lái shāo shì xiūxi [wo dow juh-lee ligh show shir shew-shee]

restaurant 餐馆 cānguǎn [tsab-gwan]

▸ are there any good restaurants around here? 这附近有什么好的餐馆吗？ zhè fùjìn yǒu shénme hǎo de cānguǎn ma? [juh foo-jin yoh sheun-muh how duh tsan-gwan ma]

at a restaurant

▸ I'd like to reserve a table for tonight 我想预定一张今天晚上的桌位 wǒ xiǎng yùdìng yī zhāng jīntiān wǎnshang de zhuōwèi [wo shyang yoo-ding yee jang jin-tyen wan-shang duh jwore-zir]

▸ can we see the menu? 我们能看菜单吗？ wǒmen néng kàn càidān ma? [wo-meun nung kan tsigh-dan ma]

▸ do you have a set menu? 你们有套餐吗？ nǐmen yǒu tàocān ma? [ni-meun yoh tow-tsan ma]

▸ rare/medium/well done, please 请来半熟的/七分熟的/全熟的 qǐng lái bàn shú de/qī fēn shú de/quán shú de [ching ligh ban shoo duh/chee feun shu duh/chwan shoo duh]

▸ can I have the check, please? 请给我结账好吗？ qǐng gěi wǒ jiézhàng hǎo ma? [ching gay wo jyeah-jang how ma]

restriction 限制 xiànzhì [shyen-jir]
  ▸ are there restrictions on how much luggage you can take? 对可以携带的行李数量有限制吗? duì kěyǐ xiédài de xíngli shùliàng yǒu xiànzhì ma? [dway kuh-yee shyea-digh shing-lee yoh shyen-jir ma]

restroom 厕所 cèsuǒ [tsuh-swore]
  ▸ is there a restroom on the bus? 公共汽车上有厕所吗? gōnggòng qìchē shang yǒu cèsuǒ ma? [gong-gong chee-chuh shang yoh tsuh-swore ma]

retired 退休的 tuìxiū de [tway-shew]
  ▸ I'm retired now 我现在退休了 wǒ xiànzài tuìxiū le [wo shyen-zigh tway-shew luh]

return (arrival back) 返回 fǎnhuí [fan-hway] ◆ (rental car) 归还 guīhuán [gway-hwan]; (smile) 回报 huíbào [hway-bow]
  ▸ when do we have to return the car? 我们必须什么时候还车? wǒmen bìxū shénme shíhou huán chē? [wo-meun bee-shoo sheun-muh shir-hoh hwan chuh]

return trip 返程 fǎnchéng [fan-chung]
  ▸ the return trip is scheduled for 6 o'clock 返程定在6点钟 fǎnchéng dìng zài liù diǎnzhōng [fan-chung ding zigh lew dyen jong]

rice (uncooked) 大米 dàmǐ [da-mee]; (cooked) 米饭 mǐfàn [mee-fan]
  ▸ I'd like steamed/boiled rice, please 请给我来点米饭 qǐng gěi wǒ lái diǎn mǐfàn [ching gay wo ligh dyen mee-fan]

ride (trip in a car) 乘坐 chéngzuò [chung-zwore]; (lift) 搭乘 dāchéng [da-chung]; (on a bike) 骑自行车 qí zìxíngchē [chee zir-shing-chuh]; (on a motorcycle) 骑摩托车 qí mótuōchē [chee mo-twore-chuh]
  ▸ do you want a ride? 你要搭车吗? nǐ yào dāchē ma? [nee yow da-chuh ma]
  ▸ where can we go for a ride around here? 这附近我们可以去哪里骑自行车? zhè fùjìn wǒmen kěyǐ qù nǎli qí zìxíngchē? [juh foo-jin wo-meun kuh-yee choo na-lee zir-shing-chuh]

riding (on horseback) 骑马 qí mǎ [chee-ma]
  ▸ to go riding 去骑马 qù qí mǎ [choo chee ma]

right (correct) 正确的 zhèngquè de [jung-chue duh]; (not left) 右边的 yòubian de [yoh-byen duh] ◆ 右边 yòubian [yoh-byen] ◆ 在右 zài yòu [zigh yoh]
  ▸ to the right (of) (在......的)右边 (zài......de) yòubian [(zigh...duh) yoh-byen]
  ▸ that's right 是的 shì de [shir duh]
  ▸ I don't think the check's right 我想账单错了 wǒ xiǎng zhàngdān cuò le [wo shyang jang-dan tswore luh]
  ▸ is this the right train for Shanghai? 这是去上海的火车吗? zhè shì qù shànghǎi de huǒchē ma? [juh shir choo shang-high duh hwore-chuh ma]

roads

In the last few years more than 300,000 kilometers of roads have been built in China. This is more than were built in the previous 50 years. Road transportation is consequently becoming more efficient and more comfortable, especially when traveling by bus, and it is becoming easier to reach very beautiful, isolated regions. However, the growth of traffic in the cities is becoming a major problem and causing increased pollution.

▸ is this the right number? 这是正确的号码吗？ **zhè shì zhèngquè de hàomǎ ma?** [juh shir jung-chue duh how-ma ma]

▸ take the next right 在下一个路口向右拐 **zài xià yī gè lùkǒu xiàng yòu guǎi** [zigh shya yee guh loo-koh shyang yoh gwigh]

▸ you have to turn right 你得向右拐 **nǐ děi xiàng yòu guǎi** [nee day shyang yoh gwigh]

right-hand 右边的 **yòubian de** [yoh-byen]

▸ it's on the right-hand side of the steering column 它在驾驶杆的右侧 **tā zài jiàshǐgān de yòucè** [ta zigh jya-shir-gan duh yoh-tsuh]

right of way 先行权 **xiānxíngquán** [shyen-shing-chwan]

▸ who has the right of way here? 在这里谁有先行权？ **zài zhèlǐ shéi yǒu xiānxíngquán?** [zigh juh-lee shay yoh shyen-shing-chwan]

road 路 **lù** [loo]

▸ which road do I take for Chengdu? 去成都我该走哪条路？ **qù chéngdū wǒ gāi zǒu nǎ tiáo lù?** [choo chung-doo wo gigh zoh na teow loo]

▸ what is the speed limit on this road? 这条路上的限速是多少？ **zhè tiáo lù shang de xiànsù shì duōshao?** [juh teow loo shang duh shyen-soo shir dwore-show]

rob *(person)* 抢劫 **qiǎngjié** [chyang-jyeah]

▸ I've been robbed 我被抢劫了 **wǒ bèi qiǎngjié le** [wo bay chyang-jyeah luh]

rock climbing 攀岩 **pān yán** [pan yan]

▸ can you go rock climbing here? 可以在这里攀岩吗？ **kěyǐ zài zhèlǐ pān yán ma?** [kuh-yee zigh juh-lee pan yan ma]

roller skate 旱冰鞋 **hànbīngxié** [han-bing-shyeah]

▸ where can we rent roller skates? 我们能在哪里租到旱冰鞋？ **wǒmen néng zài nǎli zūdào hànbīngxié?** [wo-meun nung zigh na-lee zoo-dow han-bing-shyeah]

room *(bedroom)* 房间 **fángjiān** [fang-jyen]; *(space)* 空间 **kōngjiān** [kong-jyen]

▸ do you have any rooms available? 你们还有空房吗？ **nǐmen hái yǒu kòngfáng ma?** [nee-meun high yoh kong-fang ma]

▸ how much is a room with a bathroom? 带浴室的房间多少钱？ **dài yùshì de fángjiān duōshao qián?** [digh yoo-shir duh fang-jyen dwore-show chyen]

round-trip tickets

It is not possible to buy round-trip tickets in China, so usually you buy a one-way for your outward journey, and then another one-way when you come back.

▶ I've reserved a room for tonight under the name Pearson 我用皮尔森的名字预定了一间今天晚上的房间 wǒ yòng pí'ěrsēn de míngzi yùdìngle yī jiān jīntiān wǎnshang de fángjiān [wo yong pee-er-seun duh ming-zir yoo-ding yee jyen jin-tyen wan-shang duh fang-jyen]

▶ can I see the room? 我能看房吗？ wǒ néng kàn fáng ma? [wo nung kan fang ma]

rosé (wine) 桃红的 táohóng de [tow-hong duh] ◆ 桃红葡萄酒 táohóng pútaojiǔ [tow-hong poo-tow-jew]

▶ could you recommend a good rosé? 你能推荐一种好的桃红葡萄酒吗？ nǐ néng tuījiàn yī zhǒng hǎo de táohóng pútaojiǔ ma? [nee-nung tway-jyen yee jong how duh tow-hong poo-tow-jew ma]

round trip 往返旅行 wǎngfǎn lǚxíng [wang-fang looh-shing]

▶ how long will the round trip take? 往返一次需要多少时间？ wǎngfǎn yī cì xūyào duōshao shíjiān? [wang-fan yee tsir shoo-yow dwore-show shir-jyen]

route (itinerary) 路线 lùxiàn [loo-shyen]

▶ is there an alternative route we could take? 是否有其他路线我们可以走？ shìfǒu yǒu qítā lùxiàn wǒmen kěyǐ zǒu? [shir-foh yoh chee-ta loo-sheyn wo-meun kuh-yee zoh]

row (of seats) 排 pái [pigh]

▶ can we have seats in the front row? 能给我们前排的座位吗？ néng gěi wǒmen qián pái de zuòwei ma? [nung gay wo-meun chyen pigh duh zwore-way ma]

rowboat 划艇 huátǐng [hwa-ting]

▶ can we rent a rowboat? 我们能租划艇吗？ wǒmen néng zū huátǐng ma? [wo-meun nung zoo hwa-ting ma]

rubber ring 游泳圈 yóuyǒngquān [yoh-yong-chwan]

▶ where can I buy a rubber ring? 我可以在哪里买到游泳圈？ wǒ kěyǐ zài nǎli mǎidào yóuyǒngquān? [wo kuh-yee zigh na-lee migh-dow yoh-yong-chwan]

run (on foot) 奔跑 bēnpǎo [beun-pow]; (in a car) 行驰 xíngshǐ [shing-shir]; (for skiing) 滑道 huádào [hwa-dow] ◆ (on foot) 奔跑 bēnpǎo [beun-pow]; (bus, train) 行驰 xíngshǐ [shing-shir]; (engine) 运转 yùnzhuǎn [ywan-jwan] ◆ (traffic light) 闯 chuǎng [chwung]

▶ I'm going for a run 我去跑步 wǒ qù pǎobù [wo choo pow-boo]

▸ the bus runs every half hour 公共汽车每半小时一班 gōnggòng qìchē měi bàn xiǎoshí yī bān [gong-gong chee-chuh may ban sheow-shir yee ban]

running 跑步 pǎobù [pow-boo]

▸ where can you go running here? 这里可以在哪里跑步？ zhèlǐ kěyǐ zài nǎli pǎobù? [juh-lee kuh-yee na-lee pow-boo]

run out of 用完 yòngwán [yong-wan]

▸ I've run out of gas 我汽油用完了 wǒ qìyóu yòngwán le [wo chee-yoh yong-wan luh]

S

safe 安全的 ānquán de [an-chwan duh] ♦ *(for valuables)* 保险箱 bǎoxiǎnxiāng [bow-shyen-shyang]

▸ is it safe to swim here? 在这里游泳安全吗？ zài zhèlǐ yóuyǒng ānquán ma? [zigh juh-lee yoh-yong an-chwan ma]

▸ is it safe to camp here? 在这里露营安全吗？ zài zhèlǐ lùyíng ānquán ma? [zigh juh-lee loo-ying an-chwan ma]

▸ is there a safe in the room? 房间里有保险箱吗？ fángjiān li yǒu bǎoxiǎnxiāng ma? [fang-jyen lee yoh bow-shyen-shyang ma]

sail *(of a boat)* 帆 fān [fan]

▸ we need to adjust that sail 我们需要调整帆了 wǒmen xūyào tiáozhěng fān le [wo-meun shoo-yow teow-jung fan luh]

sailboat 帆船 fānchuán [fan-chwan]

▸ can we rent a sailboat? 我们能租艘帆船吗？ wǒmen néng zū sōu fānchuán ma? [wo-meun kuh-yee zoo soh fan-chwan ma]

sailing 帆船运动 fānchuán yùndòng [fan-chwan yun-dong]

▸ to go sailing 驾驶帆船 jiàshǐ fānchuán [jya-shir fan-chwan]

▸ I'd like to take beginners' sailing classes 我想参加初级帆船课程 wǒ xiǎng cānjiā chūjí fānchuán kèchéng [wo shyang tsan-jya choo-jee fan-chwan kuh-chung]

salad 色拉 sèlā [suh-la]

▸ can I just have a salad? 我只要色拉可以吗？ wǒ zhǐ yào sèlā kěyǐ ma? [wo jir yow suh-la kuh-yee ma]

sale *(selling)* 出售 chūshòu [choo-shoh]; *(at reduced prices)* 特价 tèjià [tuh-jya]

▸ is it for sale? 这个卖吗？ zhège mài ma? [juh-guh migh ma]

▸ can you get your money back on sale items? 特价商品可以退货吗？ tèjià shāngpǐn kěyǐ tuìhuò ma? [tuh-jya shang-pin kuh-yee tway-hwore ma]

sales tax 增值税 zēngzhíshuì [zung-jir-shway]

▸ is sales tax included? 包括增值税吗？ bāokuò zēngzhíshuì ma? [bow-kwore zung-jir-shway ma]

▸ can you deduct the sales tax? 你能否减去增值税？ nǐ néngfǒu jiǎnqù zēngzhíshuì? [nee nung-foh jyang zung-jir-shway]

salt 盐 yán [yan] ◆ 在......中加盐 zài......zhōng jiā yán [zigh...jong jya yan]

▸ can you pass me the salt? 你能把盐递给我吗？ nǐ néng bǎ yán dì gěi wǒ ma? [nee nung ba yan dee gay wo ma]

▸ it doesn't have enough salt 那里面的盐不够 nà lǐmian de yán bù gòu [na lee-myen duh yan boo goh]

salty 咸的 xián de [shyen duh]

▸ it's too salty 太咸了 tài xián le [tigh shyen luh]

same 一样的 yīyàng de [yee-yang duh]

▸ I'll have the same 我要一样的 wǒ yào yīyàng de [wo yow yee-yang duh]

▸ the same (as) （与......）相同的 (yǔ......) xiāngtóng de [(yoo...) shyang-tong duh]

▸ it's the same as yours 和你的一样 hé nǐ de yīyàng [huh nee duh yee-yang]

sandwich 三明治 sānmíngzhì [san-ming-jir]

▸ a chicken sandwich, please 请来一份鸡肉三明治 qǐng lái yī fèn jīròu sānmíngzhì [ching ligh yee feun jee-roh san-ming-jir]

Saturday 星期六 xīngqīliù [shing-chee-lew]

▸ Saturday, September 13th 9月13日，星期六 jiǔ yuè shísān rì, xīngqīliù [jew yue shir-san rir shing-chee-lew]

▸ it's closed on Saturdays 星期六关门 xīngqīliù guānmén [shing-chee-lew gwan-meun]

sauce 酱 jiàng [jyang]

▸ do you have a sauce that isn't too strong? 你有口感不那么重的酱吗？ nǐ yǒu kǒugǎn bù nàme zhòng de jiàng ma? [nee yoh koh-gwan boo na-muh jong duh jyang ma]

sauna 桑拿浴 sāngnáyù [sang-na-yoo]

▸ is there a sauna? 有桑拿浴吗？ yǒu sāngnáyù ma? [yoh sang-na-yoo ma]

sausage 香肠 xiāngcháng [shyang-chang]

▸ I'd like to try some of the hot sausage 我想吃一些热的香肠 wǒ xiǎng chī yīxiē rè de xiāngcháng [wo shyang chir yee-shyeah ruh duh shyang-chang]

say 说 shuō [shwore]

▸ how do you say 'good luck' in Chinese? 'good luck' 用中文怎么说？ 'good luck' yòng zhōngwén zěnme shuō? [good luck yong jong-weun zeun-muh shwore]

scared

▸ to be scared 害怕 hàipà [high-pa]

▸ I'm scared of spiders 我怕蜘蛛 wǒ pà zhīzhū [wo pa jir-joo]

scheduled flight 定期航班 dìngqī hángbān [ding-chee hang-ban]

▸ when is the next scheduled flight to Beijing? 下一班飞往北京的定期航班是几点？ xià yī bān fēiwǎng běijīng de dìngqī hángbān shì jǐ diǎn? [shya yee ban fay-wang bay-jing duh ding-chee hang-ban shir jee dyen]

school (for children) 学校 xuéxiào [shue-sheow]; (college, university) 学院 xuéyuàn [shue-ywan]

▸ are you still in school? 你还在读大学吗？ nǐ hái zài dú dàxué ma? [nee high zigh doo da-shue ma]

scoop (of ice cream) 勺 sháo [show]

▸ I'd like a cone with two scoops 我要一个两球的冰激凌筒 wǒ yào yī gè liǎng qiú de bīngjīlíngtǒng [wo yow yee guh lyang chew duh bing-chee-ling-tong]

scooter 小型摩托车 xiǎoxíng mótuōchē [sheow-shing mo-twore-chuh]

▸ I'd like to rent a scooter 我想租一辆小型摩托车 wǒ xiǎng zū yī liàng xiǎoxíng mótuōchē [wo shyang zoo yee lyang sheow-shing mo-twore-chuh]

Scotch (whiskey) 苏格兰威士忌 sūgélán wēishìjì [soo-guh-lan way-shir-jee]

▸ a Scotch on the rocks, please 请来一杯加冰的苏格兰威士忌 qǐng lái yī bēi jiā bīng de sūgélán wēishìjì [ching ligh yee bay jya bing duh soo-guh-lan way-shir-jee]

Scotch tape® 透明胶 tòumíngjiāo [toh-ming-jeow]

▸ do you have any Scotch tape®? 你有透明胶吗？ nǐ yǒu tòumíngjiāo ma? [nee yoh toh-ming-jeow ma]

scrambled eggs 用牛奶和黄油炒的鸡蛋 yòng niúnǎi hé huángyóu chǎo de jīdàn [yong new-nigh huh hwung-yoh chow duh jee-dan]

▸ I'd like scrambled eggs for breakfast 我早餐要牛奶和黄油炒的鸡蛋 wǒ zǎocān yào niúnǎi hé huángyóu chǎo de jīdàn [wo zow-tsan yow new-nigh huh hwung-yoh chow duh jee-dan]

screen (room in a movie theater) 放映厅 fàngyìngtīng [fang-ying-ting]

▸ how many screens does the movie theater have? 这个电影院有多少个放映厅？ zhège diànyǐngyuàn yǒu duōshao gè fàngyìngtīng? [juh-guh dyen-ying-ywan yoh dwore-show guh fang-ying-ting]

scuba diving 带水下呼吸器潜水 dài shuǐ xià hūxīqì qiánshuǐ [digh shway shya hoo-shee-chee chyen-shway]

▸ can we go scuba diving? 我们能去潜水吗？ wǒmen néng qù qiánshuǐ ma? [wo-meun nung choo chyen-shway ma]

sea 海 hǎi [high]

▸ the sea is rough 海上风浪很大 hǎi shang fēnglàng hěn dà [high shang fung-lang heun da]

‣ how long does it take to walk to the sea? 步行去海边要多久？ bùxíng qù hǎibiān yào duō jiǔ？ [boo-shing choo high-byen yow dwore jew]

seasick 晕船的 yūnchuán de [yun-chwan duh]

‣ I feel seasick 我感到晕船 wǒ gǎndào yūnchuán [wo gan-dow yun-chwan]

seasickness 晕船 yūnchuán [yun-chwan]

‣ can you give me something for seasickness, please? 请你给我一些治晕船的药好吗？ qǐng nǐ gěi wǒ yīxiē zhì yūnchuán de yào hǎo ma? [ching nee gay wo yee-shyeah jir yun-chwan duh yow how ma]

seaside resort 海滨旅游胜地 hǎibīn lǚyóu shèngdì [high-bin looh-yoh shung-dee]

‣ what's the nearest seaside resort? 最近的海滨旅游胜地在什么地方？ zuì jìn de hǎibīn lǚyóu shèngdì zài shénme dìfang? [zway jin duh high-bin looh-yoh shung-dee zigh sheun-muh dee-fang]

season (of the year) 季节 jìjié [jee-jyeah]

‣ what is the best season to come here? 什么季节来最好？ shénme jìjié lái zuì hǎo? [sheun-muh jee-jyeah ligh zway how]

season ticket 长期票 chángqīpiào [chang-chee-peow]

‣ how much is a season ticket? 长期票多少钱？ chángqīpiào duōshao qián? [chang-chee-peow dwore-show chyen]

seat 座位 zuòwei [zwore-way]

‣ is this seat taken? 这个座位有人吗？ zhège zuòwei yǒu rén ma? [juh-guh zwore-way yoh reun ma]

‣ excuse me, I think you're (sitting) in my seat 对不起，我想你坐了我的位置 duìbuqǐ, wǒ xiǎng nǐ zuòle wǒ de wèizhi [dway-boo-chee wo shyang nee zwore-luh wo duh way-jir]

second (unit of time) 第二 dì-èr [dee-er]; (gear) 二挡 èrdǎng [er-dang] ◆ 第二的 dì-èr de [dee-er duh]

‣ wait a second! 等一会儿！ děng yīhuìr! [dung yee-hwayr]

‣ is it in second? 挂了二挡吗？ guàle èrdǎng ma? [gwa-luh er-dang ma]

‣ it's the second street on your right 是你右边的第二条街 shì nǐ yòubian de dì-èr tiáo jiē [shir nee yoh-byen duh dee-er teow jyeah]

second class 二等 èrděng [er-dung] ◆ 用二等 yòng èrděng [yong er-dung]

‣ your seat's in second class 你的座位在二等舱 nǐ de zuòwei zài èrděngcāng [nee duh zwore-way zigh er-dung-tsang]

‣ to travel second class 坐二等舱出行 zuò èrděngcāng chūxíng [zwore er-dung-tsang choo-shing]

see 看见 kànjian [kan-jyen]

‣ I'm here to see Dr. Brown 我来这儿见布朗医生 wǒ lái zhèr jiàn bùlǎng yīshēng [wo ligh jer jyen boo-lang yee-shung]

▸ can I see the room? 我能看一下房间吗？ wǒ néng kàn yī xià fángjiān ma? [wo nung kan yee shya fang-jyen ma]

▸ I'd like to see the dress in the window 我想看一下橱窗里的连衣裙 wǒ xiǎng kàn yī xià chúchuāng li de liányīqún [wo shyang kan yee shya choo-chwung lee duh lyen-yee-chun]

▸ see you! 再见！ zàijiàn! [zigh-jyen]

▸ see you later 一会儿见 yīhuìr jiàn [yee-hwayr jyen]

▸ see you (on) Thursday! 星期四见！ xīngqīsì jiàn! [shing-chee-sir jyen]

self-service (restaurant, gas station) 自助的 zìzhù de [zir-joo duh] ◆ 自助服务 zìzhù fúwù [zir-joo foo-woo]

▸ is it self-service? 是自助式的吗？ shì zìzhùshì de ma? [shir zir-joo-shir ma]

sell 出售 chūshòu [choo-shoh]

▸ do you sell stamps? 你们出售邮票吗？ nǐmen chūshòu yóupiào ma? [nee-meun choo-shoh yoh-peow ma]

▸ the radio I was sold is defective 卖给我的收音机是坏的 mài gěi wǒ de shōuyīnjī shì huài de [migh gay wo duh shoh-yin-jee shir hwigh duh]

send 送出 sòngchū [song-choo]; (mail) 寄 jì [jee]

▸ I'd like to send this package to Boston by airmail 我想把这个包裹用航空邮件寄往波士顿 wǒ xiǎng bǎ zhège bāoguǒ yòng hángkōng yóujiàn jìwǎng bōshìdùn [wo shyang ban juh-guh bow-gwore yong hang-kong yoh-jyen jee-wang bo-shir-dun]

▸ could you send a tow truck? 你能叫辆拖车过来吗？ nǐ néng jiào liàng tuōchē guòlai ma? [nee nung jeow lyang twore-chuh gwore-ligh ma]

separately (individually) 单独地 dāndú de [dan-doo duh]

▸ is it sold separately? 这个单独出售吗？ zhège dāndú chūshòu ma? [juh-guh dan-doo choo-shoh ma]

September 九月 jiǔ yuè [jew yue]

▸ September 9th 九月九日 jiǔ yuè jiǔ rì [jew yue jew rir]

serve (meal, drink) 端上 duānshang [dwan-shang]; (customer) 招待 zhāodài [jow-digh]; (town, station) 为......提供服务 wèi......tígōng fúwù [way...tee-gong foo-woo]

▸ when is breakfast served? 几点提供早餐？ jǐ diǎn tígōng zǎocān? [jee dyen tee-gong zow-tsan]

▸ are you still serving lunch? 你们还供应午餐吗？ nǐmen hái gōngyìng wǔcān ma? [nee-meun high gong-ying woo-tsan ma] ▸ see box on p. 150

service (in a restaurant) 服务 fúwù [foo-woo] ◆ (car) 检修 jiǎnxiū [jyen-shew]

▸ the service was terrible 服务很差 fúwù hěn chà [foo-woo heun cha]

▸ we have to have the car serviced 我们得把车送去检修了 wǒmen děi bǎ chē sòngqu jiǎnxiū le [wo-meun day ba chuh song-choo jyen-shew luh]

serving dishes

In Chinese restaurants, food is traditionally served on serving dishes rather than on individual plates. The dishes are put in the middle of the table, then everyone digs in with their chopsticks. Usually order the same number of dishes as there are guests. A business lunch or a banquet might include around twenty dishes, both hot and cold. Bear in mind that it is polite not to finish everything in the dish, or your bowl of rice or noodles, as a way of showing that you have had enough to eat (otherwise, to please you, your host might re-order the dish you have just finished!).

service charge 服务费 fúwùfèi [foo-woo-fay]
- ▸ is the service charge included? 包括服务费了吗? bāokuò fúwùfèi le ma? [biow-kwore foo-woo-fay luh ma]

set *(of cookware)* 套 tào [tow] ◆ *(sun)* 日落 rìluò [rir-lwore]
- ▸ do you have a spare set of keys? 你有一套备份的钥匙吗? nǐ yǒu yī tào bèifèn de yàoshi ma? [nee yoh yee tow bay-feun duh yow-shir ma]
- ▸ what time does the sun set? 几点钟日落? jǐ diǎnzhōng rìluò [jee dyen-jong rir-lwore]

seven 七 qī [chee]
- ▸ there are seven of us 我们有七个人 wǒmenyǒu qī gè rén [wo-meun yoh chee guh reun]

several 几个的 jǐ gè de [jee-guh duh] ◆ 几个 jǐ gè [jee-guh]
- ▸ I've been before, several years ago 我几年前去过那里 wǒ jǐ nián qián qùguo nàli [wo jee nyen chyen choo-gwore na-lee]

shade *(shadow)* 阴凉处 yīnliángchù [yin-lyang-choo]
- ▸ can we have a table in the shade? 我们能要一张阴凉处的桌子吗? wǒmen néng yào yī zhāng yīnliángchù de zhuōzi ma? [wo-meun nung yow yee jang yin-lyang-choo duh jwore-zir ma]

shake *(bottle)* 摇动 yáodòng [yow-dong] ◆ *(in agreement)* 握手为定 wòshǒu wéi dìng [wo-shoh way ding]
- ▸ to shake hands 握手 wòshuǒ [wo-shoh]
- ▸ let's shake 让我们握手为定吧 ràng wǒmen wòshǒu wéi dìng ba [rang wo-meun wo-shoh way ding ba]

shame *(remorse, humiliation)* 羞耻 xiūchǐ [shew-chir]; *(pity)* 遗憾 yíhàn [yee-jan]
- ▸ (what a) shame! 真遗憾! zhēn yíhàn! [jeun yee-han]

shampoo 洗发露 xǐfàlù [shee-fa-loo]
- ▸ do you have any shampoo? 你有洗发露吗? nǐ yǒu xǐfàlù ma? [nee yoh shee-fa-loo ma]

share 与人分享 yǔ rén fēnxiǎng [yoo reun feun-shyang]
  ▸ we're going to share it: can you bring us two plates? 我们合吃，给我们拿两个盘子好吗？ wǒmen hé chī, gěi wǒmen ná liǎng gè pánzi hǎo ma? [wo-meun huh chir gay wo-meun na lyang guh pan-zir how ma]

shared (bathroom, kitchen) 公用的 gōngyòng de [gong-yong duh]
  ▸ is the bathroom shared? 浴室是公用的吗？ yùshì shì gōngyòng de ma? [yoo-shir shir gong-yong duh ma]

shaver 电动剃须刀 diàndòng tìxūdāo [dyen-dong tee-shoo dow]
  ▸ where can I buy a new shaver? 我可以去哪里买电动剃须刀？ wǒ kěyǐ qù nǎli mǎi diàndòng tìxūdāo [wo kuh-yee choo na-lee migh dyen-dong tee-shoo-dow]

sheet (for a bed) 床单 chuángdān [chwung-dan]; (of paper) 张 zhāng [jang]
  ▸ could you change the sheets? 你能把床单换了吗？ nǐ néng bǎ chuángdān huànle ma? [nee nung ba chwung-dan hwan-luh ma]

ship 船 chuán [chwan]
  ▸ when does the ship dock? 船什么时候到港？ chuán shénme shíhou dàogǎng? [chwan sheun-muh shir-hoh dow-gang]

shoe 鞋 xié [shyeah]
  ▸ what sort of shoes should you wear? 应该穿哪种鞋？ yīnggāi chuān nǎ zhǒng xié? [ying-gigh chwan na jong shyeah]

shoe size 鞋子的尺码 xiézi de chǐmǎ [shyeah-zir duh chir-ma]
  ▸ what's your shoe size? 你鞋子的尺码是多少？ nǐ xiézi de chǐmǎ shì duōshao? [nee shyeah-zir duh chir-ma shir dwore-show]

shop (store) 商店 shāngdiàn [shang-dyen]
  ▸ what time do the shops downtown close? 市区的商店什么时候关门？ shìqū de shāngdiàn shénme shíhou guānmén? [shir-choo duh shang-dyen sheun-muh shir-hoh gwan-meun]

shopping 购物 gòu wù [goh woo]
  ▸ where can you go shopping around here? 这附近可以去哪里购物？ zhè fùjìn kěyǐ qù nǎli gòu wù? [juh foo-jin kuh-yee choo na-lee goh woo]

shopping bag 购物袋 gòuwùdài [goh-woo-digh]
  ▸ can I have a shopping bag, please? 请给我一个购物袋好吗？ qǐng gěi wǒ yī gè gòuwùdài hǎo ma? [ching gay wo yee guh goh-woo-digh how ma]

shopping center 购物中心 gòu wù zhōngxīn [goh woo jong-shin]
  ▸ I'm looking for a shopping center 我在找购物中心 wǒ zài zhǎo gòu wù zhōngxīn [wo zigh jow goh woo jong-shin]

shop window 商店橱窗 shāngdiàn chúchuāng [shang-dyen choo-chwung]
  ▸ we've been looking in the shop windows 我们在看商店橱窗里的东西 wǒmen zài kàn shāngdiàn chúchuāng li de dōngxi [wo-meun zigh kan shang-dyen choo-chwung lee duh dong-shee]

short *(time, in length)* 短的 duǎn de [dwan duh]; *(in height)* 矮的 ǎi de [igh duh]; *(of funds)* 短缺的 duǎnquē de [dwan-chue duh]

- we're only here for a short time 我们只在这里短期停留 wǒmen zhǐ zài zhèlǐ duǎnqī tíngliú [wo-meun jir zigh juh-lee dwan-chee ting-lew]
- we'd like to do a shorter trip 我们想参加时间短一点儿的旅行 wǒmen xiǎng cānjiā shíjiān duǎn yīdiǎnr de lǚxíng [wo-meun shyang tsan-jya shir-jyen dwan yee-dyenr duh loo-shing]
- I'm 2 yuan short 我差两元钱 wǒ chà liǎng yuán qián [wo cha lyang ywan chyen]

shortcut 捷径 jiéjìng [jyeah-jing]

- is there a shortcut? 有捷径吗? yǒu jiéjìng ma? [yoh jyeah-jing ma]

should 应该 yīnggāi [ying-gigh]

- what should I do? 我该怎么做? wǒ gāi zěnme zuò? [wo gigh zeun-muh zwore]

show *(at the theater)* 表演 biǎoyǎn [beow-yan]; *(at the movies)* 电影 diànyǐng [dyen-ying]; *(on TV)* 节目 jiémù [jyeah-moo] ◆ *(let see)* 显示 xiǎnshì [shyen-shir]

- what time does the show begin? 演出什么时候开始? yǎnchū shénme shíhou kāishǐ? [yan-choo sheun-muh shir-hoh kigh-shir]
- could you show me where that is on the map? 你能在地图上指给我看那个在哪里吗? nǐ néng zài dìtú shàng zhǐ gěi wǒ kàn nàge zài nǎli ma? [nee nung zigh dee-too shang jir guh wo kan na-guh zigh na-lee ma]
- could you show me the room? 你能让我看房吗? nǐ néng ràng wǒ kàn fáng ma? [nee nung rang wo kan fang ma]

shower *(device, act)* 淋浴 línyù [lin-yoo]; *(of rain)* 阵雨 zhènyǔ [jeun-yoo]

- I'd like a room with a shower, please 我想要一间带淋浴的房间 wǒ xiǎng yào yī jiān dài línyù de fángjiān [wo shyang yow yee jyen digh lin-yoo duh fang-jyen]
- how does the shower work? 这个淋浴该怎么用? zhège línyù gāi zěnme yòng? [juh-guh lin-yoo gigh zeun-muh yong]
- the shower is leaking 浴室漏水了 yùshì lòu shuǐ le [yoo-shir loh shway luh]

shower head 喷头 pēntóu [peun-toh]

- the shower head is broken 淋浴的喷头坏了 línyù de pēntóu huài le [lin-yoo duh peun-toh hway luh]

shrimp 虾 xiā [shya]

- I'm allergic to shrimp 我对虾过敏 wǒ duì xiā guòmǐn [wo dway shya gwore-min]

shut 把......关上 bǎ......guānshang [ba...gwang-shang] ◆ 关上 guānshang [gwan-shang]

- the window won't shut 窗户关不上 chuānghù guān bù shàng [chwung-hoo gwan boo shang]

shutter (on a window) 百叶窗 bǎiyèchuāng [bigh-yuh-chwung]; (on a camera) 快门 kuàimén [kwigh-meun]

- ▶ are there shutters on the windows? 窗户上有百叶窗吗? chuānghu shang yǒu bǎiyèchuāng ma? [chwung-hoo shang yoh bigh-yuh-chwung ma]

shuttle (vehicle) 穿梭巴士 chuānsuō bāshì [chwan-swore ba-shir]

- ▶ is there a shuttle to the airport? 有开往机场的穿梭巴士吗? yǒu kāiwǎng jīchǎng de chuānsuō bāshì ma? [yoh kigh-wang jee-chang duh chwan-swore ba-shir ma]

sick (unwell) 生病的 shēngbìng de [shung-bing duh]

- ▶ I feel sick 我感到恶心 wǒ gǎndào ěxīn [w gan-dow uh-shin]
- ▶ to be sick (be unwell) 生病 shēngbìng [shung-bing]; (vomit) 呕吐 ǒutù [gan-dow oh-too]

side (of the body) 侧 cè [tsuh]; (of an object) 面 miàn [myen]; (edge) 边缘 biānyuán [byen-ywan]; (opposing part) 边 biān [byen]

- ▶ I have a pain in my right side 我右侧疼 wǒ zuǒcè téng [wo zwore-tsuh]
- ▶ could we have a table on the other side of the room? 我们能要一张在房间另一边的桌位吗? wǒmen néng yào yī zhāng zài fángjiān lìng yī biān de zhuōwèi ma? [wo-meun nung yow yee jang zigh fang-jyen ling yee byen duh jwore-way ma]
- ▶ which side of the road do we drive on here? 在这里在道路的哪一边开车? zài zhèlǐ zài dàolù de nǎ yībiān kāichē? [zigh juh-lee zigh dow-loo duh na yee-byen kigh-chuh]

sidewalk 人行道 rénxíngdào [reun-shing-dow]

- ▶ the sidewalks are very clean here 这里的人行道很干净 zhèlǐ de rénxíngdào hěn gānjìng [juh-lee duh reun-shing-dow heun gan-jing]

sight (seeing) 视力 shìlì [shir-lee] ◆ **sights** (of a place) 风景 fēngjǐng [fung-jing]

- ▶ I'm having problems with my sight 我的视力有问题 wǒ de shìlì yǒu wèntí [wo duh shir-lee yoh weun-tee]
- ▶ what are the sights that are most worth seeing? 最值得看的风景是什么? zuì zhíde kàn de fēngjǐng shì shénme? [zway jir-duh kan duh fung-jing shir sheun-muh]

sign 签 qiān [chyen] ◆ **签名** qiānmíng [chyen-ming]

- ▶ do I sign here? 我在这儿签名吗? wǒ zài zhèr qiānmíng ma? [wo zigh jer chyen-ming ma]

signpost 路标 lùbiāo [loo-beow]

- ▶ does the route have good signposts? 路上路标清楚吗? lù shang lùbiāo qīngchǔ ma? [loo shang loo-beow ching-choo ma]

silver *(metal)* 银 yín [yin]

▸ is it made of silver? 这个是银做的吗? zhège shì yín zuò de ma? [juh-guh shir yin zwore duh ma]

since 自从......以来 zìcóng......yǐlái [zir-tsong...yee-ligh] ◆ *(because)* 既然 jìrán [jee-ran]

▸ I've been here since Tuesday 自从星期二以来我就在这儿了 zìcóng xīngqī'èr yǐlái wǒ jiù zài zhèr le [zir-tsong shing-chee-er yee-ligh wo jew zigh jer luh]

▸ it hasn't rained once since we've been here 我们到这儿后还没有下过一场雨 wǒmen dào zhèr hòu hái méiyou xiàguo yī chǎng yǔ [wo-meun dow jer hoh high may-yoh shya-gwore yee chang yoo]

single *(only one)* 单一的 dānyī de [dan-yee duh]; *(unmarried)* 未婚的 wèihūn de [way-hun duh]

▸ I'm single 我未婚 wǒ wèihūn [way-hun]

▸ she's a single woman in her thirties 她是一个三十多岁的未婚女人 tā shì yī gè sānshí duō suì de wèihūn nǚrén [ta shir ge guh san-shir dwore sway duh way-hun nooh-reun]

single bed 单人床 dānrénchuáng [dan-reun-chwung]

▸ we'd prefer two single beds 我们想要两张单人床 wǒmen xiǎng yào liǎng zhāng dānrénchuáng [wo-meun shyang yow lyang jang dan-reun-chwung]

single room 单人房 dānrénfáng [dan-reun-fang]

▸ I'd like to book a single room for five nights, please 我想预订一间单人房,住五个晚上 wǒ xiǎng yùdìng yī jiān dānrénfáng, zhù wǔ gè wǎnshang [wo shyang yoo-ding yee jyen dan-reun-fang joo woo guh wan-shang]

sister 姐妹 jiěmèi [jyeah-may]

▸ I have two sisters 我有两个姐妹 wǒ yǒu liǎng gè jiěmèi [wo yoh lyang guh jyeah-may]

sit 坐 zuò [zwore]

▸ may I sit at your table? 我能和你同坐一张桌子吗? wǒ néng hé nǐ tóng zuò yī zhāng zhuōzi ma? [wo mung huh nee tong zwore yee jang jwore-zir ma]

▸ is anyone sitting here? 这里有人坐吗? zhèli yǒu rén zuò ma? [juh-lee yoh reun zwore ma]

site *(of a town, a building)* 场所 chǎngsuǒ [chang-swore]; *(archeological)* 遗址 yízhǐ [yee-jir]

▸ can we visit the site? 我们能参观遗址吗? wǒmen néng cānguān yízhǐ ma? [wo-meun nung tsan-gwan yee-jir ma]

sitting *(for a meal)* 一批 pī [yee-pee]

▸ is there more than one sitting for lunch? 不止一批人来用午餐吗? bùzhǐ yī pī rén lái yòng wǔcān ma? [boo-jir yee pee reun ligh yong woo-tsan ma]

six 六 liù [lew]

▸ there are six of us 我们有六个人 wǒmenyǒu liù gè rén [wo-meun yoh lew guh reun]

sixth 第六的 dì–liù de [dee-lew duh] ◆ 第六 dì–liù [dee-lew]

▸ our room is on the sixth floor 我们的房间在六楼 wǒmen de fángjiān zài liù lóu [wo-meun duh fang-jyen zigh lew loh]

size (of a person, clothes) 尺码 chǐmǎ [chir-ma]

▸ do you have another size? 你还有其他尺码吗？ nǐ hái yǒu qítā chǐmǎ ma? [nee high yoh chee-ta chir-ma ma]

▸ do you have it in a smaller size? 这个你还有小一点儿的尺码吗？ zhège nǐ hái yǒu xiǎo yīdiǎnr de chǐmǎ ma? [juh-guh nee high yoh sheow yee-dyenr duh chir-ma ma]

▸ I take/I'm a size 38 (shoes) 我穿38码的鞋 wǒ chuān sānshíbā mǎ de xié [wo chwan san-shir-ba ma duh shyeah]; (clothes) 我穿38码的衣服 wǒ chuān sānshíbā mǎ de yīfu [wo chwan san-shir-ba ma duh yee-foo]

skate 滑冰 huábīng [hwa-bing] ◆ 溜冰鞋 liūbīngxié [lew-bing-shyeah]

▸ can you skate? 你会滑冰吗？ nǐ huì huábīng ma? [nee hway hwa-bing ma]

▸ how much is it to rent skates? 租溜冰鞋要多少钱？ zū liūbīngxié yào duōshao qián? [zoo lew-bing-shyeah yow dwore-show chyen]

skating 滑冰 huábīng

▸ where can we go skating? 我们可以去哪里滑冰？ wǒmen kěyǐ qù nǎli huábīng? [wo-meun kuh-yee choo na-lee hwa-bing]

ski boots 滑雪靴 huáxuěxuē [hwa-shue-shue]

▸ I'd like to rent ski boots 我想租滑雪靴 wǒxiǎng zū huáxuěxuē [wo shyang zoo hwa-shue-shue]

skiing 滑雪 huáxuě [hwa-shue]

▸ where can we go skiing near here? 我们可以去哪里滑雪？ wǒmen kěyǐ qù nǎli huáxuě? [wo-meun kuh-yee choo na-lee hwa-shue]

skis 滑雪板 huáxuěbǎn [hwa-shue-ban]

▸ I'd like to rent a pair of skis for the week, please 我想租一副滑雪板，租一个星期 wǒ xiǎng zū yī fù huáxuěbǎn, zū yī gè xīngqī [wo shyang zoo yee foo hwa-shue-ban zoo yee guh shing-chee]

sleep (be asleep) 睡觉 shuìjiào [shway-jeow]; (spend night) 过夜 guòyè [gwore-yuh]

▸ I slept well 我睡得好 wǒ shuì de hǎo [wo shway duh how]

▸ I can't sleep 我睡不着 wǒ shuì bù zháo [wo shway boo jow]

sleeping bag 睡袋 shuìdài [shway-digh]

▸ where can I buy a new sleeping bag? 我可以去哪里买个新睡袋？ wǒ kěyǐ qù nǎli mǎi gè xīn shuìdài? [wo kuh-yee choo na-lee migh guh shin shway-digh]

slice (of bread, ham) 片 piàn [pyen] ◆ 把......切成片 bǎ......qiēchéng piàn [ba...chyeah-chung pyen]

▸ a thin slice of ham 薄薄的一片火腿 báobáo de yī piàn huǒtuǐ [bow-bow duh yee pyen hwore-tway]

slim *(person)* 苗条的 miáotiao de [meow-teow duh]

  ▸ she's slim 她苗条 tā miáotiao [ta meow-teow]

slow 慢的 màn de [man duh]

  ▸ the fog was slow to clear 雾散得慢 wù sàn de màn [woo san duh man]

  ▸ is that clock slow? 那个钟慢了吗？ nàge zhōng màn le ma? [na-guh jong man luh ma]

slowly 慢地 màn de [man duh]

  ▸ could you speak more slowly, please? 请你说得慢一点儿好吗？ qǐng nǐ shuō de màn yīdiǎnr hǎo ma? [ching nee shwore duh man yee-dyenr how ma]

small 小的 xiǎo de [sheow duh]

  ▸ do you have anything smaller? 你有小一点儿的吗？ nǐ yǒu xiǎo yīdiǎnr de ma? [nee yoh sheow yee-dyenr duh ma]

smell *(notice a smell of)* 闻到 wéndào [weun-dow] ◆ *(have a smell)* 气味 qìwèi [chee-way]; *(have a bad smell)* 臭味 chòuwèi [choh-way]

  ▸ can you smell something burning? 你闻到烧焦的味道了吗？ nǐ wéndào shāojiāo de wèidào le ma? [nee weun-dow show-jeow duh way-dow luh ma]

  ▸ it smells in here 这里气味很难闻 zhèli qìwèi hěn nán wén [juh-lee chee-way heun nan weun]

smoke 烟 yān [yan]; *(of cigarette)* 烟味 yānwèi [yan-way] ◆ *(person)* 吸烟 xīyān [shee-yan]

  ▸ is the smoke bothering you? 烟味让你讨厌吗？ yānwèi ràng nǐ tǎoyàn ma? [yan-way rang nee tow-yan ma]

  ▸ do you mind if I smoke? 我吸烟你介意吗？ wǒ xīyān nǐ jièyì ma? [wo shee-yan nee jyeeay-yee ma]

  ▸ no thanks, I don't smoke 不，谢谢。我不吸烟 bù, xièxie. wǒ bù xīyān [shyeah-shyeah wo boo shee-yan]

smoker 吸烟者 xīyānzhě [shee-yan-juh]

  ▸ are you smokers or nonsmokers? 你们是吸烟的还是不吸烟的？ nǐmen shì xīyān de háishi bù xīyān de? [ni-meun shir shee-yan duh high-shir boo shee-yan duh]

smoking 吸烟 xīyān [shee-yan]

  ▸ is smoking allowed here? 可以在这里吸烟吗？ kěyǐ zài zhèli xīyān ma? [kuh-yee zigh juh-lee shee-yan ma]

  ▸ I can't stand smoking 我讨厌吸烟 wǒ tǎoyàn xīyān [wo tow-yan shee-yan]

smoking compartment 吸烟车厢 xīyān chēxiāng [shee-yan juh-shyang]

  ▸ I'd like a seat in a smoking compartment 我想要一个吸烟车厢的座位 wǒ xiǎng yào yī gè xīyān chēxiāng de zuòwei [wo shyang yow yee guh shee-yan juh-shyang duh zwore-way]

  ▸ is there a smoking compartment? 有吸烟车厢吗？ yǒu xīyān chēxiāng ma? [yoh shee-yan chuh-shyang ma]

smoking

The Chinese have a reputation for being heavy smokers, but it's becoming more and more difficult to find a place where you are allowed to smoke in China. Most trains are now completely nonsmoking, although you can smoke in the spaces between the cars, near the doors. Most movie theaters, theaters and concert halls do not allow smoking. In restaurants, however, there is usually no separation of smoking/nonsmoking areas. The major imported brands of cigarettes remain a highly-valued present.

smoking section 吸烟区 xīyānqū [shee-yan-choo]

▸ I'd like a table in the smoking section 我想要一张在吸烟区的桌子 wǒ xiǎng yào yī zhāng zài xīyānqū de zhuōzi [wo shyang yee jang zigh shee-yan-choo duh jwore-zir]

sneaker 运动鞋 yùndòngxié [yun-dong-shyeah]

▸ your sneakers are really trendy! 你的运动鞋真时尚！ nǐ de yùndòngxié zhēn shíshàng! [nee duh yun-dong-shyeah jeun shir-shang]

snorkel 潜水呼吸管 qiánshuǐ hūxīguǎn [chyen-shway hoo-shee-gwan]

▸ I'd like to rent a snorkel and mask, please 我想租潜水呼吸管和面具 wǒ xiǎng zū qiánshuǐ hūxīguǎn hé miànjù [wo shyang zoo chyen-shway hoo-shee-gwan huh myen-joo]

snow 下雪 xià xuě [shya shue]

▸ it's snowing 在下雪 zài xià xuě [zigh shya shue]

snowboard 踏板滑雪板 tàbǎn huáxuěbǎn [ta-ban hwa-shue-ban]

▸ I'd like to rent a snowboard 我想租一个踏板滑雪板 wǒxiǎng zū tàbǎn huáxuěbǎn [wo shyang zoo ta-ban hwa-shue-ban]

snowboarding 踏板滑雪 tàbǎn huáxuě [ta-ban hwa-shue]

▸ where can we go snowboarding near here? 这附近我们可以去哪里玩踏板滑雪？ zhè fùjìn wǒmen kěyǐ qù nǎli wán tàbǎn huáxuě? [juh foo-jin wo-meun kuh-yee choo na-lee wan ta-ban hwa-shue]

snow tire 防滑轮胎 fánghuá lúntāi [fang-hwa lun-tigh]

▸ do I need snow tires? 我需要防滑轮胎吗？ wǒ xūyào fánghuá lúntāi ma? [wo shoo-yow fang-hwa lun-tigh ma]

so *(to such a degree)* 这么 zhème [jeun-muh]; *(also)* 也 yě [yuh]; *(consequently)* 所以 suǒyǐ [swore-yee]

▸ it's so big! 真大啊！ zhēn dà a! [jeun da a]

▸ there are so many choices I don't know what to have 有这么多的选择，我都不知道该选哪个 yǒu zhème duō de xuǎnzé, wǒ dōu bù zhīdao gāi xuǎn nǎge [yoh jeun-muh dwore duh shwan-zuh, wo doh boo jir-dow gigh shwan na-guh]

▶ I'm hungry – so am I! 我饿了。 我也是！ wǒ è le. wǒ yě shì! [wo uh-luh wo yuh shir]

soap 肥皂 féizào [fay-zow]

▶ there's no soap 没有肥皂了 méiyou féizào le [may-yoh fay-zow luh]

socket (in a wall) 电源插座 diànyuán chāzuò [dyen-ywan cha-zwore]

▶ is there a socket I can use to recharge my cell? 有没有电源插座我可以给手机充电？ yǒuméiyǒu diànyuán chāzuò wǒ kěyǐ gěi shǒujī chōngdiàn? [yoh-may-yoh dyen-ywan cha-zwore wo kuh-yee gay shoh-jee chong-dyen]

solution (to a problem) 解决方法 jiějué fāngfǎ [jyeah-jue fang-fa]; (liquid) 溶液 róngyè [rong-yuh]

▶ that seems to be the best solution 那似乎是最好的解决方法 nà sìhū shì zuì hǎo de jiějué fāngfǎ [na sir-hoo shir zway how duh jyeah-jue fang-fa]

▶ I'd like some rinsing solution for soft lenses 我要用于清洗软性隐形眼镜的护理液 wǒ yào yòngyú qīngxǐ ruǎnxìng yǐnxíng yǎnjìng de hùlǐyè [wo yow yong-yoo ching-shee rwan-shing yin-shing yan-jing duh hoo-lee-yuh]

some (an amount of) 一些 yīxiē [yee-shyeah]; (a number of) 许多 xǔduō [shoo-dwore]

▶ I'd like some coffee 我要咖啡 wǒ yào kāfēi [wo yow ka-fay]

▶ some friends recommended this place 一些朋友推荐这个地方 yīxiē péngyou tuījiàn zhège difang [yee-shyeah pung-yoh tway-jyen juh-guh dee-fang]

▶ can I have some? 我能要一些吗？ wǒ néng yào yīxiē ma? [wo nung yow yee-shyeah ma]

somebody, someone 某人 mǒu rén [moh-reun]

▶ somebody left this for you 有人把这个留给了你 yǒu rén bǎ zhège liú gěi le nǐ [yoh reun ba juh-guh lew gay luh nee]

something 某事物 mǒu shìwù [moh shir-woo]

▶ is something wrong? 出问题了吗？ chū wèntí le ma? [choo weun-tee luh ma]

somewhere 某个地方 mǒu gè dìfang [moh-guh dee-fang]

▶ I'm looking for somewhere to stay 我在找住的地方 wǒ zài zhǎo zhù de dìfang [wo zigh jow joo duh dee-fang]

▶ somewhere near here 这附近的某个地方 zhè fùjìn de mǒu gè dìfang [juh foo-jin duh moh guh dee-fang]

▶ somewhere else 其他地方 qítā dìfang [chee-ta dee-fang]

son 儿子 érzi [er-zir]

▶ this is my son 这是我儿子 zhè shì wǒ de érzi [juh shir wo duh er-zir]

soon 不久 bùjiǔ [boo-jew]

▶ see you soon! 回头见！ huítóu jiàn！ [hway-toh jyen]

▶ as soon as possible 尽快 jìnkuài [jin-kwigh]

saying sorry

If you want to say 'sorry' or 'excuse me', when you are going to ask a question or ask someone to do something, you use the expression 劳驾 láojià [low-jya] in the North and in Beijing, while in the South you say 麻烦你 máfan nǐ [ma-fan nee].

sore throat 喉咙疼 hóulong téng [hoh-long tung]
- I have a sore throat 我喉咙疼 wǒ hóulong téng [wo hoh-long chung]

sorry 对不起 duìbuqǐ [dway-boo-chee]
- I'm sorry 对不起 duìbuqǐ [dway-boo-chee], 抱歉 bàoqiàn [bow-chyen]
- sorry I'm late 对不起，我迟到了 duìbuqǐ, wǒ chídào le [dway-boo-chee wo chir-dow luh], 对不起，我晚了 duìbuqǐ, wǒ wǎn le [dway-boo-chee wo wan luh]
- I'm sorry, but this seat is taken 对不起，这个座位已经有人了 duìbuqǐ, zhège zuòwei yǐjīng yǒu rén le [dway-boochee juh-guh zwore-way yee-jing yoh reun lih]
- sorry to bother you 对不起，打扰您了 duìbuqǐ, dǎrǎo nín le [dway-boo-chee da-row neen luh]
- sorry? (asking for repetition) 什么？ shénme? [sheun-muh]
- no, sorry 对不起，没有 duìbuqǐ, méiyou [dway-boo-chee may-yoh]

sound (of footsteps, conversation) 声 shēng [shung]; (of a voice) 声音 shēngyīn [shung-yin]; (of a TV, radio) 音量 yīnliàng [yin-lyang]
- can you turn the sound down? 你能把音量关小点儿吗？ nǐ néng bǎ yīnliàng guān xiǎo diǎnr ma? [nee nung ba yin-lyang gwan sheow dyenr ma]

souvenir 纪念品 jìniànpǐn [jee-nyen-pyen]
- where can I buy souvenirs? 我可以去哪里买纪念品？ wǒ kěyǐ qù nǎli mǎi jìniànpǐn? [wo kuh-yee choo na-lee migh jee-nyen-pyen]

souvenir shop 旅游品商店 lǚyóupǐn shāngdiàn [looh-yoh-pin shang-dyen]
- I'm looking for a souvenir shop 我在找旅游品商店 wǒ zài zhǎo lǚyóupǐn shāngdiàn [wo zigh jow looh-yoh-pin shang-dyen]

spa (town) 矿泉疗养地 kuàngquán liáoyǎngdì [kwung-chwan leow-yang-dee]; (health club) 矿泉疗养中心 kuàngquán liáoyǎng zhōngxīn [kwang-chwan leow-yang jong-shin]; (bathtub) 热水按摩浴缸 rèshuǐ ànmó yùgāng [ruh-shway an-mo yoo-gang]
- the spa's not working 热水按摩浴缸坏了 rèshuǐ ànmó yùgāng huài le [ruh-shway an-mo yoo-gang hway luh]

space (room) 空间 kōngjiān [kong-jyen]; (for parking) 车位 chēwèi [chuh-way]; (for a tent, a trailer) 空位 kòngwèi [kong-way]
- is there space for another bed in the room? 房间里还有位置放床吗？

fángjiān li hái yǒu wèizhi fàng chuáng ma? [fang-jyen lee high yoh way-jir fang chwung ma]

▶ I'd like a space for one tent for two days 我想要一个搭帐篷的空位，两个晚上 wǒ xiǎng yào yī gè dā zhàngpeng de kòngwèi,liǎng gè wǎnshang [wo shyang yow yee guh da jang-pung duh kong-way lyang guh wan-shang]

▶ do you have any spaces farther from the road? 不太靠近马路的地方还有没有空位了？ bù tài kàojìn mǎlù de dìfang hái yǒuméiyǒu kòngwèi le? [boo tigh kow-jin ma-loo duh dee-fang high yoh-may-yoh kong-way luh]

spade (child's toy) 小铲子 xiǎo chǎnzi [sheow chan-zir]

▶ my son's left his spade at the beach 我儿子把他的小铲子落在海边了 wǒ érzi bǎ tā de xiǎo chǎnzi là zài hǎibiān le [wo er-zir ba ta duh sheow chan-zir la zigh high-byen luh]

spare (clothes, battery) 备用的 bèiyòng de [bay-yong duh] ◆ (tire) 备用轮胎 bèiyòng lúntāi [bay-yong lun-tigh]; (part) 备件 bèijiàn [bay-jyen]

▶ should I take some spare clothes 我该带些备用的衣服吗？ wǒ gāi dài xiē bèiyòng de yīfu ma? [wo gigh digh shyeah bay-yong duh yee-foo ma]

▶ I don't have any spare cash 我没有多余的现金 wǒ méiyou duōyú de xiànjīn [wo may-yoh dwore-yoo duh shyen-jin]

▶ I've got a spare ticket for the game 我有一张多余的看比赛的票 wǒ yǒu yī zhāng duōyú de kàn bǐsài de piào [wo yoh yee jang dwore-yoo duh kan bee-sigh duh peow]

spare part 备用零件 bèiyòng língjiàn [bay-yong ling-jyen]

▶ where can I get spare parts? 我在哪里可以弄到备用零件？ wǒ zài nǎli kěyǐ nòngdào bèiyòng língjiàn? [wo zigh na-lee kuh-yee nong-dow bay-yong ling-jyen]

spare tire 备用轮胎 bèiyòng lúntāi [bay-yong lun-tigh]

▶ the spare tire's flat too 备用轮胎也没气了 bèiyòng lúntāi yě méi qì le [bay-yong lun-tigh yuh may chee luh]

spare wheel 备用方向盘 bèiyòng fāngxiàngpán [bay-yong fang-shyang-pan]

▶ there's no spare wheel 没有备用的方向盘 méiyou bèiyòng de fāngxiàng-pán [may-yoh bay-yong duh fang-shyang-pan]

sparkling 起泡的 qǐ pào de [chee-pow duh]

▶ could I have a bottle of sparkling water, please? 请给我来一瓶汽水好吗？ qǐng gěi wǒ lái yī píng qìshuǐ hǎo ma? [ching gay wo ligh yee ping chee-shway how ma]

speak 说 shuō [shwore] ◆ 说话 shuōhuà [shwore-hwa]

▶ I speak hardly any Chinese 我几乎不会说一点儿中文 wǒ jīhū bù huì shuō yīdiǎnr zhōngwén [wo jee-hoo boo hway shwore yee-dyenr jong-weun]

▶ is there anyone here who speaks English? 有人会说英语吗？ yǒu rén huì shuō yīngyǔ ma? [yoh reun hway shwore ying-yoo ma]

- could you speak more slowly? 你能说得慢一点儿吗？ nǐ néng shuō de màn yīdiǎnr ma [nee nung shwore duh man yee-dyenr ma]
- hello, I'd like to speak to Mr...; this is... 你好，我想和……通话。我是…… nǐ hǎo, wǒ xiǎng hé……tōnghuà. wǒ shì…… [nee how wo shyang huh...tong-hwa wo shir]
- who's speaking please? 请问你是谁？ qǐng wèn nǐ shì shéi? [ching weun nee shir shay]
- hello, Gary speaking 你好，我是加里 nǐ hǎo, wǒ shì jiālǐ [nee how wo shir jya-lee]

special 特选 tèxuǎn [tuh-shwan]
- what's today's special? 今天的特选是什么？ jīntiān de tèxuǎn shì shénme? [jin-tyen duh tuh-shwan shir sheun-muh]

specialist 专家医生 zhuānjiā yīshēng [jwan-jya yee-shung]
- could you refer me to a specialist? 你能把我转给专家医生治疗吗？ nǐ néng bǎ wǒ zhuǎn gěi zhuānjiā yīshēng zhìliáo ma? [nee nung ba wo jwan gay jwan-jya yee-shung zir-leow ma]

specialty 特产 tèchǎn [tuh-chan]
- what are the local specialties? 当地的特产是什么？ dāngdì de tèchǎn shì shénme? [dang-dee duh tuh-chan shir sheun-muh]

speed limit 限速 xiànsù [shyen-soo]
- what's the speed limit on this road? 这条路的限速是多少？ zhè tiáo lù de xiànsù shì duōshao? [juh teow loo duh shyen-soo shir dwore-sheow]

speedometer 速度计 sùdùjì [soo-doo-jee]
- the speedometer's broken 速度计坏了 sùdùjì huài le [soo-doo-jee hwigh luh]

speed trap 车速监测路段 chēsù jiāncè lùduàn [chuh-soo jyen-tsuh loo-dwan]
- are there lots of speed traps in the area? 在这个区有许多车速检测路段吗？ zài zhège qū yǒu xǔduō chēsù jiāncè lùduàn ma? [zigh juh-guh yoh shoo-dwore chuh-soo jyen-tsuh loo-dwan ma]

spell 拼写 pīnxiě [pin-shyeah]
- how do you spell your name? 你的名字该怎么拼写？ nǐ de míngzi gāi zěnme pīnxiě? [nee duh ming-zir gigh zeun-muh pin-shyeah]

spend 花 huā [hwa]
- we are prepared to spend up to 200 yuan 我们准备花到两百欧元 wǒmen zhǔnbèi guādào liǎngbǎi ōuyuán [wo-meun jun-bay gwa-dow lyang-bigh oh-ywan]
- I spent a month in China a few years ago 我几年前在中国呆了一个月 wǒ jǐ nián qián zài zhōngguó dāile yī gè yuè [wo jee nyen chyen zigh jong-gwore digh-luh yee guh yue]

spicy 辛辣的 xīnlà de [shin-la duh]
- is this dish spicy? 这道菜辣吗？ zhè dào cài là ma? [juh dow tsigh la ma]

spoons

These are very useful for those of us who can't manage chopsticks!: 筷子 kuàizi [kwigh-zir]. Spoons are the only type of cutlery that you can ask for in restaurants (there are no knives or forks except in big hotels or restaurants specializing in foreign food). Since the SARS epidemic, most restaurants provide disposable wooden or bamboo chopsticks. Some restaurants provide them in sealed sachets which also contain a small antiseptic towel. These have to be paid for and cost about 3 yuan.

spoon 勺子 sháozi [show-zir]
- could I have a spoon? 能给我一个勺子吗？ néng gěi wǒ yī gè sháozi ma? [nung gay wo yee guh show-zir ma]

sport 体育运动 tǐyù yùndòng [tee-yoo yun-dong]
- do you play any sports? 你参加什么体育运动吗？ nǐ cānjiā shénme tǐyù yùndòng ma? [nee tsan-jya sheun-muh tee-yoo yun-dong ma]
- I play a lot of sports 我参加许多体育运动 wǒ cānjiā xǔduō tǐyù yùndòng [wo tsan-jya shoo-dwore tee-yoo yun-dong]

sporty (person) 擅长体育的 shàncháng tǐyù de [shan-chang tee-yoo duh]
- I'm not very sporty 我不是很擅长体育运动 wǒ bù shì hěn shàncháng tǐyù yùndòng [wo shir heun shan-chang tee-yoo yun-dong]

sprain 扭伤 niǔshāng [new-shang]
- I think I've sprained my ankle 我想我扭伤了我的踝关节 wǒ xiǎng wǒ niǔshāng le wǒ de huái huānjié [wo shyang wo new-shang luh wo duh hwigh hwan-jyeah]
- my wrist is sprained 我的手腕扭了 wǒ de shǒuwàn niǔ le [wo duh shoh-wan new luh]

sports

As well as the sports traditionally associated with the Chinese (ping-pong, badminton, etc.), people also take an interest in football and basketball, while the nouveau riche have taken up golf or tennis. There is a tradition in China of participating in sports or exercise for health reasons. If you take a morning walk along the Bund in Shanghai or in a Beijing park, you'll see people practicing *tai chi* 太极 tàijí [tigh-chee] or *qigong* 气功 qìgōng [chee-gong]. You'll also see people walking backward or working out on the exercise apparatus that is available to the public alongside streets or in parks.

square *(in a town)* 广场 guǎngchǎng [gwung-chang]
- where is the main square? 主广场在哪里？ zhǔ guǎngchǎng zài nǎli? [joo-gwung–chang zigh na-lee]

stain 污渍 wūzì [woo-zir]
- can you remove this stain? 你能去除这个污渍吗？ nǐ néng qùchú zhège wūzì ma? [nee nung choo-choo juh-guh woo-zir ma]

stairs 楼梯 lóutī [loh-tee]
- where are the stairs? 楼梯在哪里？ lóutī zài nǎli? [loh-tee zigh na-lee]

stall *(car, engine)* 熄火 xīhuǒ [shee-hwore]
- the engine keeps stalling 发动机不停地熄火 fādòngjī bùtíng de xīhuǒ [fa-dong-jee boo-ting duh shee-hwore]

stamp *(for letter, postcard)* 邮票 yóupiào [yoh-peow]
- do you sell stamps? 你们出售邮票吗？ nǐmen chūshòu yóupiào ma? [nee-meun choo-shoh yoh-peow ma]

stand *(stall, booth)* 货摊 huòtān [hwore-tan]; *(in a stadium)* 看台 kàntái [kan-tigh] ◆ *(tolerate)* 忍受 rěnshòu [reun-shoh] ◆ *(be upright)* 站 zhàn [jan]; *(get up)* 起立 qǐlì [chee-lee]
- where's stand number 5? 五号看台在哪里？ wǔ hào kàntái zài nǎli? [woo how kan-tigh zigh na-lee]

start *(begin)* 开始 kāishǐ [ligh-shir]; *(function)* 启动 qǐdòng [chee-dong]
- when does the concert start? 音乐会什么时候开始？ yīnyuèhuì shénme shíhou kāishǐ? [yin-yue-hway sheun-muh shir-hoh kigh-shir]
- the car won't start 汽车发动不起来 qìchē fādòng bù qǐlái [chee-chuh fa-dong boo chee-ligh]

starving 饿 è [uh]
- I'm absolutely starving 我饿极了 wǒ èjí le [wo uh-jee luh]

States
- the States 美国 měiguó [may-gwore]
- I'm from the States 我来自美国 wǒ láizì měiguó [wo ligh-zir may-gwore]
- I live in the States 我住在美国 wǒ zhù zài měiguó [wo joo zigh may-gwore]
- have you ever been to the States? 你去过美国吗？ nǐ qùguo měiguó ma? [nee choo-gwore may-gwore ma]

station *(railroad:bus, subway)* 站 zhàn [jan]; *(TV, radio)* 台 tái [tigh]; *(police)* 局 jú [joo]
- to the train station, please! 请去火车站！ qǐng qù huǒchēzhàn [ching choo hwore-chuh-jan]
- Is there a police station near here? 这附近是否有警察局？ zhè fùjìn shìfǒu yǒu jǐngchájú? [juh foo-jin shir-foh yoh jing-cha-joo]
- where is the nearest subway station? 最近的地铁站在什么地方？ zuì jìn de

dìtiězhàn zài shénme dìfang? [zway jin duh dee-tyeah-jan zigh sheun-muh dee-fang]

stay (in a place) 停留 tíngliú [ting-lew] ◆ (visit) 逗留 dòuliú [doh-lew]

▶ we're planning to stay for two nights 我们计划住两个晚上 wǒmen jìhuà zhù liǎng gè wǎnshang [wo-meun jee-hwa joo lyang guh wan-shang]

▶ a two-week stay 逗留两周 dòuliú liǎng zhōu [doh-lew lyang joh]

steak 牛排 niúpái [new-pigh]

▶ I'd like a steak and fries 我要一块牛排和薯条 wǒ yào yī kuài niúpái hé shǔtiáo [wo yow yee kwigh new-pigh huh shoo-teow]

steal (money, wallet, necklace) 偷 tōu [toh]

▶ my passport was stolen 我的护照被偷了 wǒ de hùzhào bèi tōu le [wo duh hoo-jow bay toh luh]

▶ our car has been stolen 我们的汽车被偷了 wǒmen de qìchē bèi tōu le [wo-meun duh chee-chuh bay toh luh]

steering 转向装置 zhuǎnxiàng zhuāngzhì [jun-shyang jwung-jir]

▶ there's a problem with the steering 转向装置有问题 zhuǎnxiàng zhuāngzhì yǒu wèntí [joo-shyang jwung-jir yoh weun-tee]

steering wheel 方向盘 fāngxiàngpán [fang-shyang-pan]

▶ the steering wheel is very stiff 方向盘太重了 fāngxiàngpán tài zhòng le [fang-shyang-pan tigh jong luh]

stick shift (lever) 操纵变速杆 cāozòng biànsùgān [tsow-zong byen-soo-gan]; (car) 手动挡的车 shǒudòngdǎng de chē [shoh-dong-dang duh chuh]

▶ is it a stick shift or an automatic? 这是手动挡的车还是自动挡的车？ zhè shì shǒudòngdǎng de chē háishì zìdòngdǎng de chē? [juh shir shoh-dong-dang duh chuh high-shir zir-dong-dang chuh]

still (up to now, up to then) 仍然 réngrán [rung-ran]; (even now) 还 hái [high]

▶ how many miles are there still to go? 还要走多少英里？ hái yào zǒu duōshao yīnglǐ? [high yow zoh dwore-show ying-lee]

▶ we're still waiting to be served 我们还在等人来为我们服务 wǒmen hái zài děng rén lái wèi wǒmen fúwù [wo-meun high zigh dung reun ligh way wo-meun foo-woo]

sting (wasp, nettle) 蛰 zhē [juh]

▶ I've been stung by a wasp 我被黄蜂蛰了 wǒ bèi huángfēng zhē le [wo bay hwung-fung juh luh]

stomach 胃 wèi [way]

▶ my stomach hurts 我胃疼 wǒ wèi téng [wo way tung]

stomachache 胃疼 wèi téng [way tung]

▶ I have a really bad stomachache 我胃疼得实在厉害 wǒ wèi téng de shízài lìhai [wo way tung duh shir-zigh lee-high]

stores

Most stores, boutiques and department stores are open every day, including Sunday, and don't close for lunch. Many department stores specialize in a particular type of product, such as clothes and shoes, fabrics, antiques, souvenirs, etc. These shopping centers rent sales units to independent traders who offer the same products at competing prices. A tip: be sure to mention competitors' prices when you're haggling over a deal with a shopkeeper!

stop 站 zhàn [jan] ◆ 使......停止 shǐ......tíngzhǐ [shir...ting-jir] ◆ 停止 tíngzhǐ [ting-jir]

- is this the right stop for...? 到......是在这一站下吗？ dào......shì zài zhè yī zhàn xià ma? [dow...shir zigh juh yee jan shya ma]
- stop it! 别这样！ bié zhèyàng! [byeah juh-yang]
- where in town does the shuttle stop? 在市区机场大巴在哪里停？ zài shìqū jīchǎng dàbā zài nǎli tíng? [zigh shir-choo jee-chang da-ba zigh na-lee ting]
- please stop here 请在这里停下 qǐng zài zhèli tíngxia [ching zigh juh-lee ting-shya]
- which stations does this train stop at? 这辆火车停靠哪几个站？ zhè liàng huǒchē tíngkào nǎ jǐ gè zhàn? [juh lyang hwore-chuh ting-kow na jee guh jan]
- do we stop at Nanjing? 我们在南京停吗？ wǒmen zài nánjīng tíng ma? [wo-meun zigh nan-jing ting ma]

store *(place selling goods)* 商店 shāngdiàn [shang-dyen]

- are there any bigger stores in the area? 在这个地区有大一点儿的商店

in a store

- no, thanks, I'm just looking 不用，谢谢。我只是看看 bù yòng,xièxie. wǒ zhǐ shì kànkan [boo yong shyeah-shyeah wo jir shir kan-kan]
- how much is this? 这个多少钱？ zhège duōshao qián? [juh-guh dwore-show chyen]
- I take a size 38/I'm a size 38 我穿38码的 wǒ chuān sānshíbā mǎ de [wo chwan san-shir-ba ma duh]
- can I try this coat on? 我可以试穿这件外套吗？ wǒ kěyǐ shìchuān zhè jiàn wàitào ma? [wo kuh-yee shir-chwan juh jyen wigh-tow ma]
- can it be exchanged? 可以调换吗？ kěyǐ diàohuàn ma? [kuh-yee deow-hwan ma]

吗？ zài zhège dìqū yǒu dà yīdiǎnr de shāngdiàn ma? [zigh juh-guh dee-choo yoh da yee dyenr duh shang-dyen ma]

store window 商店橱窗 shāngdiàn chúchuāng [shang-dyen choo-chwung]

▸ the store windows are beautifully decorated at Christmas 在圣诞节，商店橱窗被装饰得非常漂亮 zài shèngdàn jié,shāngdiàn chúchuāng bèi zhuāngshì de fēicháng piàoliang [zigh shung-dan jyeah shang-dyen choo-chwung bay jwung-shir duh fay-chang peow-lyang]

storm 暴风雨 bàofēngyǔ [bow-fung-yoo]

▸ is there going to be a storm? 要来暴风雨了吗？ yào lái bàofēngyǔ le ma? [yow ligh bow-fung-yoo luh ma]

straight 直的 zhí de [jir dih] ◆ *(in a straight line)* 直地 zhí de [jir duh]

▸ you have to keep going straight 你得一直向前走 nǐ děi yīzhí xiàng qián zǒu [nee day yee-jir shyang chyen zoh]

street 街 jiē [jyeah]

▸ will this street take me to the station? 我沿着这条街走可以到车站吗？ wǒ yánzhe zhè tiáo jiē zǒu kěyǐ dào chēzhàn ma? [wo yan-juh juh teow jyeah zoh kuh-yee dow chuh-jan ma]

streetcar 有轨电车 yǒu guǐ diànchē [yoh gway dyen-chuh]

▸ can you buy tickets on the streetcar? 可以在电车上买票吗？ kěyǐ zài diànchē shang mǎi piào ma? [kuh-yee zigh dyen-chuh shang migh peow ma]

▸ which streetcar line do we have to take? 我们该乘坐哪一路电车？ wǒmen gāi chéngzuò nǎ yī lù diànchē? [wo-meun gigh chung-zwore na yee loo dyen-chuh]

▸ where is the nearest streetcar stop? 最近的电车车站在哪里？ zuì jìn de diànchē chēzhàn zài nǎli? [zway jin duh dyen-chuh chuh-jan zigh na-lee]

street map 街道图 jiēdào tú [jyeah-dow too]

▸ where can I buy a street map? 我可以在哪里买到街道图？ wǒ kěyǐ zài nǎli mǎidào jiēdào tú? [wo kuh-yee zigh na-lee migh-dow jyeah-dow too]

strong *(wind, current)* 强劲的 qiángjìng de [chyang-jing duh]; *(current)* 湍急的 tuānjí de [twan-jee duh]; *(smell, taste)* 浓郁的 nóngyù de [nong-yoo duh]

▸ is the current very strong here? 这里的水流非常湍急吗？ zhèli de shuǐliú fēicháng tuānjí ma? [juh-lee duh shway-lew fay-chang twan-jee ma]

stuck

▸ to be stuck *(jammed)* 不能动的 bù néng dòng de [boo nung dong duh]; *(trapped)* 被困住的 bèi kùnzhù de [bay kun-joo duh]

▸ someone is stuck in the elevator 有人被困在电梯里了 yǒu rén bèi kùn zài diàntī li le [yoh reun bay kun zigh dyen-tee lee luh]

student 学生 xuésheng [shue-shung]

▸ I'm a student 我是名学生 wǒ shì míng xuésheng [wo shir ming shue-shung]

subway

Big cities like Beijing, Shanghai or Canton have subway systems, but they don't cover a very wide area. Beijing has launched a vast program for the building of several new lines in time for the Olympic Games in 2008. Tickets can be bought singly at the stations. They may be at a set price (Beijing) or priced according to how far you travel (Shanghai). On average they cost about 2 to 6 yuan. All the names of stations are given in Chinese characters, *pinyin* and English.

student discount 学生折扣 xuéshēng zhékòu [shue-shung juh-koh]
- do you have student discounts? 有学生折扣吗？ yǒu xuéshēng zhékòu ma? [yoh shue-shung juh-koh ma]

studio (apartment) 单间公寓 dānjiān gōngyù [dan-jyen gong-yoo]
- I'm renting a studio apartment 我租了一个单间公寓 wǒ zūle yī gè dānjiān gōngyù [wo zoo-luh yee guh dan-jyen gong-yoo]

style *(manner, design)* 风格 fēnggé [fung-guh]; *(elegance)* 风度 fēngdù [fung-doo]
- she has a lot of style 她很有风度 tā hěn yǒu fēngdù [ta heun yoh fung-doo]

subway 地铁 dìtiě [dee-tyeah]
- can I have a map of the subway? 能给我一张地铁图吗？ néng gěi wǒ yī zhāng dìtiě tú ma? [nung gay wo yee jang dee-tyeah too ma]

subway train 地铁 dìtiě [dee-tyeah]
- when's the last subway train from this station? 从这个站出发的最后一班地铁是几点？ cóng zhège zhàn chūfā de zuìhòu yī bān dìtiě shì jǐ diǎn? [tsong juh-guh jan choo-fa duh zway-hoh yee ban dee-tyeah shir jee dyen]

sudden 突然的 tūrán de [too-ran duh]
- all of a sudden 突然 tūrán [too-ran]

sugar 糖 táng [tang]
- can you pass me the sugar? 你能把糖递给我吗？ nǐ néng bǎ táng dì gěi wǒ ma? [nee nung ba tang dee gay wo ma]

suggest *(propose)* 建议 jiànyì [jyen-yee]
- do you have anything else you can suggest? 你还有什么要建议的？ nǐ hái yǒu shénme yào jiànyì de? [nee high yoh sheun-muh yow jyen-yee duh]

suit *(be convenient for)* 适合 shìhé [shir-huh]
- that suits me perfectly 那个对我很合适 zhège duì wǒ hěn shìhé [juh-guh dway wo heun shir-huh]
- it doesn't suit me 那不适合我 nà bù shìhé wǒ [na boo shir-huh wo]

suitcase 手提箱 shǒutíxiāng [shoh-tee-shyang]
- one of my suitcases is missing 我的一个手提箱找不到了 wǒ de yī gè shǒutíxiāng zhǎo bù dào le [wo duh yee guh shoh-tee-shyang jow boo dow luh]
- my suitcase was damaged in transit 我的手提箱在搬运过程中被损坏了 wǒ de shǒutíxiāng zài bānyùn gòuchéng zhōng bèi sǔnhuài le [wo duh shoh-tee-shyang zigh ban-yun gwore-chung jong bay sun-hway luh]

summer 夏天 xiàtiān [shya-tyen]
- in (the) summer 在夏天 zài xiàtiān [zigh shya-tyen]

summer vacation 暑假 shǔjià [shoo-jya]
- we've come here for our summer vacation 我们过来过暑假 wǒmen guòlai guò shǔjià [wo-meun gwore-ligh gwore shoo-jya]

sun 太阳 tàiyáng [tigh-yang]
- the sun's very strong at this time of day 每天的这个时候太阳都非常大 měi tiān de zhège shíhou tàiyáng dōu fēicháng dà [may tyen duh juh-guh shir-hoh tigh-yang doh fay-chang da]

sunburn 晒伤 shàishāng [shigh-shang]
- I've got a bad sunburn 我被严重晒伤了 wǒ bèi yánzhòng shàishāng le [wo bay yan-jong shigh-shang luh]
- do you have cream for a sunburn? 你有治晒伤的药膏吗? nǐ yǒu zhì shàishāng de yàogāo ma? [nee yoh jir shigh-shang duh yow-gow ma]

Sunday 星期天 xīngqītiān [shing-shee-tyen]
- where can I find a doctor on a Sunday? 星期天我可以去哪里看病? xīngqītiān wǒ kěyǐ qù nǎli kànbìng? [shing-shee-tyen wo kuh-yee choo na-lee kan-bing]
- are the stores open on Sunday? 星期天商店开门吗? xīngqītiān shāngdiàn kāimén ma? [shing-shee-tyen shang-dyen kigh-meun ma]

sun deck 阳台 yángtái [yang-tigh]
- how do I get onto the sun deck? 我要去阳台该怎么走? wǒ yào qù yángtái gāi zěnme zǒu? [wo yow choo yang-tigh gigh zeun-muh zoh]

sunglasses 太阳眼镜 tàiyáng yǎnjìng [tigh-yang yan-jing]
- I've lost my sunglasses 我的太阳眼镜丢了 wǒ de tàiyáng yǎnjìng diū le [wo-duh tigh-yang dew luh]

sunny (day, weather) 晴朗的 qínglǎng de [ching-lang duh]
- it's sunny 天气晴朗 tiānqì qínglǎng [tyen-chee ching-lang]

sunrise 日出 rìchū [rir-choo]
- what time is sunrise? 日出是几点? rìchū shì jǐ diǎn? [rir-choo shir jee dyen]

sunset 日落 rìluò [rir-lwore]
- isn't the sunset beautiful? 日落难道不美吗? rìluò nándào bù měi ma? [rir-lwore nan-dow boo may ma]

suntan lotion 防晒霜 fángshàishuāng [fang-shigh-shwung]

▸ I'd like SPF 30 suntan lotion 我要防晒指数是30的防晒霜 wǒ yào fángshài zhǐshù shì sānshí de fángshàishuāng [wo yow fang-shigh jir-shoo shir san-shir duh fang-shigh-shwung]

supermarket 超市 chāoshì [chow-shir]

▸ is there a supermarket nearby? 附近有超市吗？ fùjìn yǒu chāoshì ma? [foo-jin yoh chow-shir ma]

surcharge 附加费 fùjiāfèi [foo-jya-fay]

▸ do I have to pay a surcharge? 我需要支付附加费吗？ wǒ xūyào zhīfù fùjiāfèi ma? [wo shoo-yow jir-foo foo-jya-fay ma]

surfboard 冲浪板 chōnglàngbǎn [chong-lang-ban]

▸ is there somewhere we can rent surfboards? 是否有地方我们可以租到冲浪板？ shìfǒu yǒu dìfang wǒmen kěyǐ zūdào chōnglàngbǎn? [shir-foh yoh dee-fang wo-meun kuh-yee zoo-dow chong-lang-ban]

surfing 冲浪 chōnglàng [chong-lang]

▸ can we go surfing around here? 我们可以在这附近冲浪吗？ wǒmen kěyǐ zài zhè fùjìn chōnglàng ma [wo-meun kuh-yee zigh juh foo-jin chong-lang ma]

surprise 吃惊 chījīng [chir-jing]

▸ what a nice surprise! 真是个惊喜！ zhēn shì gè jīngxǐ! [jeun shir guh jing-shee]

surrounding area 周围地区 zhōuwéi dìqū [joh-way dee-choo]

▸ Beijing and the surrounding area 北京及其周围地区 běijīng jí qí zhōuwéi dìqū [bay-jing jee chee joh-way dee-choo]

swallow 吞下 tūnxia [tun-shya] ◆ 吞咽 tūnyàn [tun-yan]

▸ the ATM outside has swallowed my credit card 外面的自动取款机吞了我的信用卡 wàimian de zìdòng qǔkuǎnjī tūnle wǒ de xìnyòngkǎ [wigh-myen duh zir-dong choo-kwan-jee tun luh wo duh shin-yong-ka]

▸ it hurts when I swallow 我吞咽的时候感到疼 wǒ tūnyàn de shíhou gǎndào téng [wo tun-yan duh shir-hoh gan-dow tung]

swim 游泳 yóuyǒng [yoh-yong] ◆ 游 yóu [yoh]

▸ is it safe to swim here? 在这里游泳安全吗？ zài zhèlǐ yóuyǒng ānquán ma? [zigh juh-lee yoh-yong an-chwan ma]

▸ to go for a swim 去游泳 qù yóuyǒng [choo yoh-yong]

swimming pool 游泳池 yóuyǒngchí [yoh-yong-chir]

▸ is there an open-air swimming pool? 有露天游泳池吗？ yǒu lùtiān yóuyǒngchí ma? [yoh loo-tyen yoh-yong-chir ma]

switch 开关 kāiguān [kigh-gwan]

▸ the switch doesn't work 开关坏了 kāiguān huài le [kigh-gwan hwigh luh]

switch off *(light, appliance, radio)* 关 guān [gwan]; *(electricity)* 切断 qiēduàn [chyeah-dwan]

▸ where do you switch the light off? 在哪里关灯？ zài nǎli guān dēng? [zigh na-lee gwan dung]

▸ my cell was switched off 我的手机关机了 wǒ de shǒujī guānjī le [wo duh shoh-jee gwan-jee luh]

switch on *(light, heating, TV)* 打开 dǎkāi [da-kigh]; *(engine)* 开启 kāiqǐ [kigh-chee]

▸ where do I switch this light on? 这灯在哪里开？ zhè dēng zài nǎli kāi? [juh dung zigh na-lee kigh]

synagogue 犹太教会堂 yóutàijiào huìtáng [yoh-tigh-jeow hway-tang]

▸ where's the nearest synagogue? 最近的犹太教会堂在哪里？ zuì jìn de yóutàijiào huìtáng zài nǎli? [zway jin duh yoh-tigh-jeow hway-tang zigh na-lee]

table 桌子 zhuōzi [jwore-zir]

▸ I've reserved a table in the name of... 我用......的名字预定了一个桌位 wǒ yòng......de míngzi yùdìngle yī gè zhuōwèi [yong...duh ming-zir yoo-ding-luh yee guh jwore-way]

▸ a table for four, please! 请给一张四个人的桌子！ qǐng gěi yī zhāng sì gè rén de zhuōzi! [ching gay yee jang sir guh reun duh jwore-zir]

table tennis 乒乓球 pīngpāngqiú [ping-pang-chew]

▸ are there tables for table tennis? 有打乒乓球的桌子吗？ yǒu dǎ pīngpāngqiú de zhuōzi ma? [yoh da ping-pang-chew duh jwore-zir]

table wine 佐餐酒 zuǒcānjiǔ [zwore-tsan-jew]

▸ a bottle of red table wine 一瓶佐餐红葡萄酒 yī píng zuǒcān hóng pútaojiǔ [yee ping zwore-tsan hong poo-tow-jew]

take *(get hold of)* 拿 ná [na]; *(steal)* 偷走 tōuzǒu [toh-zoh]; *(carry)* 携带 xiédài [shyeah-digh]; *(accompany)* 伴随 bànsuí [ban-sway]; *(transport)* 运载 yùnzài [ywan-zigh]; *(require)* 需要 xūyào [shoo-yow]; *(wear)* 穿 chuān [chwan]; *(time)* 花费 huāfèi [hwa-fay]

▸ someone's taken my bag 有人拿了我的包 yǒu rén nále wǒ de bāo [yoh reun na-luh wo duh bow]

▸ can you take me to this address? 你是否能把我送到这个地址？ ní shìfǒu néng bǎ wǒ sòngdào zhège dìzhǐ? [nee shir-foh nung ba wo song-dow juh-guh dee-jir]

▸ are you taking the plane or the train to Beijing? 你是坐飞机还是火车去北京？ ní shì zuò fēijī háishi huǒchē qù běijīng? [nee shir zwore fay-jee high-shir hwore-chir choo bay-jing]

- which road should I take? 我该走哪条路呢？ **wǒ gāi zǒu nǎ tiáo lù ne?** [wo gigh zoh na teow loo nuh]
- I take a size 40 我穿40码的 **wǒ chuān sìshí mǎ de** [wo chwan sir-shir ma duh]
- how long does the trip take? 行程需要多久？ **xíngchéng xūyào duō jiǔ?** [shing-chung shoo-yow dwore jew]
- how long does it take to get to Beijing? 到北京要多久？ **dào běijīng yào duō jiǔ?** [dow bay-jing yow dwore-jew]
- could you take a photo of us? 你能给我们拍张照片吗？ **nǐ néng gěi wǒmen pāi zhāng zhàopiàn ma?** [nee nung gay wo-meun pigh jang jow-pyen ma]

take back (to a store) 退还 **tuìhuán** [tway-hwan]; (to one's home) 带回 **dàihui** [digh-hway]

- I'm looking for a present to take back to my son 我在找一份带回去给我儿子的礼物 **wǒ zài zhǎo yī fèn dàihuiqu gěi wǒ érzi de lǐwù** [wo zigh jow yee feun digh-hway-choo gay gay wo er-zir duh lee-woo]

take down (bags, luggage) 把......拿下来 **bǎ......náxialai** [ba...na-shya-ligh]

- could you take these bags down, please? 请问，你能把这些行李拿下来吗？ **qǐng wèn, nǐ néng bǎ zhèxiē xínglǐ náxialai ma?** [ching weun nee nung ba juh-shyeah shing-lee na-shya-ligh ma]

take in (bags, luggage) 把......拿进去 **bǎ......nájìnqu** [ba...na-jin-choo]

- can you have someone take in my bags, please? 请问，你能找人把我的行李拿进去吗？ **qǐng wèn, nǐ néng zhǎo rén bǎ wǒ de xínglǐ nájìnqu ma?** [ching weun nee nung jow reun ba wo duh shing-lee na-jin-choo ma]

taken (seat) 已被占用的 **yǐ bèi zhànyòng de** [yee bay jang-yong duh]

- sorry, this seat is taken 对不起，这个位置已经有人了 **duìbuqǐ, zhège wèizhi yǐjīng yǒu rén le** [dway-boo-chee juh-guh way-juh yee-jing yoh reun luh]

take up (bags, luggage) 把......拿上去 **bǎ......náshangqu** [ba...na-shang-choo]

- can someone take our bags up to our room? 有人能把我们的行李拿到上面我们的房间吗？ **yǒu rén néng bǎ wǒmen de xínglǐ nádào shàngmian wǒmen de fángjiān ma?** [yoh reun nung ba wo-meun duh shing-lee na-dow shang-myen wo-meun duh fang-jyen ma]

talk 说话 **shuōhuà** [shwore-hwa]

- could I talk with you for a moment? 我能和你说会儿话吗？ **wǒ néng hé nǐ shuō huìr huà ma?** [wo nung huh nee shwore hwayr hwa ma]
- you have no right to talk to me like that 你没有权利对我那样说话 **nǐ méiyou quánlì duì wǒ nàyàng shuōhuà** [nee may-yoh chwan-lee dway wo na-yang shwore-hwa]

tall (person, tree, building) 高的 **gāo de** [gow duh]

- what's that tall building over there? 那边的那个高大的建筑物是什么？ **nàbiān de nàge gāodà de jiànzhùwù shì shénme?** [na-byen duh na-guh gow-da duh jyen-joo-woo shir sheun-muh]

tastes

The ancient Chinese *Five Elements* philosophy recognizes five different basic tastes: sweet 甜 tián [tyen], salty 咸 xián [shyen], sour 酸 suān [swan], bitter 苦 kǔ [koo], and spicy 辣 là [la]. Gourmets also appreciate differences in the texture of foods (crisp, soft), and how peppery or fermented they are.

tank *(for gas)* 油箱 yóuxiāng [yoh-shyang]
  ▸ is the tank full? 油箱满了吗? yóuxiāng mǎn le ma? [yoh-shyang man luh ma]

taste 味道 wèidao [way-dow] ◆ *(sense)* 尝出 chángchū [chang-choo]; *(try)* 体验 tǐyàn [tee-yan] ◆ 品尝 pǐncháng [pin-chang]
  ▸ I can't taste anything 我什么味道也尝不出来 wǒ shénme wèidao yě cháng bù chūlái [wo sheun-muh way-dow yuh chang boo choo-ligh]
  ▸ would you like to taste the wine? 你想尝一下葡萄酒吗? nǐ xiǎng cháng yī xià pútaojiǔ ma? [nee shyang chang yee shya poo-tow-jew ma]
  ▸ it tastes funny 它味道奇怪 tā wèidao qíguài [ta way-dow chee-gwigh]

tax 税 shuì [shway]
  ▸ does this price include tax? 这个价格里面含税吗? zhège jiàgé lǐmian hán shuì ma? [juh-guh jya-guh lee-myen han shway ma]

taxi 出租车 chūzūchē [choo-zoo-chuh]
  ▸ how much does a taxi cost from here to the station? 从这里到车站坐出租车要多少钱? cóng zhèli dào chēzhàn zuò chūzūchē yào duōshao qián? [tsong juh-lee dow chuh-jan zwore choo-zoo-chuh yow dwore-show chyen]
  ▸ I'd like to reserve a taxi to take me to the airport, please 请给我预定一辆出租车去机场 qǐng gěi wǒ yùdìng yī liàng chūzūchē qù jīchǎng [ching gay wo yoo-ding yee lyang choo-zoo-chuh choo jee-chang]

taxis

The prices vary according to the degree of comfort (and safety) of the vehicle. Prices are per kilometer (generally between 1 and 2 yuan) and according to the time taken, plus a charge of about 10 yuan (in Beijing), a rate which increases after 11 p.m. They are a relatively cheap means of transportation and by far the most practical way of getting around in the busy cities. Remember to hold on to the ticket given to you by your taxi driver as this will be how you can track the car down should you leave something behind in it. You can also arrange for taxis to take you to far-flung places such as the *Great Wall* 长城 chángceng [chang-chung] (from the center of Beijing). For this sort of trip you can negotiate a total price for the journey before you leave, rather than using the meter.

taxi driver

Another word for a taxi driver is a 师傅 shīfu [shir-foo]. This respectful term, which means 'master,' can also be used to address anyone whose job requires specialist technical knowledge (a plumber or an electrician, for example).

taxi driver 出租车司机 chūzūché sījī [choo-zoo-chuh sir-jee]

▸ can you ask the taxi driver to wait? 你能叫出租车司机等一下吗？ nǐ néng jiào chūzūché sījī děng yī xià ma? [nee nung jeow choo-zoo-chee-chuh sir-jee dung yee shya ma]

taxi stand 出租车候车点 chūzūché hòuchēdiǎn [choo-zoo-chuh hwore-chuh-dyen]

▸ where can I find a taxi stand? 我在哪里能找到出租车候车点？ wǒ zài nǎli néng zhǎodào chūzūché hòuchēdiǎn? [wo zigh na-lee nung jow-dow choo-zoo-chuh hoh-chuh-dyen]

tea *(drink)* 茶 chá [cha]

▸ tea with milk 加奶的茶 jiā nǎi de chá [jya nigh duh cha]
▸ tea without milk 不加奶的茶 bù jiā nǎi de chá [boo jya nigh duh cha] ▸ see box on p. 174

teach 教 jiāo [jeow]

▸ so, you teach Chinese? maybe you could help me! 那么，你是教中文的？你也许可以帮助我！ nàme, nǐ shì jiāo zhōngwén de? nǐ yěxǔ kěyǐ

---

taking a taxi

▸ could you call me a taxi, please? 请你为我叫一辆出租车好吗？ qǐng nǐ wèi wǒ jiào yī liàng chūzūché hǎo ma? [ching nee way wo jeow yee lyang choo-zoo-chuh how ma]
▸ to the station/airport, please 请去车站/机场 qǐng qù chēzhàn/jīchǎng [ching choo chuh-jan/jee-chang]
▸ stop here/at the lights/at the corner, please 请在这里/红绿灯前/拐角处停车 qǐng zài zhèli/hónglǜdēng qián/guǎijiǎochù tíng chē [ching zigh juh-lee/hong-looh-dung chyen/gwigh-jeow-choo ting chuh]
▸ can you wait for me? 你能等我吗？ nǐ néng děng wǒ ma? [nee nung dung wo ma]
▸ how much is it? 多少钱？ duōshao qián? [dwore-show chyen]
▸ keep the change 不用找零了 bù yòng zhǎolíng le [boo yong jow-ling luh]

tea

Tea is without doubt the most popular drink in China. It is made using tea leaves rather than from tea bags (though you may find these in your hotel room). Tea-making is an art and a gastronomic delight. Tea is not usually drunk during a meal but separately or with small light dishes (especially in Canton). This is because of its delicate flavor. Many Chinese people carry small Thermos® flasks of tea with them during the day. These can be filled with hot water at any time. A tip: China has some wonderful, very restful tea houses, especially in Sichuan and the South of China.

bāngzhù wǒ! [na-muh nee shir jeow jong-weun duh nee yuh-shoo kuh-yee bang-joo wo]

teacher 教师 jiàoshī [jeow-shir]
- I'm a teacher 我是个教师 wǒ shì gè jiàoshī [wo shir-guh jeow-shir]

tea house 茶室 cháshì [cha-shir]
- is there a tea house near here? 附近有没有比较好的茶室？ fùjìn yǒuméiyǒu bǐjiào hǎo de cháshì? [foo-jin yoh-may-yoh bee-jeow how duh cha-shir]

telephone 电话 diànhuà [dyen-hwa] ◆ 给……打电话 gěi……dǎ diànhuà [gay...da dyen-hwa] ◆ 打电话 dǎ diànhuà [da...dyen-hwa]
- can I use the telephone? 我能用电话吗？ wǒ néng yòng diànhuà ma? [wo nung yong dyen-hwa ma]

telephone booth 电话亭 diànhuàtíng [dyen-hwa-ting]
- is there a telephone booth near here? 这附近有电话亭吗？ zhè fùjìn yǒu diànhuàtíng ma? [juh foo-jin yoh dyen-hwa-ting ma]

telephones

There are a lot of public telephones on Chinese streets. These are called 公用电话 gōngyòng diànhuà [gong-yong dyen-hwa], and they are useful and inexpensive for local calls. For international calls, you can buy a prepaid *IP card* (pronounced using the English 'IP'): IP卡 ip kǎ [igh-pee-ka]. Note that the amount shown on the card indicates the time credit, but that the price of the phone card can sometimes be negotiated. You should also note that although some cellphone packages allow for calls to be received free of charge, many of your Chinese friends will pay to take calls on their cellphones.

television

There are a lot of national and local television channels in China. International channels are available via cable in the big hotels, and channel CCTV9 broadcasts programs in English. You will notice that many Chinese programs are subtitled because of the regional differences in dialect.

telephone call 电话 diànhuà [dyen-hwa]

> I'd like to make a telephone call 我想打个电话 wǒ xiǎng dǎ gè diànhuà [wo shyang da guh dyen-hwa]

television *(system)* 电视 diànshì [dyen-shir]; *(broadcasts)* 节目 jiémù [jyeah-moo]; *(set)* 电视机 diànshìjī [dyen-shir-jee]

> what's on television tonight? 今晚电视上播什么？ jīnwǎn diànshì shang bō shénme? [jin-wan dyen-shir shang bo sheun-muh]

tell 告诉 gàosu [gow-soo]

> can you tell me the way to the museum? 你能告诉我去博物馆的路吗？ nǐ néng gàosu wǒ qù bówùguǎn de lù ma? [nee nung gow-soo wo choo bo-wo-gwan duh loo ma]

> can you tell me what time it is? 你能告诉我现在是几点吗？ nǐ néng gàosu wǒ xiànzài shì jǐ diǎn ma? [nee nung gow-soo wo shyen-zigh shir jee dyen ma]

temperature *(meteorological)* 温度 wēndù [weun-doo]; *(fever)* 发烧 fāshāo [fa-show]

> what's the temperature? 温度是多少？ wēndù shì duōshao? [weun-doo shir dwore-show]

> I've got a temperature 我发烧了 wǒ fāshāo le [wo fa-show luh]

temple 庙宇 miàoyǔ [meow-yoo]

> could you tell me where the temple is, please? 请你告诉我庙宇在什么地方好吗？ qǐng nǐ gàosu wǒ miàoyǔ zài shénme dìfang hǎo ma? [ching gow-soo wo meow-yoo zigh sheun-muh dee-fang how ma]

temples

Temples are magnificent havens of peace and spirituality amidst the bustling life of Chinese towns. There are Buddhist, Taoist and Confucian temples. Many are still in use and you will be welcomed by the monks. The architecture is often superb. Note especially the wooden frames. A tip: you can sometimes eat at temples, buy good luck charms, and have your fortune told.

ten 十 shí [shir]
- there are ten of us 我们有十个人 wǒmenyǒu shí gè rén [wo-meun yoh shir guh reun]

tennis 网球 wǎngqiú [wang-chew]
- where can we play tennis? 我们可以在哪里打网球? wǒmen kěyǐ zài nǎli dǎ wǎngqiú? [wo-meun kuh-yee zigh na-lee da wang-chew]

tennis racket 网球拍 wǎngqiúpāi [wang-chew-pigh]
- can you rent tennis rackets? 可以租到网球拍吗? kěyǐ zūdào wǎngqiúpāi ma? [kuh-yee zoo-dow wang-chew-pigh ma]

tent 帐篷 zhàngpeng [jang-pung]
- I'd like to book space for a tent, please 我想预定一个搭帐篷的位置 wǒ xiǎng yùdìng yī gè dā zhàngpeng de wèizhi [wo shyang yoo-ding yee guh da jang-pung duh way-jir]
- can you put up your tent anywhere? 是否可以在任何地方搭帐篷? shìfǒu kěyǐ zài rènhé dìfang dā zhàngpeng? [shir-foh kuh-yee zigh reun-huh dee-fang da jang-pung]

tent peg 帐篷桩 zhàngpengzhuāng [jang-pung-jwung]
- we're short of tent pegs 我们没帐篷桩了 wǒmen méi zhàngpengzhuāng le [wo-meun may jang-pung-jwung luh]

terminal *(in airport)* 航站楼 hángzhànlóu [hang-jan-loh]
- where is terminal one? 一号航站楼在哪里? yī hào hángzhànlóu zài nǎli? [yee how hang-jan-loh zigh na-lee]
- is there a shuttle between terminals? 航站楼之间是否有穿梭巴士? hángzhànlóu zhī jiān shìfǒu yǒu chuānsuō bāshì? [hang-jan-loh jir jyen shir-foh yoh chwan-swore ba-shir]

tetanus 破伤风 pòshāngfēng [po-shang-fung]
- I've been vaccinated for tetanus 我已经注射过破伤风的疫苗了 wǒ yǐjīng zhùshèguo pòshāngfēng de yìmiáo le [wo yee-jing joo-shuh-gwore po-shang-fung duh yee-meow luh]

thank 感谢 gǎnxiè [gan-shyeah] ◆ **thanks** 谢谢 xièxie [shyeah-shyeah]
- thanks for everything (you've done) 谢谢你所做的一切 xièxie nǐ suǒ zuò de yīqiè [shyeah-shyeah nee swore zwore duh yee-chyeah]

thank you! 谢谢! xièxie! [shyeah-shyeah]
- thank you very much! 非常感谢! fēicháng gǎnxiè! [fay-chang gan-shyeah]

that *(demonstrative use)* 那个 nàge [na-guh] ◆ 那 nà [na]
- who's that? 那是谁? nà shì shéi? [na shir shay]
- that's right 那是对的 nà shì duì de [na shir sway duh]
- the road that goes to Dalian 通往大连的路 tōngwǎng dàlián de lù [tong-wang da-lyen duh loo]

I'll have that one 我要那个 wǒ yào nàge [wo yow na-guh]

theater *(for plays)* 剧院 jùyuàn [joo-ywan]

▸ where is there a theater? 哪里有剧院？ nǎli yǒu jùyuàn? [na-lee yoh joo-ywan]

theft 偷窃 tōuqiè [toh-chyeah]

▸ I'd like to report a theft 我来报案，有桩盗窃案 wǒ lái bào'àn, yǒu zhuāng dàoqiè'àn [wo ligh bow-an yoh jwung dow-chyeah-an]

then *(at a particular time)* 当时 dāngshí [dang-shir]; *(next)* 然后 ránhòu [ran-hoh]; *(in that case)* 那么 nàme [na-muh]

▸ I'll see you then 我们到时候见 wǒmen dào shíhou jiàn [wo-meun dow shir-hoh jyen]

▸ I'll see you at six then 那我们就6点钟见 nà wǒmen jiù liù diǎnzhōng jiàn [wo-meun jew lew dyen-jong jyen]

there *(in that place)* 在那里 zài nàli [zigh na-lee]; *(to that place)* 去那里 qù nàli [choo na-lee]

▸ he's over there 他在那里 tā zài nàli [ta zigh na-lee]

▸ there is/are... 有...... yǒu...... [yoh...]

▸ there's a problem 出问题了 chū wèntí le [choo weun-tee luh]

▸ are there any restrooms near here? 这附近有休息室吗？ zhè fùjìn yǒu xiūxíshì ma? [juh foo-jin yoh shew-shee-shir ma]

▸ there you are *(handing over something)* 给你 gěi nǐ [gay nee]

thermometer 温度计 wēndùjì [weun-doo-jee]

▸ do you have a thermometer? 你有温度计吗？ nǐ yǒu wēndùjì ma? [nee yoh weun-doo-jee ma]

▸ the thermometer shows 18 degrees (Celsius) 温度计显示18（摄氏）度 wēndùjì xiǎnshì shíbā (shèshì)dù [weun-doo-jee shyen-shir shir-ba shuh-shir doo]

---

saying thank you

▸ thank you 谢谢 xièxie [shyeah-shyeah]

▸ thanks, that's very kind of you 谢谢，您真是太好了 xièxie, nín zhēn shì tài hǎo le [shyeah-shyeah neen jeun shir tigh how luh]

▸ I can't thank you enough 我实在太感谢您了 wǒ shízài tài gǎnxiè nín le [wo shir-zigh tigh gan-shyeah neen luh]

▸ thank you for your help 谢谢你的帮助 xièxie nǐ de bāngzhù [shyeah-shyeah nee duh bang-joo]

▸ I wanted to thank you for inviting me 谢谢您邀请我 xièxie nín yāoqǐng wǒ [shyeah shyeah neen yow-ching wo]

thin *(person)* 瘦的 shòu de [shoh duh]; *(slice, layer, material)* 薄的 báo de [bow duh]

> isn't that jacket too thin for a cold evening like this? 晚上这么冷，那件夹克难道不是太薄了吗？ wǎnshang zhème lěng, nà jiàn jiākè nándào bù shì tài báo le ma? [wan-shang juh-muh lung na jyen jya-kuh nan-dow boo shir tigh bow luh ma]

thing *(object)* 东西 dōngxi [dong-shee]; *(matter)* 事情 shìqing [shir-ching]
◆ **things** *(possessions, clothes)* 个人物品 gèrén wùpǐn [guh-reun woo-pin]

> what's that thing for? 那个东西是干什么用的？ nàge dōngxi shì gàn shénme yòng de? [na-guh dong-shee shir-gan shuen-muh yong duh]
> I don't know what the best thing to do is 我不知道最好该怎么办 wǒ bù zhīdao zuì hǎo gāi zěnme bàn [wo boo jir-dow zway how gigh zeun-muh ban]
> could you look after my things for a minute? 你能照看一会儿我的东西吗？ nǐ néng zhàokàn yīhuìr wǒ de dōngxi ma? [nee nung jow-kan yee-hway wo duh dong-shee ma]

think *(believe)* 认为 rènwéi [reun-way] ◆ *(use mind)* 想 xiǎng [shyang]

> I think (that)… 我想…… wǒ xiǎng…… [wo shyang]
> I thought service charge was included 我认为服务费已经包括在内了 wǒ rènwéi fúwùfèi yǐjīng bāokuò zài nèi le [wo reun-way foo-woo-fay yee-jing bow-kwore zigh nay luh]
> I don't think so 我不这么认为 wǒ bù zhème rènwéi [wo boo juh-muh reun-way]

third 第三的 dì–sān de [dee-san duh] ◆ *(fraction)* 三分之一 sān fēn zhī yī [sa feun jir yee]; *(gear)* 三挡 sāndǎng [san-dang]

> this is my third time in China 这是我第三次来中国 zhè shì wǒ dì–sān cì lái zhōngguó [juh shir wo dee san tsir ligh jong-gwore]

thirsty

> to be thirsty 感到渴 gǎndào kě [gan-dow kuh]
> I'm very thirsty 我很渴 wǒ hěn kě [wo heun kuh]

three 三 sān [san]

> there are three of us 我们有三个人 wǒmenyǒu sāngè rén [wo-meun yoh san-guh ren]

throat 喉咙 hóulong [hoh-long]

> I have a fish bone stuck in my throat 一根鱼刺卡在了我的喉咙里 yī gēn yú cì kǎ zài le wǒ de hóulong li [yee geun yoo tsir ka zigh luh wo duh hoh-long lee]

throat lozenge 润喉糖 rùnhóutáng [run-hoh-tang]

> I'd like some throat lozenges 我想要一些润喉糖 wǒ xiǎng yào yīxiē rùnhóutáng [wo shyang yow yee shyeah run-hoh-tang]

buying train tickets (i)

It is not possible to buy round-trip tickets in China, so usually you buy a single for your outward journey, and then another single when you come back. It's also not possible to buy tickets more than a few days before departure. If you want to avoid long queues at the station, you can go to a travel agent, who will buy your ticket for you, in return for a commission. Hotel reception desks also offer this service. At the train station, tickets are checked before you go onto the platform, and then again when you get on the train. Once on board, if you are on a long journey, the inspector may exchange your ticket for a pass. This is a good idea as he will return it to you just before your stop, so you will know it's nearly time to get off! A word of warning: you must keep your ticket on you as it is often checked as you leave the station.

thunderstorm 雷雨 léiyǔ [lay-yoo]

▸ will there be a thunderstorm? 会有雷雨吗？ huì yǒu léiyǔ ma? [hway yoh lay-yoo ma]

Thursday 星期四 xīngqīsì [shing-chee-sir]

▸ we're arriving/leaving on Thursday 我们星期四到/离开 wǒmen xīngqīsì dào/líkāi [wo-meun shing-chee-sir dow/lee-kigh]

ticket 票 piào [peow]

▸ I'd like a ticket to... 我想要一张去......的票 wǒ xiǎng yào yī zhāng qù......de piào [wo shyang yow yee jang choo...duh peow]

▸ how much is a ticket to...? 去......的票多少钱？ qù......de piào duōshao qián? [choo...duh peow swore-show chyen]

▸ I'd like to book a ticket 我想定一张票 wǒ xiǎng dìng yī zhāng piào [wo shyang ding yee jang peow]

▸ I'd like three tickets for... 我要三张......的票 wǒ yào sān zhāng......de piào [wo yow san jang...duh peow]

tide 潮汐 cháoxī [chow-shee]

▸ what time does the tide turn? 潮汐什么时候改变？ cháoxī shénme shíhou gǎibiàn? [cho-shee sheun-muh shir-hoh gigh-byen]

tight *(piece of clothing)* 紧的 jǐn de [jin duh]

▸ these pants are too tight 裤子太紧了 kùzi tài jǐn le [koo-zir tigh jin luh]

time 时间 shíjiān [shir-jyen]; *(occasion)* 时候 shíhou [shir-hoh]

▸ do we have time to visit the town? 我们有时间参观城市吗？ wǒmen yǒu shíjiān cānguān chéngshì ma? [wo-meun yoh shir-jyen tsan-gwan chung-shir ma]

▸ what time is it? 现在是几点？ xiànzài shì jǐ diǎn? [shyen-zigh shir jee dyen]

time

Punctuality is paramount as a sign of Chinese politeness. If invited to dinner, a banquet or a party, it is sometimes even advisable to arrive a little early.

- what time do you close? 你们几点关门？ nǐmen jǐ diǎn guānmén? [nee-meun jee dyen gwan-men]
- could you tell me if the train from Beijing is on time? 你是否能告诉我从北京开来的火车准点吗？ nǐ shìfǒu néng gàosu wǒ cóng běijīng kāilai de huǒchē zhǔndiǎn ma? [nee shir-foh nung gow-soo wo tsong bay-jing kigh-ligh duh hwore-chuh jun-dyen ma]
- maybe some other time 也许以后 yěxǔ yǐhòu [yuh-shoo yee-hoh]
- three times 三次 sān cì [san tsir]
- at the same time 同时 tóngshí [tong-shir]
- the first time 第一次 dì–yī cì [dee-yee tsir]

timetable 时刻表 shíkèbiǎo [shir-kuh-beow]

- do you have local bus timetables? 你有当地的公共汽车时刻表吗？ nǐ yǒu dāngdì de gōnggòng qìchē shíkèbiǎo ma? [nee yoh dang-dee duh gong-gong chee-chuh shir-kuh-beow ma]

tip *(gratuity)* 小费 xiǎofèi [sheow-fay] ◆ *(give a gratuity to)* 付小费给 fù xiǎofèi gěi [foo sheow-fay gay]

tire *(for a vehicle)* 轮胎 lúntāi [lun-tigh]

- the tire's flat 轮胎没气了 lúntāi méi qì le [lun-tigh may chee luh]
- the tire's punctured 轮胎被扎破了 lúntāi bèi zhāpò le [lun-tigh bay ja-po luh]

to *(indicating place, direction)* 向 xiàng [shyang]; *(in telling time)* 之前 zhīqián [jir-chyen]

- when is the next train to Shenyang? 下一班去沈阳的火车是几点？ xià yī bān qù shěnyáng de huǒchē shì jǐ diǎn? [shya yee ban choo sheun-yang duh hwore-chuh shir jee dyen]
- it's twenty to nine 现在是9点差20分 xiànzài shì jiǔ diǎn chà èrshí fēn [shyen-zigh shir jew dyen cha er-shir feun]

tipping

Tipping is not widespread in China, except for in large international-class hotels and some restaurants, and it is never compulsory. Never leave money on the table. Hand it over directly (e.g. to the floor supervisor in your hotel) or say 'keep the change' 不用找零了 bù yòng zhǎoling le [boo yong jow-ling luh] (in a restaurant or a taxi).

tobacco stores

ⓘ

There aren't any tobacco stores as such in China. Cigarettes are often sold in small stores that sell drinks and alcohol as well. You can spot them by the characters 烟 yān [yan] and 酒 jiǔ [jew] (tobacco and alcohol). You can also buy cigarettes at shopping malls or in some supermarkets. Watch out for counterfeit cigarettes, usually of international brands. These are often sold in the street.

tobacco store 烟草店 yāncǎodiàn [yan-tsow-dyen]
 ▸ where is the nearest tobacco store? 最近的烟草店在哪儿？ zuì jìn de yāncǎodiàn zài nǎr? [zway jin duh yan–tsow–dyen zigh nar]

today 今天 jīntiān [jin-tyen]
 ▸ what's today's date? 今天是几月几日？ jīntiān shì jǐ yuè jǐ rì? [jin-tyen shir jee yue jee rir]

toe 脚趾 jiǎozhǐ [jeow-jir]
 ▸ I think I've broken my toe 我想我的脚趾骨折了 wǒ xiǎng wǒ de jiǎozhǐ gǔzhé le [wo shyang wo duh jeow-jir goo-juh luh]

together 一起 yīqǐ [yee-chee]
 ▸ let's go together 我们一起去吧 wǒmen yīqǐ qù ba [wo-meun yee-chee choo ba]

toilet 厕所 cèsuǒ [tsuh-swore]
 ▸ I need to go to the toilet 我要上厕所 wǒ yào shàng cèsuǒ [wo yow shang tsuh-swore]
 ▸ do you have to pay to use the toilet? 上厕所需要付费吗？ shàng cèsuǒ xūyào fù fèi ma? [shang tsuh-swore shoo-yow foo fay ma]

toilet paper 卫生纸 wèishēngzhǐ [way-shung-jir]
 ▸ there is no toilet paper 没有卫生纸了 méiyou wèishēngzhǐ le [may-yoh way-shung-jir luh]

toll (for a road, a bridge) 费 fèi [fay]
 ▸ do you have to pay a toll to use the bridge? 过桥需要付费吗？ guòqiáo xūyào fù fèi ma? [gwore-chew shoo-yow foo fay ma]

toll-free (number, call) 免费的 miǎnfèi de [myen-fau duh] ◆ (call) 免费 miǎnfèi [myen-fay]
 ▸ there's a toll-free number you can call 有一个免费的电话号码你可以打 yǒu yī gè miǎnfèi de diànhuà hàomǎ nǐ kěyǐ dǎ [yoh yee guh myen-fay duh dyen-hwa how-ma nee kuh-yee da]

tomato 番茄 fānqié [fan-chyeah], 西红柿 xīhóngshì [shee-hong-shir]
 ▸ a kilo of tomatoes 一公斤番茄 yī gōngjīn fānqié [yee gong-jin fan-chyeah], 一公斤西红柿 yī gōngjīn xīhóngshì [yee gong-jin shee-hong-shir]

tomato juice 番茄汁 fānqiézhī [fan-chyeah-jir]
- I'd like a tomato juice 我要一杯番茄汁 wǒ yào yī bēi fānqiézhī [wo yow yee bay fan-chyeah-jir]

tomorrow 明天 míngtiān [ming-tyen]
- can you hold my reservation until tomorrow? 你能把我的预定保留到明天吗？ nǐ néng bǎ wǒ de yùdìng bǎoliúdào míngtiān ma? [nee nung ba wo duh yoo-ding bow-lew-dow ming-tyen ma]
- I'm leaving tomorrow morning 我明天早晨出发 wǒ míngtiān zǎochén chūfā [wo ming-tyen zow-cheun choo-fa]
- see you tomorrow night 明天晚上见 míngtiān wǎnshang jiàn [ming-tyen wan-shang jyen]

tonight 今晚 jīnwǎn [jin-wan]
- do you have any beds available for tonight? 今晚你们有空床位吗？ jīnwǎn nǐmen yǒu kòng chuángwèi ma? [jin-wan ni-meun yoh kong chwung-way ma]

too (also) 也 yě [yuh]; (excessively) 太 tài [tigh]
- enjoy your meal! – you too 祝你吃得开心！– 你也一样 zhù nǐ chī de kāixīn! – nǐ yě yīyàng [joo nee chir duh kigh-shin nee yuh yee-yang]
- she's too tired to... 她太累了以至于...... tā tài lèi le yīzhìyú...... [nee yuh yee-yang...]
- it's too expensive 那太贵了 nà tài guì le [na tigh gway luh]
- there are too many people 人太多了 rén tài duō le [reun tigh dwore luh]

tooth 牙 yá [ya]
- I've broken a tooth 我的一颗牙掉了 wǒ de yī kē yá diào le [wo duh yee kuh ya deow luh]

toothache 牙疼 yá téng [ya tung]
- I have a toothache 我牙疼 wǒ yá téng [wo ya tung]

toothbrush 牙刷 yáshuā [ya-shwa]
- I forgot my toothbrush 我忘了带我的牙刷了 wǒ wàngle dài wǒ de yáshuā [wo wang-luh digh wo duh ya-shwa]

toothpaste 牙膏 yágāo [ya-gow]
- I'd like to buy some toothpaste 我要买牙膏 wǒ yào mǎi yágāo [wo yow migh yow-gow]

top (of a bottle, a tube) 顶部 dǐngbù [ding-boo]; (of a jar) 盖子 gàizi [gigh-zir]
- (maximum) 最高的 zuì gāo de [zway gow duh]
- the car drove away at top speed 汽车以最快的速度开走了 qìchē yǐ zuì kuài de sùdù kāizǒu le [chee-chuh yee zway kway duh soo-doo kigh-zoh luh]

tour 旅行 lǚxíng [looh-shing]
- I'm planning to do a two-week tour of the country 我正计划在国内旅行两周 wǒ zhèng jìhuà zài guónèi lǚxíng liǎng zhōu [wo jung jee-hwa zigh gwore-nay looh-shing lyang joh]

tourist 游客 lǚkè [looh-kuh] ♦ *(season)* 旅游旺的 lǚyóu wàng de [looh-yoh wang duh]

> do you get many tourists here? 这里有很多游客吗？ zhèli yǒu hěn duō yóukè ma? [juh-lee yoh heun dwore yoh-kuh ma]

tourist attraction 旅游景点 lǚyóu jǐngdiǎn [loo-yoh jing-dyen]

> what are the main tourist attractions in the area? 这里最主要的旅游景点是哪个？ zhèli zuì zhǔyào de lǚyóu jǐngdiǎn shì nǎge? [juh-lee zway joo-yow dun loo-yoh jing-dyen shir na-guh]

tourist class 硬席 yìngxí [ying-shee]

> in tourist class, please 请给硬席 qǐng gěi yìngxí [ching gay ying-shee]

tourist guide 导游 dǎoyóu [dow-yoh]

> we have a good tourist guide with a lot of up-to-date information 我们的导游不错，知道许多最新消息 wǒmen de dǎoyóu bùcuò, zhīdao xǔduō zuì xīn xiāoxi [wo-meun duh dow-yoh boo-tswore jir-dow shoo-dwore zway shin sheow-shee]

tourist office 旅游信息中心 lǚyóu xìnxī zhōngxīn [loo-yoh shin-shee jong-shin]

> I'm looking for the tourist office 我在找旅游信息中心 wǒ zài zhǎo lǚyóu xìnxī zhōngxīn [wo zigh jow looh-yoh shin-shee jong-shin]
> can I get a street map at the tourist office? 我去旅游信息中心是否能拿到街道图？ wǒ qù lǚyóu xìnxī zhōngxīn shìfǒu néng nádào jiēdào tú？ [wo choo looh-yoh shin-shee jong-shin shir-foh nung na-dow jyeah-dow too]

tow 拖 tuō [twore]

> could you tow me to a garage? 你能把我的车拖到修车厂吗？ nǐ néng bǎ wǒ de chē tuōdào xiūchēchǎng ma? [nee nung ba wo duh chuh twore-dow shew-chuh-chang ma]

toward *(in the direction of)* 向着 xiàngzhe [shyang-juh]

> we're heading toward Shanghai 我们正前往上海 wǒmen zhèng qiánwǎng shànghǎi [wo-meun jung chyen-wang shang-high]

tow away 拖走 tuōzǒu [twore-zoh]

> my car's been towed away 我的车被拖走了 wǒ de chē bèi tuōzǒu le [wo duh chuh bay twore-zoh luh]

towel 毛巾 máojīn [mow-jin]

> we don't have any towels 我们没有毛巾了 wǒmen méiyou máojīn le [wo-meun may-yoh mow-jin luh]
> could we have more towels? 能再给我们一些毛巾吗？ néng zài gěi wǒmen yīxiē máojīn ma? [nung zigh gay wo-meun yee-shyeah mow-jin ma]

tower *(of a church, a castle)* 塔 tǎ [ta]

> can you visit the tower? 可以参观这座塔吗？ kěyǐ cānguān zhè zuò tǎ ma? [kuh-yee tsan-gwan juh zwore ta ma]

getting around town

▸ which bus goes to the airport? 哪一路公共汽车去机场？ nǎ yī lù gōnggòng qìchē qù jīchǎng? [na yee loo gong-gong chee-chuh choo jee-chang]

▸ where does the bus to the station leave from? 开往火车站的公共汽车从哪里出发？ kāiwǎng huǒchēzhàn de gōnggòng qìchē cóng nǎli chūfā? [kigh-wang hwore-chuh-jan duh gong-gong chee-chuh tsong na-lee choo-fa]

▸ I'd like a one-way (ticket) to… 我要一张去……的单程票 wǒ yào yī zhāng qù……de dānchéngpiào [wo yow yee jang choo…duh dan-chung-peow]

▸ could you tell me where I have to get off to go to…? 你能否告诉我去……该在哪里下车？ nǐ néngfǒu gàosu wǒ qù……gāi zài nǎli xià chē [nee nung-foh gow-soo wo choo…gigh zigh na-lee shya chuh]

town 城市 chéngshì [chung-shir]
  ▸ to go into town 进城 jìn chéng [jin chung]

town hall 市政厅 shìzhèngtīng [shir-jung-ting]
  ▸ where is the town hall? 市政厅在哪里？ shìzhèngtīng zài nǎli? [shir-jung-ting zigh nar]

traffic (vehicles) 车辆 chēliàng [chuh-lyang]
  ▸ is there a lot of traffic on the freeway? 高速公路上车辆多吗？ gāosù gōnglù shang chēliàng duō ma? [gow-soo gong-loo shang chuh-lyang dwore ma]

traffic circle 环形交叉路口 huánxíng jiāochā lùkǒu [hwan-shing jeow-cha loo-koh]
  ▸ you turn right at the traffic circle 你到环形交叉路口的时候向左拐 nǐ dào huánxíng jiāochā lùkǒu de shíhou xiàng zuǒ guǎi [nee dow hwan-shing jeow-cha loo-koh duh shir-hoh shyang zwore gwigh]

traffic jam 交通阻塞 jiāotōng zǔsè [jeow-tong zoo-suh]
  ▸ we got stuck in a traffic jam 我们碰到了交通阻塞 wǒmen pèngdàole jiāotōng zǔsè [wo-meun pung-dow-luh jeow-tong zoo-suh]

traffic lights 红绿灯 hónglǜdēng [hong-looh-dung]
  ▸ turn left at the traffic lights 到红绿灯后向左拐 dào hónglǜdēng hòu xiàng zuǒ guǎi [dow hong-looh-dung hoh shyang zwore yoh gwigh]

traffic lights

Be careful at crossroads in big towns as it is often legal to turn right while the lights are on red for traffic going straight ahead. This means you have to take particular care when you are crossing the road. At major crossroads, there are sometimes traffic wardens with red armbands who supervise the flow of pedestrians and will tell you when you can cross.

trains

Chinese trains have four main classes: hard seat 硬座 yìngzuò [ying-zwore], soft seat 软座 ruǎnzuò [rwan-zwore], hard sleeper 硬卧 yìngwò [ying-wo] and soft sleeper 软卧 ruǎnwò [rwan-wo]. Standing tickets are also available: 站票 zhànpiào [jan-peow]. You can take a seat with a standing ticket, if one is available. China recently finished building one of the world's highest railway lines. It runs between Qinghai province and Tibet, and half of it is laid on permafrost. A tip: the restaurant car is usually worth a visit. Dishes are prepared on the train and served at your table for a very reasonable price.

trail *(path)* 小路 xiǎolù [sheow-loo]
  ▸ will this trail take us back to the parking lot? 沿着这条路我们能到停车场吗？ yánzhe zhè tiáo lù wǒmen néng dào tíngchēchǎng ma? [yan-juh juh teow loo wo-meun nung dow ting-chuh-chang ma]

train *(on the railroad)* 火车 huǒchē [hwore-chuh]; *(on the subway)* 地铁 dìtiě [dee-tyeah]
  ▸ when is the next train to Hangzhou? 下一班开往杭州的火车是几点？ xià yī bān kāiwǎng hángzhōu de huǒchē shì jǐ diǎn? [shya yee ban kigh-wang hang-joh duh hwore-chuh shir jee dyen]
  ▸ do you have reduced-price train tickets for seniors? 有给老人的特价票吗？ yǒu gěi lǎoren de tèjiàpiào ma? [yoh gay low-reun duh tuh-jya-peow ma]
  ▸ which platform does the train for Beijing leave from? 开往北京的火车从哪个站台出发？ kāiwǎng běijīng de huǒchē cóng nǎge zhàntái chūfā? [kigh-wang bay-jing duh hwore-chuh tsong na-guh jan-tigh choo-fa]
  ▸ the train was fifteen minutes late 火车晚点了15分钟 huǒchē wǎndiǎnle shíwǔ fēnzhōng [hwore-chuh wan-dyen shir-woo feun-jong]

tram 有轨电车 yǒu guǐ diànchē [yoh gway dyen-chuh]
  ▸ can you buy tickets on the tram? 能在电车上买票吗？ néng zài diànchē shang mǎi piào ma? [nung zigh dyen-chuh shang migh peow ma]
  ▸ which tram line do we have to take? 我们该乘坐哪一路电车？ wǒmen gāi chéngzuò nǎ yī lù diànchē? [wo-meun gigh chung-zwore na yee loo dyen-chuh]
  ▸ where is the nearest tram stop? 最近的电车车站在哪里？ zuì jìn de diànchē chēzhàn zài nǎli? [zway jin duh dyen-chuh chuh-jan zigh na-lee]

transfer *(of money)* 转账 zhuǎnzhàng [jwan-jang] ♦ *(money)* 转 zhuǎn [jwan]
  ▸ I'd like to transfer some money from my savings account 我想从我的储蓄账户里转点钱 wǒ xiǎng cóng wǒ de chǔxù zhànghù li zhuǎn diǎn qián [wo shyang tsong wo duh choo-shoo jang-hway lee jwan dyen chyen]

travel 旅行 lǚxíng [looh-shing]

▸ I'd like a window seat facing the direction of travel 我想要一个朝着车开的方向的靠窗的座位 wǒ xiǎng yào yī gè cháozhe chē kāi de fāngxiàng de kào chuāng de zuòwei [wo shyang yow yee guh chow-juh chuh kigh duh fang-shyang duh kow chwung duh zwore-way]

▸ I'm traveling on my own 我独自一人旅行 wǒ dúzì yī rén lǚxíng [wo doo-zir yee reun looh-shing]

travel agency 旅行社 lǚxíngxshè [looh-shing-shuh]

▸ I'm looking for a travel agency 我在找旅行社 wǒ zài zhǎo lǚxíngshè [wo zigh jow looh-shing-shuh]

traveler's check 旅行支票 lǚxíng zhīpiào [looh-shing jir-peow]

▸ do you take traveler's checks? 你们收旅行支票吗？ nǐmen shōu lǚxíng zhīpiào ma? [nee-meun shoh looh-shing jir-peow ma]

tree 树 shù [shoo]

▸ what type of tree is that? 那是棵什么树？ nà shì kē shénme shù? [na shir kuh sheun-muh shoo]

trip *(journey)* 旅行 lǚxíng [looh-shing]

▸ have a good trip! 祝你旅途愉快！ zhù nǐ lǚtú yúkuài! [zhoo nee looh-too yoo-kwigh]

trouble *(difficulty)* 困难 kùnnan [kun-nan]; *(effort)* 麻烦 máfan [ma-fan]

▸ we didn't have any trouble finding the hotel 我们没费一点劲儿就找到了旅馆 wǒmen méi fèi yīdiǎn jìngr jiù zhǎodàole lǚguǎn [wo-meun may fay yee-dyenr jingr jew jow-dow luh looh-gwan]

▸ I don't want to be any trouble 我不想添麻烦 wǒ bù xiǎng tiān máfan [wo boo shyang tyen ma-fan]

▸ it's no trouble 不麻烦 bù máfan [boo ma-fan]

trunk *(of a car)* 行李箱 xínglixiāng [shing-shyang]; *(piece of luggage)* 大旅行箱 dà lǚxíngxiāng [da looh-shing-shyang]

▸ my things are in the trunk of the car 我的东西在汽车的行李箱里 wǒ de dōngxi zài qìchē de xínglixiāng li [wo duh dong-shee zigh chee-chuh duh shing-shyang lee]

---

traveling

As a rule it is safe and quite easy to travel around in China. Public transportation is extensive and cheap, but conditions (especially in hard seat or hard sleeper class) can be cramped, and over-crowding, especially during holiday periods, is common. Most of China is now open for tourists, except for a few isolated areas.

▸ I've got two small bags and a large trunk 我有两个手提箱和一个大的旅行箱 wǒ yǒu liǎng gè shǒutíxiāng hé yī gè dà de lǚxíngxiāng [wo yoh lyang guh shoh-tee-shyang huh yee guh da looh-shing-shyang]

try *(attempt)* 努力做 nǔlì zuò [noo-lee zwore]; *(sample)* 尝试 chángshì [chang-shir]

▸ I'd like to try the local beer 我想试试本地的啤酒 wǒ xiǎng shìshi běndì de píjiǔ [wo shyang shir-shir beun-dee duh pee-jew]

try on *(dress, shoes)* 试穿 shìchuān [shir-chwan]

▸ I'd like to try on the one in the window 我想试穿橱窗里的那个 wǒ xiǎng shìchuān chúchuāng li de nàge [wo shyang shir-chwan choo-chwung lee duh na-guh]

tub *(of ice cream)* 盒 hé [huh]

▸ do you sell tubs of ice cream to take home? 你们卖可以带回家的盒装冰激淋吗？ nǐmen mài kěyǐ dài huí jiā de hézhuāng bīngjīlín ma? [nee-meun migh kuh-yee digh hway jya duh huh-jwang bing-jee-lin ma]

Tuesday 星期二 xīngqī'èr [shing-chee-er]

▸ we're arriving/leaving on Tuesday 我们星期二到/离开 wǒmen xīng'qīèr dào/líkāi [wo-meun shing-chee-er dow/lee-kigh]

tunnel 隧道 suìdào [sway-dow]

▸ is there a toll for using the tunnel? 过隧道要付钱吗？ guò suìdào yào fù qián ma? [gwore sway-dow yow foo chyen ma]

turn *(in a game, order)* 机会 jīhuì [jee-hway]; *(off a road)* 转弯处 zhuǎnwānchù [jwan-wan-choo] ◆ *(change direction)* 转弯 zhuǎnwān [jwan-wan]

▸ it's your turn 轮到你了 lúndào nǐ le [lun-dow nee luh]

▸ is this the turn for the campground? 去野营地是在这儿转弯吗？ qù yěyíngdì shì zài zhèr zhuǎnwān ma? [choo yuh-ying-dee shir zigh jur jwan-wan ma]

▸ turn left at the lights 到了红绿灯向左转 dàole hónglǜdēng xiàng zuǒ zhuǎn [dow-luh hong-looh-dung shyang zwore jwan]

▸ you have to turn right 你得向右转 nǐ děi xiàng yòu zhuǎn [nee day shyang yoh jwan]

turn down *(radio, volume, gas)* 关小 guānxiǎo [gwan-sheow]

▸ can we turn the air-conditioning down? 我们能把空调关小点儿吗？ wǒmen néng bǎ kōngtiáo guānxiǎo diǎnr ma? [wo-meun nung ba kong-teow gwan-sheow dyenr ma]

▸ how do you turn the volume down? 怎样才能把音量关小？ zěnyàng cái néng bǎ yīnliàng guānxiǎo? [zeun-yang tsigh nung ba yin-lyang gwan-sheow]

turn off *(light, appliance)* 关上 guānshang [gwan-shang]

▸ where do you turn the light off? 灯在哪里关？ dēng zài nǎli guān? [dung zigh na-lee gwan]

▸ my cell was turned off 我的手机关机了 wǒ de shǒujī guānjī le [wo duh shoh-jee gwan-jee luh]

turn on *(light, radio)* 打开 dǎkāi [da-kigh]

▸ where do I turn this light on? 我该在哪里把灯打开? wǒ gāi zài nǎli bǎ dēng dǎkāi? [wo gigh zigh na-lee ba dung da-kigh]

▸ can you turn on the ignition? 汽车能启动吗? qìchē néng qǐdòng ma? [chee-chuh nung chee-dong ma]

turn up *(sound, central heating)* 开大 kāidà [kigh-da]

▸ how do you turn up the heating? 怎样才能把暖气开大? zěnyàng cái néng bǎ nuǎnqì kāidà? [zeun-yang tsigh nung ba nwan-chee kigh-da]

TV *(system)* 电视系统 diànshì xìtǒng [dyen-shir shee-tong]; *(broadcasts)* 电视节目 diànshì jiémù [dyen-shir jyeah-mu]; *(set)* 电视机 diànshìjī [dyen-shir-jee]

▸ the TV in our room is broken 我们房间的电视机坏了 wǒmen fángjiān de diànshìjī huài le [wo-meun fang-jyen duh dyen-shir-jee hwigh luh]

TV lounge 有电视机的休息室 yǒu diànshìjī de xiūxishì [yoh dyen-shir-jee duh shew-shir]

▸ is there a TV lounge? 是否有带电视机的休息室? shìfǒu yǒu dài diànshìjī de xiūxishì? [shir-foh yoh digh dyen-shir-jee duh shew-shir]

twelve 十二 shí'èr [shir-er] ◆ *(noon)* 中午十二点 zhōngwǔ shí'èr diǎn [jong-woo shir-er dyen]; *(midnight)* 凌晨零点 língchén líng diǎn [ling-cheun ling dyen]

▸ there are twelve of us 我们有十二个人 wǒmen yǒu shí'èr gè rén [wo-meun yoh shir-er guh reun]

▸ it's twelve o'clock *(noon)* 现在是中午十二点 xiànzài shì zhōngwǔ shí'èr diǎn [shyen-zigh shir jong-woo shir-er dyen]; *(midnight)* 现在是凌晨零点 xiànzài shì língchén líng diǎn [shyen-zigh shir ling-cheun ling dyen]

twice 两次 liǎng cì [lyang tsir]

▸ the ferry runs twice a day 渡船一天开两次 dùchuán yī tiān kāi liǎng cì [doo-chwan yee tyen kigh lyang tsir]

twin 双胞胎 shuāngbāotāi [shwang-bow-tigh] ◆ 双胞胎的 shuāngbāotāi de [shwang-bow-tigh duh]

▸ twin brother 双胞胎兄弟 shuāngbāotāi xiōngdì [shwang-bow-tigh shyong-dee]

▸ twin sister 双胞胎姐妹 shuāngbāotāi jiěmèi [shwang-bow-tigh jyeah-may]

twin beds 两张单人床 liǎng zhāng dānrénchuáng [lyang jang dan-reun-chwung]

▸ a room with twin beds 有两张单人床的房间 yǒu liǎng zhāng dānrénchuáng de fángjiān [yoh lyang jang dan-reun-chwung duh fang-jyen]

two 二 èr [er], 两 liǎng [lyang]

▸ there are two of us 我们有两个人 wǒmenyǒu liǎng gè rén [wo-meun yoh lyang guh reun]

umbrella 雨伞 yǔsǎn [yoo-san]
- could you lend me an umbrella? 你能借给我一把雨伞吗？ nǐ néng jiè gěi wǒ yī bǎ yǔsǎn ma? [nee nung jyeah gay wo yee ba yoo-san ma]

unacceptable 不能接受的 bù néng jiēshòu de [boo nung jyeah shoh duh]
- it's completely unacceptable! 这根本让人无法接受！ zhè gēnběn ràng rén wúfǎ jiēshòu! [juh geun-beun rang reun woo-fa jyeah-shoh]

underpass 地下通道 dìxià tōngdào [dee-shya tong-dow]
- is the underpass safe at night? 晚上地下通道安全吗？ wǎnshang dìxià tōngdào ānquán ma? [wan-shang dee-shya tong-dow an-chwan ma]

understand 理解 lǐjiě [lee-jyeah] ◆ 知道 zhīdao [jir-dow]
- I can understand Chinese, but I can't really speak it 我听得懂中文，但是不怎么会说 wǒ tīng de dǒng zhōngwén, dànshì bù zěnme huì shuō [wo ting duh dong jong-weun dan-shir boo zeun-muh hway shwore]
- I understand a little 我只知道一点儿 wǒ zhǐ zhīdao yīdiǎnr [wo jir jir-dow yee-dyenr]
- I don't understand a word 我一个字也不懂 wǒ yī gè zì yě bù dǒng [wo yee guh zir yuh boo dong]
- do you understand? 你明白了吗？ nǐ míngbaile ma? [nee ming-bigh luh ma]

unit *(of condominium complex)* 公寓 gōngyù [gong-yoo]
- we'd prefer a unit with air conditioning 我们想要一个有空调的公寓 wǒmen xiǎng yào yī gè yǒu kōngtiáo de gōngyù [wo-meun shyang yow yee guh yoh kong-teow duh gong-yoo]

---

saying that you have understood/not understood

- oh, I see…! 哦，我知道了…… ò, wǒ zhīdao le…… [o wo jir-dow luh]
- sorry, but I didn't understand 对不起，我不明白 duìbuqǐ,wǒ bù míngbai [dway-boo-chee wo boo ming-bigh]
- I'm a little confused… 我有点儿糊涂…… wǒ yǒu diǎnr hútu…… [wo yoh dyenr hoo-too]
- I don't understand your question 我不明白你的问题 wǒ bù míngbai nǐ de wèntí [wo boo ming-bigh nee duh weun-tee]
- sorry, but I still don't understand 对不起，但是我还是不理解 duìbuqǐ, dànshì wǒ háishi bù lǐjiě [dway-boo-chee dan-shir wo high-shir boo lee-jyeah]

United States (of America)

- the United States 美国 měiguó [may-gwore]
- I'm from the United States 我来自美国 wǒ láizì měiguó [wo ligh-zir may-gwore]
- I live in the United States 我住在美国 wǒ zhù zài měiguó [wo joo zigh may-gwore]
- have you ever been to the United States? 你去过美国吗？ nǐ qùguo měiguó ma? [nee choo-gwore may-gwore ma]

unleaded (gas) 不含铅的 bù hán qiān de [boo han chyen duh] ◆ 无铅汽油 wúqiān qìyóu [woo-chyen chee-yoh]

- do you have premium or just regular unleaded? 你有高级汽油还是普通无铅汽油？ nǐ yǒu gāojí qìyóu háishi pǔtōng wúqiān qìyóu? [nee yoh gow-jee chee-yoh high-shir poo-tong woo-chyen chee-yoh]

until 直到 zhídào [jir-dow]

- I'm staying until Sunday 我会呆到星期天 wǒ huì dāi dào xīngqītiān [wo hway digh dow shing-chee-tyen]
- until noon 直到中午 zhídào zhōngwǔ [jir-dow jong-woo]

up (to or in a higher position) 在上面 zài shàngmian [zigh shang-myen] ◆ (wrong) 出事了的 chūshìle de [choo-shir-luh duh] ◆ **up to** 正忙于 zhèng máng yú [jung mang yoo]

- what's up? (what's wrong?) 出什么事了？ chū shénme shì le? [choo sheun-muh shir luh]; (as greeting) 你好吗？ nǐ hǎo ma? [nee how ma]
- what are you up to tonight? 今晚你干什么？ jīnwǎn nǐ gàn shénme? [jin-wang nee gan sheun-muh]
- up to now 直到现在 zhídào xiànzài [jir-dow shyen-zigh]

urgent 紧急的 jǐnjí de [jin-jee suh]

- it's not urgent 不着急 bù zháojí [boo jow-jee]

urgently 紧急地 jǐnjí de [jin-jee duh]

- I have to see a dentist urgently 我得马上去看牙医 wǒ děi mǎshàng qù kàn yáyī [wo day ma-shang choo kan ya-yee]

US(A)

- the US 美国 měiguó [may-gwore]
- I'm from the US 我来自美国 wǒ láizì měiguó [wo ligh-zir may-gwore]
- I live in the US 我住在美国 wǒ zhù zài měiguó [wo joo zigh may-gwore]
- have you ever been to the US? 你去过美国吗？ nǐ qùguo měiguó ma? [nee choo-gwore may-gwore ma]

use 使用 shǐyòng [shir-yong]

- could I use your cellphone? 我能用你的手机吗？ wǒ néng yòng nǐ de shǒujī ma? [wo nung yong nee duh shoh-jee ma]

vacancy 空房 kòngfáng [kong-fang]

▸ do you have any vacancies for tonight? 今晚你们有空房吗？ jīnwǎn nǐmen yǒu kòngfáng ma？ [jin-wang nee-meun yoh kong-fang ma]

vacation 假期 jiàqī [jya-chee]

▸ are you here on vacation? 你在放假吗？ nǐ zài fàngjià ma？ [nee zigh fang-jya ma]

▸ I'm on vacation 我在放假 wǒ zài fàngjià [wo zigh fang-jya]

valid 有效的 yǒuxiào de [yoh-sheow duh]

▸ is this ticket valid for the exhibit too? 这张票也能用于参观展览吗？ zhè zhāng piào yě néng yòngyú cānguān zhǎnlǎn ma？ [juh jang peow yuh nung yong-yoo tsan-gwan jan-lan ma]

▸ how long is this ticket valid for? 这张票多久有效？ zhè zhāng piào duōjiǔ yǒuxiào？ [juh jang peow dwore-jew yoh-sheow]

▸ my passport is still valid 我的护照还有效 wǒ de hùzhào hái yǒuxiào [wo duh hoo-jow high yoh-sheow]

vegetable 蔬菜 shūcài [shoo-tsigh]

▸ does it come with vegetables? 配有蔬菜吗？ pèiyǒu shūcài ma？ [pay-yoh shoo-tsigh ma]

vegetarian 素食的 sùshí de [soo-shir duh] ◆ 素食者 sùshízhě [soo-shir-juh]

▸ I'm a vegetarian 我是素食者 wǒ shì sùshízhě [wo shir soo-shir-shuh]

▸ do you have vegetarian dishes? 你们有给素食者吃的菜吗？ nǐmen yǒu gěi sùshízhě chī de cài ma？ [nee-meun yoh gay soo-shir-juh chir duh tsigh ma]

vending machine 自动售货机 zìdòng shòuhuòjī [zir-dong shoh-hwore-jee]

▸ the vending machine isn't working 自动售货机坏了 zìdòng shòuhuòjī huài le [zir-dong shoh-hwore-jee hwigh luh]

---

vegetables

Chinese cuisine uses a lot of vegetables that are eaten as dishes in their own right. In a restaurant, you order them separately from the meat or fish, which are served without any accompaniment. Vegetarians will be in their element as there are a multitude of dishes that are made from vegetables alone, with different sauces, cooking methods, etc. However, beware: many vegetable dishes have bits of meat, fish or shrimp added, so be sure to check.

vertigo 晕眩 yūnxuàn [yun-shwan]
> ▶ I suffer from vertigo 我感到晕眩 wǒ gǎndào yūnxuàn [wo gan-dow yun-shwan]

very 很 hěn [heun]
> ▶ I'm very hungry 我很饿 wǒ hěn è [wo heun uh]
> ▶ very much 非常 fēicháng [fay-chang]
> ▶ very near 很近 hěn jìn [heun jin]

view *(panorama)* 景色 jǐngsè [jing-suh]
> ▶ I'd prefer a room with an ocean view 我想要一间海景房 wǒ xiǎng yào yī jiān hǎijǐngfáng [wo shyang yow yee jyen high-jing-fang]

villa 度假别墅 dùjià biéshù [doo-jya byeah-shoo]
> ▶ we'd like to rent a villa for one week 我们想租一个星期的度假别墅 wǒmen xiǎng zū yī gè xīngqī de dùjià biéshù [wo-meun shyang zoo guh shing-chee duh doo-jya byeah-shoo]

virus 病毒 bìngdú [bing-doo]
> ▶ I must have picked up a virus 我一定是感染病毒了 wǒ yīdìng shì gǎnrǎn bìngdú le [wo yee-ding shir gan-rang bing-doo luh]

visa 签证 qiānzhèng [chyen-jung]
> ▶ do you need a visa? 你需要签证吗？ nǐ xūyào qiānzhèng ma? [nee shoo-yow chyen-jung ma]

visit 游览 yóulǎn [yoh-lan] ◆ 参观 cānguān [tsan-gwan]
> ▶ is this your first visit to Beijing? 这是你第一次来北京吗？ zhè shì nǐ dì-yī cì lái běijīng ma? [juh shir nee dee-yee tsir ligh bay-jing ma]
> ▶ I'd like to visit the castle 我想去参观城堡 wǒ xiǎng qù cānguān chéngbǎo [wo shyang tsan-gwan chung-bow]

voicemail 语音信箱 yǔyīn xìnxiāng [yoo-yin shin-shyang]
> ▶ I need to check my voicemail 我需要查看我的语音信箱 wǒ xūyào chákàn wǒ de yǔyīn xìnxiāng [wo shoo-yow cha-kan wo duh yoo-yin shin-shyang]

voucher 代金券 dàijīnquàn [digh-jin-chwan]
> ▶ I haven't received the voucher 我还没有收到代金券 wǒ hái méiyou shōudào dàijīnquàn [wo high may-yoh shoh-dow digh-jin-chwan]

waist 腰 yāo [yow]
▸ it's a little bit tight at the waist 腰部有点儿紧 yāobù yǒu diǎnr jǐn [yow-boo yoh dyenr jin]

wait 等 děng [dung]
▸ have you been waiting long? 你等了很久吗？ nǐ děngle hěn jiǔ ma? [nee dug-luh heun jew ma]

waiter 服务员 fúwùyuán [foo-woo-ywan]
▸ waiter, could we have the check, please? 服务员，请给我们买单好吗？ fúwùyuán, qǐng gěi wǒmen mǎidān hǎo ma? [foo-woo-ywan ching gay wo-meun migh-dan how ma]

wait for 等 děng [dung]
▸ are you waiting for the bus? 你在等公共汽车吗？ nǐ zài děng gōnggòng qìchē ma? [nee zigh dung gong-gong che-chuh ma]
▸ I'm waiting for them to call back 我在等他们给我打电话 wǒ zài děng tāmen gěi wǒ dǎ diànhuà [wo zigh dung ta-meun gay wo da dyen-hwa]
▸ don't wait for me 别等我了 bié děng wǒ le [byeah dung wo luh]

waiting room *(for train)* 候车室 hòuchēshì [hoh-chuh-shir]; *(for a doctor, a dentist)* 候诊室 hòuzhěnshì [hoh-jeun-shir]
▸ is there a waiting room near the platform? 站台附近有候车室吗？ zhàntái fùjìn yǒu hòuchēshì ma? [jan-tigh foo-jin yoh hoh-chuh shir ma]

waitress 女服务员 nǚ fúwùyuán [nooh- foo-woo-ywan]
▸ the waitress has already taken our order 女服务员已经给我们点过菜了 nǚ fúwùyuán yǐjīng gěi wǒmen diǎnguo cài le [nooh- foo-woo-ywan yee-jing gay wo-meun dyen-gwore tsigh luh]

wake 唤醒 huànxǐng [hwan-shing] ◆ 醒来 xǐnglái [shing-ligh]
▸ could you wake me at 6:45? 你能在6点45分叫醒我吗？ nǐ néng zài liù diǎn sìshíwǔ fēn jiàoxǐng wǒ ma? [nee nung zigh lew dyen sir-shir-woo feun jeow-shing wo ma]
▸ I always wake early 我总是醒得早 wǒ zǒng shì xǐng de zǎo [wo zong-shir shing duh zow]

wake up 把......唤醒 bǎ......huànxǐng [ba...hwan-shing] ◆ 醒来 xǐnglái [shing-ligh]
▸ a noise woke me up in the middle of the night 半夜一阵喧闹把我吵醒 bànyè yī zhèn xuānnào bǎ wǒ chǎoxǐng [ban-yuh yee jeun shwan-now ba wo chow-shing]

▸ I have to wake up very early tomorrow to catch the plane 明天我得起得很 早去赶飞机 míngtiān wǒ děi qǐ de hěn zǎo qù gǎn fēijī [ming-tyen wo day chee duh heun zow choo gan fay-jee]

walk 步行 bùxíng [boo-shing] ◆ *(person)* 陪......走 péi......zǒu [pay...zoh]; *(distance)* 走 zǒu [zoh]

▸ are there any interesting walks in the area? 在这个地区有没有比较好的步 行路线？ zài zhège dìqū yǒuméiyǒu bǐjiào hǎo de bùxíng lùxiàn? [zigh juh-guh dee-choo yoh-may-yoh bee-jeow how duh boo-shing loo-shyen]

▸ let's go for a walk 我们出去散步吧 wǒmen chūqù sànbù ba [wo-meun choo-choo san-boo ba]

▸ how long would it take me to walk there? 我走去要多久？ wǒ zǒuqu yào duō jiǔ? [wo zoh-choo yow dwore jew]

walking boots 步行靴 bùxíngxuē [boo-shing-shue]

▸ do you need walking boots? 要穿步行靴吗？ yào chuān bùxíngxuē ma? [yow chwan boo-shing-shue ma]

wallet 钱包 qiánbāo [chyen-bow]

▸ I've lost my wallet 我丢失了我的钱包 wǒ diūshīle wǒ de qiánbāo [wo dew shir-luh wo duh chyen-bow]

want *(wish, desire)* 想要 xiǎng yào [shyang yow]

▸ I don't want to go there 我不想去那里 wǒ bù xiǎng qù nàli [wo boo shyang choo na-lee]

warm 温暖的 wēnnuǎn de [weun-nwan duh]

▸ it's warm 挺暖和 tǐng nuǎnhuo [ting nwan-hwore]

▸ where can I buy some warm clothing for the trip? 我可以去哪里为这次旅 行买一些保暖的衣服？ wǒ kěyǐ qù nǎli wèi zhè cì lǚxíng mǎi yīxiē bǎonuǎn de yīfu? [wo kuh-yee choo na-lee way juh tsir looh-shing ma yee-shyeah bow-nwan duh yee-foo]

warn 警告 jǐnggào [jing-gow]

▸ no one warned me about that! 没有人提醒过我那个！ méiyou rén tíxǐngguo wǒ nàge! [may-yoh reun tee-shing-gwore wo na-guh]

wash 洗 xǐ [shee] ◆ 洗涤 xǐdí [shee-dee]

▸ where can I wash my hands? 我可以在哪里洗手？ wǒ kěyǐ zài nǎli xǐ shǒu? [wo kuh-yee zigh na-lee shee shoh]

watch 手表 shǒubiǎo [shoh-beow] ◆ *(look at)* 看 kàn [kan]; *(guard)* 看守 kānshǒu [kan-shoh]

▸ my watch has been stolen 我的手表被偷了 wǒ de shǒubiǎo bèi tōu le [wo duh shoh-beow bay toh luh]

▸ can you watch my bags for a minute? 你能看一会儿我的行李吗？ nǐ néng kān yīhuìr wǒ de xíngli ma? [nee nung kan yee-hwayr wo duh shing-lee ma]

water

The Chinese don't drink tap water unless it is boiled, so you will not be brought a jug of water to your restaurant table. On a train, you'll find Thermos® flasks of boiled water so that you can make a cup of tea or a bowl of noodles. In your hotel room, you'll be provided with a kettle so that you can boil water. Bottles of mineral water are inexpensive and sold almost everywhere.

water 水 shuǐ [shway]

▸ could I have some hot water, please? 请给我一些热水好吗? qǐng gěi wǒ yīxiē rèshuǐ hǎo ma? [ching gay wo yee-shyeah ruh-shway how ma]

▸ there's no hot water 没有热水 méiyou rèshuǐ [may-yoh ruh-shway]

water ski 滑水橇 huáshuǐqiāo [hwa-shway-cheow]

▸ can I rent water skis here? 我能在这里租滑水橇吗? wǒ néng zài zhèli zū huáshuǐqiāo ma? [wo nung zigh juh-lee zoo hwa-shway-cheow ma]

water skiing 滑滑水橇 huá huáshuǐqiāo [hwa hwa-shway-cheow]

▸ can I go water skiing anywhere around here? 这附近有什么地方我能滑滑水橇? zhè fùjìn yǒu shénme dìfang wǒ néng huá huáshuǐqiāo? [juh foo-jin yoh sheun-muh dee-fang wo nung hwa hwa-shway-cheow]

wave *(of water)* 浪 làng [lang]

▸ the waves are very big today 今天浪很大 jīntiān làng hěn dà [jin-tyen lang heun da]

way *(means)* 办法 bànfǎ [ban-fa]; *(route)* 路 lù [loo]

▸ what's the best way of getting there? 去那里最好的路线是哪一条? qù

asking the way

▸ can you show me where we are on the map? 你能在地图上指给我们看我们的位置吗? nǐ néng zài dìtú shang zhǐ gěi wǒmen kàn wǒmen de wèizhi ma? [nee nung zigh dee-too shang jir gay wo-meun kan wo-meun duh way-jir ma]

▸ where is the station/the post office? 车站/邮局在哪儿? chēzhàn/yóujú zài nǎr? [chuh-jan/yoh-jew zigh nar]

▸ excuse me, how do you get to Jingshan Houjie? 劳驾,去景山后街该怎么走? láojià, qù jǐngshān hòujiē gāi zěnme zǒu? [low-jya choo jing-shan hoh-jyeah gigh zeun-muh zoh]

▸ is it far? 远吗? yuǎn ma? [ywan ma]

▸ is it within walking distance? 走过去不远吧? zǒu guòqu bù yuǎn ba? [zoh gwore-choo boo ywan ba]

nàli zuì hǎo de lùxiàn shì nǎ yī tiáo? [choo na-lee zway how duh loo-shyen shir na yee teow]

- which way is it to the bus station? 哪条路是去公共汽车站的？ nǎ tiáo lù shì qù gōnggòng qìchēzhàn de? [na teow loo shir choo gong-gong chee-chuh-jan duh]
- I went the wrong way 我走错路了 wǒ zǒu cuò lù le [wo zoh tswore loo luh]
- on the way 在途中 zài tú zhōng [zigh too jong]
- no way! 没门儿！ méi ménr! [may meun-r]

way out 出口 chūkǒu [choo-koh]

- where's the way out? 出口在哪里？ chūkǒu zài nǎli? [choo-koh zigh na-lee]

weak *(person)* 虚弱的 xūruò de [shoo-rwore duh]; *(drink)* 淡的 dàn de [dan duh]

- I feel very weak 我感到很虚弱 wǒ gǎndào hěn xūruò [wo gan-dow heun shoo-rwore]
- could I have a very weak coffee? 我能要一杯很淡的咖啡吗？ wǒ néng yào yī bēi hěn dàn de kāfēi ma? [wo nung yow yee bay heun dan duh ka-fay ma]

wear *(piece of clothing, glasses)* 穿戴 chuāndài [chwan-digh]

- is what I'm wearing all right? 我穿戴得体吗？ wǒ chuāndài détǐ ma? [wo chwan-digh duh-tee ma]

weather 天气 tiānqì [tyen-chee]; *(on the TV, the radio)* 气象 qìxiàng [chee-shyang]

- what is the weather like today? 今天天气怎么样？ jīntiān tiānqì zěnmeyàng? [jin-tyen tyen-chee zeun-muh-yang]
- is the weather going to change? 天气会变吗？ tiānqì huì biàn ma? [tyen-chee hway byen ma]

weather forecast 气象预报 qìxiàng yùbào [chee-shyang yoo-bow]

- what's the weather forecast for tomorrow? 明天的气象预报是什么？ míngtiān de qìxiàng yùbào shì shénme? [ming-tyen duh chee-shyang yoo-bow shir sheun-muh]

website address 网址 wǎngzhǐ [wang-jir]

- can you give me your website address? 你能给我你的网址吗？ nǐ néng gěi wǒ nǐ de wǎngzhǐ ma? [nee nung gay wo nee duh wang-jir ma]

Wednesday 星期三 xīngqīsān [shing-chee-san]

- we're arriving/leaving on Wednesday 我们星期三到/离开 wǒmen xīngqīsān dào/líkāi [wo-meun shing-chee-san dow/lee-kigh]

week 星期 xīngqī [shing-chee]; 周 zhōu [joh]

- how much is it for a week? 一星期多少钱？ yī xīngqī duōshao qián? [yee shing-chee dwore-show chyen], 一周多少钱？ yī zhōu duōshao qián? [yee joh dwore-show chyen]
- I'm leaving in a week 我一个星期后离开 wǒ yī gè xīngqī hòu líkāi [wo yee guh shing-chee hoh lee-kigh], 我一周后离开 wǒ yī zhōu hòu líkāi [wo yee joh hoh lee-kigh]

- two weeks 两周 liǎng zhōu [lyang joh]，两个星期 liǎng gè xīngqī [lyang guh shing-chee]

weekly 一周的 yī zhōu de [yee joh duh]
- is there a weekly rate? 有一周的价格吗？ yǒu yī zhōu de jiàgé ma? [yoh yee joh duh jya-guh ma]

welcome 欢迎 huānyíng [hwan-ying]
- welcome! 欢迎！ huānyíng! [hwan-ying]
- you're welcome (in reply to thanks) 不客气 bù kèqi [boo kuh-chee]
- you're welcome to join us 欢迎你加入我们 huānyíng nǐ jiārù wǒmen [hwan-ying nee jya-roo wo-meun]

well (in health) 健康的 jiànkāng de [jyen-kang duh] ◆ 好地 hǎo de [how duh]
- I'm very well, thank you 我很好，谢谢 wǒ hěn hǎo, xièxie [wo heun how shyeah-shyeah]
- get well soon! 祝你早日康复！ zhù nǐ zǎo rì kāngfù! [joo nee zow rir kang-foo]
- well played 干得漂亮 gàn de piàoliang [gan duh peow-lyang]

well done (steak) 全熟的 quán shú de [chwan-shoo duh]
- well done, please 请来全熟的 qǐng lái qún shú de [ching ligh chun-shoo duh]

what 什么 shénme [sheun-muh]
- what? (asking for repetition) 什么？ shénme? [sheun-muh]
- what is it? (what's this thing?) 那是什么？ nà shì shénme? [na shir sheun-muh]; (what's the matter?) 怎么了？ zěnme le? [zeun-muh luh]
- what's up? (what's wrong?) 出什么事了？ chū shénme shì le? [choo sheun-muh shir luh]; (as greeting) 你好吗？ nǐ hǎo ma? [nee how ma]
- what's your name? 你叫什么名字？ nǐ jiào shénme míngzi? [nee jeow sheun-muh ming-zir]
- what's it called? 这叫什么？ zhè jiào shénme? [juh jeow sheun-muh]
- what time is it? 几点了？ jǐ diǎn le? [jee dyen luh]
- what day is it? 今天星期几？ jīntiān xīngqī jǐ? [jin-tyen shing-chee jee]
- what desserts do you have? 你们有什么甜点？ nǐmen yǒu shénme tiándiǎn? [nee-meun yoh sheun-muh tyen-dyen]

wheel 轮胎 lúntāi [lun-tigh]
- could you help me change the wheel? 你能帮我换轮胎吗？ nǐ néng bāng wǒ huàn lúntāi ma? [nee nung bang wo hwan lun-tigh ma]

when 什么时候 shénme shíhou [sheun-muh shir-hoh]
- when was it built? 那是什么时候建造的？ nà shì shénme shíhou jiànzào de? [na shir sheun-muh shir-hoh jyen-zow duh]
- when is the next train to Beijing? 下一班开往北京的火车是几点？ xià yī bān kāiwǎng běijīng de huǒchē shì jǐ diǎn? [shya yee ban kigh-wang bay-jing duh hwore-chuh shir jee dyen]

where 哪里 nǎli [na-lee]

- where do you live? 你住在哪里？ nǐ zhù zài nǎli? [nee joo zigh na-lee]
- where are you from? 你从哪里来？ nǐ cóng nǎli lái? [nee tsong na-lee ligh]
- excuse me, where is the nearest bus stop, please? 劳驾，请问最近的公共汽车站在什么地方？ láojià, qǐng wèn zuì jìn de gōnggòng qìchēzhàn zài shénme dìfang? [low-jya ching weun zway jin duh gong-gong chee-chuh-jan zigh sheun-muh dee-fang]

which 哪一个 nǎ yī gè [na yee guh]

- which hotel would you recommend for us? 你向我们推荐哪一家旅馆？ nǐ xiàng wǒmen tuījiàn nǎ yī jiā lǚguǎn? [nee shyang wo-meun tway-jyen na yee jya looh-gwan]
- which way should we go? 我们应该走哪条路呢？ wǒmen yīnggāi zǒu nǎ tiáo lù ne? [wo-meun ying-gigh zoh na teow loo nuh]
- which do you prefer? 你更喜欢哪个？ nǐ gèng xǐhuan nǎ gè? [nee gung shee-hwan na guh]

while 一会儿 yīhuìr [yee-hwayr]

- I'm only planning to stay for a while 我只是打算呆一会儿 wǒ zhǐ dǎsuan dāi yīhuìr [wo jir da-swan digh yee-hwayr]

white (in color) 白色的 báisè de [bigh-suh duh]

- I need a white T-shirt 我需要一件白色的短袖汗衫 wǒ xūyào yī jiàn báisè de duǎn xiù hànshān [wo shoo-yow yee jyen bigh-suh duh dwan-shew han-shan]

white wine 白葡萄酒 bái pútaojiǔ [bigh poo-tow-jew]

- a glass of white wine, please 请来一杯白葡萄酒 qǐng lái yī bēi bái pútaojiǔ [ching ligh bay bigh poo-tow-jew]

who 谁 shéi [shay]

- who are you? 你是谁？ nǐ shì shéi? [nee shir shay]
- who should I speak to about the heating? 关于暖气的问题我该和谁讲？ guānyú nuǎnqì de wèntí wǒ gāi hé shéi jiǎng? [gwan-yoo nwan-chee duh weun-tee wo gigh huh shay jyang]
- who's calling? 你是哪位？ nǐ shì nǎ wèi? [nee shir na way]

whole 全部的 quánbù de [chwan-boo duh] ♦ **on the whole** 总体而言 zǒngtǐ ér yán [zong-tee er yan]

- we spent the whole day walking 我们步行了了一整天 wǒmen bùxíngle yī zhěngtiān [wo-meun boo-shing-luh yee jung-tyen]
- on the whole we had a good time 总体而言，我们过得挺开心 zǒngtǐ ér yán, wǒmen guò de tǐng kāixīn [zong-tee er yan wo-meun gwore ting kigh-shin]

whole-wheat 全麦的 quánmài de [chwan-migh duh]

- I'd like some whole-wheat bread 我想要一些全麦面包 wǒ xiǎng yào yīxiē quánmài miànbāo [wo shyang yow yee-shyeah chwan-migh myen-bow]

why 为什么 wèi shénme [way sheun-muh]

▸ why not? 为什么不呢? wèi shénme bù ne? [way sheun-muh boo nuh]

wide *(river, road)* 宽的 kuān de [kwan duh]

▸ 2 meters wide 两米宽 liǎng mǐ kuān [lyang mee kwan]

will *(to express future tense)* 将 jiāng [jyang]; *(indicating willingness)* 愿 yuàn [ywan]

▸ I'll be arriving at six 我会6点钟到 wǒ huì liù diǎnzhōng dào [wo hway lew dyen-jong dow]

win *(competition, race)* 赢 yíng [ying] ◆ *(be ahead)* 赢 yíng [ying]

▸ who's winning? 谁赢了? shéi yíng le? [shay ying luh]

wind 风 fēng [fung]

▸ there's a strong West wind 有猛烈的西风 yǒu měngliè de xīfēng [yoh mung-lyeah duh shee-fung]

window *(of a building)* 窗户 chuānghu [chwung-hoo]; *(of a store)* 橱窗 chúchuāng [choo-chwung]; *(at a station, in a post office)* 窗口 chuāngkǒu [chwung-koh]

▸ I can't open the window 我打不开窗户 wǒ dǎ bù kāi chuānghu [wo da boo kigh chwung-hoo]

▸ I'm cold: could you close your window? 我冷。你能把窗户关上吗? wǒ lěng. nǐ néng bǎ chuānghu guānshang ma? [wo lung nee nung ba chwung-hoo gwan-shang ma]

▸ I'd like to see the dress in the window 我想看看橱窗里的那件连衣裙 wǒ xiǎng kànkan chúchuāng li de liányīqún [wo shyang kan-kan choo-chwung lee duh lyen-yee-chun]

▸ where's the window for buying tickets? 买票在哪个窗口? mǎi piào zài nǎge chuāngkǒu? [migh peow zigh na-guh chwung-koh]

window seat 靠窗的位置 kào chuāng de wèizhi [kow chwung duh way-jir]

▸ I'd like a window seat if possible 如有可能,我想要一个靠窗的位置 rú yǒu kěnéng, wǒ xiǎng yào yī gè kào chuāng de wèizhi [roo yoh kuh-nung wo shyang yow yee guh kow chwung duh way-jir]

windshield 挡风玻璃窗 dǎngfēng bōlichuāng [dang-fung bo-lee-chwung]

▸ could you clean the windshield? 你能把挡风玻璃窗擦干净吗? nǐ néng bǎ dǎngfēng bōlichuāng cā gānjìng ma? [nee nung ba dang-fung bo-lee-chwung tsa gan-jing ma]

windsurfing 风帆冲浪 fēngfān chōnglàng [fung-fan chong-lang]

▸ is there anywhere around here I can go windsurfing? 在这附近有什么地方我可以进行风帆冲浪? zài zhè fùjìn yǒu shénme dìfang wǒ kěyǐ jìnxíng fēngfān chōnglàng? [zigh juh foojin yoh sheun-muh dee-fang wo kuh-yee jin-shing fung-fan chong-lang]

wishes and regrets

- I hope it won't be too busy 希望人不会太多 xīwàng rén bù huì tài duō [shee-wang reun boo hway tigh dwore]
- it'd be great if you stayed 如果你能留下来，那就太好了 rúguǒ nǐ néng liú xiàlai, nà jiù tài hǎo le [roo-gwore nee nung lew shya-ligh na jew tigh how luh]
- if only we had a car! 真希望我们有辆车啊！ zhēn xīwàng wǒmen yǒu liàng chē a! [jun shee-wang wo-meun yoh lyang chuh a]
- unfortunately, we couldn't get there in time 非常不幸，我们无法及时到那里 fēicháng bùxìng, wǒmen wúfǎ jíshí dào nàli [fay-chang boo-shing womeun wu-fa jee-shir dow na-lee]
- I'm really sorry you couldn't make it 真遗憾你来不了 zhēn yíhàn nǐ lái bù liǎo [jeun yee-han nee ligh boo leow]

windy (day, weather) 风大的 fēng dà de [fung da duh]
- it's windy 今天风大 jīntiān fēng dà [jin-tyen fung da]

wine 葡萄酒 pútaojiǔ [poo-tow-jew]
- this wine is not chilled enough 这葡萄酒不够凉 zhè pútaojiǔ bù gòu liáng [juh poo-tow-jew boo goh lyang]

wine list 酒水单 jiǔshuǐdān [jew shway-dan]
- can we see the wine list, please? 请给我们看一下酒水单好吗？ qǐng gěi wǒmen kàn yī xià jiǔshuǐdān hǎo ma? [ching gay wo-meun kan yee shya jew-shway-dan how ma]

wish 愿望 yuànwàng [ywan-wang] ◆ 祝愿 zhùyuàn [joo-ywan]
- best wishes! 祝你一切顺利！ zhù nǐ yīqiè shùnlì! [joo nee yee-chyeah shun-lee]

wishing someone something

- Happy Birthday! 生日快乐！ shēngrì kuàilè! [shung-rir kwigh-luh]
- Merry Christmas! 圣诞快乐！ shèngdàn kuàilè! [shung-dan kwigh-luh]
- Happy New Year! 新年快乐！ xīnnián kuàilè! [shin-nyen kwigh-luh]
- enjoy your vacation! 祝你假期愉快！ zhù nǐ jiàqī yúkuài! [joo nee jya-chee yoo-kwigh]
- enjoy your meal! 吃得开心！ chī de kāixīn! [chir duh kigh-shin]
- good night! 晚安！ wǎn'ān! [wan-an]
- congratulations! 恭喜！ gōngxǐ! [gong-shee]

▶ we wish you good luck 我们祝你好运 wǒmen zhù nǐ hǎoyùn [wo-meun joo nee how-yun]

with 和……在一起 hé……zài yīqǐ [huh...zigh yee-chee]

▶ thanks, but I'm here with my boyfriend 谢谢，但是我在这儿和我的男朋友在一起 xièxie, dànshì wǒ zài zhèr hé wǒ de nánpéngyou zài yīqǐ [shyeah-shyeah dan-shir wo zigh juh huh wo duh nan-pung-yoh zigh yee-chee]

withdraw (money) 提取 tíqǔ [tee-choo]

▶ I'd like to withdraw 100 yuan 我想取100元 wǒ xiǎng qǔ yībǎi yuán [wo shyang choo yee-bigh ywan]

without 没有 méiyou [may-yoh]

▶ a chicken sandwich without mayonnaise 不加蛋黄酱的鸡肉三明治 bù jiā dànhuángjiàng de jīròu sānmíngzhì [boo jya dan-hwang-jyang duh jee-roh san-ming-jir]

woman 女人 nǚrén [nooh-reun]

▶ where's the women's changing room? 女更衣室在哪里？ nǚ gēngyīshì zài nǎli? [nooh gung-yee-shir zigh na-lee]

wonderful 令人高兴的 lìng rén gāoxìng de [ling reun gow-shing duh]

▶ that's wonderful! 那太好了！ nà tài hǎo le! [na tigh how luh]

▶ the weather was wonderful 天气很好 tiānqì hěn hǎo [tyen-chee heun how]

word 词 cí [cir]

▶ I don't know what the word is in English 我不知道在英语里是哪个词 wǒ bù zhīdao zài yīngyǔ li shì nǎge cí [wo boo jir-dow zigh ying-yoo lee shir na-guh tsir]

▶ I don't understand a word 我一个字也不懂 wǒ yī gè zì yě bù dǒng [wo yee guh tsir yuh boo dong]

work (employment) 工作 gōngzuò [gong-zwore] ◆ (do a job) 做工作 zuò gōngzuò [zwore gong-zwore]; (function) 运转 yùnzhuǎn [yun-jwan]

▶ to be out of work 失业 shīyè [shir-yuh]

▶ I work in marketing 我从事行销工作 wǒ cóngshì xíngxiāo gōngzuò [wo tsong-shir shing-sheow gong-zwore]

▶ the heating's not working 暖气失灵了 nuǎnqì shīlíng le [nwan-chee shir-ling luh]

▶ how does the shower work? 淋浴器该怎么用？ línyùqì gāi zěnme yòng? [lin-yoo-chee gigh zeun-muh yong]

workday 工作日 gōngzuòrì [gong-zwore-rir]

▶ is tomorrow a workday? 明天是工作日吗？ míngtiān shì gōngzuòrì ma? [ming-tyen shir gong-zwore-rir ma]

world 世界 shìjiè [shir-jyeah]
- what part of the world are you from? 你来自世界的哪个地方？ nǐ láizì shìjiè de nǎge dìfang? [nee ligh-zir shir-jyeah duh na-guh dee-fang]

worried 担心的 dānxīn de [dan-shin duh]
- I'm worried about his health 我担心他的健康 wǒ dānxīn tā de jiànkāng [wo dan-shin ta duh jyen-kang]

worry 担心 dānxīn [dan-shin]
- don't worry! 别担心！ bié dānxīn! [byeah dan-shin]

worth (in value) 值......钱 zhí......qián [jir...chyen]; (deserving of) 值得 zhíde [jir-duh]
- how much is it worth? 这个值多少钱？ zhège zhí duōshao qián? [juh-guh jir dwore-show chyen]
- it's well worth a visit 这很值得一看 zhè hěn zhíde yī kàn [juh heun jir-duh yee kan]
- what's worth seeing in this town? 在这个城市里，哪些值得一看？ zài zhège chéngshì li, nǎxiē zhíde yī kàn? [zigh juh-guh chung-shir lee na-shyeah jir-duh yee kan]

wound 伤口 shāngkǒu [shang-koh]
- I need something for disinfecting a wound 我需要消毒伤口的东西 wǒ xūyào xiāodú shāngkǒu de dōngxi [wo shoo-yow sheow-doo shang-koh duh dong-shee]

wrap (up) 把......包起来 bǎ......bāo qǐlai [ba...bow chee-ligh]
- can you wrap it (up) for me? 你能帮我把这个包起来吗？ nǐ néng bāng wǒ bǎ zhège bāo qǐlai ma? [nee nung bang wo ba juh-guh bow chee-ligh ma]

wrist 手腕 shǒuwàn [shoh-wan]
- I've sprained my wrist 我把手腕扭了 wǒ bǎ shǒuwàn niǔ le [wo ba shoh-wan new luh]

write 写 xiě [shyeah]
- I have some letters to write 我要写几封信 wǒ yào xiě jǐ fēng xìn [wo yow shyeah jee fung shin]

wrong (incorrect) 错误的 cuòwù de [cwore-woo duh]; (amiss) 有毛病的 yǒu máobìng de [woh mow-bing duh]
- to be wrong (person) 错误的 cuòwù de [tswore-woo duh]
- I'm sorry, but I think you're wrong 对不起，但是我想你错了 duìbuqǐ, dànshì wǒ xiǎng nǐ cuò le [dway-boo-chee dan-shir wo shyang nee cwore luh]
- sorry, I dialed the wrong number 对不起，我拨错电话号码了 duìbuqǐ, wǒ bō cuò diànhuà hàomǎ le [dway-boo-chee wo bo tswore dyen-hwa how-ma luh]
- you've got the wrong number 你拨错电话号码了 nǐ bō cuò diànhuà hàomǎ le [nee bo tswore dyen-hwa how-ma luh]

- this is the wrong train 不是这辆火车 bù shì zhè liàng huǒchē [boo shir juh lyang hwore-chuh]
- what's wrong? 怎么了？ zěnme le? [zeun-muh luh]
- there's something wrong with the switch 开关有问题 kāiguān yǒu wèntí [kigh-gwan yoh weun-tee]

x, y, z

X-ray X光片 x-guāngpiàn [x-gwung-pyen]
- do you think I should have an X-ray? 你认为我需要拍X光片吗？ nǐ rènwéi wǒ xūyào pāi x-guāngpiàn ma? [nee reun-way wo shoo-yow pigh x-gwung-pyen ma]

year 年 nián [nyen]
- we came here last year 我们去年来的 wǒmen qùnián lái de [wo-meun choo-nyen ligh duh]
- I'm 21 years old 我21岁 wǒ èrshíyī suì [wo er-shir-yee sway]

yellow 黄色的 huángsè de [hwang-suh duh]
- the yellow one 黄色的那个 huángsè de nàge [hwang-suh duh na-guh]

Yellow Pages® 电话黄页 diànhuà huángyè [dyen-hwa hwung-yuh]
- do you have a copy of the Yellow Pages®? 你有电话黄页吗？ nǐ yǒu diànhuà huángyè ma? [nee yoh dyen-hwa hwung-yuh ma]
- why don't you look in the Yellow Pages®? 你为什么不查电话黄页呢？ nǐ wèishénme bù chá diànhuà huángyè ne? [nee way-sheun-muh boo cha dyen-hwa hwung-yuh nuh]

yes *(in agreement)* 好的 hǎo de [how duh]; *(in disagreement)* 不 bù [boo]
- yes, please 好的，请 hǎo de, qǐng [how duh ching]
- it doesn't matter – yes it does! 那不要紧。 不，要紧的 nà bù yàojǐn. bù, yàojǐn de [na boo yow-jin boo yow-jin duh]

saying yes

While it is possible to translate 'no' into Chinese, 'yes' is more difficult, as the latter is usually expressed by repeating the verb in the question. For example, the question 'are you American?' should be answered, if you want to say 'yes', by 是 shì [shir] which means 'to be.' But if you want to answer 'yes' to the question 'have you any children?,' you should use the verb 'to have' 有 yǒu [yoh].

yet *(up to now)* 还 hái [high]; *(at the present time)* 现在 xiànzài [shyen-zigh]
  ▸ I've not been there yet 我还没有去过那里 wǒ hái méiyou qùguo nàli [wo high may-yoh choo-gwore na-lee]

yogurt 酸奶 suānnǎi [swan-nigh]
  ▸ do you have any yogurt? 你们有酸奶吗? nǐmen yǒu suānnǎi ma? [nee-meun yoh swan-nigh ma]

young man 年轻男子 qīngnián nánzǐ [nyen–ching nan-zir]
  ▸ who is that young man? 那个青年男子是谁? nàge qīngnián nánzǐ shì shéi? [na-guh nyen–ching nan-zir shir shay]

young person 年轻人 niánqīngrén [nyen-ching-reun]
  ▸ are there any discounts for young people? 年轻人是否有折扣? niánqīng-rén shìfǒu yǒu zhékòu? [nyen-ching-reun shir-foh yoh juh-koh]

young woman 年轻女子 niánqīng nǚzǐ [nyen–ching nooh-zir]
  ▸ who is the young woman he's with? 和他在一起的年轻女子是谁? hé tā zài yīqǐ de niánqīng nǚzǐ shì shéi? [huh ta zigh yee-chee duh nyen–ching nooh-zir shir shay]

youth hostel 青年旅舍 qīngnián lǚshè [ching-nyen looh-shuh]
  ▸ I'd like to book two beds for three nights in a youth hostel 我想在青年旅舍定两个床位，三个晚上 wǒ xiǎng zài qīngnián lǚshè dìng liǎng gè chuángwèi, sān gè wǎnshang [wo shyang zigh ching-nyen looh-shuh ding lyang guh chwung-way san guh wan-shang]

zone *(on public transportation)* 区 qū [choo]
  ▸ I'd like a ticket for zones one to four 我想要一张用于一区到四区的票 wǒ xiǎng yào yī zhāng yòngyú yī qū dào sì qū de piào [wo shyang yow yee jang yong-yoo yee choo dow sir choo duh peow]

Chinese language and culture

Modern Chinese usage

Chinese (汉语 Hànyǔ, 华语 Huáyǔ or 中文 Zhōngwén) is part of the Sino-Tibetan family of languages, a language family comprising about 250 languages of East Asia. More than 1.3 billion people, or about one fifth of the world's population speak some form of Chinese as their native language, making it the language with the most native speakers in the world.

In general, all varieties of Chinese are **tonal** (i.e. each word has a high-low pitch pattern permanently associated with it) and **analytic** (i.e. the meaning of each word or phrase is indirectly expressed through several or many words). However, Chinese is also distinguished by its high level of internal diversity. Regional variation between the different variants/dialects is comparable to the Romance language family: many variants of spoken Chinese are different enough to be mutually incomprehensible. There are between six and twelve main regional groups (depending on the classification scheme), of which the most populous are **Mandarin**, **Wu**, and **Cantonese**. Mandarin Chinese is spoken by 833 million people worldwide, **Wu** by 77 million people, and **Cantonese** by 71 million.

The standardized form of spoken Chinese is based on the Beijing dialect. **Standard Mandarin** is the official language of the People's Republic of China (including Hong Kong and Macao), and of the Republic of China (including Taiwan and other islands), and it is one of the four official languages of Singapore. It is also spoken in Malaysia, Indonesia, Thailand, Vietnam, Burma and Cambodia, and parts of Japan, North Korea, South Korea, and the Philippines.

The Chinese government is promoting **Standard Mandarin** as the 'common language' of communication, and as such it is used in all government communication, in the media, and as the official language of instruction in schools. It is common for speakers of Chinese to be able to speak several varieties of the language, typically **Standard Mandarin**, the local dialect, and occasionally a regional lingua franca, such as **Cantonese**. Speakers of several different Chinese languages tend to switch between **Standard Mandarin** and their local dialect, depending on the situation.

History and development of the language

Spoken Chinese

The Chinese language has always consisted of a wide variety of dialects. Spoken variations of Chinese have been evolving since at least the late Han Dynasty (206 BC – AD 220), but it isn't until the Ming Dynasty (1368 – 1644) and the Qing Dynasty (1644 – 1912) that we find mention of a standard spoken language, guānhuà (官话) ('official speech'), a reference to the speech used at the courts. During the early part of this period the standard was based on the Nanjing dialect, but later the Beijing dialect became increasingly influential.

In the 17th century, the Chinese Empire set up Orthoepy Academies in an attempt to make pronunciation conform to the Beijing standard. These attempts were not successful. As late as the 19th century the emperor had difficulty understanding some of his own ministers in court, who did not always follow a standard pronunciation.

By 1909, the dying Qing Dynasty had established the Beijing dialect as guóyǔ (国语), or the 'national language.' The Republic of China was established in 1912, and a commission, represented by delegates from all over the country, was convened to promote a common national language. The Beijing dialect subsequently became the major source of standard national pronunciation, an effort that was continued under the administration of the People's Republic of China, established in 1949.

In 1955, Standard Mandarin was renamed pǔtōnghuà (普通话), or 'common speech.' Today the elementary school education systems of both mainland China and Taiwan are committed to teaching Mandarin, and Standard Mandarin is spoken by most people in these regions. In Hong Kong, the language of education and formal speech remains Cantonese but Standard Mandarin is becoming increasingly influential.

There have been many significant changes in Standard Mandarin during the course of the 20th century. Many of the respectful terms that were in use in imperial China have almost entirely disappeared in modern-day daily conversation. Words such as jiàn (贱 'my humble') and guì (贵 'your honorable'), common in ancient spoken Chinese, are now no longer used. This reflects the shift from an imperial society to the modern communist state.

Written Chinese

The written language has changed much less. Although the system has been altered over time due to revolutions and political changes, the principles of the written language, along with the symbols and characters, have remained basically the same.

The Chinese language is the oldest written language in the world. Chinese character inscriptions have been found on turtle shells dating back to the Shang dynasty (1766 – 1123 BC). This proves that the written language has existed for more than 3,000 years, though experts estimate that it was first applied at least 3,000 years before this time.

Until the 20th century, most formal Chinese writing was done in wényán (文言) (*classical Chinese or literary Chinese*). This was very different from any spoken variety of Chinese, much as Classical Latin differs from the modern Romance languages. Since the May Fourth Movement (a period of anti-imperialist, cultural, and political action) in 1919, the formal standard for written Chinese has been báihuà (白话), or vernacular Chinese. The term *standard written Chinese* now refers to vernacular Chinese. This is the one formal standard written language, and it is used by speakers of all the various different forms of Chinese.

With the existence of so many Chinese dialects, the written language is thus the common form of communication. However, written Chinese can be further subdivided into two forms: **simplified** and **traditional**. There is also a system called **pinyin**, which is the Chinese language transcribed using a Roman spelling.

Simplified characters

Simplified Chinese is the form most commonly used in mainland China. Characters have fewer pen-strokes than traditional Chinese characters. Simplified characters have existed for hundreds of years, but only became officially acceptable in formal writing in the 1950s after the founding of the People's Republic of China. This was an attempt to improve literacy. People who are literate in simplified Chinese characters may not be literate in traditional Chinese.

Traditional or classical Chinese

Traditional or classical Chinese characters are taught and used by Chinese people in Hong Kong, Taiwan, Malaysia, Korea, Japan, and elsewhere. Many textbooks, newspapers, and Chinese subtitled movies use traditional characters. In the United States, the Chinese newspapers, **Ming Pao** and **Sing Tao** use traditional Chinese characters as these papers are generally read by Cantonese-speaking Chinese people from Hong Kong.

Pinyin

The most common Romanization system for Standard Mandarin is **Hanyu pinyin** (汉语拼音 Hànyǔ pīnyīn), also known simply as **pinyin**. Pinyin was approved in 1958 and adopted in 1979 by the government in the People's Republic of China in order to teach Standard Mandarin pronunciation and to make the Chinese language more understandable to the Western world. The pinyin system uses the Western alphabet and spelling to pronounce Chinese words.

A large Chinese dictionary usually contains 40,000 characters. In order to read a newspaper, you need to be able to recognize between 2,000 and 3,000. In secondary schools in China the number of characters taught is 5,000.

Influence of Chinese language and culture

With China's rapid development, huge market potential, and increasing influence on the rest of the world, **Standard Mandarin** has become an increasingly popular choice among students of foreign languages in the Western world. In North America the study of Chinese is spreading to places where, only a decade ago, such a widespread and sustained interest in the language seemed unimaginable.

Chinese cultural exports are also winning favor in 21st century America. Traditional practices such as *feng shui*, the ancient Chinese art of placement and arrangement of space, have become popular in the US in recent years. The practice is estimated to be more than three thousand years old. It has its origins in **Taosim**, the ancient Chinese philosophy advocating a simple honest life and non-interference with the cause of natural events. **Chinese astrology**, **cuisine**, several **Chinese martial arts**, **traditional Chinese medicine**, and many styles of **qigong** breath training disciplines also have some relationship with Taoism, and many of these are also becoming popular in the US today.

Chinese cuisine has been prevalent in the US since the 19th century, initially catering to railroad workers, and these days it can be found in towns and cities across the country.

Chinese astrology, often referred to as the Chinese zodiac, is also popular in the US. The United States Postal Service issues postage stamps featuring the 12-year cycle of animals each year to honor this Chinese heritage.

In modern times, **Chinese martial arts** have become widely practiced across the US. These have also spawned the genre of cinema known as martial arts movies or **Kung Fu** movies. The movies of **Bruce Lee** were the first to be popular in the West. More recently, martial artists and actors such as **Jet Li** and **Jackie Chan** have given Chinese martial arts films even more of a boost.

Big-budgeted **Chinese-language cinema** is starting to compete with the best Hollywood films. The movie **Hero** topped the US box office for two weeks in 2002, making enough in the US alone to cover all of its production costs. The cast and crew featured many of China's most famous actors, some of whom have been known in the US since the 1999 movie **Crouching Tiger, Hidden Dragon**, a breakthrough Chinese movie that provided many Americans with their first introduction to Chinese cinema.

Chinese and English: differences and similarities

There are very few similarities between Chinese and English. Both the spoken and written languages have little in common. As if to underline this, the Chinese word for *head* (头 tóu) very much resembles the English word *toe*. The differences between the two languages far outweigh the points of comparison!

Grammar

This is the area in which English and Chinese are most alike. The basic structure of sentences is similar. Note, however, the following key differences:

♦ There is no definite article (*the*) or indefinite article (*a*) in Chinese.

♦ There are no plural forms in Chinese – noun endings remain the same whether singular or plural.

♦ In Chinese the verb never changes its form, no matter who/what is performing the action or what tense you are using.

Vocabulary

There are very few words in Chinese that bear any resemblance to English. Those that do, do so because they have been transliterated from English: motorbike – 摩托车 (mótuōchē).

But Chinese is changing, and an increasing number of loanwords (words taken directly into the language from other languages, with little or no translation) are making their way into everyday Chinese usage. New words can be created by combining existing words. For example, the word for *vacuum cleaner* in Chinese is 吸尘器 (xīchénqì). This translates literally as *suck dust machine*.

Chinese is increasingly borrowing English words and phrases that are neither translated nor transliterated in their daily speech. Most prominently, **bye** and **bye-bye** have more or less replaced the Chinese 再见 (zàijiàn – bye-bye) among more Westernized Chinese people.

Other English words that have become popular in everyday Chinese conversation include **okay**, **free**, **enjoy**, **care**, **anyway** and **work**.

Below are examples of their use in regular conversation:

我们明天再说, okay? (wǒmen míngtiān zàishuō, okay) – *let's talk about it tomorrow, okay?*
我的打印机不 work 了 (wǒ de dǎyìnjī bù work le) – *my printer is not working*
我根本不 care (wǒ gēnběn bù care) – *I don't care at all*

Pronunciation

This is the area in which Chinese and English most differ. Like the other Sino-Tibetan languages, Chinese is tonal, i.e., different tones distinguish words that would otherwise be pronounced alike. Mandarin has four tones: a high tone, a rising tone, a tone that combines a falling and a rising inflection, and a falling tone.

Pronouncing a word incorrectly can result in your referring to your mother as a horse or your boss as your wife – but Chinese people will usually give you the benefit of the doubt!

Modern developments in the language

In modern-day China, political discourse has shifted from discussion on making sacrifices to that of making money. Accordingly, Chinese expressions for age-old concepts such as model workers, marriage prospects, and exemplary behavior are rarely used. These days socialist slogans have become mere kitsch, and popular transliterations of English words such as *cool* (酷 kù) and *taxi* (的士 dīshì) can be seen and heard with increasing frequency.

Below are some examples of other new, commonly used Chinese words and phrases:

贸易战 (màoyìzhàn)	*trade war*
人权 (rénquán)	*human rights*
发 (fā)	*to become prosperous and successful, to get rich*
侃 (kǎn) or 瞎掰 (xiābāi)	*to talk nonsense, to brag*
二百五 (èrbǎiwǔ)	*stupid, idiot (lit. two hundred and fifty)*
够呛 (gòuqiàng)	*terrible, that's tough!*
蛮 (mán)	*quite, pretty, as in 蛮好 (mán hǎo) – pretty good; and 蛮好吃 (mán hǎo chī) – really delicious*
回见 (huíjiàn)	*see you later!, see you around!*

Not so long ago, when there was still a revolutionary spirit in China, 同志 (tóngzhì – *comrade*) was the best and the only way to address another person – man or woman, old or young. At that time, couples were not husband and wife, but 爱人 (àirén – *lovers*). 小姐 (xiǎojiě – *Miss*), 先生 (xiānsheng – *Mr.*) and 女士 (nǚshì – *lady*) were considered feudal usage, and therefore banned.

Today, these once-tabooed terms have replaced 同志 (tóngzhì – *comrade*) and have once again become the polite form of address. Meanwhile, the term *comrade* (同志 tóngzhì – tóng: *the same*; zhì: *will* – lit. *people of the same will*) has taken on a new level of meaning – it now refers to homosexuals. Thus:

男同志 (nán tóngzhì) means *gay man*
女同志 (nǚ tóngzhì) means *lesbian*

The increasing use of instant messaging, both on cell phones and the Internet is introducing a whole new and different range of slang into the Chinese language. You may see the following in text messages or email communications in China:

pp	片片 (piàn piàn)	*picture*
mm	美眉 (měi méi)	*girl (lit. beautiful eyebrows)*
ppmm	漂亮美眉 (piàoliang měi méi)	*pretty girl*
fb	腐败 (fǔbài)	*dining out (formal meaning = corruption)*
opa	好的 (hǎo de)	*OK*
ding	顶 (dǐng)	*support, agree*
3x	谢谢 (xièxie)	*thanks*
88	再见 (zàijiàn)	*bye-bye*
BB	小孩 (xiǎohái)	*baby*
偶	我	*I*
泥	你	*you*
东东	东西	*thing*
偶稀饭	我喜欢	*I like*

Cultural highlights

There are three things China is most famous for: **silk**, **porcelain** and **tea**.

The invention of **porcelain** in China was arguably China's greatest contribution to world civilization. Porcelain made China so famous that in the West we named our plates and cups after it.

Jingdezhen in north-eastern Jiangxi province has been the leading center of China's porcelain industry for a thousand years. Today it is under state protection as an important historical city. It has 133 ancient buildings and cultural sites, and attracts large numbers of visitors from home and abroad.

Silk and silk-making is a vital feature of Chinese history and its ancient civilization. Silk was first produced in China in 3000 B.C., and archaeological evidence of its existence dates back to about 5,500 years ago.

The Chinese **Silk Road** was constructed under the western Han Emperor Wudi (156 BC – 87 BC). Wudi wanted to build an alliance with neighboring countries to guard against military threats. He succeeded in establishing a very lucrative trade in silk and other inventions.

Tea has always been a prominent feature of Chinese culture and an important Chinese export. It is believed that tea shrubs were cultivated in China as early as two thousand years ago, and many of China's legends and lore was based on tea. In ancient China special ways of preparing and drinking tea emerged, and these customs developed into an art form. Modern-day Japanese tea ceremonies are based on the original Chinese method.

There are five kinds of Chinese tea: **green tea**, **oolong tea**, **compressed tea**, **black tea**, and **scented tea**. Green tea is China's most popular tea. Scented tea, using flowers such as jasmine and magnolia, is especially well-liked among tourists in China.

Myths and legends

Chinese mythology focuses on the origin of Chinese culture. Like many mythologies, it is believed to be a factual recording of history. Chinese mythology began in about the 12th century BC. Myths and legends were then passed down in oral format for over a thousand years, before settling into three major but related belief systems – **Confucianism**, **Taoism**, and **Buddhism**.

Confucianism was founded by the philosopher **Confucius**, who believed in the importance of familial ties and cooperation over individual accomplishments. As a belief system, **Confucianism** identifies the importance of developing a responsible and moral person, such as respecting one's family, ancestors, traditions, and the law.

Taoism, or 'the Way,' is a religion of mysticism focused on obtaining higher spiritual awareness beyond perceptual or intellectual apprehension. **Taosim** holds that everything has a purpose and a way in life and nature.

Buddhism holds that a person's actions in his or her past or present life will influence the destiny of his or her reincarnated life. **Buddhists** believe that in order to achieve nirvana (true reality, or liberation) one should purify and train the mind and act according to the laws of karma and of cause and effect: perform positive actions, and positive results will follow.

For the most part, Chinese myths often revolve around moral issues, which inform people of their culture and values.

One of the most important and mythical figures in Chinese mythology is the **dragon**. The dragon is considered to be the most powerful and divine creature. Many people in China believe that dragons can fly and that they make clouds with their breath.

Traditional Chinese music

Chinese music dates back to the dawn of Chinese civilization – documents and artifacts provide evidence of a well-developed musical culture as early as the Zhou Dynasty (1122 BC – 256 BC). In ancient China music was considered to be central to the harmony and longevity of the state. Most emperors placed importance on folk music, and sent officers to collect folk songs as a means of inspecting the popular will.

During the height of the **Cultural Revolution** (1966 –1976), musical composition and performance were greatly restricted in China. Today musical institutions have been reinstated and musical composition and performances have been revived.

Among the oldest known musical instruments in China are the bamboo pipes and the **qin** (琴 *lit. ancient stringed instrument*). Plucked and bowed stringed instruments are popular, as are flutes, cymbals, gongs, and drums.

Chinese dress

The traditional clothing of the Han Chinese, the predominant ethnic group of China, is the **Hanfu** (汉服 *lit. clothing of the Han people*). **Hanfu** can be traced back to the Yellow Emperor in the 27th century BC. It encompasses all forms of Han Chinese dress up to the 17th century, when the **Manchus**, a semi-nomadic people from Manchuria, formed the Qing Dynasty (1644 – 1911).

The **Manchus** subjugated the native Han Chinese population by forcing them to adopt the Manchu hairstyle (the pigtail) and Manchu-style clothing. Manchu women typically wore a one-piece dress that came to be known as the **qipao** (旗袍 or *banner dress*). The **qipao** survived the political turmoil of the revolution that toppled the Qing, and has become, with few changes, the archetypal dress for Chinese women.

These days Han Chinese people generally wear Western-style clothing. Traditional Chinese dress is usually reserved for celebrations, in themed restaurants (targeted at tourists), and other special events. At a typical Chinese wedding, the bride will wear a white bridal gown just the same as those worn in the West. Business attire is also similar to that worn anywhere in the industrialized world for a given trade.

China's 55 other officially recognized minority groups differ widely in their folkways and customs, and this is most visible in their clothing. The traditional dress of many western Chinese minority groups is particularly elaborate and colorful. Many ethnic minority people in western China still wear traditional costume today.

Typical traits and habits

Both traditional and modern Chinese ways of life are quite unique and very different from those of Western cultures. In traditional China, family life was central to Chinese culture, as Chinese people lived in large family units. As many as 100 or more relatives lived together under the rule of the oldest male. The ideal was *five generations under one roof*.

Today Chinese people tend to live in smaller family units, usually just parents and their children, and sometimes grandparents as well. Almost all adults – both men and women – have jobs. In many families a grandparent looks after the house and children during the day. An increasing number of children are also attending nursery schools.

In modern China many young households share in the shopping, housecleaning, cooking, and childcare activities. But equality between the sexes is more widely accepted in the cities than it is in the countryside, where boys are still valued more than girls.

Face

One of the most unique cultural features of China is the concept of 'face.' 'Face' is related to the image or credibility of the person you are dealing with. You should never, insult, embarrass, shame, yell at or otherwise demean a person in China. If you do, they will lose 'face.' In ancient times, the Chinese warrior chief might have committed suicide after losing a battle because of the loss of 'face.' While this may no longer occur, awareness of 'face' and its impact remains an important cultural issue.

In the business world, negotiations should be conducted so as to ensure everybody you are dealing with retains 'face' even if the deal does not conclude successfully. This means bringing negotiations to a close in a manner that will satisfy everybody's superiors. By the same token, it can be difficult to get straight or honest answers in business negotiations. Information that does not present a company in a positive light may simply be excluded from view. Suggestions for improvements to existing services or systems should be worded carefully, and presented in a positive light where at all possible.

Meeting people

When meeting people in China, handshaking is normal though the handshake may be longer and may not be as firm as a Western-style handshake. Kissing and hugging are generally not practiced. Back slapping and shoulder squeezing are OK for good friends and acquaintances.

When exchanging business cards, you should always give or receive the card with two hands. It is usually good to study the card for a moment to show your interest. Two hands should also be used when somebody gives you a gift, food, tea or any other item. Note that gifts are almost never opened in front of the gift-giver.

Food

Chinese daily life revolves around food. It is present at almost every holiday or family event and it is usually the center of activity.

Chinese cuisine is known for its exotica. Almost all creatures are eligible for eating. This is a tradition that goes back to times when food may have been scarce. Shark fin soup, for example, harkens back to the days of famine along the coast of China. When there was not enough food to go around, the fin was all that was left to be eaten. In general, it is polite to try everything that is offered, even if it looks unpalatable. Your hosts will usually be aware if they are giving you something very exotic, and will not press you to eat anything that makes you feel truly squeamish.

In the big cities, a wide variety of food is available, but this is not true of the rural areas. Diet depends largely upon the region. Common staples include rice, potatoes, cornmeal, tofu, and other grains. Noodles are also popular. Dairy products are rare.

Chinese people tend to eat their meals earlier than Americans. Morning meetings end at around 11:30 a.m. to allow everyone to go to lunch. Dinners are usually at 6 p.m.

Table manners may range from the rustic to the urbane, depending on the status of the diners. One commonality is the acceptance of smacking the lips, belching at the table and slurping soup. These gestures signify that the diner is enjoying the food.

Do not use your fingers to touch food if at all possible, and do not insert your fingers into your mouth at any time. Toothpicks are used after meals, with the left hand covering the mouth while the right hand manipulates the toothpick. You should also avoid picking up

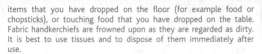

items that you have dropped on the floor (for example food or chopsticks), or touching food that you have dropped on the table. Fabric handkerchiefs are frowned upon as they are regarded as dirty. It is best to use tissues and to dispose of them immediately after use.

Finally, table conversation typically revolves around discussing food preparation and different types of cuisine. Controversial topics such as religion, politics and money are usually ignored. You should not eat too fast or finish all the food on your plate as this gives the impression that you do not have enough to eat.

At a restaurant

If you are invited to a meal, the person who invites you will almost always pay the bill. You should offer to pay, but give up after about three attempts. The same should apply in the reverse – if you invite people to a meal, you should pay regardless of the battle presented by your guests.

When dining, you should place bones or other food scraps on a separate plate or dish. It is usually acceptable in mid-range restaurants to spit bones or other inedibles onto the table. In general, watch what other people are doing.

Your host will probably ensure that your teacup or beer glass etc. is always full. If pouring tea or any other drink, ensure that you fill the glasses/cups of your host and other guests first. You can thank someone who does this for you by tapping on the table top.

Finally, a word about tipping – it is neither standard nor expected in most service businesses, including restaurants.

In a Chinese home

Chinese people enjoy hosting visitors at their home and are very hospitable and courteous. You should avoid calling on a Chinese home unannounced, but if you are invited make sure that you arrive on time. It is customary to bring a simple gift of food, drink or flowers. Gifts from abroad are particularly welcome – chocolates, fine tea or coffee, and even crafts will all be well received.

When entering the home of a Chinese person it is generally advisable to take off your shoes even if your hosts tell you not to worry. This is because shoes that are worn outside the house are considered to carry dirt. You will usually be supplied with slippers while you are indoors.

Shopping

Many stores and markets require you to bargain and to negotiate. The rough rule in the markets is to start a counter-offer that is as low as 30% of the first offer you receive. In stores, most places now have fixed prices, but you can still make an offer, provided you are willing to carry it through at that price.

Popular leisure activities

The growth of new leisure industries as well as new technologies in China is changing the way that Chinese people spend their free time.

Changes in leisure patterns mostly find expression in changes and upgrades to popular consumer goods. Radios have made way for hi-fis, and black-and-white TVs for color TVs, flat-panel TVs, and so on. Cellphones can be seen everywhere in China, and digital and video cameras and MP3 players are picking up the pace. People are getting around more easily too – office workers in Shanghai are driving their new cars and motorbikes to the countryside to be 'one-day farmers' during their days off.

Just a few years ago, bowling used to be a highly popular pastime. These days sports such as **tennis**, **badminton** and **snooker** have overtaken it in popularity and even accessibility. New sports venues are catering to business parties and individuals with vast, disposable incomes. More people belong to **gyms** than ever before.

Other sports played in China include **basketball**, **ping pong** and **volleyball**. **Golf** is also becoming increasingly popular. There are now a number of major golf tournaments in China, receiving significant international sponsorship.

Soccer was introduced in the 1990s and has become one of the most well-supported sports in China. The Chinese Super League, China's premier soccer league, was founded in 2004. The women's national team has been particularly successful, and also has a strong following.

Other sports that are popular among Chinese spectators include **Formula 1 car racing**. The Chinese Grand Prix is a Formula 1 event held annually at the Shanghai International Circuit.

Interestingly, while more Chinese people try to make time for leisure and even hire domestic helpers in order to do so, home improvement and **DIY** have emerged as surprisingly popular pastimes. **Gardening** is another increasingly popular leisure activity in urban areas.

Elderly people in China enjoy more traditional leisure activities such as **Tai Chi**, **jogging** and other forms of **morning exercise**, **chess games**, **dancing**, **fashion shows** for the elderly, **singing**, going to traditional Chinese operas or ballad singing concerts, and attending **calligraphy**, **painting**, **musical instrument** or **flower arrangement classes** at old people's universities.

Chinese–English
dictionary

signs in public places

问讯处
wènxùnchù
[weun-shun-choo]
information desk

电话亭
diànhuàtíng
[dyen-hwa-ting]
telephone booth

入口
rùkǒu
[roo-koh]
entrance

出口
chūkǒu
[choo-koh]
exit

公用电话
gōngyòng diànhuà
[gong-yong dyen-hwa]
public telephone

洗手间 男
xǐshǒujiān nán
[shee-shoh-jyen nan]
toilets (men)

洗手间 女
xǐshǒujiān nǚ
[shee-shoh-jyen nooh]
toilets (women)

推
tuī
[tway]
push

拉
lā
[la]
pull

紧急出口
jǐnjí chūkǒu
[jin-jee choo-koh]
emergency exit

故障中
gùzhàng zhōng
[goo-jang jong]
break down

出入请下车
chūrù qǐng xià chē
[choo-roo ching shya chuh]
please leave your bicycle at the
entrance

停车场
tíngchēchǎng
[ting-chuh-chang]
parking lot

慢
màn
[man]
slow

停
tíng
[ting]
stop

禁止入内
jìnzhǐ rùnèi
[jin-jir roo-nay]
no entrance

未成年人禁止入内
wèichéngniánrén jìnzhǐ rùnèi
[way-chung-nyen-reun jin-jir roo-nay]
no minors

禁止停车
jìnzhǐ tíngchē
[jin-jir ting-chuh]
no parking

营业时间
yíngyè shíjiān
[ying-yuh shir-jyen]
business hours

游客止步
yóukè zhǐbù
[yoh-ke jir-boo]
no visitors

旅馆
lǚguǎn
[looh-gwan]
hotel

不准随地吐痰
bù zhǔn suídì tǔ tán
[boo-jun sway-dee too tan]
no spitting

旅社
lǚshè
[looh-shuh]
hostel

禁止游泳
jìnzhǐ yóuyǒng
[jin-jir yoh-yong]
no bathing

银行
yínháng
[yin-hang]
bank

禁止钓鱼
jìnzhǐ diào yú
[jin-jir dyow yoo]
no fishing

邮局
yóujú
[yoh-joo]
post office

at the airport

机场
jīchǎng
[jee-chang]
airport

检疫站
jiǎnyìzhàn
[jyen-yee-jan]
quarantine

海关
hǎiguān
[high-gwan]
customs

边防检查站
biānfáng jiǎncházhàn
[byen-fang jyen-cha-jan]
border police

外汇兑换处
wàihuì duìhuànchù
[wigh-hway dway-hwan-choo]
foreign currency exchange

候机厅
hòujītīng
[hoh-ji-ting]
lounge

贵宾候机厅
guìbīn hòujītīng
[gway-bin hoh-ji-ting]
VIP lounge

登机口
dēngjīkǒu
[dung-jee-koh]
boarding gate

国内离港
guónèi lígǎng
[gwore-nay lee-gang]
domestic terminal

国际离港
guójì lígǎng
[gwore-jee lee-gang]
international terminal

国内抵达
guónèi dǐdá
[gwore-nay dee-da]
domestic arrivals

国际抵达
guójì dǐdá
[gwore-jee dee-da]
international arrivals

检票处
jiǎnpiàochù
[jyen-peow-choo]
ticket desk

问讯处
wènxùnchù
[weun-shun-choo]
information desk

电话亭
diànhuàtíng
[dyen-hwa-ting]
telephone booth

公用电话
gōngyòng diànhuà
[gong-yong dyen-hwa]
public telephone

停车场
tíngchēchǎng
[ting-chuh-chang]
parking lot

洗手间 男
xǐshǒujiān nán
[shee-shoh-jyen nan]
toilets (men)

洗手间 女
xǐshǒujiān nǔ
[shee-shoh-jyen nooh]
toilets (women)

行李寄存处
xíngli jìcúnchù
[shing-lee jee-tsun-choo]
left luggage

机场巴士
jīchǎng bāshì
[jee-chang ba-shir]
airport shuttle bus

禁止停车
jìnzhǐ tíngchē
[jin-jir ting-chuh]
no parking

入口
rùkǒu
[roo-koh]
entrance

出租车站
chūzūchēzhàn
[choo-zoo-chuh-jan]
taxi stand

出口
chūkǒu
[choo-koh]
exit

...... 方向
......fāngxiàng
[fang-shyang]
in the direction of...

finding your way

东
dōng
[dong]
East

后
hòu
[hoh]
back

南
nán
[nan]
South

左
zuǒ
[zwore]
left

西
xī
[shee]
West

右
yòu
[yoh]
right

北
běi
[bay]
North

中
zhōng
[jong]
center

前
qián
[chyen]
front

上
shàng
[shang]
up

下
xià
[shya]
down

大街
dàjiē
[da-jyeah]
avenue
▸ 长安大街 Chang'an Avenue

街
jiē
[jyeah]
street

路
lù
[loo]
road
▸ 东风北路 Dongfeng North Road

门
mén
[men]
gate
▸ 地安门 Gate of Earthly Peace

胡同
hútong
[hoo-tong]
lane (North China)

巷
xiàng
[shyang]
alley

桥
qiáo
[chyeow]
bridge

里弄
lǐlòng
[lee long]
lane

江
jiāng
[jyang]
river

河
hé
[huh]
river

湖
hú
[hoo]
lake

沟
gōu
[goh]
gully

运河
yùnhé
[yun-huh]
canal

going out

电影院
diànyǐngyuàn
[dyen-ying-ywan]
cinema

剧院
jùyuàn
[joo-ywan]
theater

音乐厅
yīnyuètīng
[yin-yue-ting]
concert hall

木偶剧场
mù'ǒu jùchǎng
[mu-oh joo-chang]
puppet theater

京剧
jīngjù
[jing-joo]
Peking Opera

博物馆
bówùguǎn
[bo-woo gwan]
museum

单号
dān hào
[dan-how]
odd-numbered seats

双号
shuāng hào
[shwung-how]
even-numbered seats

楼上
lóushàng
[loh-shang]
balcony

楼下
lóuxià
[loh-shya]
stalls

入口
rùkǒu
[roo-koh]
entrance

紧急出口
jǐnjí chūkǒu
[jin-jee choo-koh]
emergency exit

衣帽间
yīmàojiān
[yee-mow-jyen]
cloakroom

公园
gōngyuán
[gong-ywan]
park

游乐场
yóulèchǎng
[yoh-luh-chang]
amusement park

出租车站
chūzūchēzhàn
[choo-zoo-chuh-jan]
taxi stand

茶馆
cháguǎn
[cha-gwan]
tea-house

酒吧
jiǔbā
[jew-ba]
bar

歌厅
gētīng
[guh-ting]
karaoke hall

舞厅
wǔtīng
[woo-ting]
dance hall

迪厅
dítīng
[dee-ting]
discotheque

休闲娱乐中心
xiūxián yúlè zhōngxīn
[shyew-shyen yoo-luh jong-shin]
recreation center

剧院
jùyuàn
[joo-ywan]
theater

原声加字幕
yuánshēng jiā zìmù
[ywan-sheng jya-zir-moo]
subtitles

存衣处
cúnyīchù
[tsun-yee-choo]
cloakroom

曲艺表演
qǔyì biǎoyǎn
[choo-yee byeow-yan]
folk performance

曲艺节目
qǔyì jiémù
[choo-yee jyeah-moo]
folk program

歌舞
gēwǔ
[guh-woo]
song and dance

杂技
zájì
[za-jee]
acrobatics

杂技剧团
zájì jùtuán
[za-jee joo-twan]
acrobatic troupe

public transportation

公共汽车站
gōnggòng qìchēzhàn
[gong-gong chee-chuh-jan]
bus stop

空调车
kōngtiáochē
[kong-teow-chuh]
air-conditioned bus

无轨电车
wú guǐ diànchē
[woo-gway dyen-chuh]
trolley bus

长途汽车站
chángtú qìchēzhàn
[chang-too-chee-chuh-jan]
long-distance bus station

先下后上
xiān xià hòu shàng
[shyen-shya hoh-shang]
passengers off first

老弱病残孕专座
lǎo ruò bìng cán yùn zhuānzuò
[low rwore bing tsan yoon jwan-zwore]
seats reserved for the elderly, the infirm, disabled people and pregnant women

头班车
tóubānchē
[toh-ban-chuh]
first bus/train

末班车
mòbānchē
[mo-ban-chuh]
last bus/train

夜班车
yèbānchē
[yuh-ban-chuh]
night service

月票
yuèpiào
[yue-peow]
monthly ticket

小面包车
xiǎo miànbāochē
[shyow myen-bow-chuh]
minibus

停车场
tíngchēchǎng
[ting-chuh-chang]
parking lot

推
tuī
[tway]
push

拉
lā
[la]
pull

慢
màn
[man]
slow

停
tíng
[ting]
stop

女厕
nǔ cè
[nooh-tsuh]
toilets (women)

入口
rùkǒu
[roo-koh]
entrance

长途汽车站
chángtú qìchēzhàn
[chang-too chee-chuh-jan]
long-distance bus station

出口
chūkǒu
[choo-koh]
exit

提取行李
tíqǔ xínglì
[tee-choo shing-lee]
baggage claim

男厕
nán cè
[nan-tsuh]
toilets (men)

站台通道
zhàntái tōngdào
[jan-tigh tong-dow]
to the platforms

at the hospital

医院
yīyuàn
[yee-ywan]
hospital

急诊（室）
jízhěnshì
[jee-jeunshir]
emergency room

北京医院
beijīng yīyuàn
[bay-jing yee-ywan]
Beijing Hospital

医生
yīshēng
[yee-sheng]
doctor

卫生院
weishēngyuàn
[way-sheng-ywan]
health center

牙医
yáyī
[ya-yee]
dentist

停车场
tíngchēchǎng
[ting-chuh-chang]
parking lot

门诊部
ménzhěnbù
[meun-jeun-boo]
outpatient department

挂号处
guàhàochù
[gwa-how-choo]
reception

收费处
shōufèichù
[shoh-fay-choo]
payment desk

取药处
qǔyàochù
[choo-yow-choo]
(in a hospital) pharmacy

住院部
zhùyuànbù
[joo-ywan-boo]
hospitalization department

内科
nèikē
[nay-kuh]
general medicine department

外科
wàikē
[wigh-kuh]
department of surgery

耳科
ěrkē
[er-kuh]
ear department

眼科
yǎnkē
[yan-kuh]
opthalmology department

牙科
yákē
[ya-kuh]
dental department

创伤外科
chuāngshāng wàikē
[chwung-shang wigh-kuh]
trauma surgery

中医科
zhōngyīkē
[jong-yee kuh]
Traditional Chinese Medicine department

病房
bìngfáng
[bing-fang]
ward

化验室
huàyànshì
[hwa-yan-shir]
laboratory

透视室
tòushìshì
[toh-shir-shir]
radioscopy room

观察室
guāncháshì
[gwan-cha-shir]
observation room

治疗室
zhìliáoshì
[jir-leow-shir]
treatment room

护士台
hùshitái
[hoo-shir-tigh]
nurse desk

诊所
zhensuǒ
[jeun-swore]
dispensary

静
jìng
[jing]
quiet

药店
yàodiàn
[yow-dyen]
pharmacy

禁止吸烟
jìnzhǐ xīyān
[jin-jir shee-yan]
no smoking

official offices

使馆
shǐguǎn
[shir-gwan]
embassy

......部
......bù
[boo]
department of..., ministry of...
▶ 外交部 Ministry of Foreign Affairs

大使馆
dàshǐguǎn
[da-shir-gwan]
embassy

中国银行
zhōngguó yínháng
[jong-gwore yin-hang]
Bank of China

美国使馆
měiguó shǐguǎn
[may-gwore shir-gwan]
US embassy

英国使馆
yīngguó shǐguǎn
[ying-gwore shir-gwan]
British embassy

......委员会
......wěiyuánhuì
[way-ywan-hway]
committee of...
▶ 宗教事务委员会
Religious Affairs Committee

警察局
jǐngchájú
[jing-cha-joo]
police station

出生日期
chūshēng rìqī
[choo-shung rir-chee]
date of birth

派出所
pàichūsuǒ
[pigh-choo-swore]
local police station

出生地点
chūshēng dìdiǎn
[choo-shung dee-dyen]
birthplace

护照号码
hùzhào hàomǎ
[hoo-jow how-ma]
passport number

签证
qiānzhèng
[chyen-jung]
visa

收发室
shōufāshì
[shoh-fa-shir]
mail room

消防站
xiāofángzhàn
[sheow-fang-jan]
fire station

at the restaurant

饭馆
fànguǎn
[fan-gwan]
restaurant

粤菜
yuècài
[yue-tsigh]
Cantonese cuisine

餐馆
cānguǎn
[tsan-gwan]
restaurant

淮扬菜
huáiyángcài
[hwigh-yang tsigh]
Huaiyang cuisine

饭庄
fànzhuāng
[fan-jwung]
restaurant

上海本帮菜
shànghǎi běnbāngcài
[shang-high beun-bang-tsigh]
Shanghai cuisine

素菜馆
sùcàiguǎn
[soo-tsigh-gwan]
vegetarian restaurant

菜单
càidān
[tsigh-dan]
menu

川菜
chuāncài
[chwan-tsigh]
Sichuan cuisine

......风味
......fēngwèi
[fung-way]
...flavor

鲁菜
lǔcài
[loo-tsigh]
Shandong cuisine

烤鸭
kǎoyā
[kow-ya]
roast duck

涮羊肉
shuàn yángròu
[shwan yang-roh]
lamb hotpot

云吞
yúntūn
[yun-tun]
dumpling soup

火锅
huǒguō
[hwore-gwore]
hotpot

蒸饺
zhēngjiǎo
[jung-jeow]
steamed dumplings

主食
zhǔshí
[jew-shir]
staple food (rice, noodles etc.)

粥
zhōu
[joh]
congee

面条
miàntiáo
[myen-teow]
noodles

冰糖莲子粥
bīngtáng liánzǐ zhōu
[bing-tang lyen-zir joh]
sugared lotus grain congee

炒面
chǎomiàn
[chow-myen]
fried noodles

馒头
mántou
[man-toh]
steamed bun

包子
bāozi
[bow-zir]
steamed bun

饼
bǐng
[bing]
cake

花卷
huājuǎn
[hwa-jwan]
steamed twisted roll

春卷
chūnjuǎn
[chun-jwan]
spring roll

饺子
jiǎozi
[jeow-zir]
boiled dumplings

（白）米饭
(bái) mǐfàn
[(bigh) mee-fan]
(plain) rice

馄饨
húntun
[hun-tun]
dumpling soup

蛋炒饭
dàn chǎo fàn
[dan chow-fan]
egg fried rice

甜点
tiándiǎn
[tyen-dyen]
dessert

月饼
yuèbǐng
[yue-bing]
moon cake

汤圆
tāngyuán
[tang-ywan]
boiled rice dumpling

拔丝苹果
básī píngguǒ
[ba-sir ping-gwore]
toffee apple

杏仁酪
xìngrénlào
[shing-reun-low]
almond cream

花生糊
huāshēnghú
[hwa-shung-hoo]
peanut congee

麻团
mátuán
[ma-twan]
sesame rice ball

豌豆黄
wāndòu huáng
[wan-doh hwang]
pea cake

冰糖葫芦
bīngtáng húlu
[bing-tang hoo-loo]
caramelized haw

凉菜
liángcài
[lyang-tsigh]
hors-d'œuvre

五香牛肉
wǔxiāng niúròu
[woo-shyang new-roh]
five-spiced beef

什锦冷盘
shíjǐn lengpán
[shir-jin lung-pan]
assortment of hors-d'œuvres

凉拌海蜇
liáng bàn hǎizhé
[lyang ban high-juh]
jellyfish salad

炸花生米
zhá huāshēngmǐ
[ja hwa-shung-mee]
peanut fries

泡菜
pàocài
[pow-tsigh]
marinated vegetables

萝卜丝
luóbosī
[lwore-bo-sir]
shredded turnip

腌肉
yānròu
[yen-roh]
salted pork

腊肉
làròu
[la-roh]
smoked pork

火腿
huǒtuǐ
[hwore-tway]
ham

香肠
xiāngcháng
[shyang-chang]
sausage

松花蛋
sōnghuādàn
[song-hwa-dan]
thousand year-old egg (duck eggs preserved in lime)

鹌鹑蛋
ānchúndàn
[an-chun-dan]
quail's egg

热菜
rècài
[ruh-tsigh]
hot plate

鱼香肉丝
yúxiāng ròusī
[yoo-shyang roh-sir]
fish-flavored pork strips

宫爆鸡丁
gōng bào jī dīng
[gong bow jee ding]
peanut spiced chicken

辣子肉丁
là zǐ ròu dīng
[la zir roh ding]
spicy pork

红烧肉
hóng shāo ròu
[hong show roh]
pork stew

回锅肉
huí guō ròu
[hway gwore roh]
twice-cooked pork

烤乳猪
kǎo rǔzhū
[kow roo-joo]
roasted piglet

香酥鸡
xiāng sū jī
[shyang soo jee]
crispy fragrant chicken

红烧牛肉
hóngshāo niúròu
[hong-show new-roh]
beef stew

炖牛肉
dùn niúròu
[dun new-roh]
beef casserole

烤羊肉
kǎo yángròu
[kow yang-roh]
roast lamb

烤羊肉串
kǎo yáng ròu chuàn
[kow yang roh chwan]
roast lamb skewer

鱼
yú
[yoo]
fish

松鼠鱼
sōngshǔ yú
[song-shoo yoo]
*squirrel-shaped fish in sweet and
sour sauce*

清蒸鱼
qīngzhēng yú
[ching-jung yoo]
steamed fish

干烧鱼
gānshāo yú
[gan-show yoo]
dry-cooked fish

炸鱼
zhá yú
[ja yoo]
fried fish

鱼片
yúpiàn
[yoo-pyen]
slivers of fish

鱼丸
yúwán
[yoo-wan]
fish ball

虾
xiā
[shya]
shrimp

清炒虾仁
qīngchǎo xiārén
[ching-chow shya-reun]
shelled shrimp

龙虾
lóngxiā
[long-shya]
lobster

软炸大虾
ruǎnzhá dàxiā
[rwan-ja da-shya]
shrimp fritter

炸虾球
zhá xiāqiú
[ja shya-chew]
fried shrimp ball

蔬菜
shūcài
[shoo-tsigh]
vegetables

麻婆豆腐
mápó dòufu
[ma-po doh-foo]
spicy tofu

干煸豆角
gānbiān dòujiǎo
[gan-byen doh-jeow]
dry-cooked beans

鱼香茄子
yú xiāng qiézi
[yoo shyang chyeah-zir]
fish-flavored eggplant

糖醋藕
táng cù ǒu
[tang tsoo oh]
sweet and sour lotus root

海米冬瓜
hǎimǐ dōngguā
[high-mee dong-gwa]
white gourd and dried shrimps

砂锅豆腐
shāguō dòufu
[sha-gwore doh-foo]
tofu in a terracotta pot

西红柿鸡蛋汤
xīhóngshì jīdàn tāng
[shee-hong-shir jee-dan tang]
tomato and egg soup

蘑菇菜心
mógu càixīn
[mo-goo tsigh-shin]
cabbage with mushroom

酒水
jiǔshuǐ
[jin-shway]
drinks

饮料
yǐnliào
[yin-lyow]
drinks

白酒
báijiǔ
[bigh-jew]
clear spirit

啤酒
píjiǔ
[pee-jew]
beer

葡萄酒
pútaojiǔ
[poo-tow-jew]
wine

椰汁
yēzhī
[yuh-jir]
coconut milk

杏仁露
xìngrénlù
[shing-ren-loo]
almond milk

酸枣汁
suānzǎozhī
[swan-zow-jir]
wild jujube juice

绿茶
lǜchá
[looh-cha]
green tea

花茶
huāchá
[hwa-cha]
scented tea

红茶
hóngchá
[hong-cha]
black tea

菊花茶
júhuāchá
[joo-hwa-cha]
chrysanthemum tea

煎饼
jiānbǐng
[jyen-bing]
savory pancake

咖啡馆
kāfēiguǎn
[ka-fay-gwan]
coffee shop

买单
mǎidān
[migh-dan]
the check

账单
zhàngdān
[jang-dan]
the check

主食
zhǔshí
[joo-shir]
staple food (rice, noodles etc.)

结账
jiézhàng
[jyeah-jang]
the check

小吃店
xiǎochīdiàn
[shyow-chir-dyen]
snack bar

套餐
tàocān
[tow-tsan]
set meal

shopping

......商场
......shāngchǎng
[shang-chang]
store
▸ 王府井商场 Wangfujing store

衣服
yīfu
[yee-foo]
clothes

......商店
......shāngdiàn
[shang-dyen]
store

鞋帽
xié mào
[shyeah mow]
shoes and hats

......市场
shìchǎng
[shir-chang]
market
▸ 东安市场 Dong'an market

食品
shípǐn
[shir-pin]
food

推
tuī
[tway]
push

酒类
jiǔlèi
[jew-lay]
wines and spirits

拉
lā
[la]
pull

糕点
gāodiǎn
[gow-dyen]
pastries

熟食
shúshí
[shoo-shir]
(catering) cooked dishes

日用品
rìyòngpǐn
[rih-yong-pin]
articles for everyday use

家用电器
jiāyòng diànqì
[jya-yong dyen-chee]
household electric appliances

礼品
lǐpǐn
[lee-pin]
gifts

办公用品
bàngōng yòngpǐn
[ban-gong yong-pin]
office equipment

烟酒
yān jiǔ
[yan jew]
cigarettes and alcohol

手工艺品
shǒugōngyìpǐn
[shoh-gong-yee-pin]
handicrafts

特价
tèjià
[tuh-jya]
special offer

优惠
yōuhuì
[yoh-hway]
special offer

大礼包
dà lǐbāo
[da lee-bow]
bonus gift

减价
jiǎnjià
[jyen-jya]
sale

请勿吸烟
qǐng wù xīyān
[ching woo shee-yan]
no smoking please

收款台/收银台
shōukuǎntái/shōuyíntái
[shoh-kwan-tigh/shoh-yin-tigh]
check-out

营业时间
yíngyè shíjiān
[ying-yuh shir-jyen]
business hours

紧急出口
jǐnjí chūkǒu
[jin-jee choo-koh]
emergency exit

花店
huādiàn
[hwa-dyen]
florist

旅游纪念品店
lǚyóu jìniànpǐndiàn
[loo-yoh jee-nyen-pin-dyen]
souvenir store

水果店
shuǐguǒdiàn
[shway-gwore-dyen]
fruit store

咖啡馆
kāfēiguǎn
[ka-fay-gwan]
coffee shop

花市
huāshì
[hwa-shir]
flower market

菜市场
càishìchǎng
[tsigh-shir-chang]
food market

灯具市场
dēngjù shìchǎng
[deng-joo shir-chang]
lamp market

家具市场
jiājù shìchǎng
[jya-joo shir-chang]
furniture market

建材市场
jiàncái shìchǎng
[jyen-tsigh shir-chang]
building materials market

汽配市场
qìpèi shìchǎng
[chee-pay shir-chang]
automobile parts market

入口
rùkǒu
[roo-koh]
entrance

出口
chūkǒu
[choo-koh]
exit

男厕
nán cè
[nan-tsuh]
toilets (men)

女厕
nǚ cè
[nooh-tsuh]
toilets (women)

商业中心
shāngyè zhōngxīn
[shang-yuh jong-shin]
commercial center

烟铺
yānpù
[yan-poo]
(store) tobacco store

food stores

市场
shìchǎng
[shir-chang]
market

熟食店
shúshídiàn
[shoo-shir-jyen]
store selling cooked foods

糕点房
gāodiǎnfáng
[gow-dyen-fang]
confectionery store

副食店
fùshídiàn
[foo-shir dyen]
grocery store

早点铺
zǎodiǎnpù
[zow-dyen-poo]
breakfast stop

面包店
miànbāodiàn
[myen-bow-dyen]
bakery

营业时间
yíngyè shíjiān
[ying-yuh shir-jyen]
business hours

超市
chāshì
[chow-shir]
supermarket

numbers

一 壹
yī
[yee]
one

二 贰
èr
[er]
two

三 叁
sān
[san]
three

四 肆
sì
[sir]
four

五 伍
wǔ
[woo]
five

六 陆
liù
[lew]
six

七 柒
qī
[chee]
seven

八 捌
bā
[ba]
eight

九　玖
jiǔ
[jew]
nine

十　拾
shí
[shir]
ten

十一　拾壹
shíyī
[shir-yee]
eleven

二十　贰拾
èrshí
[er-shir]
twenty

二十一　贰拾壹
èrshíyī
[er-shir-yee]
twenty-one

三十　叁拾
sānshí
[san-shir]
thirty

百　佰
bǎi
[bigh]
one hundred

一百零一　壹佰零壹
yībǎi líng yī
[yee-bigh ling yee]
one hundred and one

千　仟
qiān
[chyen]
one thousand

万　萬
wàn
[wan]
ten thousand

十万　拾萬
shí wàn
[shir wan]
one hundred thousand

百万　佰萬
bǎi wàn
[bigh wan]
one million

千万仟萬
qiān wàn
[chyen wan]
ten million

亿　億
yì
[yee]
one hundred million

十亿　拾億
shí yì
[shir yee]
one billion

百亿　佰億
bǎi yì
[bigh yee]
ten billion

千亿　仟億
qiān yì
[chyen yee]
one hundred billion